MAKERS OF MODERN ENGLAND

Makers of Modern England

THE FORCE OF INDIVIDUAL
GENIUS IN HISTORY

by Giovanni Costigan

THE MACMILLAN COMPANY, NEW YORK
COLLIER-MACMILLAN LIMITED, LONDON

Library of Congress Catalog Card Number: 66-26144

FIRST PRINTING

The Macmillan Company, New York
Collier-Macmillan Canada Ltd., Toronto, Ontario
Printed in the United States of America

to AMNE

Contents

Introduction

THE EXTENT TO WHICH single individuals may influence the course of history is an endlessly fascinating subject. For centuries literary historians tended to magnify the role of the heroic leader. Carlyle's famous dictum that history is but the biography of great men was only a modern restatement of an ancient tradition. In the contemporary world of great political states and great industrial organizations, however, the individual has come gradually to count for less and less. The more history has approached the condition of sociology the more this tendency has been accentuated. Sixty years ago, Professor J. B. Bury declared that the single individual no longer counted in modern politics. However weak a particular prime minister or president might be, the political system of a democracy, Bury thought, was so strong and so stable that it would remain undamaged. In his recent book *What Is History?* Professor E. H. Carr similarly depreciates the role of the individual as compared with the vast impersonal forces at work in the twentieth century.

Yet a generation that has seen the emergence of figures as powerful as Hitler, Stalin, Mussolini, Churchill, and de Gaulle is forced to recognize once more the fact that individuals do really matter in history, and that within certain limits their action may be decisive for good or ill. That Germany would some day seek revenge for the humiliation of defeat in 1918 seemed exceedingly probable, but no one could have predicted as the accompaniment of this the mass murder of six million Jews: that tragedy would not have occurred save for the paranoiac delusions of one man. That Soviet Russia would one day transform itself into a powerful industrial state would also seem to have been inevitable, but that the process should involve the Moscow Trials and the blood purges of the thirties seems less a function of historical inevitability than of Stalin's lust for power.

Perhaps the career of Churchill affords the most striking illustration in modern times both of the incalculable importance of a single individual at a given moment in history and also of the limits imposed even upon such a one by the inexorable development of forces beyond his control. Churchill could summon up the defiant spirit of a nation at a moment of utmost peril and lead it on to victory, but not even he could galvanize a dying empire into life or avert its inevitable liquidation.

Even allowing for the formidable power of modern political organization, the individual, then, may still exert a significant influence upon his time. And in an age which is indebted to Freud one may perhaps observe that should all other systems and theories of history—Hegelian, Marxian, Crocean, Nietzschean, Spenglerian, Toynbeian, and the rest—prove invalid, there still remains as the basic unit of history, now as in the Stone Age, the single individual, alone yet not alone, endowed with immemorial loves and hatreds, anxieties and joys, desires and regrets. Some knowledge of his psychology, therefore, may afford a clue to the understanding of whatever patterns may be discerned in history.

The series of sketches that follow is designed to show how eight men—or to be exact, eight men and one woman—profoundly affected the life of modern England. It is, of course, always difficult to estimate the degree of influence individuals have over the society in which they live. It is above all difficult to determine how far purely intellectual influences help to modify or transform society. That England would not be the same today had statesmen like Gladstone and Disraeli, Lloyd George and Churchill never lived is self-evident. But it is almost equally certain that twentieth-century England would never have emerged in its present form save for the ideas of thinkers like Bentham, John Stuart Mill, and the Webbs. They, too, must be numbered among the Makers of Modern England.

Perhaps the only figure discussed here whose claim to inclusion in such a group might be questioned is Cardinal Newman. He alone among them did his best to arrest or avert the emergence in England of a modern democratic industrial society. He alone was totally out of sympathy with the aims of the contemporary world. He alone looked back nostalgically to the imagined charm of former ages and deplored their passing. Yet man is far from being a wholly rational being, and far from satisfied with the material abundance he himself has created; and Newman may speak for all those who find themselves alienated, in England as elsewhere, by the pressures of the modern world—with its commercialism, its crassness, it vulgarity. Moreover, since today Newman's co-religionists form the largest single body in England of religious believers, his beliefs, romantic as they are, have not lost their importance in the contemporary scene.

Apart from Newman, the personalities examined here may be said to epitomize the essential development of English political and social life during the last century and a half. Utilitarian philosophers like Bentham and Mill provided the rationale for the reforms so urgently needed to transform the rural aristocratic England of the eighteenth century into the industrial democratic England of the nineteenth. After the thinkers came the statesmen, men like Gladstone and Disraeli, who carried out many of the reforms that Bentham and Mill had advocated.

The blueprint for the further transformation of England from the political democracy of the nineteenth century to the social democracy of the twentieth was in large measure the work of the Fabians and especially of those selfless and tireless collectivists Sidney and Beatrice Webb. In its early stages, the welfare state they projected was realized through the social reforms effected by Lloyd George and Winston Churchill. Later, the extraordinary political verve of this unrivaled pair carried Britain triumphantly through the perils of the two world wars. With the coming of peace in 1945, the Labour government completed the construction of the welfare state the Fabians had envisaged half a century earlier.

The unifying principle underlying all these efforts was the attempt to realize in England the idea of the greatest happiness of the greatest number. The Utilitarians expected this to result from laissez faire; but when laissez faire led unexpectedly to monopoly, the Fabians sought to realize the greatest happiness principle through the collective will of society as expressed in Parliament.

The means changed, but the underlying principle remained the same. As for the statesmen—Gladstone and Disraeli, Lloyd George and Churchill—whatever their personal differences and whatever else they may have accomplished, each certainly did something in a practical way—through legislation—to establish English society more securely on the basis of the general-happiness principle. As a result, today the English people, despite the ravages of two world wars, enjoy a higher level of well-being—particularly in matters such as health, housing, and education—than they have ever known in the past. The material foundation for happiness has been laid. How far this alone is adequate to achieve happiness is of course a very different question—one that belongs to the realm of psychology and ethics.

In presenting these nine distinguished individuals, I have emphasized their personalities rather than their achievements or philosophy. My main aim has been to restore them briefly to life in the imagination of the reader. Of the nine, only two—Newman and Gladstone—had any firm belief in immortality. Yet all of them no doubt wished to be not wholly forgotten by their countrymen—or by future ages. All surely hoped to achieve some portion of what Pater calls "that secondary existence, that warm place still left, in thought at least, beside the living, the desire for which is actually, in various forms, so great a motive with most of us."

MAKERS OF MODERN ENGLAND

I

Jeremy Bentham

(1748-1832)

JEREMY BENTHAM probably did more than any single man to change the climate of opinion in England during the nineteenth century with respect to politics and law. John Stuart Mill did not exaggerate when he called him one of the "great seminal minds" of his age. With irrefutable logic Bentham demolished the foundations on which the old order, with all its corruption and cruelty, had been built. "He swept away," wrote Mill, "the accumulated cobwebs of centuries; he untied knots which the efforts of the ablest thinkers, age after age, had only drawn tighter; and it is no exaggeration to say of him, that, over a great part of the field, he was the first to shed the light of reason." On the two hundredth anniversary of Bentham's birth, the London *Times*—his bitter enemy during his lifetime—wrote that he could "confidently be ranked among the greatest Englishmen of all ages."

Bentham was an infant prodigy. His parents had once found him at the age of three absorbed in a huge folio of Rapin's *History of England*, a lighted candle on either side of his desk. The boy followed the ruthless wars of Edward III "with eager sympathy," and his delight grew with "the number of Frenchmen left dead in the field of battle." Like other children, he loved to read of battles and of slaughter. As an adult, however, Bentham developed a moral sensibility of great delicacy and tenderness and could not bear the thought of suffering inflicted upon any creature. His concern included animals as well as human beings.

To a nature such as this, military "glory" made no appeal—since it could only be purchased at the price of the suffering of others. The very sound of the word was offensive to Bentham, who de-

nounced with vigor what he termed "passion-kindling appella-
tives" like "honour" and "glory." "The duty of a king to his
subjects and the world," he wrote in 1789, "is to compass war, by
any means, and at any price; and the less the profit or pretence,
the greater the glory." In the vocabulary of politics, he observed,
moral values were inverted: "In this dictionary, peace and tranquillity are represented by sloth, obscurity and insignificance;
bloodshed and destruction by vigour, spirit, activity, a sense of
national glory, and so on." Instead, therefore, of seeking to stimu-
late a warlike spirit, Bentham—among his innumerable projects—
devoted his energy to sketching a *Plan for a Universal and Perpetual Peace*, which was, in some respects, more imaginatively
conceived than that of Kant. It has been suggested that Woodrow
Wilson may have borrowed the idea for his famous Fourteen
Points from the fourteen points of Bentham's Plan.

Contemptuous of glory, Bentham was without personal ambition and indifferent to fame. The object of his life was to abolish
corruption and injustice, to increase happiness and minimize pain;
and the means by which these things could best be accomplished,
he thought, was the deliberate and constant application of reason
in the affairs of daily life.

To trace the genesis of an idealism as disinterested as that of
Jeremy Bentham is a difficult psychological problem. He was an
elder son, and till the age of nine an only child. His mother,
whom he loved, died when he was eleven. His father, an attorney,
was inordinately proud of the boy's precocity and stimulated his
premature mental growth in every possible way. At the age of
five Jeremy was reading Latin and Greek under his father's
tutelage, and at twelve he had already matriculated at Oxford.

To the child's intense embarrassment, his father used to boast of
his knowledge and exhibit him as a prodigy. "He was always
talking to me and to others of my powers," Bentham recalled
long after. Once, at Oxford, the father made the timid boy walk
the whole length of Christ Church Hall, under the scrutiny of
every undergraduate, to see if he could recognize any former
schoolmates. As Bentham later confessed, he had been "ready to
faint—to sink into the earth with agony." He was taught to despise other boys. From an early age, his father let him know that

he expected to see him one day sitting on the woolsack as Lord Chancellor of England. " 'Pushing,' " he would say, " 'pushing' was the one thing needful; but 'pushing,' " said Bentham plaintively, "was not congenial to my character." The conviction that he could not or would not fulfill his father's expectations produced strong feelings of guilt in the boy. "Throughout life," as his earliest biographer, Sir John Bowring, put it, "the apprehension of blame was strong in Bentham's mind." As long as his father lived, Bentham addressed him as "Honoured Sir." His private opinion, however, was that his father was "a mixture of hectoring and puffing, and self-complacency and cringing and self-ostentation and forced civility."

Bentham had to wait till he was forty-four before experiencing the sense of liberation springing from what Freud has called the greatest event in any man's life—the death of his father. Indeed, had Bentham lived a century later, it is probable that with his keen intellectual curiosity, he would have discerned in his own relations with his father a classical example of what Freud was to term the Oedipus complex.

Bentham's difficulties as a child were compounded by the fact that he was tiny in size and so weak that in going upstairs "he could not mount the stairs without bringing one leg up to the other at every step." When his father tried to make him learn dancing at the age of seven, it proved to be a torment, since, apart from his extreme shyness, the boy could not support himself on tiptoe. Of his attempts to play cricket, Bentham remembered only that he "was a dwarf, and too weak to enjoy it." "Aware of his defects," wrote Bowring, "he supplied them by thought and care, and no one was more alert and active than he. His adroitness served for strength: and physical infirmity was counteracted by intellectual activity."

Intensely solitary, the child had no companions of his own age. Reading—chiefly in history and literature—was his passion. "When I got hold of a novel," he later recalled, "I identified myself with all the personages, and thought more of their affairs than of any affairs of my own." At an early age he read books such as Plutarch's *Lives*, *Gulliver's Travels*, Voltaire's *Candide* and *History of Charles XII*, *Gil Blas*, *Clarissa Harlowe*, and Stow's *Chronicles*, and invariably he sympathized with the suffering and oppressed. His imagination was lively; hence, after reading *Pilgrim's Progress* he dreamed constantly of the devil, and *Paradise Lost* frightened him half to death. Even at Oxford he still believed in ghosts and was afraid of the gloomy rooms that had been allotted to him in college.

His earliest politics were naturally those of his father—Tory and Royalist: Charles I was a "blessed martyr." On the death of George II, he wrote an ode on "the dead god," which Dr. Johnson praised as a "very pretty performance of a young man." Bentham's mature judgment, tersely expressed, was that "it was a mediocre performance, on a trumpery subject, written by a miserable child."

At Oxford the "miserable child" found a more imposing authority than the parental one in the impressive person of Sir William Blackstone, Vinerian Professor of Law and author of the *Commentaries on the Laws of England*. Little could Sir William have realized the critical intellect embodied in the smallest member of his audience. To Bentham's astonishment—he was only fifteen at the time—he heard a legal system that he had already come to regard as archaic, obscure, and contradictory, praised as the height of human wisdom. "Blackstone was a formal, precise and affected lecturer," he recalled, "cold, reserved and wary—exhibiting a frigid pride." Later, in his *Commonplace Book,* in memorable words he pilloried the famous professor: "His hand was formed to embellish and corrupt everything it touches. . . . His is the treasury of vulgar errors, where all the errors that are, are collected and improved. . . . In him every prejudice has an advocate. . . . He is the dupe of every prejudice, and the abettor of every abuse." No doubt Bentham had long measured himself against his father's narrow intelligence, and found scant pleasure in the ease of victory; but to pit himself against the greatest legal pundit of the age and find himself superior—this must have given him an enduring basis for confidence in his own intellectual ability.

In challenging Blackstone, Bentham was of course assaulting the principle of authority itself. For Blackstone symbolized Oxford. "The genius of the place," wrote Bentham in disdain, "is a compound of orthodoxy and corruption." On first entering the university, he had been shocked by the necessity of subscribing to the Thirty-Nine Articles of the Church of England, some of which he found unintelligible, others absurd. "I signed, but by the view I found myself forced to take of the whole business, such an impression was made, as will never depart from me but with life." "Mendacity and insincerity," he later declared, were "the sure and only effects of an English university education." He was revolted by the coarseness and drunkenness of undergraduate life, and mortified by the physical smallness that made him the butt of persecution. On one occasion, a burly future parson had seized him and held him at arm's length, suspended upside down.

Slowly, Bentham must have become conscious that it was his destiny to challenge a system that was supported by powerful vested interests as well as by centuries of inherited prejudice. It was the story of the Emperor's Clothes, and Jeremy was the child crying out that the Emperor had nothing on. His first work after leaving Oxford, the famous *Fragment on Government* in 1776, was a refutation of Blackstone. Though the work was circulated anonymously at Bentham's wish, his father could not help letting out the secret; and not long after, the great Whig peer Lord Shelburne climbed the stairs one day to the young lawyer's "doghole in the Temple," where he was living in "obscurity—perfect obscurity." The period of such obscurity was over.

At the age of twenty-one, pursuant to his father's wishes, Bentham was admitted to the bar. In his first law suit, he told his client that the only profit from it would accrue to the lawyers. Hence he advised him to drop the case. Such advice was hardly the road to riches or to forensic success.

Bentham's sense of order and justice was outraged by the gross abuses with which both common law and equity were encrusted. The existing system, from which his father expected him to make his fortune, he found monstrous. Under it, said Bentham, justice was denied to nine-tenths of the people and sold to the rest at a great price. Lawyers, he declared, were "the only persons in whom ignorance of the law was not punished." It was "as impossible to a lawyer to wish men out of litigation, as for a physician to wish them in health."

Personal factors, too, may have played a part in his determination to renounce a legal career for a life of solitary work and contemplation. With his weak voice, unimposing presence, and diminutive stature—though, as he said, he had "shot up" since childhood—Bentham was, from a practical point of view, well advised to give up the practice of law, into which his father had pushed him. "I went to the bar," he said, "as a bear to the stake." In any case, considerable moral courage was required both to disappoint his father's hopes and cut himself off from all promise of place and profit. It was not so much that he was without ambition as that his ambition was entirely disinterested. "What Bacon was to the physical world," he wrote at the age of thirty, "Helvetius was to the moral. The moral world has therefore had its Bacon, but its Newton is yet to come." It is clear, then, that Bentham already cherished in private an immense intellectual ambition—to be the Newton of the moral world.

He determined thenceforth to devote his life not to the manipulation of the law for his own advantage, but to its reformation—on the one hand to a thorough and systematic exposure of its abuses and on the other to an equally thorough and systematic program for its improvement. Not content to be merely a critic, Bentham wished to construct a scientific foundation for law. His mind was not only minutely analytical, but powerfully synthesizing as well. Indeed, the master passion of his life, to which he was to remain faithful for fifty years, was to codify existing law, and beyond that, to frame a constitutional code that might serve as a basis for the legal system of any country in the world.

Two key concepts formed the philosophical basis of the legal reforms he proposed—the greatest happiness of the greatest number, and the principle of utility. Some of the ideas that have most influenced the course of history have been of an extreme simplicity. It is, in fact, difficult to conceive their novelty when they were first propounded or to realize either the fierce opposition they aroused or the severe and protracted struggle that was necessary before they could gain acceptance. In the words of the eminent Victorian jurist Sir FitzJames Stephen, if few read Bentham today, it is largely because his works lie buried among the ruins of the superstitions they destroyed.

The philosophers of the Enlightenment—French, English, Scottish, and Italian—exerted the chief formative influence upon Bentham's mature thought. From their writings he elaborated the ideas that were to underlie his future work. "Priestley was the first (unless it was Beccaria)," he wrote, "who taught my life to pronounce this sacred truth: that the greatest happiness of the greatest number is the foundation of morals and legislations."

Utility was the criterion by which all customs, laws, and institutions were to be judged—by the degree, that is, to which they ministered to human happiness or reduced human pain. "Montesquieu, Barrington, Beccaria and Helvetius, but most of all, Helvetius, set me on the principle of utility." Nor did he forget the teacher of his teachers. "O Locke!" he exclaimed. "First master of intellectual truth! without whom those who have taught *me* would have been as nothing! let thy blest spirit, if now it looketh down upon the affairs of men, acknowledge my obedience to the first great lesson of thy life, in the assertion of independence."

Yet for a nature trained from childhood in habits of obedience, and which now transferred to these great minds the homage that had once been paid to his father, the habit of mental independence did not come easily. From the embarrassments and humiliations of his early life, he had to overcome an ingrained sense of his own inadequacy and unworthiness. That eccentric and enigmatic statesman Lord Shelburne gave the young man his first feeling of self-confidence. "He raised me up," wrote Bentham gratefully in after years, "from the bottomless pit of humiliation. He made me feel that I was something." Yet even after this encouragement, real confidence was long in coming. "Even after he had become known as an author," says Bowring, "a sense of his own insignificance pursued him. 'I have done nothing,' he often said, 'but I could do something—I am of some value—there are materials in me, if anyone would but find it out. I feel like a cat or a dog that is used to be beaten by everybody it meets.'"

The question, What is genius? haunted Bentham for years. Once, when he was six, his father had sought to parade the little prodigy by getting him to define the word "genius" before some adult friends. "A pretty question to ask a poor, raw, timid boy!" Bentham commented years later. Reading Helvetius gave him an answer to the problem. "Have I a *genius* for anything?" he asked himself at one agonizing crucial moment and then, "What of all earthly pursuits is the most important? Legislation, was the an-

swer Helvetius gave. . . . And have I indeed a genius for legislation? I gave myself the answer—fearfully and trembling—Yes!"
From the depths of his being sprang this moment of revelation,
this sudden crystallization of a self-confidence that would thenceforth sustain him through life.

Bentham had found his vocation. With scarcely an intermission,
for fifty years, secluded in his house from six in the morning
until ten at night, he was to work, writing, analyzing, projecting
new reforms, drafting a rational and comprehensive code of laws,
intended for the use of all mankind. The labor of composition
Bentham always found—partly from his anxiety to express himself with absolute precision and lack of ambiguity—extremely
irksome. "Inconceivably difficult," he once called it; and his room
was littered with scattered paper fragments—the *disjecta membra*
of his thought.

The result of all these years of labor was the gradual construction of a systematic mental philosophy. Following such
thinkers as Locke, Hume, and Hartley, Bentham came to regard
consciousness as dependent upon a bundle of sensations that could
ultimately be classified under two headings—those which produced pleasure and those which produced pain. Since the pursuit
of happiness was the fundamental purpose of human life, for
Bentham morality consisted in promoting whatver factors led
to the increase of pleasure and in suppressing those which pro-
moted pain. Law, therefore, ought to be the regulations drawn
up by society whereby this maximizing of pleasure and min-
imizing of pain could be most comprehensively effected. For the
benefit of legislators Bentham drew up an ingenious and extremely elaborate table of pleasures and pains, showing which
actions should be encouraged and which punished by law. This
hedonistic calculus was the basis of Utilitarian morality.

Like the positivists of a later generation, Bentham believed that
sensations, and indeed all mental qualities, were susceptible of
exact measurement. Morality, therefore, could be a science as
exact as mathematics. Unfortunately Bentham made no *qualitative*
distinctions in his "felicific calculus." In his often quoted phrase,
the pleasures of push pin were equal to the pleasure of poetry,
and hence worthy of equal encouragement. Bentham's table of

pleasure and pain proved to be an arid schematism, a dissection of the human psyche conducted in a mechanical and lifeless fashion.

It is not surprising that in this psychological tabulation from which value judgments are omitted, aesthetic pleasures count for very little. Bentham was, in fact, exceedingly deficient in aesthetic awareness. Art was to the grown man, he once observed, as toys were to the child. Like religion, art was in effect a survival from the primitive, which civilized man could readily dispense with. Poetry consisted of tricks of rhyme or meter, which tickled the ear but added nothing to the sense. He made no distinction whatever between verse and poetry. There was nothing to be found in the latter that could not better be expressed in prose. Indeed Bentham once defined poetry contemptuously as writing where the lines don't go clear across the page. He wasted no time reading Shakespeare or Pope, or the great romantic poets who were his own contemporaries—Wordsworth, Coleridge, Blake, Shelley, Keats, Byron. To the appeal of painting and sculpture he was equally indifferent. As for music, though he learned to play Bach fugues upon the organ, it seems likely that the pleasure he derived from them was not of a sensuous but of a purely formal sort—based upon the mathematical order inherent in the notes of the score.

Bentham's insensibility in the field of aesthetics carried with it its own penalty. For his writing was so devoid of charm, his language so empty of beauty, that once it had served the practical purpose for which it was intended—the demolition of abuse and prejudice—it was read no more. One may still read Bentham out of curiosity, or for instruction, but hardly for pleasure—an ironic fate for one who rated pleasure as the end of life, but a just fate for one who was indifferent to the aesthetic value of literature.

The death of his father in 1792 left Bentham a competence and a house (the house in which Milton had once written *Paradise Lost*). It was situated in Queen Square Place, Westminster, looking out upon St. James's Park. From a Freudian point of view, it is significant that the years immediately following his father's death were among the most productive of Bentham's whole life. It was as though he had been liberated at length from psychic bondage. "Meantime, here am I sitting and scribbling on in this my hermitage," he wrote a friend, "never seeing anybody but for some special reason, always bearing reference to the service of mankind." Each day regularly he covered between ten and fifteen sheets—his "sibylline leaves"—in a minute and almost illegible handwriting, then laid them aside without rereading or correction—to write a similar amount next day.

"Is there any one of these my pages," he asked, "in which the love of humankind has been for a moment forgotten? Show it to me, and this hand shall be the first to tear it out." Yet, strangely enough, he seldom sought to make known what he had written. He was no more able to "push" his ideas than he had been to "push" himself. He had been content to have the famous *Fragment on Government* appear anonymously, and had been amused to hear the names of great men canvassed as the possible author. There was a sudden decline in interest when the real authorship finally became known. Bentham's *Introduction to the Principles of Morals and Legislation*, which was later to exert so much influence in Europe and America, was published in 1789, but it was fated to be pushed out of sight almost immediately by the controversies which arose over the French Revolution. Fearful of contention Bentham was reluctant to send other manuscripts to the printer. Hence year by year they began to accumulate, and even though rats ate them, he still did nothing about them.

The failure to publish was due partly to Bentham's obsessive quest for perfection, a quest which left him perpetually dissatisfied with what he had done, and partly to the restless intellectual curiosity which diverted him from one project to another, without completing any of them. "I have seen him," said his friend Dumont, "suspend a work almost finished, and compose a new one, only to assure himself of the truth of a single proposition which seemed to be doubtful." There was, indeed, some truth in the complaint of another friend that Bentham always seemed to "running from a good scheme to a better. In the meantime life passes away and nothing is completed."

From the danger of failing to exert the influence that his writings deserved, Bentham was rescued by the devotion of a small band of friends and disciples who, recognizing his genius, put themselves at its service. "Bentham," Mill recalled, "began the contest as a young man and had grown old before he had any followers." But when the followers finally appeared, they rendered him most loyal support. They felt, indeed, to quote a later authority, that Bentham's works "constituted a veritable treasure-house for legal reformers, as well as a rich mine for statesmen and publicists." The earliest was Etienne Dumont, a Swiss pastor and philosopher who came to England as tutor to Lord Lansdowne's son. He devoted himself to the herculean task of deciphering, editing, and translating Bentham's manuscripts. Dumont also had to struggle against inertia, and although Bentham entrusted manuscripts to him as early as 1788, it was twelve years later before the first of them appeared in print. Then, between 1802 and 1823, Dumont published five volumes in French. They established Bentham's name throughout Europe. In 1792, Bentham was made a citizen of France, an honor he never ceased to cherish. Thirty-one years later, when he paid a casual visit to one of the highest courts of justice in France, "the whole body of advocates rose and paid him the highest marks of respect, and the court invited him to the seat of honour."

In England, a group of reformers that included some of the most eminent lawyers of the time—Sir Samuel Romilly and Henry Brougham, later Lord Brougham—as well as philosophers like James Mill, colonizers like Edward Gibbon Wakefield, and practical politicians like Francis Place, the radical tailor of Charing Cross Road, looked up to Bentham as their mentor. From the next generation was to come the greatest Utilitarian of all—John Stuart Mill, one of the leading spirits in the *Westminster Review*, founded in 1824 for the propagation of Utilitarian principles. Their combined efforts helped to establish in England a new order of society—the humanizing of the penal code, the curtailment of religious intolerance, the widening of the franchise, the emancipation of colonies, the extension of education. Bentham himself, along with Brougham, was one of the founders in 1827 of University College, London, "the godless institution of Gower Street"—a secular establishment designed to challenge the theological monopoly of learning enjoyed by the two ancient seminaries of Oxford and Cambridge.

Especially was Bentham's influence felt in the sphere of criminal law and prison reform. To his championship humanitarian movements owed much—the protection of children and lunatics, the prevention of cruelty to animals, the abolition of the slave trade. Modern sanitation in England began with Edwin Chadwick, one of Bentham's admirers and for some time his private secretary. More than any other man, Chadwick was responsible for freeing the country from the dread scourge of cholera, the last severe outbreak of which ravaged England in the year of Bentham's death.

The influence, however, of the founder of the Utilitarian school extended far beyond his own time and place. Naturally it showed itself first in his chosen field of law. He "found the philosophy of law a chaos, he left it an exact science," wrote John Stuart Mill, the most distinguished of all his disciples. In his Harvard *Lectures on the Relation between Law and Public Opinion during the Nineteenth Century*, Professor Albert V. Dicey justified at some length his often-quoted conclusion that "the history of legal reform in England in the nineteenth century is the story of the shadow cast by one man—Bentham." "The first and greatest of legal philosophers," he termed him. "I do not know a single law reform effected since Bentham's day which cannot be traced to his influence," said another Oxford professor, Sir Henry Maine. In the opinion of his contemporary, Lord Chancellor Brougham: "The age of Law Reform and the age of Jeremy Bentham are one and the same. He is the father of the most important of all the branches of Reform, the leading and ruling department of human improvement. No one before him had ever seriously thought of exposing the defects in our English system of Jurisprudence." On the second centenary of his birth, the London *Times* declared that Bentham "still exerts a post-humous despotism over English politics and on the whole, it is a benevolent despotism."

But if an intellectual elite admired him, a much larger section of the public condemned his ideas as dangerously radical. Arnold of Rugby—Matthew Arnold's father—declared that such ideas should be tolerated only in the convict station at Botany Bay. Transcendentalists and conservatives were both outraged by the new rationalism. In his *Journal* in 1831, Emerson denounced "the stinking philosophy of the Utilitarian." With equal vehemence, Carlyle expressed his detestation of "Benthamee formulas, barren as the east wind."

The Tory radical William Cobbett ridiculed "Jerry Bentham"

as a "miserable queer old coxcomb," and commented in his *Rural
Rides* upon "the total insignificance of the miserable conundrums
that he was continually putting upon paper." Such was Cobbett's
estimate of reforms that were to transform English law. "Well,
great as Jerry was," jeered Cobbett in 1832, "death smote the
great mortal at last." Bentham was equally vilified from the opposite political extreme. He had always opposed socialism; hence
in the footnotes to *Das Kapital*, Karl Marx spattered him with
abuse: "the arch-Philistine, Jeremy Bentham, that insipid, pedantic, leather-tongued oracle of the ordinary bourgeois intelligence
of the nineteenth century. In no time and in no century," he
wrote, "has the most homespun commonplace strutted about in
so self-satisfied a way. . . . I should call Mr. Jeremy a genius in
the way of bourgeois stupidity."

Less abusive but no less unenlightened was young Gladstone
in the eighteen-thirties; for that "rising hope of the stern unbending Tories" could see no more in Benthamism than "a school
which taught that success is the only criterion of merit." And
in the twentieth century, that fastidious conservative, Lord Balfour, regarded the Utilitarians with the same supercilious distaste
that he felt for a gaucherie in conduct or a solecism in speech.
"The speculative outlook of the philosophical Radicals," wrote
Balfour in his *Autobiography*, "filled me with contempt."

The founder of Utilitarianism was even more famous abroad
than at home. "His name is little known in England," wrote
Hazlitt in a brilliant essay on Bentham in his scintillating *Spirit
of the Age*, "better known in Europe, best of all in the plains of
Chile and the mines of Mexico. He has offered constitutions for
the New World, and legislated for future times." Aaron Burr
did, in fact, visit Bentham in 1808, and found the latter especially
interested in talking with him, since he was then thinking of
emigrating to Mexico so as to escape the cold of the London
winter. Bentham was even willing to sacrifice his "wicked books"
—Rousseau, Helvetius, and Voltaire—should these be on the *Index
Expurgatorius* in Mexico.

Colonel Burr once described to his "intellectual and glamorous"
daughter Theodosia, wife of Governor Allston of South Carolina,
how Bentham had invited him to stay as his guest. "He met me at

the gate, with the frankness and affection of an old friend." It was impossible, said Burr, "to conceive a physiognomy more strongly marked with ingenuousness and philanthropy." The philosopher he considered to be "second to no one, ancient or modern, in profound thinking, in logical and analytical reasoning." The American was interested in editing some of Bentham's manuscripts, and went up to the attic to inspect them. He found only a "horrid confusion," and the dust of forty years, "a great portion of it being transferred to my person." He sent some of Dumont's translations, however, to the beautiful Theodosia, who wished "to have the honour of becoming his translator" by rendering them back into English. Unfortunately, she drowned at sea in 1812.

Aaron Burr was one of Bentham's first disciples in America. Twenty years earlier he had brought him to the notice of Albert Gallatin, the future Secretary of the Treasury; and the latter, meeting Bentham in London in 1814, told him that from that time he considered himself his pupil. John Quincy Adams, too, while Minister in London, became a friend of Bentham and used to accompany him on a daily seven-mile walk through the London parks. The philosopher presented him with twenty-five sets of his collected writings, "to be distributed, one copy to the Governor of every state in the Union." In 1815, Bentham himself wrote a circular letter to each of the Governors. He had, of course, already suggested to President Madison that he be allowed to codify the laws of the United States, and he was to approach Andrew Jackson on the same subject.

It was, however, chiefly through the work of the distinguished Louisiana jurist Edward Livingston, whom Sir Henry Maine calls "the first legal genius of modern times," that Bentham's influence passed over to the United States. Later his thought influenced the historian Richard Hildreth, whom Herbert Schneider of Columbia has termed "America's only Bentham." Curiously enough, it was the newest portion of the New World that paid most heed to the philosopher of the Old. For the frontier states of the West were the first to adopt legal codes patterned after Bentham's ideas. "Would it not," asked Francis Gilmer, a Virginian correspondent of Bentham, in 1818, "be a more glorious destination for a philosopher from his closet in London, to control the principles of legislation and jurisprudence on the banks of the Missouri, or the shores of the Chesapeake, than to leave his researches to the casual, capricious and ineffectual patronage of an executive office?" In the classical language of the period, Mr. Gilmer expressed the hope that should Bentham's philosophy be submerged in England, it would yet emerge "in a clear and tranquil Arethusa in America."

In South America, Bentham was even more widely read than in the United States, and by 1830 no less than forty thousand copies of Dumont's translations of his works had been sold there. Among his earliest disciples and correspondents were the liberal leaders Miranda and Santander in Venezuela. The Liberator himself, Simón Bolívar, was proud to have met Bentham in London, and congratulated him on having "reduced matters of legislation to mathematical certainty." Bentham's name, he added, was "never pronounced, even in these savage regions of America, without veneration and without gratitude." In Guatemala, the first constitution bore the impress of Bentham's ideas; President José del Vallé, who addressed him privately as "My ever dear Father," and in public as "Legislator del Mundo," declared that "the greatest good of the greatest number was the only true principle of legislation," and that Bentham was "the oracle" of all who were concerned with drafting constitutions. "You live in all civilized countries," he exclaimed. "You will live in all ages. The light from Westminster shall illumine these lands." In the Argentine, President Bernardino Rivadavia, and in Chile, Professor Lastarria, the eminent reformer, were among those who later called themselves Utilitarians.

In Europe, Bentham's works were translated during his lifetime from Dumont's French edition into German, Russian, Hungarian, and Spanish. The Cortes in Lisbon formally voted that they should also be translated into Portuguese. One may imagine with what delight Bentham heard that, at a time when his works were still unknown at Oxford and Cambridge, he was being studied with enthusiasm at Coimbra and Salamanca. At the University of Bologna, "none but Greeks and foreigners" were allowed to read him. The first Italian edition of Bentham did not appear till 1848. Even a romantic like Stendahl admired Bentham warmly and had the hero of his autobiographical novel *Armance* converted from Christianity to Utilitarianism by reading "bad books like Bentham, Bayle and Helvetius."

Catherine the Great and Alexander I of Russia, the Egyptian dictator, Mehemet Ali, and others were interested in Bentham's projects. Count Szechenyi in Hungary used his arguments to attack the obsolete Hungarian constitution, and Louis Kossuth, the champion of Magyar freedom, regarded Szechenyi as Bentham's pupil. Through Lord William Bentinck and Macaulay, Bentham's ideas were taken up in Bengal by the East India Company, and thereby came to influence the lives of millions of Hindus and Moslems in the great subcontinent. As Talleyrand once remarked, the whole world had plundered Bentham—and yet, what treasures still remained! Bentham was more entitled to the name of "genius," Talleyrand told Bowring on one occasion, "than any man he had ever known."

Of all the tributes paid to the philosopher-hermit, however, the most exotic is that recorded by the incorrigible optimist George Borrow, who went to Spain to sell Bibles. In an obscure and flea-bitten village in Galicia in the eighteen-thirties Borrow discovered an *alcalde* who was rapturous in praise of the "great Baintham, he who invented laws for all the world, the most universal genius which the world ever produced—a Solon, a Plato, and Lope de Vega." Since the vendor of Bibles had never read a word of Bentham, his embarrassment may be imagined. "How surprising!" said the mayor, "I see indeed that you know nothing of his writings though an Englishman. Now here am I, a simple *alcalde* of Galicia, yet I possess all the writings of Baintham on that shelf, and I study them day and night."

Sixty years later, the philosopher was being read with equal enthusiasm in an obscure village at the other end of Europe. "The utility of Bentham," wrote Leon Trotsky, "seemed to me the last word in human thought. For several months I was a staunch Benthamist." Later he passed over to communism—a system Bentham abhorred.

What manner of man was it who thus developed from a failure at the bar into the greatest legal philosopher of Europe, and from a timid frightened boy into one of the outstanding father figures of the age? A childless bachelor, Bentham was regarded by many of his followers as standing to them *in loco parentis*. They showered him with filial affection, which he reciprocated. In 1827, the unscrupulous Brougham, whose invective was more feared than that of any other man in Parliament, and who was then close upon fifty, was addressed by Bentham as "My dearest best boy," or "Dear sweet little poppet," salutations to which Brougham responded with "Dear sweet Grandpapa." The dour-visaged, hard-headed Francis Place was likewise, at the age of sixty, Bentham's "Dear good boy." When the closest disciple of his last years, Sir John Bowring, was released after a brief imprisonment in France, Bentham embraced him effusively: "As the hart panteth for the water-brooks, so panted my heart for thee, my son." Even the ebullient son of Kerry, Daniel O'Connell, terror of law-abiding Englishmen, was lamblike in dealing with Bentham, whom he called "Benefactor of the Human Race," "Respected and revered Master," while the philosopher in return hailed him as "Dan, dear child," overlooking the duel in which O'Connell had once killed his opponent. Not that Bentham approved of dueling; for when the Duke of Wellington fought Lord Winchelsea, Bentham sent him a sharp reproof beginning with the stern admonition: "Misguided man!"

Sir Leslie Stephen later spoke of Bentham as having been endowed with "the elephantine humour of one who was all his life a philosopher and a child." The curious mingling in one person of the gravity of age with the playfulness of youth was observed by most visitors to Queen Square Place. "Mr. Bentham's general appearance," wrote Hazlitt, was "a singular mixture of boyish simplicity and of the venerableness of age." "He never knew prosperity and adversity, passion nor satiety," said John Stuart Mill. "He never had even the experiences which sickness gives; he lived from childhood to eighty-five in boyish health. He knew no dejection, no heaviness of heart. He never felt life a sore and weary burden. He was a boy to the last."

Mill of course knew Bentham only in old age, by which time the philosopher had achieved an almost perfect serenity of mind. The unhappiness of Bentham's early life was never known to Mill. The tranquillity of his later years was the result partly of a frank enjoyment of the esteem which time had brought ("now at length, when I am just ready to drop into the grave," he wrote, "my fame has spread itself all over the civilized world") and partly of the gradual failing, with increasing age, of the affective side of his nature. It is a serious mistake to consider Bentham—as contemporaries like Carlyle and Emerson were prone to do—only as a man devoid of feeling, a mere logic-grinder. Indeed it seems likely that Bentham developed his analytical powers to such an extreme degree as a defense aga st the too disturbing challenge of his emotional needs. For the minute analysis of feeling can be an anodyne against the pain that may result from an excessive capacity to feel.

If the perpetual youthfulness of Bentham, remarked by observers like Hazlitt and Mill, was the source of some of his chief virtues, it was also responsible for certain defects in his thinking. The habit of endless questioning, "the disposition to demand the *why* of everything," as Mill put it, and the refusal to be put off by illogical or evasive answers derive essentially from the insatiable curiosity of childhood and furnish the materials for intellectual growth. In most lives, this ceaseless curiosity diminishes during the normal process of growing up, or else is harnessed to selfish and practical ends. ("Compare," says Freud, "the feeble mentality of the average adult with the radiant intelligence of the normal healthy child.") Jeremy Bentham, therefore, in failing to develop the usual unquestioning acceptance of mediocrity, and of the world as it exists, may be regarded as an example of fortunately arrested development.

This childlike candor of mind, and utter transparency of intention, was what made him dare to question what others, like Blackstone or his father, had accepted without hesitation. "During so many generations," wrote Mill, "in each of which thousands of well-educated young men were successively placed in Bentham's position and with Bentham's opportunities, he alone was found with sufficient moral sensibility and self-reliance to say to himself, that these things, however profitable they might be, were frauds. Who, before Bentham," Mill continued, "(whatever controversies might exist on points of detail), dared to speak disrespectfully, in express terms, of the British Constitution and the English Law? He did so, and his arguments and his example together encouraged others." The calm and confident belief in the correctness of his convictions was as important an element in Bentham's success as his extraordinary intellectual power.

This same innocence of mind, sustained over the years by Bentham's philosophic seclusion and withdrawal from the practical business of life, was also, however, the cause of his inadequate notions about human psychology. For a long time Bentham tended to believe that merely to expose an abuse would lead to its disappearance. His *Book of Fallacies* (1824) is perhaps the most masterly exposé in English of the sophistries that underlie most public speaking, and it is no less cogent today than when it was written, a century and a quarter ago. Of all Bentham's works, it is perhaps the one which has best defied "the iniquity of oblivion."

Bentham, however, allowed himself to believe that a day would come when the rhetorical fallacies of a public speaker would immediately be detected by the intelligence of his audience, so that a speaker misled by emotion would at once be interrupted by impatient cries of "Stale! Stale! Fallacy of Authority! Fallacy of Distrust!" To this naive optimism about the possibility of developing a disinterested and widely diffused public intelligence, Bentham united a touching but childish faith in the purity of men's motives. Believing that others were as idealistic as himself, he was slow to realize the lengths to which, in order to protect their own interests, the wielders of power would go. "I was a great reformist," he plaintively recalled when he was eighty, "but never suspected that the people in power were against reform. I supposed they only wanted to know what was good in order to embrace it."

A similar innocence led him to underrate the complexities and contradictions of human nature, as they had developed under the sway of differing customs and traditions. His "sanguine and almost boyish fancy" led him to overestimate the feasibility of reform. Thus he had not the least conception of the extraordinary variety of cultures, religions, languages, and customs that go to make up India, and believed that he could conjure away the problems which beset the English rulers of that teeming subcontinent with a wave of the hand. "I could, with the same facility, turn my hand to the concerns of that distant country," he once wrote, "as to those of the parish in which I live." At a given moment he was willing to legislate for Britain, India, or Russia equally with Venezuela, Spain, or Greece, or for the United States along with Egypt. In actual fact, however, he could not even convince his own countrymen of the truth of ideas that to him were self-evidently true and useful.

To such a degree did Bentham's alienation from the world increase with its persistent rejection of his ideas that he began to exhibit many characteristics of the obsessional neurotic. He could scarcely tolerate the presence of more than one visitor at a time. He, who had once been fond of company, began to develop a morbid shyness and fear of strangers. An elaborate ritual came to regulate the first introduction of a guest. To minimize pain, he would determine in advance the precise place, in the doorway or on the staircase, which he and his visitor would occupy as they were introduced. In his *Autobigraphy* Robert Owen records the philosopher's nervous agitation at the prospect of their first meeting and how when this had been effected, Bentham exclaimed with evident relief, "Well, well! It is all over. We are introduced." He would write letters to philosophers like Voltaire and d'Alembert and then be too shy to send them. No doubt there was also something obsessional about the daily ritual by means of which, in a sedentary occupation, Bentham safeguarded his health—as in "the ante-jentacular and post prandial circumgyrations" around his garden, exercises in which his visitors were invited to accompany him.

One interesting manifestation of Bentham's neurosis was an obsessional hatred of the king. In boyhood he had, of course, been taught to revere George III, but as he matured and struggled to establish his own identity, he came to displace some of the antagonism which he felt toward his father upon the chief father figure of the realm. His father's death did not resolve the conflict: indeed, his hostility to the sovereign increased. One result of it was a curious production entitled *A History of the Warfare between Jeremy Bentham and George III, by One of the Belligerents*. Possibly Bentham's rejection of deity derived from the same root feeling.

Apart from these obsessional traits, Bentham had known weariness and depression, and had striven to overcome them. As a young man he had been plagued by what he called "the blue devils," a mood of despondency from which he sought to free himself by going into society. "How I was tormented!" he exclaimed, on reading in old age through one of his youthful diaries. "I went on very slowly in my father's conception, but it was the result of dejection of spirits." Surely it was of himself that he was speaking when, in a work on political economy, he commented incidentally on the "timidity which labours in grief, in darkness, in awkwardness, embarrassment—and false shame . . . the frequent and afflictive companions and most cruel enemies of merit and solitary genius."

So far as the public was concerned, at the age of sixty Bentham was still unknown and of all the projects which he had attempted and which had come to grief, his ideal prison, or Panopticon, caused him more distress than all the rest. To "this mill for grinding rogues honest and idle men industrious," he had devoted twenty years of his life and a considerable part of his fortune. The only result was that he was "not only a laughing stock, but a ruined man." In the end it had all come to nothing, though in 1814 Parliament voted him £23,000 compensation for the money he had spent on it. (The state penitentiary at Joliet, Illinois, however, was later modeled on the Panopticon.) In 1795, Wilberforce had described "poor Bentham" as "dying of sickness of hope deferred." "Never was anyone worse used," he declared. "I have seen the tears run down the cheeks of that strong-minded man, through vexation at the pressing importunity of creditors and the insolence of official underlings." To represent Bentham as a man without feeling is to substitute a crude caricature for a living person.

The truth is that, though he was lacking in passion, Bentham's nature was warm and affectionate, his sensibilities tender and easily bruised. "In point of appetite," he wrote his father at the age of twenty-seven, "I am as cool as any Anchorite could wish to be." Yet once at least, by his own admission, he had "been shot through and through with a pair of black eyes." As a young man he had even given advice about affairs of the heart to his younger brother (later Sir Samuel Bentham, the distinguished naval engineer), for whose education he considered himself responsible. "Apply thyself to the young girls about thee, not as matter of anxiety, but of amusement. Kiss their hands: be not sparing of their lips: and use soft violence. Whatever they take patiently, do thou a little more. In general, they will sooner forgive thee for doing too much than too little."

Solitary in childhood, set apart in youth by mental precocity and physical smallness, Bentham had never been exposed to the chances and challenges of normal life. As a guest of Lord Shelburne in 1781, at his beautiful house of Bowood, he had been, for the first time in his life, thrown in the company of ladies. He pleased them with his skill at chess and on the harpsichord, and by his general amiability and liveliness. He even gained the entrée to Lady Shelburne's dressing room. Mild flirtations developed in such a setting, and he found himself—perhaps to his surprise—a little in love with two ladies, one after the other— with Miss Caroline Vernon, sister of Lady Shelburne, and after her departure, with Lord Holland's sister Lady Caroline Fox, then a girl of thirteen. Bentham was thirty-three—an odd little creature, intelligent, good-natured and—in his own phrase—full of "foolish sensibilities."

With Miss Vernon he got on famously: they were "mighty social merry" over the chessboard, and Bentham quoted Lord Shelburne as having observed that "he never saw her laugh with anybody as much as with me." But the lady's visit came to an end, and despite "the air of cordiality and attention with which I took my leave of her at night," Bentham lacked the courage to bid her farewell next morning, "thinking it might be deemed an act of impertinence." He was fearful of gossip, and aware of "the great gulfs of a hundred kinds that are fixed between us." In other words, he was unable to profit by the good advice he had given to his brother Samuel. Doubtless he was timid, self-conscious, and painfully inhibited.

After Miss Vernon's departure, Lady Caroline Fox came to stay at Bowood in that delightful summer. "We are very good friends: she too plays at chess; she is very fond of it. . . . Her face—I had like to have forgot her face," Bentham remarks roguishly, "is far from unpleasing." To his father—"Honoured Sir"—he wrote gaily that it was "absolutely necessary" that he should be "in readiness to play at chess with Miss F., whose *Cavaliere Servente* I have been ever since she came here. . . . Would you have thought of my being in such favour with the ladies?" But something always went awry: nothing ever came of these sentimental attachments. All his life, however, Bentham was persuaded that Lord Shelburne had "had many projects for marrying me to ladies of his acquaintance." If so, such plans miscarried.

"To the end of his days," said Sir John Bowring, "Bentham spoke of Bowood and its inhabitants with intense affection. I have often seen tears roll down his cheeks when reverting to some of the loved inhabitants of that mansion. Nearly fifty years later, when he was almost eighty, Bentham wrote to one of "the fair ladies of Bowood"—his friend and biographer is too discreet to mention which—and reminded her of the flower she had given him "in the green lane." "Since that day," said Bentham—and he was given to precision—"not a single one has passed (not to speak of nights), in which you have not engrossed more of my thoughts than I could have wished." At his death he promised to send her a ring, with his profile and a lock of snow-white hair. "You will not, I hope, be ashamed of me." To this letter he received an answer that was "cold and distant . . . and he was indescribably hurt and disappointed by it." He sat "a long time, greatly moved." At last he said to Bowring, "Take me forward, I entreat you, to the future—do not let me go back to the past—talk of something—find out something to remove my thoughts from the time of my youth!" It is curious to remember that even John Stuart Mill believed that Bentham "knew no dejection, no heaviness of heart."

What Bentham lost in personal happiness, the world gained in the flow of sympathy for oppressed and suffering things which was released by the quick springs of his lively imagination. All whom society condemned found in him their champion—not only the familiar persecuted minorities, the Catholic, the Jew, the Negro, but also the felon in the pillory, the soldier under the lash, the unwed mother, the unsuccessful suicide, the homosexual. (Individuals in those last three categories, he argued, lay outside the field of penal legislation.) Like his contemporary Samuel Rogers, he might well have seen some morning in London "a cartload of young girls, in dresses of various colours, on their way to be executed at Tyburn"; and we know that from his hermitage he could hear the screams of soldiers being flogged in the neighboring barracks. Such sights and sounds must have been anguish to a man of so delicate a sensibility. Generations ahead of his time, he was opposed to capital punishment.

Animals, he believed, deserved the same consideration as human beings. Yet he was not one whose championship of animals was the obverse of a revulsion from mankind, for he thought even vivisection justified if it really served the interests of humanity. One of the most fruitful friendships of his life—it led to the humanizing of the penal code—was with Sir Samuel Romilly. It began with their common fondness for cats. "Our love for pusses, our mutual respect for animals," said Bentham, "was a bond of union. For pusses and mouses we had both of us great kindness."

In his workshop Bentham used to tame mice and allowed them to run about freely. He was delighted to see them playing among his papers, and only regretted that the time spent in stroking them was lost to legislation. At his farmhouse at Hendon, he had "a beautiful pig," which "loved to come and lie down to be rubbed, and took to following me like a dog"; while at Ford Abbey, in Devonshire, "there was a young ass of great symmetry and beauty, to which I was much attached, and which grew much attached to me—each fondling the other."

The same playful nature and innocence of mind extended to the naming of the inanimate objects of his daily use—Dapple, his walking stick, or Dick, his "sacred tea-pot." Perhaps such names served also as magical incantations to ward off evil. But where ultimate matters were concerned, Bentham's regard for truth was absolute. His anthropomorphism stopped short of the world of nature. He had no belief in God, in the soul, or in immortality. Orthodox Christianity he called the great "Juggernaut;" the Bible, the "Jugg Book." These terms he invented so as not to scandalize his servants, in case they should hear religious topics discussed between himself and his friends, while they were waiting at table. In any conventional sense, Bentham was without religion—though he might perhaps have subscribed to Tom Paine's saying that his religion was to do good to mankind. For Bentham, at all events, morality and religion had no necessary connection.

When his own hour came, he faced death with the same cheerful composure that had carried him so equably through life. Right up to the end he was at work, "codifying like any dragon." To Bowring, who was with him in his last moments, he observed characteristically: "I now feel that I am dying; our care must be to minimize pain." He asked that the servants be dismissed, since the sight of him would only make them unhappy. "Yet I must not be alone: *you* will remain with me, and you only; and then we shall have reduced the pain to the least possible amount." 'His head reposed on my bosom," Bowring recalled. "After he had ceased to speak, he smiled, and grasped my hand. He looked at me affectionately, and closed his eyes. There was no struggle—no suffering—life faded into death."

Bentham left his body to be dissected for scientific purposes in the presence of his friends. Today one may see him in a glass case in University College, London. The clothed skeleton is seated, wearing Bentham's everyday clothes, his wide-brimmed straw hat upon his head, and the faithful Dapple in his hand. Despite the fact that the head is stuffed, while the philosopher's skull lies between his feet, the general affect is astonishingly lifelike.

Bentham's epitaph may best be spoken by one who, if the most influential of his followers, was also the most perceptive of his critics: "A place, therefore," says John Stuart Mill, "must be assigned to Bentham among the masters of wisdom, the great teachers and permanent intellectual ornaments of the human race. He is among those who have enriched mankind with imperishable gifts." It is fitting also to remember Bentham's modest and realistic estimate of his own motivation. "I am a selfish man," he noted in one of the last entries in his *Commonplace Book*, "as selfish as any man can be. But in me, somehow or other, so it happens, selfishness has taken the shape of benevolence."

II

John Stuart Mill

(1806-73)

JOHN STUART MILL possessed one of the most lucid and rational minds that ever existed in England. He is the author of perhaps the finest vindication of the principle of democracy which has yet been written in the English language—the essay *On Liberty*. He is also an illuminating example of the way in which a child prodigy may fulfill in adult life the promise of his youth. For owing to his father's detestation of the training then given in English schools and universities, with their pronounced clerical bias, the boy was never sent to school but was educated wholly by his father at home.

The mental training of which Mill left so absorbing an account in his *Autobiography* constitutes one of the most notable educational experiments in history. It violated all the principles that today are regarded as fundamental in the training of children. It was grim, unremitting, and loveless, but it produced that unique figure in the history of English thought, John Stuart Mill. "It proved," he said, "how much more than is commonly supposed may be taught, and well taught, in those early years which, in the common modes of what is called instruction, are little better than wasted." Mill used to say that by nature he was less quick of apprehension, less retentive of memory, and less resolute in character than the average child; and that if he had been able to achieve any distinction in life, it was due to the education he had received from his father. "What I could do, could assuredly be done by any boy or girl of average capacity and healthy physical constitution: and if I have accomplished anything, I owe it, among other fortunate circumstances, to the fact that through the early training bestowed on me by my father, I started, I may fairly say, with an advantage of a quarter of a century over my contemporaries."

At the age of three, Mill began to read Aesop's *Fables* in Greek; and then went on to Herodotus and Xenophon. By the time he was seven, he had read the first six *Dialogues* of Plato. "I have no remembrance of the time when I began to learn Greek," he later recalled. At twelve he had gone beyond his father in mathematics and had also read his way through much of Livy, Cicero, Sallust, and Tacitus as well as through Virgil, Horace, Ovid, Lucretius, and Juvenal.

History he discovered for himself in the works of Robertson, Hume, and Gibbon. Like Bentham as a boy, he particularly loved stories of soldiers and battles, and identified himself with forlorn or desperate causes—with the Dutch against the Spanish Inquisition, with Frederick the Great or with Paoli in Corsica against the odds that each had faced. Though he was taught little poetry, he was excited by the martial romances of Scott—*Marmion,* perhaps, or *The Lay of the Last Minstrel.* Already at five, he had favored the wife of a first Lord of the Admiralty with a discussion of the respective merits of Marlborough and Napoleon, and at six he composed a history of Rome in fifteen hundred words.

Two considerations dominated the father's educational psychology: the early training of memory in order to amass a copious and exact store of knowledge; and the training of mind, so that the boy should learn to think and judge for himself on the basis of the knowledge he had acquired.

James Mill, the father, was an ex-Presbyterian preacher and the self-made son of a Scottish shoemaker. His special interest was psychology, and he was extremely positive in his opinions. "If I had time to write a book," he once observed blandly, "I would make the human mind as plain as the road from Charing Cross to St. Paul's." Those who differed from him he condemned. Early in his reading of the *Critique of Pure Reason,* he turned aside in disgust with the patronizing remark that he saw "clearly enough what poor Kant is about." His contempt for aristocracy is well conveyed by his comment on one occasion that he had just seen "Lord Paget and another well-dressed animal whose name I did not hear." In spite of these shortcomings, he was,

Blanco White declared, "a very superior man. Though severe and almost stiff in the forms of his mind, he was a man of profound observation, and worthy of the name of a philosopher. He was also a man of great virtue and benevolence, though reverend gentlemen considered him an Atheist."

At the age of thirty-five James Mill had become the personal friend and ardent disciple of Jeremy Bentham, so that the ideas in which his eldest son was educated were those of the Utilitarian philosopher. The whole family stayed frequently with Bentham, and the boy learned to revere him as a sort of spiritual grandparent. Had James Mill died, Bentham was to have become the boy's legal guardian.

In the *Autobiography*, forty years later, Mill was to write: "The 'principle of utility,' understood as Bentham understood it —fell exactly into its place as the keystone which held together the detached and fragmentary components of my knowledge and beliefs. It gave unity to my conception of things. I now had opinions; a creed, a doctrine, a philosophy: in one among the best senses of the word, a religion."

The boy's education was wholly rational and scientific in character. Religious training played no part in it: religion was not so much attacked as ignored. Mill's formal criticism of the education he had received was not that it had been too little concerned with literature and the arts, but that it had been too speculative in nature, and too little practical in aim.

Mill's childhood was not solitary, as Bentham's had been for the first nine years of his life. On the contrary, Mill was the first of a long line of brothers and sisters—there were nine in twenty years—each one of whom received his or her education primarily from their eldest brother. The latter acted, therefore, as a kind of monitor inside his father's household. The direct responsibility for the mental training of so many other children induced at an early age a degree of self-reliance and maturity which was quite as remarkable as the boy's intellectual precocity.

This self-contained world of a single family, to which no playmates or companions were admitted from outside, was responsible for a strongly marked trait of character in which Mill much resembled the youthful Bentham: innocence and unworldliness. At the age of fourteen Mill had not the least idea that he knew more than other children at his age, or that his education had been in any way peculiar. Far from being conceited, he remembered only how at different times he had failed to live up to his father's expectations. Like Bentham, he developed an uncompromising devotion to truth, which was to mark him all his life. His unquestioned status as—under his father—head of the family removed from him all fear of rivalry and gave him a sense of complete confidence and security. "He was," as Professor Bain wrote, "absolutely without feeling of rivalry, or jealousy of other men's success." Francis Place, who knew Mill well as a boy, once prophesied of him: "He will be a truly astonishing man; but he will probably be morose and selfish." Neither part of this prophecy came true.

The chief defect in this singular education was its rigid repression of feeling—its almost total absence of love. Bentham had early noted of his new disciple, Mill's father, that "his creed of politics results less from love of the many, than from hatred of the few." In his *Autobiography*, Mill's son recalled how "constitutionally irritable" his father had been, how he had often lost his temper with him, and how severe had been his punishments, though they were never corporal. For a mistake in a single word, the children would be denied their dinner at the usual hour of one and kept waiting for it till six. Whenever the father entered the room, silence fell on the family. The children never cried or showed any emotion. Fear and respect were the basis of Mill's relation to his father. "I had no one to whom I desired to express everything which I felt," he wrote in a portion of the *Autobiography* which was not included in the first published version, "and the only person I was in communication with to whom I looked up, I had far too much fear of to make the communication to him of any act or feeling ever a matter of frank impulse or spontaneous inclination." "He could help the mass," wrote Place of James Mill, "but he could not help the individual, not even himself, or his own."

It is curious how little Mill's mother figures in all this, or in Mill's later memories. A friend of the family recalled her as "a tall, handsome lady, sweet-tempered, with pleasant manners, fond of her children." She was not, however, in the least intellectual, as a result of which she appears to have been excluded from a large part of the family life—that part which consisted of the educational establishment presided over by her husband and conducted by her eldest son. In an unpublished fragment, Mill remarked of his mother that her children "liked her because she was kind to them; but to make herself loved, looked up to, or even obeyed, required qualities which she unfortunately did not possess." It is impossible to know how just or unjust this judgment may have been: no doubt to love in such a loveless household, presided over by so tyrannical a patriarch, was impossible. Mill's opinion was emphatic: "I grew up in the absence of love and in the presence of fear; and many and indelible are the effects of this bringing up in the stunting of my moral growth." The most blameworthy act in Mill's life was perhaps the abruptness, not to say the cruelty, with which, immediately after his marriage, he virtually cut his mother and his family out of his life. In his *Autobiography* his brothers and sisters are rarely mentioned, his mother not at all.

At fourteen, when he was sent alone to live for a year in the south of France in the house of Jeremy Bentham's younger brother Sir Samuel, the naval engineer, Mill gained his first idea of the outside world. He was sent abroad to learn French and to study French history, politics, and literature. The sudden exposure to a cheerful, noisy, gregarious, extrovert family must have been a shock. In vain the boy tried to put in his usual nine hours' daily reading. For the first time in his life he must have realized that his own experience had been not, as he supposed, normal, but highly exceptional. Self-consciousness no doubt enhanced the sense of isolation.

Several years later—at the age of twenty—when his education was finished and he was employed, like his father, by the East India Company, in whose service he remained for the greater part of his life, Mill experienced the most profound emotional crisis of his life. Without knowing why, he suddenly fell into a deep mental dejection. It lasted through one dreadful London winter, and he was powerless to shake it off. The habits of study he had acquired were of no avail: all his learning seemed useless. Having prepared himself so assiduously, under his father's tutelage, for his life's work—to contribute to the greatest happiness of the greatest number—he found to his astonishment that his own personal happiness had vanished, apparently forever. With dismay he realized that even should he attain his goal—the happiness of mankind—his own existence would be no happier than before. It was the mental affliction that the medieval monks had called "accidie," and which they had regarded as the worst of misfortunes.

Many years later, in his *Autobiography*, Mill related the astonishing way in which his malaise found unexpected and instantaneous relief. He was reading Marmontel's *Memoirs* and had just reached the passage in which the playwright told how his father's sudden death had left the family ruined and how, at that same moment, though still a boy, he realized that it was his duty to take his father's place and fend for the rest of the family. In reading this passage, Mill suddenly found himself in tears, and unaccountably possessed by joy. "I was no longer hopeless: I was not a stick or a stone. I had still, it seemed, some of the material out of which all worth of character, and all capacity for happiness, are made." Earlier biographers attributed this emotional breakdown, which Mill calls "A Crisis in my Mental History," to fatigue from prolonged overwork. More plausible, however, is the psychoanalytical suggestion that Mill was probably suffering from a severe unconscious death wish against his tyrannical father, which the passage in Marmontel, by making explicit his own unconscious fantasies, enabled him spontaneously to resolve.

James Mill died in 1836. His eldest son was thirty, and only then did he print the critical estimate of Bentham which he had written in 1833, but had kept back out of regard for his father's feelings. "As good may be drawn out of evil," he wrote Bulwer-Lytton, "the event which has deprived the world of the man of the greatest philosophical genius it possessed . . . has made it far easier . . . to soften the harder and sterner features of its Radicalism and Utilitarianism."

Yet throughout life Mill bore the marks of the ordeal through which he had passed. The intense nervous strain to which he had been subjected was evident in the spasmodic twitching of a muscle over one eye and in the anguished look, as of one holding sternly in check an almost uncontrollable grief, which haunts us in Mill's later photographs. It was manifest also in the consuming loneliness that possessed him—save during the years of his love for Harriet Taylor. "There is now no human being (with whom I can associate on terms of equality) who acknowledges a common object with me."

The legend that Mill was a dry rationalist, devoid of feeling and without understanding of life, was one that was sedulously propagated while he was alive by political enemies like Disraeli and by false friends like Carlyle. "Mill's character has generally been regarded as somewhat cold and impassive," wrote one of his earliest biographers. Charlotte Brontë thought that Mill, despite his defense of women's rights, "would make a hard dry dismal world of it," and rejoiced to see how Ruskin made the Utilitarians "fret and fume." Writings such as the essay *On Liberty* and *The Subjection of Women*, in which one may sense underlying the argument the presence of feeling, intense but controlled, should have sufficed to dispel so false an idea of Mill's personality. He was, in fact, as Thirlwall, bishop of St. David's, discerned, "a man of vehemently passionate susceptibility. The snow covers a volcano." Even in Mill's *Utilitarianism*, a set piece in defense of the new philosophy, one notices a degree of passion that was lacking in Bentham. "It is better to be Socrates dissatisfied," he wrote in one place, "than a fool satisfied"; in another, he said that though he doubted "whether a noble character is always the happier for its nobleness, yet it always contributes to the sum of greatest happiness." The ability to do without happiness, he suggested, affords the best hope of actually being happy. He denied that Utilitarianism was either selfish or coldhearted, and asserted that the teachings of Christ represented "the complete spirit of the ethics of utility."

Mill's private correspondence also reveals a nature that is anything but "cold and impassive." There is, for example, a decided energy about some of his political observations. Thus, in 1831, at the age of twenty-five, Mill was so exasperated by Tory attempts to wreck the Great Reform Bill, that he was capable of telling his friend John Sterling: "I should not care though a revolution were to exterminate every person in Great Britain and Ireland who has £500 a year. Many very amiable persons would perish, but what is the world the better for such amiable persons?" "Highly incendiary stuff," says Michael St. John Packe,

Mill's latest biographer: yet so completely have such feelings vanished from Mill's published works, that the reader of them can scarcely even guess at their existence. The London *Times* he stigmatized as "the meanest, most malicious, and most hypocritical among our very low newspaper press." For Napoleon III, who had slaughtered the workingmen of Paris, he entertained an almost personal hatred; and when he suspected Lord John Russell of having "a sentimental affection" for the tyrant, he felt "a strong desire to kick the rascal." Much more discerning than some better placed observers was the able New York journalist George Smalley, who, after visiting Mill at Avignon, came away with the decided impression that here was a man who felt strongly about things, and who could hate as well as love.

The story of Mill's boyhood, however, as described by Mill himself, seems to warrant the view of him as a man of less than average feeling; and admirers such as Professor Bain, who insisted that the bent of his mind was logical and abstract rather than concrete or poetic, provided confirmation of the idea. Even Gladstone's tribute to Mill—"the Saint of Rationalism"—may have done something to propagate the myth that he was nothing more than a dry rationalist.

The strongest influence contributing to this caricature was the spiteful gossip of Mill's jealous rival, Carlyle. "He seemed to me," wrote the latter, "to be withering or withered into the miserablest meta-physical scrae [old shoe], body and mind, that I had almost ever met within the world. His eyes go twinkling and jerking with wild lights and twitches; his head is bald, his face brown and dry—poor fellow after all." Mill's *Autobiography* he characterized as "wholly the life of a logic-chopping machine, little more of human in it than if it had been done by a thing of mechanized iron. Autobiography of a steam-engine. . . ." After Mill's death, Carlyle derided his successful editorship of the *London & Westminster Review* as "sawdust to the masthead, and a croakery of crawling things, instead of a speaking by men."

Time has revealed the truth to be almost the opposite. The works which were so influential during Mill's lifetime—the *System of Logic* (1843), which dominated the study of logic in British universities for fifty years, and the *Principles of Political Economy* (1848), which went through thirty-two editions in the same space of time, and nearly as many more since then—

are now no longer popular. The treatise on logic, says Bertrand Russell, is, from a modern point of view, less cogent than Duns, Scotus or William of Occam; while, according to Packe, the work on political economy was not abreast of contemporary knowledge even at the time it was written and in fact retarded the study of that subject for a generation.

One may agree with Russell that the writings that have really kept alive Mill's name and influence are the essay *On Liberty* (1859) and *The Subjection of Women* (1869). Professor F. A. Hayek, the editor of Mill's letters, believes, however, that it is the *Autobiography* which will live longest of all Mill's works, and that it has already exerted a greater influence than any other. In any event, these writings are distinguished not only by Mill's usual clarity of thought and persuasiveness of style but by the imprint of deep personal feeling. In Lord Russell's view, the immense effect Mill had upon his own age was due more to moral elevation than to any special capacity for abstruse reasoning.

Professor Hayek goes so far as to consider Mill as having been essentially a romantic. For example, Mill regarded marriage as justified not by any prudential consideration, but solely by mutual love. "Surely it is wrong, wrong in every way, and on every view of morality," he wrote in 1831 (twenty years before his own marriage), "that there should exist any motives to marriage excepting the happiness which two persons who love one another feel in associating their own existence." Certainly he was remote from his own father and from Bentham when he wrote: "The highest natures are of course impassioned natures," or again, that "the *justification* of passion, and one of its greatest beauties and glories, is that in an otherwise fine character it weakens *no* feeling which deserves to subsist, but would naturally strengthen them all." Actually, Mill's bias toward feeling led him, almost in the manner of Plato, to hypostatize ideas. He inclined, wrote the eminent Danish critic George Brandes not long after Mill's death, "to serve not a cause but its personal incarnation." Mill's worship of Harriet Taylor is of course the supreme example of such a tendency.

To demonstrate that, for all his splendid gifts of argumentation, Mill was more than a dry logician, and to recognize that the secret of his influence lay in the fact that he was a man of profound feeling, is to explain another facet of Mill's nature which has puzzled biographers. More than once he came under the influence of minds plainly inferior to his own: he seemed even to rejoice in the temporary surrender of his personality to them. This was true of his relations with F. D. Maurice and John Sterling, and above all, with Thomas Carlyle. It may also, despite his own disclaimer, throw light on the influence which, almost from the moment they met, Mrs. Harriet Taylor exercised upon him.

Carlyle was the least systematic and the most intuitive of thinkers. His writings are full of unexamined assumptions and violent prejudices—religious, political, social, even racial. What he lacks in reason and credibility he makes up for by confident dogmatism and by bullying the reader. It has been observed that for more than forty years he preached the doctrine of silence at the top of his voice. "A moral desperado," Matthew Arnold called him. "We begin with introspection and the eternal verities," said Lord Morley, "and we end with blood and iron." Carlyle was not merely a hero worshiper of the Great Man—Frederick the Great or Bismarck—but a spiritual precursor of twentieth-century fascism. What, one wonders, was the appeal of such a man—with his intolerance of ideas he did not share, his reactionary politics, his contempt for democracy, his belief in master races—for so convinced a believer in the power of reason and in the process of democracy as John Stuart Mill?

At first reading, Carlyle's writings seemed to the philosopher to be only "a haze of poetry and German metaphysics"; *Sartor Resartus*, which Mill considered Carlyle's "best and greatest work," he read with "enthusiastic admiration and the keenest delight." Mill's considered estimate of his rival found expression in his *Autobiography*: "I was during a long period one of his most fervent admirers; but the good his writings did me was not as philosophy to instruct, but as poetry to animate. . . . I felt that he was a poet, and that I was not; that he was a man of intuition, which I was not; and that as such, he not only saw many things long before me, which I could only, when they were pointed out to me, hobble after and prove, but that it was highly probable he could see many things which were not visible to me even after they were pointed out." It may be doubted whether any distinguished thinker has ever paid so generous a tribute to a contemporary and rival. Carlyle, at any rate, was willing to tolerate and patronize Mill so long as he remained his disciple; but when the latter, having assimilated what he could, left him to follow his native bent, Carlyle never forgave what he regarded as apostasy. The essay *On Liberty* he regarded as a personal affront. His cold anger followed Mill thereafter to the grave.

It is evident in Mill that his habit of temporary subjection to natures the opposite of his own, however much it may have been rooted in psychological necessity, was the source of his greatest virtue as a thinker—his ability to understand and portray sympathetically ideas with which, from the general bent of his mind, he might have been expected to be wholly out of sympathy. His essay on Coleridge—and the plea made therein for moderate conservatism as a counterpoise to certain arid tendencies in Bentham's philosophy—is an excellent illustration of the comprehensiveness and tolerance of Mill's mental outlook. He is, indeed, justly remembered as the prince of debaters, the fairest and most scrupulous of antagonists. "His treatment of opponents," says Professor Bain, "was a model of the ethics of controversy." In argument it was his practice—one which was capable of producing devastating results—to state his adversary's case better than that adversary had been able to do; and then, having built it up, to demolish it by revealing its fallacies and undermining its logic.

Sir Arthur Salter once declared that Mill was able to evoke in his readers, and especially in the young, a sort of "intellectual ecstasy." This irresistible power of Mill as a thinker is the result of a twofold attraction: on the surface, a lucid and orderly marshaling of arguments; and just below, the ever-present pulse of passion—precisely the same quality of controlled emotion which was stamped upon his features. As Jung might put it, Mill deliberately cultivated the recessive parts of his personality and strengthened those which had been repressed through training and environment. "The whole course of my intellectual cultivation," wrote Mill, "had made precocious and premature analysis the inveterate habit of my mind." Hence he deliberately determined to adjust the balance between emotion and reason. Thus, unlike Bentham, he could affirm that "the cultivation of the feelings became one of the cardinal points in my ethical and philosophical creed."

Mill's urgent desire that the rational mind should enter fully into the realm of feeling is best illustrated in his relationship with Harriet Taylor. Most biographers have been embarrassed or apologetic about an "infatuation" seemingly so unaccountable. Yet the most recent and best-informed students of Mill's life are agreed that he did not greatly err in his own estimate of his wife's influence, an estimate that his contemporaries considered so extravagant as to indicate something approaching mental derangement on his part.

John Stuart Mill and Harriet Taylor fell in love at first sight. From their initial meeting at a dinner party in 1830, neither could put the other out of mind. Mill had not believed it possible that such a combination of beauty, intelligence, and passion could exist in any one human being as he now found in his "lovely friend." "Tall and slight," a contemporary described her, "with a slightly drooping figure, the movements of undulating grace. A small head, swan-like throat, and a complexion like a pearl. Large dark eyes, not soft or sleepy, but with a look of quiet command in them. A low sweet voice with very distinct utterance."

To those who knew her only in society, wrote Mill, "she was a beauty and a wit, with an air of natural distinction, felt by all who approached her"; but to those who came to know her more intimately, she was "a woman of deep and strong feeling, of penetrating and intuitive intelligence, and of an eminently meditative and poetic nature." She put him in mind of Shelley, whom they read together, yet he felt that the poet, "so far as his powers were developed in his short life, was but a child compared with what she ultimately became." She it was who delivered him from his emotional dependence on Carlyle, and who enabled him at last to make a rational estimate of the Scottish philosopher. "I never dreamed to judge him with any definiteness," wrote Mill, "until he was interpreted to me by one greatly the superior of us both—who was more a thinker than he, and more a poet than I—whose own mind and nature included his, and infinitely more."

One may imagine the growling anger with which, after Mill's death, the dyspeptic curmudgeon of Cheyne Row read this passage in the *Autobiography*.

As for what Harriet Taylor saw in Mill, her "companion spirit and heart's desire," we have her own characterization of him, and it is just. "You are in advance of your age in culture of the intellectual faculties," she told him, "you would be the most remarkable man of your age if you had no other claim to be so than your perfect impartiality and your fixed love of justice. These are the two qualities . . . which I believe to be the rarest and most difficult to human nature."

The Carlyles had, from the first, been interested spectators of the friendship—a friendship whose piquancy consisted in the fact that Mrs. Taylor was married and had two children, while a third was born in the year following her first meeting with Mill. Carlyle first mentions her as "a young beautiful reader of mine and 'dearest Friend' of Mill's." A few weeks later, having seen her walking in Regent's Park, he noted in his journal: "pale she, passionate and sad looking: really felt a kind of interest in her"; while later, over the gulf of many years, he evoked for his American friend Charles Eliot Norton, the memory of "those great dark eyes, that were flashing unutterable things while he [Mill] was discoursin' the unutterable concernin' all sorts o' high topics." Jane Welsh Carlyle was likewise a fascinated onlooker, absorbed but cautious: "There is a Mrs. Taylor whom I could really love, if it were safe and she were willing; but she is a dangerous looking woman and engrossed with a dangerous passion, and no useful relation can spring up between us."

Harriet Taylor was two years younger than Mill, and at the time of their first meeting had been married four years. When they had known each other for about two years, she was writing that they must not meet again; to which Mill replied that for him life on such terms would be impossible—nevertheless, to obey her wishes was for him a necessity. By the next summer they were spending much time together, and making full avowal of their love. Her husband, John Taylor, a druggist, had been informed of their feelings for each other and agreed to a trial separation of six months from his wife. Mrs. Taylor wrote later, that from the beginning of her intimacy with Mill, her relations with her husband had been purely platonic. Now, at the end of the six months, she set up a separate household, where Mill visited her several times a week. Both were agreed they could not live together, since divorce was impossible and scandal unthinkable. To all outward appearances, the husband's position was preserved. "Her affection for him," wrote Mill, "is now the sole obstacle to our being together—for the present there seems absolutely no prospect of that obstacle's being got over. She believes—and she knows him better than any of us can—that it would be the breaking up of his whole future life—*that* she is determined never to be the cause of, and I am as determined never to urge her to it, and convinced that if I did I should fail."

So this curious triangular relationship subsisted for sixteen years—till eventually cancer removed John Taylor in 1849. In his last illness, day and night, his wife nursed him with devotion for two agonizing months. "He besides you," she wrote Mill at this time, "is the only life I value in this wretched world." Even after the death of John Taylor—"a most upright, brave and honourable man," Mill calls him in his *Autobiography*—two years passed before the lovers were finally married in a registry office in Dorset. "Ardently as I should have aspired to this complete union of our lives," wrote Mill after his wife's death, "I, as much as my wife, would far rather have foregone that privilege forever, than have owed it to the premature death of one for whom I had the sincerest respect, and she the strongest affection." Seven and a half years of mutual happiness were left until Harriet Mill died at Avignon in 1858. During that period the Mills practically ceased going out into society, living wholly and with perfect contentment in each other's company.

For Mill the death of his wife was an overwhelming disaster. The unspeakable loneliness of his early years, which she had banished, now fell on him again. In order to be near her grave, which he visited daily, he bought a house at Avignon and lived there with her unmarried daughter, Helen Taylor, for the greater part of every year. "I can say nothing," he wrote in his *Autobiography*, "which could describe even in the faintest manner, what that loss was and is. But because I know that she would have wished it, I endeavor to make the best of what life I have left, and to work on for her purposes with such diminished

strength as can be derived from thoughts of her, and communion
with her memory. . . . Her memory is to me a religion, and her
approbation the standard by which, summing up as it does all
worthiness, I endeavour to regulate my life."

The year 1859 saw the publication of two great books, both
of them landmarks in Western thought, one scientific, the other
political—Darwin's *Origin of Species,* and Mill's essay *On Liberty.*
The latter is perhaps the most eloquent plea that has ever been
made in English on behalf of the rights of minorities. Mill did
not assume, like Bentham, that in a democracy the rule of the
majority would automatically involve "the greatest happiness of
the greatest number." Largely as the result of reading Alexis de
Tocqueville's classic, *Democracy in America* (1835), a book
which impressed him profoundly, Mill had come to fear the possibility of tyranny developing within a democratic society, a
tyranny operating not so much from the actual laws, as from
the steady and uniform pressure of popular, and increasingly
standardized, opinion. (In the era of the Organization Man, such
fears have been abundantly realized). Hence the essay is not only
a defense of minority groups, but a moving plea for the fullest
possible realization of each individual personality. It also contains
trenchant criticisms of the shams underlying social conventions,
and of the hollowness of conventional Christianity. Typical of
its uncompromising defense of freedom are such famous passages
as these:

> If all mankind minus one were of one opinion, and only one person
> were of the contrary opinion, mankind would be no more justified
> in silencing that one person, than he, if he had the power, would be
> justified in silencing mankind.
> No one can be a great thinker who does not recognize, that as a
> thinker it is his first duty to follow his intellect to whatever conclu-
> sions it may lead. Truth gains more even by the errors of one who,
> with due study and preparation, thinks for himself, than by the
> true opinions of those who only hold them because they do not
> suffer themselves to think. Not that it is solely, or chiefly, to form
> great thinkers, that freedom of thinking is required. On the con-
> trary, it is as much and even more indispensable to enable average
> human beings to attain the mental stature which they are capable of.

Readers with mystical tendencies, who preferred to glimpse
ideas through a penumbra of obscurity, were perplexed or dis-

mayed by the challenge of Mill's essay: "that terrible little book," the pious Quaker Caroline Fox called it, "so clear, and calm, and cold." "Mill makes me shiver," she remarked "his blade is so keen and so unhesitating." Carlyle was beside himself with rage. "He rose angrily from the table with the book in his hand," wrote the luckless clergyman who chanced upon him at this manic moment, "and gave vent to such a torrent of anathema, glancing at Christianity itself, as filled me with pain and amazement. He addressed himself directly to me, almost as if *I* had written the book."

When, on the other hand, Thomas Hardy, then only nineteen, discovered Mill's essay, he found in it an evangel. He knew it, he said, almost by heart; and after his death, his copy of *On Liberty* was found to be more underlined than any other book in his possession.

By a curious coincidence, the idea for a brief but convincing defense of liberty had started into Mill's mind at the identical place where, nearly a hundred years before, Gibbon had been inspired to write about the decline and fall of the Roman Empire: on the steps leading up to the Capitol in Rome. In the last two years of her life, Mill and his wife had worked on it together. "None of my writings," he said, "have been either so carefully composed, or so sedulously corrected as this." It was twice written out in full, and then they went through it again, "reading, weighing and criticizing every sentence." The essay, he wrote, "was more directly and literally our joint production than anything else which bears my name, for there was not a sentence of it that was not several times gone through by both of us together." Her death at Avignon in 1858 cut short the final revision they had planned. To see the little book through the press in 1859 was Mill's first homage to his wife's memory, and his first means of keeping himself alive. "I have made no alteration or addition to it," he wrote, "nor shall I ever. Though it wants the last touch of her hand, no substitute for that touch shall ever be attempted by mine."

When the essay came out, it had an immediate success. Many readers, no doubt, never having heard of Mrs. Mill (so absolute had been the Mills' withdrawal from the world), must have wondered at the dedication "to the beloved and deplored memory of her who was the inspirer, and in part the author, of all that is best in my writings—the friend and wife, whose exalted sense of truth and right was my strongest incitement, and whose approbation was my chief reward. . . . Were I but capable," added Mill, "of interpreting to the world one half the great thoughts and noble feelings which are buried in her grave, I should be the medium of a greater benefit to it, than is ever likely to arise from anything that I can write, unprompted and unassisted by her all but unrivalled wisdom."

"There is a touch of fatuousness in all this," complained Leonard Courtney. Mill's praise of his wife, wrote Sir Leslie Stephen, was "so hysterical as to check full sympathy." Professor Bain suggested that Mill overrated his wife's intellect because she was skillful in giving him back his own ideas. Most of his biographers have repeated these criticisms. It is of interest, then, to note that Professor Hayek's recent edition of Mill's correspondence with Mrs. Taylor, and Mr. Michael Packe's more recent full-scale biography of Mill, provide greater factual warrant for Mill's tribute than had been supposed possible. In numerous instances, her thought can be shown to have preceded his, and at times to have given his a new direction. Thus, she believed in capital punishment in exceptional cases, while he did not; she was opposed to the secret ballot, believing that no one should be ashamed to let others know how he had voted, while he favored it: yet on both of these questions he came to reverse his opinion and accept hers. Hers was the chief influence which led him away from laissez-faire ideas toward an increasing sympathy with socialism. The chapter in his *Political Economy* where this influence was first evident. ("The Probable Future of the Labouring Classes"), he declared was "entirely due to her." Most of it "was wholly an exposition of her thought, often in words taken from her own lips." On a question of specific fact, Mill's word cannot be doubted for, like Bentham, he was the most scrupulously truthful of men. The abstract part of his thought, he affirmed, was entirely his own but in the application of theory to actual human conditions, "I was her pupil, alike in boldness of speculation and cautiousness of practical judgment."

Curiously enough, in the one area of thought and action where Mill might be supposed to have been most influenced by his wife—that affecting the emancipation of women—his mind had been made up before he met her. It was the strength of his convictions in this respect, he wrote, that had been "more than anything else, the originating cause of the interest she felt in me." He only regretted that she had not lived to see his book devoted to this subject, and that his "imperfect statement of the case" had not had the benefit of her revision and improvement.

The Subjection of Women, which Mill kept by him for eight years before publishing it in 1869, reveals the same lucid and orderly mind, the same grasp of fundamental principles, the same beautiful development of ideas that marked the essay *On Liberty*. No more persuasive defense of women's rights has appeared in the century that has elapsed since then. What we are likely to forget, in a century which has seen the triumph of so many of the causes he fought for, is the startling, or shocking, originality of his ideas as they must have appeared to most of his contemporaries. Even Bentham, who had been convinced of the justice of equal political rights for men and women, had shrunk from avowing such a belief in public—perhaps understandably, since there were already so many who regarded him as a crackpot. "Interesting and well written, but in parts extravagant and absurd," was the radical John Bright's comment on reading Mill's book. Within a few weeks *The Subjection of Women* had made its way to Russia, for an American visitor to Moscow that summer heard "four dazzling princesses," living in a country house, declare "in perfect English that Mill's book demanding freedom for women was their Bible." The eldest proudly proclaimed; "I sleep with that book under my pillow."

It was largely in order to promote the cause of women's rights that Mill allowed himself to be elected M.P. for Westminster, the most distinguished seat in Parliament, in 1865. In one of the oddest elections in English history, Mill declined either to canvass his constituents or to contribute a penny to his election expenses. Like Burke at Bristol nearly a century before, he refused if elected to be merely the mouthpiece of his constituents. He promised them faithfully that he would always put national before local interests, and that none of those he represented need look to him for personal favors. "A well-known literary man," Mill reported subsequently, "was heard to say that the Almighty himself would have no chance of being elected on such a programme." Elected Mill was nonetheless; for so great was his reputation, that even with these self-imposed handicaps, he was returned as a Liberal to the House of Commons. There he introduced the first bill in English history to grant votes to women. It mustered only seventy-three votes in a House of more than six hundred. Yet, in the struggle for the emancipation of women, it constituted a landmark.

The other innovation that Mill was proud to have brought before the notice of the House of Commons—though it, too, was defeated—was his proposal for proportional representation, after the contemporary plan propounded by Thomas Hare. This alone, in Mill's opinion, would secure adequate representation of minority groups, and adequate statement of their views, in Parliament. Mill, of course, was familiar only with a two-party system of government and never allowed for the possibility that in a multiparty system proportional representation might hamstring the executive power.

In general, while in the House of Commons, Mill went out of his way to champion neglected or unpopular causes. Thus, in defending Ireland, he was compelled to vote against his own party, some of whose members thought him too eccentric and too little responsive to party discipline. As for the Tories, "the hon. member for Westminster is a great deal too clever for us in this House," complained a conservative intellectual, Robert Lowe. "The finishing governess," sneered Disraeli. After all, Mill had written that the Tories were "the stupidest party" in the state.

Concerning his actual attendance in the House, the historian Goldwin Smith calls him "the most strictly conscientious man" he ever knew. Night after night, "an image of patience," Mill would sit giving his full attention to debates whose intellectual level was so low that listening to them was patently a waste of his time.

"We well knew," wrote Gladstone subsequently, "Mr. Mill's intellectual eminence before he entered Parliament. What his conduct there principally disclosed, at least to me, was his singular moral elevation . . . of all the motives, stings and stimulants that reach men through their egoism in Parliament, none could move or even touch him. His conduct and his language were, in this respect, a sermon; . . . for the sake of the House of Commons at large, I rejoiced in his advent, and deplored his disappearance. He did us all good. In whatever party, whatever forum of opinion, I sorrowfully confess that such men are rare." Henry Fawcett, Gladstone's blind Postmaster General, himself a man universally respected, was of the opinion that Mill, in his three years in Parliament, had raised the whole moral tone of the House.

As for Mill's physical presence in the Commons, what honorable members beheld, according to Sir Leslie Stephen, was "a slight frail figure, trembling with nervous irritability. He poured out a series of perfectly formed sentences with an extraordinary rapidity suggestive of learning by heart: and when he lost the thread of his discourse closed his eyes for two or three minutes till, after regaining his composure, he could again take up his parable. Although his oratory was defective, he was clearly speaking with intense feeling and was exceedingly sensitive to his reception by his audience." The Tory country gentlemen, however, Sir Leslie observed, soon discovered that the animal's hide could be pierced by scornful laughter, and faced by such interruptions, Mill "could neither keep his temper nor conceal his contempt."

Occasionally Mill even spoke to the public at large. Once, passing by Trafalgar Square, George Smalley saw Mill standing below Nelson's column, absolutely calm and composed, but unable to make himself heard because of the howling of the mob below; and on another occasion Thomas Hardy heard him speaking outside the classical portico of St. Paul's, Covent Garden:

> The religious sincerity of his speech was jarred on by his environment—a group on the hustings who, with few exceptions, did not care to understand him fully, and a crowd below who could not. He stood bareheaded, and his vast pale brow, so thin-skinned as to show the blue veins, sloped back like a stretching upland, and conveyed to the observer a curious sense of perilous exposure. . . . It would not be right to say that the throng was absolutely unimpressed by his words; it felt that they were weighty, though it did not quite know why.

Mill's influence was widely felt outside of Britain. The Irish Quaker pacifist Francis Sheehy Skeffington introduced the study of Mill to Dublin, and himself became the leader in Ireland of the movement for the emancipation of women. John Butler Yeats spread the gospel in Trinity College, having heard Mill speak to an audience of workingmen. "Both as a speaker and a man," he wrote in his charming autobiography, "he was of all men the most winning." From Mill, he said, he himself had first learned the real meaning of humanitarianism. In the United States, according to Lionel Trilling, Justice Holmes was "perhaps the greatest and most effective exponent of Mill's philosophy." Louis Brandeis and Benjamin Cardozo could certainly be named along with Holmes in this regard. "Who shall integrate," asked a contemporary, "all the vibrations of enlightening thought and ennobling reason that Mill set in motion?"

On the continent of Europe he was widely known. Thus George Brandes, whose works had wide influence outside his native Denmark, succinctly admonished his readers: "Study John Stuart Mill." In his autobiography, the Danish critic declared that Mill constituted his ideal of what a great man should be. He had visited Mill in retirement at Avignon, and had there observed how, unlike most great authors, whose lives failed to match the quality of their works, in Mill's case there was no disparity whatever between the man and his writings. To find his equal, wrote Brandes, one would have to go back to Marcus Aurelius.

During his year of military service with the Austrian army in 1886, Sigmund Freud translated into German *The Subjection of Women*. The founder of psychoanalysis greatly admired Victorian liberalism and saw in Mill its incarnation. Hence the striking tribute he paid to Mill's memory: "He was perhaps the man of the century who best managed to free himself from the domination of customary prejudices." The future King Peter I of Serbia, during his student days in exile at Geneva, was so impressed with the essay *On Liberty*, that he made the first translation of it into Serbo-Croatian. The same little book, wrote Count Karolyi in his *Memoirs*, so "deeply impressed" him that it helped him to emancipate himself from the feudal and Catholic tradition in which, as a great Hungarian landowner, he had been raised. (Later Karolyi, like Mill himself, rejected the undiluted laissez faire of the Manchester school, and became a socialist—in which capacity he endeavored unsuccessfully, after the Second World War, to deliver Hungary from communism.)

In prewar Turkey, Mustafa Kemal Ataturk, then a military student at Salonica, studied Mill along with the philosophers of the eighteenth century; and so, in his student days at Changsha, while still a liberal and not yet a Marxist, did Mao Tse-tung. Karl Marx himself had read Mill with almost as much disgust as he had read Bentham. "He registers the dogmatism of a disciple," he declared, "the confusion of his master's thought." Mill was nothing but a plagiarist; his philosophy only a "shallow syncretism." Even allowing for the fact that Mill's ardent individualism was obnoxious to the spirit of communism, Marx's obtuseness here is as evident as his spite.

No public issue in Mill's whole life more deeply engaged his sympathies than the American Civil War. He was of course an ardent champion of the Union, and from the outset regarded the struggle as a supreme turning point not only in American history but in the history of the world. With a prescience that few of his contemporaries possessed, he realized that victory for the South would not only prolong the monstrous practice of slavery but would strengthen everywhere in Europe the movement of antidemocratic forces of which Napoleon III was then the leader. At stake was a fundamental moral issue. Mill had always admired the abolitionists, and now he found in John Brown "a true hero." The South was guilty of "an aggressive enterprise of the slaveowners to extend the territory of slavery"; if successful, it would be "a victory of the powers of evil." "For these reasons," Mill wrote, "I cannot join with those who cry Peace, peace. . . . War is an ugly thing; but not the ugliest of things; the decayed and degraded state of moral and patriotic feeling which thinks nothing *worth* a war is worse." He was deeply shocked, but not surprised, to find that Lord Palmerston's government as well as the majority of the aristocracy were, for selfish political reasons, supporting the slaveowners. This consciousness bound him all the more closely to the handful of intellectuals who, along with the working class, supported the cause of the Union. "No question of our time," he wrote, "has been such a touchstone of men, has so tested their sterling qualities of mind or heart as this one, and I shall all of my life feel united by a sort of special tie with those, whether personally known to me or not, who have been faithful when so many were faithless." For Abraham Lincoln he felt the deepest admiration, and movingly compared his death to that of Socrates. It "puts the seal of universal remembrance upon his worth," he said. "He has now a place among the great names of history."

It is hard to think of a single liberal cause in the twentieth century—whether it was the attainment of democracy, the granting to labor of a decent standard of life, the realization of the rights of women, the freedom of Ireland, racial and religious toleration, the emancipation of colonies, or the voluntary restriction of population—which did not find an advocate in John Stuart Mill. Though he lived to see some progress in politics toward the goals he desired, in his last years Mill occasionally expressed a melancholy reminiscent of Bentham's in old age. "In my youth," he told George Brandes, when the Danish critic visited him at his home near Blackheath, "I did not believe that man could retrograde; now I know it." An American visitor noted that "although in his countenance there was a tinge of melancholy, it was serene; and there was some twinkle in his eyes when he uttered an epigrammatic criticism on one or another politician who had acquired popularity or power."

As he had received from Jeremy Bentham the tradition of rationalism as an instrument for political reform and social improvement, so Mill transmitted, though in an altered form, to the Fabian socialists, the Utilitarian zeal for "the greatest happiness of the greatest number." As laissez-faire economics had led in fact to its opposite, monopoly capitalism, so did the desire to safeguard individualism lead Mill toward the close of his life to espouse socialism, though he was by no means blind to the dangers of centralized control. "The social problem of the future," he wrote of himself and his wife, "we considered to be how to unite the greatest individual liberty of action, with a common ownership in the raw material of the globe, and an equal participation of all in the benefits of combined labour."

If Mill's success in energizing the concept of democracy has been more marked than that of Bentham, it is due in no small measure to the greater richness of his nature and the wider scope of his sympathies. Save where falsehood or cruelty (the only two things he could not tolerate), were concerned, Mill was inclined to see two sides to every question. But he also did justice to his predecessor in acknowledging that unless Bentham had been deliberately and systematically one-sided, he could not possibly have succeeded in his pioneer and herculean assault upon the system of corruption and privilege.

Mill's greater breadth of understanding was due to the fact that, while retaining Bentham's essential innocence of heart and truthfulness of mind, he had both loved and suffered more than had his teacher. However withdrawn, Mill had yet entered into the intimate world of one other human being, and into the world of men. "That no human being ever did or ever will comprehend the mind of another," was a thought that Harriet Taylor, at the age of twenty-five, had entered in her notebook; to which comment she had added that to attempt such comprehension was nonetheless "the spring and the food of all fineness of heart and mind."

Though Bentham enjoyed the formal aspects of music and played both the harpsichord and the organ, Mill's more fully developed sensibilities gave him a much finer appreciation of literature and art. Mill and his wife were both devoted to the piano, and he would improvise for hours—but only in her presence—upon themes suggested by imagery drawn from nature, or from conflicts in human affairs. Bentham had declared that "all poetry was misrepresentation." He would no doubt have agreed with Sir Isaac Newton that poetry was but "an ingenious form of nonsense." But for Mill, poetry was one of the most rewarding experiences of life.

The quality of Mill's poetic appreciation is perhaps best seen in his early championship of Tennyson against the derision of tory critics on the *Quarterly*. Mill especially admired "The Lady of Shalott," which he printed in full during the course of his review of the poem. When one remembers the depressing effect of hostile criticism upon the youthful and as yet unknown poet—Tennyson was to publish nothing in the next ten years—one may judge how gratifying must have been such a defense.

Bentham took a modest pleasure in his garden; Mill, who was an ardent botanist, preferred the challenge of mountains. "It is curious," he wrote when almost fifty, "that when I am too tired or too weak to do anything else, I can climb mountains: that is if they are steep enough, for a long ascending slope fatigues me

greatly." He loved nature in all its aspects, majestic or humble—
"the wild flowers, the ways of insects and the notes of birds"
equally with the majesty of the Alps or the Apennines. As a young
man, he used to fill his pockets with wild violet seed and scatter
it so as to embellish the hedgerows he passed in his walks. Above
all, he loved the nightingale, and listened for its first notes every
spring in England. "He was impatient for the song of the nightingale," wrote John Morley, one of the last friends to see him
alive; and it is fitting that today at Avignon, where Mill lies beside
his wife, the hot, dry, southern air, alive with cicadas, dissolves
each evening into a velvet coolness whence nightingales are heard
from a neighboring grove.

"You know that I have done my work," murmured Mill on his
deathbed to his stepdaughter. Those were the last words he uttered, and though he was half delirious when he spoke them, they
constitute the perfect summation of his life. No ode by any laureate, like that of Tennyson on the death of the Duke of Wellington, commemorated the passing of Mill, for the heroes of the spirit
are seldom recognized in so public a fashion.

III

John Henry Newman

(1801-90)

JOHN HENRY NEWMAN was to the nineteenth century what John Wesley was to the eighteenth: its chief religious figure. Not only was he the most illustrious convert to Catholicism in England since the Reformation, he also succeeded—partly by virtue of an almost childlike candor, and partly through literary genius—in overcoming the prejudices of his fellow countrymen and in winning their affectionate regard. Newman's career is fascinating also because of its unusual dramatic interest. Halfway through life, when his influence was at its height, he renounced everything for the sake of conscience, the beauty of Oxford for the slums of Birmingham, and voluntarily embraced a life of almost complete obscurity.

From the profound spiritual crisis through which he passed and from the ordeal of loneliness and virtual exile which followed, his nature emerged purified—its pride transformed into humility, its ambition sublimated into selflessness. He was rescued from obscurity, as if in his own despite, by a sudden personal attack, which had the unexpected effect of raising him to the highest national and international esteem. The cardinal's hat was bestowed on him: and so the story had a happy ending. "He became," said Lord Coleridge, "a Roman Cardinal in title, but the light and guide of multitudes of grateful hearts outside his own communion and beyond the limits of these small islands."

Newman's life falls into two almost exactly equal halves: the Anglican period, from 1801 to 1845, centered in Oxford, and the Catholic period, from 1845 to 1890, centered in Birmingham. Educated in a small private school at Ealing, he went up to Oxford at

the age of fifteen—little older than Bentham when he had matriculated, about fifty years earlier. After a solitary childhood, Newman loved Oxford from the moment he first saw "the stream-like
windings of that glorious street," and from the moment he first
heard the silvery music of her chimes. "The Sunday evening bells
are pealing," he wrote. "It leads my mind to a longing, after I
know not what. . . . What do they do to me? I have a kind of
longing after something dear to me, and well known to me, very
soothing. Such is my feeling at this minute as I hear the evening
bells of Oxford." So, too, he loved the snapdragon which grew
on the walls of Trinity, beholding in it an emblem of his own life,
which, he hoped, would thenceforward be rooted always in Oxford. As for the city itself, it must be borne in mind that in those
days "the pleasant country ran up to the walls and gates of the
colleges; no fringe of mean or commonplace suburbs interposed
between the coronal of spires and towers and its green setting."

In his autobiographical memoir, written over fifty years later,
Newman transcribed a passage from his novel *Loss and Gain*,
written in 1848, to show what had been his original thoughts on
first admittance to Oxford:

> He recollected with what awe and transport he had at first come
> to the University, as to some sacred shrine; and how from time to
> time hopes had come over him that some day or other he should
> have gained a title to residence on one of its old foundations. One
> night, in particular, came across his memory, how a friend and
> he had ascended to the top of one of its many towers with the
> purpose of making observations on the stars; and how, while his
> friend was busily engaged with the pointers, the earthly-minded
> youth had been looking down into the deep, gas-lit, dark-shadowed
> quadrangles, and wondering if he should ever be Fellow of this or
> that College, which he singled out from the mass of academical
> buildings.

As an undergraduate, Newman often worked twelve hours
daily: if he fell to nine hours one day, he made it up by fifteen the
next. In winter he rose at five, in summer at half past four, and
slept four hours a night. Like Shelley a few years before, he got
small help from his tutors—"a very sorry and unsatisfactory teaching it was." "I went to the University with an active mind, and
with no thought but that of hard reading; but when I got there, I
had as little tutorial assistance or guidance as it is possible to con-

ceive, and found myself left almost entirely to my own devices."
His own estimate of the result of his labor was that "few have
attained the facility of comprehension which I have arrived at
from the regularity and constancy of my reading, and the laborious and nerve-bracing and fancy-repressing study of Mathematics." He had worked equally hard through the vacations—
"Herodotus, Thucydides and Gibbon have employed me nearly
from morning to night," he wrote a friend during one vacation.

Yet when, in November 1820, he sat for his final examination
the result was almost total failure. In the middle of the ordeal he
collapsed, and was awarded third-class honors instead of the first
for which he had striven. The conventional explanation of Newman's breakdown is that it was due to prolonged overwork; but
Geoffrey Faber, in his brilliant book *The Oxford Apostles,* argues
convincingly that this spectacular failure was more likely due to
a conflict in the unconscious mind between Newman's strong
personal ambition and his equally powerful need to humble himself, coupled with genuine fear of failure. In his journal Newman
noted that "success would not be good for me, but my heart boils
over with vainglorious anticipation of success." Even after his
disgrace he observed: "How active still are the evil passions of
vainglory, ambition, etc., within me. After my failure last November I thought they would never be unruly again."

Against all expectation, Newman retrieved his failure in school
by winning, a little over a year later, one of the most coveted
prizes that Oxford had to offer—a fellowship at Oriel College. The
day of his election to Oriel, April 12, 1822, he remembered as "the
turning point of his life, and of all days most memorable. It raised
him from obscurity and need to competency and reputation. He
never wished anything better or higher than to live and die a
fellow of Oriel."

In 1824 he took orders as a priest in the Church of England, and
four years later became vicar of St. Mary's, the University Church.
His area of influence was thus enlarged from a single college to
include the whole university. From 1828 to 1843, Newman occupied the pulpit of St. Mary's, and gradually his voice became the
dominant one in Oxford. "The centre," wrote Gladstone many
years later, "from which his power went forth was the pulpit of
St. Mary's, with those wonderful afternoon sermons. Sunday after

Sunday, month after month, year by year, they went on, each continuing and deepening the impression the last had made." So when the Anglo-Catholic movement was launched in 1833 against Erastianism on the one hand and Evangelicalism on the other, Newman quickly became its central inspiration; for at Oxford he had thrown off the Calvinist influences of his early religious training. All the rest were ciphers, wrote Froude of the leaders of the Oxford movement: Newman alone was the indicating number.

Such leadership as Newman exerted was due solely to the inspiration which he furnished through his sermons and his writings. These apart, he had no gifts of formal leadership; of organizing or administrative capacity he had not a trace. A friend once applied to him his own verse about St. Gregory Nazianzen: "Thou couldst a people raise, but couldst not rule." "I had special impediments," Newman frankly acknowledged, "in the way of such an exercise of power; but at no time could I exercise over others that authority, which under the circumstances was imperatively required—I never had the staidness or dignity necessary for a leader." But if he was aware of the narrow scope of his own gifts, he also recognized their unique value. "Living movements do not come out of committees," he once observed.

Over a century later, it is still intriguing to speculate on the nature of the ascendency that Newman established over the minds and hearts of his hearers.

His physical presence was unimpressive. Frail, thin, bespectacled, he seemed like a phantom as he glided rather than walked through the streets of Oxford, looking neither to the right nor to the left, and recognizing neither friend nor foe. "Robust and ruddy sons of the Church," said his brother-in-law, the Reverend Thomas Mozley, "looked on him with condescending pity, as a poor fellow whose excessive sympathy, restless energy, and general unfitness for this practical world would soon wreck him. Thin, pale and with large lustrous eyes ever piercing through this veil of men and things, he hardly seemed made for this world."

His voice was weak, yet surprisingly it could rivet the attention of his hearers. Many years later, Archbishop Benson wondered how it had happened that "this timid-looking, little, weak-voiced man had so moved England." In the pulpit Newman used no gestures, but kept his arms motionless. He employed none of the

devices of the practiced orator. He never tried to be witty or
clever or epigrammatic. Since it was felt in Oxford that to ex-
temporize in the pulpit was Low Church and vulgar, Newman read
his manuscript in an even, almost monotonous voice, never looking
at the congregation. He had a curious habit of reading several
sentences, or perhaps a paragraph, rapidly but with great clearness,
then suddenly pausing for perhaps half a minute. His whole
manner seemed to deprecate the possibility of attention being
drawn to himself rather than to what he was saying. "He used,"
wrote Principal Shairp of St. Andrew's, "no vehemence, no declaration, no show of elaborated argument. . . . To call these sermons eloquent would be no word for them, high poems they
rather were, as of an inspired singer, or the outpourings of a
prophet, rapt yet self-possessed. And the tone of voice in which
they were spoken, once you grew accustomed to it, sounded like
a fine strain of unearthly music. Through the silence of that high
Gothic building, the words fell on the ear like the measured drip-
pings of water in some vast dim cave."

Thirty years later Matthew Arnold was to evoke for his American audiences the recollection of what had once captivated his
youth. "Who could resist the charm of that spiritual apparition,"
he asked,

> gliding in the dim afternoon light through the aisles of St. Mary's,
> rising into the pulpit, and then in the most entrancing of voices,
> breaking the silence with words and thoughts which were religious
> music—subtle, sweet, mournful? I seem to hear him still saying,
> "After the fever of life, after wearinesses and sicknesses, fightings
> and despondings, languor and fretfulness, struggling and succeed-
> ing; after all the changes and chances of this troubled, unhealthy
> state, at length comes death, at length the white throne of God, at
> length the beatific vision."

It is noteworthy that some upon whom Newman thus laid his
spell were nevertheless not converted by him. The historian James
Anthony Froude vehemently espoused in later life causes which
were objectionable to Newman, yet he, too, remembered that
voice which he had heard when an undergraduate at Oxford. A
vivid moment of one sermon he has captured forever:

> Newman described closely some incidents of our Lord's passion; he
> then paused. For a few moments there was a breathless silence.

Then, in a low, clear voice, of which the faintest vibration was audible in the farthest corner of St. Mary's, he said, "Now, I bid you recollect that He to whom these things were done was Almighty God." It was as if an electric stroke had gone through the church, as if every person present understood for the first time the meaning of what he had all the time been saying. I suppose it was an epoch in the mental history of more than one of my Oxford contemporaries.

From a passage in the delightful diary of the Reverend Francis Kilvert, we also learn how indelible could be the impression left by Newman upon his hearers. "As we came in at the orchard door together after the morning service," wrote Kilvert, "my dear Father said: 'As you were preaching there came back upon my ear an echo of the tones of the sweetest human voice I ever heard, the voice of John Henry Newman. No voice but yours ever reminded me of him.'" Such a remark goes far to explain the secret of the unique power Kilvert exercised over the hearts of his simple hearers in country churches in the valley of the Wye.

The key to Newman's success was his absolute sincerity. His attention was fixed solely, to the exclusion of every other thought, upon what he had to say. Thomas Mozley once wrote that Newman was more in earnest, and more thoroughly convinced of the truth of what he was saying than any other man he had ever known. In his sermons, said Froude, Newman semed to be addressing himself to the secret consciousness of every person present, just as the eyes of a portrait often seem fixed upon everyone looking at it, no matter where one may be in the room. "The look and bearing of the preacher," said Principal Shairp, "were as of one who dwelt apart, who, though he knew his age well, did not live in it. From the seclusion of study, and abstinence, and prayer, from habitual dwelling in the unseen, he seemed to come forth that one day of the week to speak to others of the things he had seen and known."

A further clue is supplied by Newman's chief biographer, who heard him in the pulpit in old age. "In his own preaching," wrote Wilfrid Ward, "the simplicity and reality he inculcated was accompanied by an intense shyness of which he was quite conscious." "From a child," Newman once wrote to a friend, "a description of Ulysses' eloquence in the *Iliad* seized my imagination and touched my heart. 'When he began he looked like a fool.' This is the only way in which I have done anything." The nature of his influence was realized by Newman himself, though he never spoke of it to others. For when he was made a cardinal, he chose as his motto the words *Cor ad cor loquitur* (Heart speaketh unto heart), a phrase that was also embroidered upon the pall at his funeral.

Dean Lake, a friend of Arnold, wrote of the eighteen-forties that "the one great power which then ruled and inspired Oxford was John Henry Newman, the influence of whose singular combination of genius and devotion has had no parallel there, either before or since." Gladstone only twice heard Newman preach, but remembered those two occasions for the rest of his life. "In presence, voice, manner and language," he wrote, "he was of marvellous harmony and completeness, grave, earnest, simple, impressive, absolutely without action." Already by 1840, without striving for publicity, Newman had become a legendary figure in Oxford. Undergraduates imitated mannerisms such as the way he held his head. His rather shabby long-tailed coat became their badge. "The influence he has gained," wrote Principal Shairp, "apparently without setting himself to seek it, was something altogether unlike anything else seen in our time. A mysterious veneration had by degrees gathered round him, till now it was almost as though some Ambrose or Augustine of elder ages had reappeared. . . . In Oriel Lane lighthearted undergraduates would drop their voices and whisper: 'There's Newman!' when, head thrust forward, and gaze fixed as though on some vision seen only by himself, with swift, noiseless step he glided by. Awe fell on them for a moment, almost as if it had been some apparition that had passed."

Yet, while his fame was steadily increasing, and more and more the youth of Oxford looked to him for guidance, Newman himself had been undergoing a prolonged spiritual ordeal. For he was beginning to be assailed by doubts about the credentials of the Church of England, and therefore about the validity of his own orders. In the *Tracts for the Times,* and from the pulpit of St. Mary's, he had been conducting a war upon two fronts: he had been defending his beloved Anglicanism against attacks from the left and from the right—from Low Church evangelicals and from the Church of Rome. His hostility to the latter was expressed both publicly and privately, in speech and in writing, on many occasions during the eighteen-thirties; and in his *Apologia*, written thirty years later, he was candid enough to draw attention to what he termed his own previous "savage and ungrateful words" against the Bishop of Rome.

In boyhood, Newman had been "most firmly convinced" that the Pope was "the Antichrist predicted by Daniel, St. Paul and St. John," and in one of his earliest appearances in the pulpit at Oxford he preached a sermon to that effect.

In 1832 he termed Catholicism "polytheistic, degrading and idolatrous;" and when, for the first time in his life, he found himself in the Eternal City in 1833, it filled him with horror. "Rome, as a city, the Rome of Daniel and the Gospels," he told his friend Pusey, "has not yet drank [*sic*] out the fullness of judgment destined for her: so that the blood of the martyrs which was shed on her soil rather cries out against her, then hallows her. It is most melancholy, with a feeling of this kind, to look upon this beautiful city." As late as 1840, he recalled penitentially in the *Apologia* "what I fancied was a fact—the unscrupulousness, the deceit, and the intriguing spirit of the agents and representatives of Rome." One of his *Tracts* in the eighteen-thirties characterized the Roman Church as "crafty, obstinate, malicious, wilful, cruel as madmen are. She is her real self only in name, and till God vouchsafe to restore her, we must treat her as if she were that Evil One which governs her."

It is, of course, well known that people assailed by secret doubts as to the validity of their beliefs often seek to relieve their anxiety by proclaiming in public their adherence to the very views which in private they are beginning to question. Such defiant affirmation is often a sort of rearguard action before the citadel of belief is finally abandoned to the enemy. So it was with Newman: while publicly sounding the alarm, in his inmost being he felt himself drawn more and more to the Mother Church of Christendom.

Desperately homesick at Palermo in Sicily in 1833, he found consolation in the churches of the city:

For thou dost soothe the heart, thou Church of Rome . . .
There, on a foreign shore,
The homesick solitary finds a friend.

How powerful was the attraction for him of the Roman Church is seen even in one of the earliest *Tracts*, in which he declared: "Considering the high gifts and the strong claims of the Church of Rome and its dependencies on our admiration, reverence, love and gratitude, how could we withstand it, as we do, how could we refrain from being melted into tenderness, and rushing into communion with it, but for the word of Truth itself?" Temperamentally, of course, he had always admired the Church's "zealous maintenance of the doctrine and rule of celibacy." He himself had taken a vow of perpetual virginity while still a boy.

Later, in 1839, when Newman began his study of the Monophysite heresy in the fifth century, he was "seriously alarmed" to find what he regarded as a close parallel between the beliefs of that sect and those of the Anglican Church. "There was an awful similitude, more awful, because so silent and unimpassioned, between the dead records of the past and the feverish chronicle of the present. The shadow of the fifth century was on the sixteenth. It was like a spirit rising from the troubled waters of the old world, with the shape and lineaments of the new." He looked into the mirror of the past: "I saw my face in that mirror, and I was a Monophysite."

He constantly heard ringing in his ears, he tells us, "the palmary words of St. Augustine," in which that doctor had exalted the Universal Church: *Securus judicat orbis terrarum*, The whole world securely sits in judgment on the single errant member. Those words, thought Newman, "absolutely pulverized" the theory of the Via Media, on which the English Church was built. Two years later, delving still deeper into the past, he came to the Arians, and found that there, too, the parallel with Protestantism held good. "The pure Arians were the Protestants."

The modern reader is likely to suspect that in thus finding his way circuitously to Rome along the path of historical analogy, Newman was actually listening to the promptings of his own heart—a view which is supported by his own words. "For myself it was not logic that carried me on; as well might one say that the quick-silver in the barometer changes the weather." Yet he found himself in an embarrassing situation, maintaining one position at one moment, and seemingly its opposite the next. It was to be expected that his enemies would charge him—as did Charles Kingsley at a later date—with duplicity. Yet no man, as the *Apologia* proves, was more sincere than Newman—sincere, but perplexed, to use one of his favorite words. His difficulties were increased by the fact that to him especially the undergraduates looked for guidance in their spiritual problems: "I kept back all persons," he wrote, "who were disposed to go to Rome with all my might."

The realization that he was responsible for the spiritual welfare of so many others, who placed implicit trust in him, was troubling. "How could I in any sense direct others," he asked, "who had to be guided in so momentous a matter myself? . . . How could I presume to unsettle them, as I was unsettled, when I had no means of bringing them out of such unsettlement? And if they were unsettled already, how could I point to them a place of refuge, when I was not sure I should choose it for myself?"

He was likewise aware that, through his writings, his influence had penetrated far beyond the walls of Oxford—into many a quiet rural rectory and busy urban parish. "There were a number of tender, eager hearts of whom I knew nothing at all, who were watching me, wishing to think as I thought, and to do as I did, if they could but find it out." They "felt the weariness of waiting, and the sickness of delayed hope, and being of more sensitive complexion of mind than myself, were made ill by the suspense. . . . I ask their pardon as far as I was really unkind to them," he added twenty years later.

No wonder that these years were a time of ever-increasing "perplexity and distress which weighed upon him"; to be forced, years later, to recollect them in the *Apologia* was like "practising on himself a cruel operation, the ripping up of old griefs. . . . It is both to head and heart an extreme trial, thus to analyze what has long gone by, and to bring out the results of that examination." In 1841, in the famous *Tract 90*, he made a last desperate but unconvincing attempt to reconcile the Thirty-Nine Articles of the Church of England with Roman Catholic belief. This tract was officially condemned by the authorities at Oxford. From the end of that year, wrote Newman, "I was on my death-bed, as regards my membership in the Anglican Church." He only wished, like Pascal, to be allowed to die in peace, and die alone. Yet so strong were the ties of affection that bound him to his friends and followers, to the church of his youth, to the city that he loved above all other places, that four years were to pass before he took the final irrevocable step.

In 1843, he resigned his living at St. Mary's, cut himself off from all but a handful of friends, and went into seclusion at the village of Littlemore, two miles outside Oxford. This withdrawal from the world he whimsically compared to Wellington's strategic withdrawal to Lisbon in 1810 behind the fortified line of Torres Vedras. "I called Littlemore my Torres Vedras, and thought that some day we might advance again inside the Anglican Church." Two years later, on October 9, 1845, on a wild day of wind and rain, he was received by the Passionist Father Dominic into the Roman Catholic Church. Only two days before, at the Sorbonne, the great French writer and agnostic Ernest Renan had left the Church and renounced the priesthood to which he had been destined. Asked the young English Catholic poet Lionel Johnson:

Did after-joy with angel hosts outweigh
Grief for the anguish of an earlier day?

In his novel *Loss and Gain*, written during the following winter in Rome, Newman described his grief at leaving Oxford—as he supposed, forever. "Bees, by the instinct of nature, do love their hives, and birds their nests," he remembered Archbishop Bramhall saying. So had he loved Oxford. On a bleak February day in 1846 he walked for the last time through Christ Church Meadow to the confluence of the Cherwell and the Isis. "There was no one to see him; he threw his arms around the willows so dear to him, and kissed them; he tore off some of the black leaves and put them in his bosom. 'I am like Undine,' he said, 'killing with a kiss.'" He was then forty-five, and save for glimpsing its spires while passing in the train, he was not to see Oxford again for thirty-two years, by which time he was an old, broken man of seventy-seven.

The story of Newman's life as a Catholic is well known. His spiritual odyssey was over. He had discovered for himself the profound pychological truth expressed by St. Augustine: "Thou hast made us for Thyself, and our hearts are restless till they rest in Thee." Never for a moment did he regret his decision, or seek to count its cost. "I have been in perfect peace and contentment," he wrote in the *Apologia*. "I have never had one doubt." Such was his inner life: the outer was far different. Instead of the brilliant new ecclesiastical career that had been prophesied for him—one such as actually raised his fellow convert Manning to the archbishopric of Westminster and the cardinalate—it was Newman's fate to become "the forgotten man" of the Catholic Church. He was relegated to thirty years' obscurity in a dreary suburb of Birmingham. In all that time his gift for preaching lay unused. He failed in everything he attempted—the Catholic University at Dublin, the editorship of the *Rambler*, the new translation of the Bible, the establishment of a branch of the Oratory at Oxford. He even became suspect at Rome, where some of his writings barely escaped condemnation. He was opposed to the definition of infallibility in 1870, but accepted the decree when it was announced. Liberal Catholics like Lord Acton did not respect such intellectual legerdemain, and though Acton accepted the decree, it was with a heavy heart, and perhaps with mental reservations.

"Because I have not retailed gossip," Newman wrote in his journal in 1860,

> flattered great people, and sided with this or that party, I am nobody. I have no friend at Rome. I have laboured in England, to be misrepresented, backbitten and scorned. I have laboured in Ireland, with a door ever shut in my face. I seem to have had many failures, and what I did well was not understood. I do not think that I am saying this in any bitterness.

It must not be thought that such complaints were occasional or untypical: for the next quarter of a century they form a large part of the burden of Newman's thoughts. "I go to Rome to be snubbed," he wrote in 1856 to his dear friend Ambrose St. John, who had preceded him into the Church. "I come to Dublin to be repelled by Dr. MacHale and worn away by Dr. Cullen. The Cardinal taunts me with his dedications, and Father Faber insults me with his letters. I have no means of defending myself more than if my hands and tongue were tied."

"I know anyhow," he complained twelve years later, "that, however honest are my thoughts, and earnest my endeavours to keep rigidly within the lines of Catholic doctrine, every word I write will be malevolently scrutinized, and every expression which can possibly be perverted sent straight to Rome—that I shall be fighting *under the lash*, which does not tend to produce vigorous efforts in the battle, or to inspire either courage or presence of mind." "My Lord had some purpose," he sadly concluded, "in letting me be so long forgotten and calumniated."

It was galling to be patronized by worldly and successful ecclesiastics like Monsignor Talbot, who had the ear of Pius IX and whose penitents were Roman dowagers. "Poor Newman!" sighed the monsignor, "by living almost ever since he has been a Catholic surrounded by a set of inferior men who idolize him, I do not think he has ever acquired the Catholic instincts." Talbot once intimated that Newman likewise might go to Rome and be confessor to an aristocratic clientele. "But Birmingham people have souls too," said Newman drily.

The youthful preacher who had captivated the university had turned prematurely into an old man. Already at Littlemore in his early forties, he had lamented: "My days are gone like a shadow and I am withered like grass." "I feel like a person," he wrote from Birmingham, "who has long been out in the dust and rain, and whose hat, coat and shoes show it." Yet his personal charm seems never to have deserted him. The poet Aubrey de Vere thus described him in old age at the Birmingham Oratory: "He was thin and pale almost to emaciation, swift of pace, but when not walking, intensely still, with a voice sweet and pathetic, and so distinct that you could count each vowel and consonant in every word."

His feeling for Oxford remained. Nearly twenty years after his departure, he wrote to Isaac Williams, his former curate at St. Mary's: "Of all human things perhaps Oxford is nearest my heart. . . . I cannot ever realize to myself that I shall never see what I so much love again. . . . But why should I wish to see what is no longer what I loved? All things change; the past never returns here. My friends, I confess, have *not* been kind." Though he never set foot in Oxford during all these years, he ventured once as close as Littlemore: there one day, a passer-by observed a shabbily dressed old man, leaning on the lych gate of the churchyard, and weeping. It was Newman.

Presently, his love for Oxford receded so far into the dimness of the past that it seemed but the shadow of a dream. In 1866 he wrote his old friend Dr. Pusey that he could not bear to revisit the city of his youth. "It would be as painful a step as I could be called upon to make. Oxford never can be to me what it was. It and I are severed. It would be like the dead visiting the dead. I should be a stranger in my dearest home." Yet he was once to revisit Oxford before he died.

From twenty years' obscurity and oblivion—"the world forgetting, by the world forgot"—Newman was dramatically rescued by an enemy's attack. In 1863 a redoubtable Protestant controversialist, Charles Kingsley, both parson and novelist, wrote an article in a leading magazine impugning Father Newman's good faith in having entered the Church of Rome. Newman's answer, in which he triumphantly vindicated himself, was the story of his life: the *Apologia pro Vita Sua*, written under stress of deep emotion, often in tears, sometimes for ten or twelve hours at a stretch. Here the genius of a master of style blended with the moral sensibility of a deeply wounded man to produce a masterpiece of English prose. His adversary, who made an ineffectual reply, failed to make any impression on a public that was moved by the spectacle of what it regarded as a maligned man seeking to establish his innocence. Even the Tory *Quarterly* confessed that Kingsley had become "the embedded fly in the clear amber of his antagonist's apology." "I wish poor dear Thackeray had been alive," moaned Kingsley. "He was too true a liberal to pat lies and bigotry on the back."

The *Apologia* brought Newman what most of all, outside of religion, he desired in life—the esteem of his fellow countrymen. He had, in fact, thrown himself upon their mercy, and his appeal had not been without a certain artfulness. "I consider Englishmen," he wrote in the Preface, "the most suspicious and touchy of mankind; I think them unreasonable and unjust in their seasons of excitement, but I had rather be an Englishman (as in fact I am) than belong to any other race under heaven. They are as generous as they are hasty and burly; and their repentance for their injustice is greater than their sin."

One of Newman's most recent admirers, James M. Cameron, calls the *Apologia* "a perfect work of art," and asserts that, in contrast to Mill's *Autobiography*, which "apart from a few precious pages" will only interest the historian of ideas, the *Apologia* "will always be read." This verdict needs considerable qualification. The candid judgment even of those in sympathy with Newman may well be that a large part of the work is dated—the minutiae of Oxford ecclesiastical politics equally with the disquisitions on heresies in the Dark Ages. Nor is the modern reader likely to find himself convinced by Newman's arguments. In appealing to the public, Newman declared that "controversies should be decided by the reason," but his own conversion he rested, as we have seen, on quite other grounds.

Superficially, Newman's approach to controversy suggests Mill's scrupulous fairness, as, for example, when Newman describes himself as one "who has ever been fair to the doctrines and arguments of his opponents." He was criticized, he complains, because "I had set out the cause which I was combatting to the best advantage." We must remember, however, that by the word "opponents" Newman here means only Roman Catholics, not evangelicals, still less rationalists. For liberals, Newman had nothing but scorn, nor did he think they even merited a hearing; as for the Low Church, "I had a thorough contempt for the controversial position of the latter." Such intolerance as this is far removed from the patience and justice with which Mill approached opinion that he held to be thoroughly mischievous.

As a controversialist, Newman was a master of rhetorical devices that Mill eschewed. In his original reply to Kingsley (omitted from subsequent editions of the *Apologia*), he overwhelmed him more by irony and sarcasm than by argument. John Holloway has called attention to Newman's fondness for the *argumentum ad hominem*. Even the *Apologia* is by no means free from this device, which the author sometimes uses in the very moment he disclaims it. It is impossible to imagine Mill indulging, as Newman admits he did, in tricks like "tit for tat" and "two can play at that." At times, as when he equates the principle of "utility," which he detested, with simple expediency, Newman uses elementary bad logic. At other times he indulges in casuistry, as when he remarks that Protestants misjudge Catholic books of moral theology: "They are intended for the Confessor, and Protestants view them as intended for the Preacher." It was this sort of disingenuousness that led Lord Acton to make the surprising judgment on his co-religionist that Newman was "the most careful and artful of apologists," and "a sophist, the manipulator and not the servant of truth."

The appeal of the *Apologia* is to our sympathies and not to our reason. Newman does not, of course, reject rational arguments in favor of deity, but frankly admits that they "do not warm or enlighten me; they do not take away the winter of my desolation, or make the buds unfold and the leaves grow within me, and my moral being rejoice." Yet who can refrain from sympathy with that sensitive, perplexed, and subtle personality as, with transparent honesty, he disarms us by laying bare his motives and his sufferings? Newman indeed "united in his own luminous and lovable being," as Llewelyn Powys put it, "the attributes of the subtle Schoolman with the simplicity and the passionate sincerity of the true saint."

Newman's *Apologia* is worth comparing with the *Autobiography* of John Stuart Mill, written about the same time and likewise under stress of deep emotion. Each represents the most persuasive expression of a significant movement of thought in the nineteenth century; and each is wholly antagonistic to the other. The mind of Newman was religious, romantic, mystical, and devout; that of Mill, secular, rational, scientific, and skeptical.

Personally, the two men had much in common: both were kindly, modest, generous, and humane; both were solitary, unworldly, sensitive, and idealistic. Yet the ideal of each was abhorrent to the other. Neither mentions the other in his own autobiography. The silence explains a good deal, for while Mill must have deplored the influence of Newman, the latter certainly regarded the Utilitarians as proof of Satan's direct intervention in human affairs.

Each was the eldest son in a large family, and each virtually renounced his mother, as well as his brothers and sisters. In the two autobiographies, there is scarcely a reference to their respective family situations. Newman is even more reserved than Mill. Thus, in the *Apologia*, he mentions that in the year 1827 he was "rudely awakened" from the dream in which his life had been drifting "by two great blows—illness and bereavement." The illness was his own, but he refrains from telling the reader that the death was that of his youngest, favorite sister, Mary.

About his own ancestry, Newman was reticent to the point of evasiveness. Not only in the *Apologia* but in all his autobiographical fragments, he suppressed the very existence of his paternal grandfather, a grocer; and while stating briefly that his father was a banker, he omits to mention that the latter had adopted a questionable coat of arms, and that, as a result of failure in business, he had sunk first to the status of brewer and then to that of tavern keeper. "He was despised, and we esteemed him not." These words from Isaiah were intoned by Newman at his father's graveside in 1825. Perhaps they served an expiatory purpose. From the official biography of Newman, written by Wilfrid Ward in 1912, references to his two younger brothers, both of whom were unusual personalities, were almost entirely expunged: the elder, Charles, atheist and bohemian, became an Owenite socialist, while the younger, Francis, a brilliant double first at Oxford, became a Plymouth Brother, then a freethinker and radical humanitarian. No doubt these facts in themselves constituted sufficient grounds for their omission from the Cardinal's biography. It is also interesting to note that while Charles Reding, the central figure in Newman's autobiographical novel *Loss and Gain*, like Newman has three sisters, he has no brothers at all. As for the sisters, "my sisters are nothing to me, or rather foreign to me," Newman wrote a friend. As his friend Isaac Williams, curate at St. Mary's, shrewdly noted in his autobiography, Newman "partly under the false guise of mortification stifled his domestic affections."

Remembering that Newman was the only member of the Oriel Common Room who was not a gentleman by birth, it is understandable why the rising young Fellow of Oriel should have been sensitive about being identified with such humble relations. Yet from the *Apologia* itself, we learn that the grounds for Newman's rejection of his family lay deeper than any purely social considerations, lay indeed at the very center of his being. To Newman the existence of other human beings seemed hardly endowed with objective reality at all.

"I used to wish that the Arabian Tales were true," wrote Newman, recalling his childhood. "My imagination ran on unknown influences, on magical powers, and talismans. . . . I thought life might be a dream, or I an angel, and all this world a deception." As an adult, he believed that angels were responsible for "the Economy of the Visible World. I considered them as the real causes of motion, light and life, and of those elementary principles of the physical universe which . . . suggest to us the notion of cause and effect, and of what are called the laws of nature." This angelic theory of physics, learned from the Alexandrian school, he propounded from the pulpit of St. Mary's in 1831. He also held with the Fathers that "though Satan fell from the beginning, the Angels fell before the deluge, falling in love with the daughters of men." Besides demons and evil spirits, he believed in "a middle race, neither in heaven nor hell; partially fallen, capricious, wayward; noble or crafty, benevolent or malicious, as the case might be. These beings gave a sort of inspiration or intelligence to races, nations and classes of men." Such was Newman's explanation of the varying psychologies of different peoples. "Take England with many high virtues, and yet a low Catholicism. It seems to me that John Bull is a spirit neither of heaven nor hell." As a contribution to knowledge, the angelic derivation of John Bull seems even more whimsical than celestial physics. In addition to all this, Newman, like Wesley, was a firm believer in ghosts and loved to talk about them. Hearing peculiar noises on one occasion during his stay at Malta, he reminded himself in his journal: "Evil spirits are always about us."

As a child Newman had usually been alone. He played no games and had few companions. "My habitual feeling then and since has been," he wrote, "that it was not I who sought friends, but friends who sought me." Like T. E. Lawrence later, he shrank from the physical touch of others, including that of his own mother. Like Mill, as a child Newman thought himself unloved. "I who am conscious to myself I never thought anything more precious than her sympathy and praise, had none of it."

At fifteen he underwent the profound experience of "conversion"—a fact, he wrote, "of which I am more certain than that I have hands and feet." Knowing that he had been "elected to eternal glory," this profound religious experience, he declared, emphasized the tendency of those "childish imaginings . . . in isolating me from the objects which surrounded me, in confirming me in my distrust of the reality of material phenomena, and making me rest in the thought of two and two only absolute and luminously self-evident beings, myself and my Creator—for while I considered myself predestined to salvation, my mind did not dwell upon others."

This sense of the unreality of the physical world, the belief that life was but a dream, dominated Newman's whole life. He would no doubt have agreed with Burke—"what shadows we are, and what shadows we pursue." His early and strong inclination toward celibacy strengthened, as he fully recognized, these solipsistic tendencies. Like his dear friend Hurrell Froude, "he had a high severe idea of the intrinsic excellence of virginity"; and at fifteen, Newman took a vow of perpetual chastity. That an idealistic boy whose education had been conducted wholly on celibate lines should have taken such a vow is perhaps not very surprising; what is more remarkable is that, so far as one can tell, Newman never seems to have had any difficulty in remaining faithful to this vow. "I am obliged to mention," he wrote in the *Apologia*, "though I do it with great reluctance, another deep imagination, which at this time, the autumn of 1816, took possession of me—there can be no mistakes about the fact; viz. that it would be the will of God that I should lead a single life. This anticipation . . . strengthened my feeling of separation from the visible world." As for the marriage of others, whether of his sisters or of his clerical colleagues, he was opposed to it. "Everyone when he marries is a lost man," he told his friends. There was, from Newman's point of view, more than a tincture of truth in the facetious remark. When, in *Loss and Gain*, the hero sees a young clergyman take a pretty bride, he feels as faint as a seasick man bidden to eat pork chops. (The joke is repeated in one of Newman's letters.) Santayana's hero in *The Last Puritan* felt similarly.

Several consequences flowed inevitably from this pronounced sense of detachment from the world, and incapacity or unwillingness to distinguish between the real and the imaginary. One was a readiness, even an anxiety, to believe in miracles. Again like his friend Froude, Newman believed that miracles abounded during the Dark and Middle ages. This predilection was carried so far that in his later years it became embarrassing to his co-religionists. The greater the strain on his credulity—as in the case of the house of Loreto miraculously flown through the air from Palestine to Italy in 1294, "in three hops," as Lytton Strachey put it—the greater was Newman's willingness to accept the alleged miracle. His superior, Bishop Ullathorne, realizing the scandal to which, even among his fellow Catholics, this credulity would give rise, had actually to restrain Newman's ardor of belief—as in his devotion to the legend of St. Winifred walking with her head under her arm after her decapitation.

"I want to ask your opinion," Newman once wrote Ward, "of this argument [for miracles] which has just occurred to me. I take this paper-knife, I push the inkstand with it. Here is distinctly through my free will an interference with the laws of nature. If these laws were left to themselves, the knife would remain still and the pen-knife unmoved. Take a stronger case, I fire a gunpowder train. See what a tremendous effect I produce in changing the ordinary course of nature. Now surely it is little to grant that if there *be* a God, He can do what I can do: and yet, so far as we know, a miracle amounts to no more than this." Such are the consequences of regarding man not as part of nature, but as altogether distinct from it.

A second result of Newman's subjective divorce from material reality was an indifference to science and to scientific method—an indifference bordering upon contempt, and which is the more striking, since in his undergraduate days at Oxford, he had been keenly interested in such subjects as chemistry and mineralogy. Geology, he had then written, was "most entertaining and opens an amazing field to imagination and to poetry." But when the full implications of the new science, with its challenge to the literal interpretation of Genesis, became evident in the epoch-making work of Lyell, Newman's enthusiasm was succeeded by distaste. "I have a profound misgiving of geological theories," he wrote to Pusey in 1858, "though I cannot be sure that facts of considerable importance are not proved. But in the whole scientific world men seem going ahead most recklessly with their usurpation on the domain of religion." His brother-in-law Thomas Mozley reports him as saying that he "considered physical science a waste of time." "Newman as a rule," he added, "indeed I cannot remember an exception—would have nothing to say to physical science. He abstained from it as much as he did from material undertakings and worldly affairs generally. He would be impatient of it, as something in the way, not worth precious time." Newman, in fact, was a fundamentalist and believed in the literal inspiration of Scripture. Arguing for the teaching of theology in universities, he gravely asked, How else could science have known of the existence of Noah's ark, save for revealed religion? And in the

Apologia he wrote: "I think it could be shown that physical science on the one hand, or again mathematics, affords but an imperfect training for the intellect."

Though he took no interest whatever in the revolution in thought effected during his own lifetime by scientists such as Darwin and Huxley, he could not help being aware of the unsettling results of their discoveries. "We live in a wonderful age," he wrote five years after the *Origin of Species* had been published. "The enlargement of the circle of secular knowledge just now is simply a bewilderment, and the more so, because it has the promise of continuing, and that with greater rapidity, and more signal results." Many "religious and sincere minds," he continued, were "simply perplexed, frightened or rendered desperate, as the case may be, by the utter confusion into which late discoveries or speculations have thrown their most elementary ideas of religion." Despite this admission of grounds for doubt, two pages later in the *Apologia* he stated flatly that there could be no conflict between science and religion, the unfortunate case of Galileo being dismissed as simply the exception that proved the rule.

A third consequence of Newman's profound self-absorption—and as Sean O'Faoláin, has observed, no one was more egocentric than he, or more "deeply introspective, constantly self-concerned, tirelessly self-recording"—was the weakness of his social sense, and his complete indifference to social problems. Save for a few personal friends, to whom he was deeply devoted, and who may be said to have become part of his personality, he had little sense of the individuality of others, including the members of his own family. How *could* he, in view of that entire absorption in the "two and two only absolute and luminously self-evident beings" which we have already noticed?

The urgent social problems of contemporary England, problems arising basically from the Industrial Revolution, he totally ignored. "Actual England is too sad to look upon. The Poet," said Newman, speaking of Keble, "seems to turn away from the sight; else, in his own words would it 'bruise too sore his tender heart.'" Of factory legislation, poor law reform, the abolition of slavery, Corn Law Repeal, the Chartist movement, not a word is to be found in the fifteen years of Newman's sermons at Oxford, though they are entitled *Sermons for the Day*. It was not the business of the Church, Newman declared from the pulpit, to make men good citizens, to produce good members of society, or to help in reforming any of the social evils against which the Utilitarians were then contending. The business of Christianity was to save individual souls, not to reform society. The idea of progress he termed a dream, "because revelation contradicts it."

Newman was, in truth, mentally more at home in the first centuries of the Christian era, listening to the Fathers of the Church, than in what he regarded as his own degenerate century. His vivid historical imagination compensated for his total lack of scientific interest. While still an Anglican, he imagined Archbishop Laud as seeing and hearing what was going on in nineteenth-century Oxford, and even walking in her streets; and after his conversion to Rome, he visualized St. Athanasius and St. Ambrose as coming to Oxford, declaring that if they were to do so, "they would go to Mass at St. Clement's."

His political ideas were few but definite. Hatred of liberalism was the compass of his creed. "The spirit of Liberalism," he proclaimed in the *Apologia*, was "the characteristic of the destined Antichrist. . . . The spirit of lawlessness came in with the Reformation, and Liberalism is its offspring." In his book on the Arian heresy in 1833, he called it "Satan's chief instrument in deluding the nations," and asserted that its coming had long ago been foreshadowed by Julian the Apostate. He stated, without elaboration, his belief in the divine right of kings, and opposed all revolutions, including the American and the French. The leaders of the Oxford movement (among whom he was the chief) could not possibly "subscribe to the revolutionary doctrines of 1776 and 1789, which they felt to be absolutely and entirely out of keeping with theological truth." His toryism was as obstinate and unyielding as that of Dr. Johnson. In his study at Oriel, he kept safely under lock and key the pernicious works of Tom Paine, and "would lend them with much caution to such as could bear the shock." In later years, much as he admired Gladstone personally, he deplored the liberalism that was associated with that statesman's name. "The great deluge is pouring in," wrote Newman despairingly in 1865, "and his boat is as good as another's." Twenty years later, he bemoaned the further extension of the franchise. "What a dreadful thing this democracy

is. How I wish Gladstone had retired into private life." As for
Home Rule, while admitting that an Irishman had reason to desire
such a measure, he himself, as a staunch Englishman, was absolutely opposed to it.

Of the liberal revolution in Paris in 1830, which delighted
Bentham's old age and Mill's early manhood, Newman wrote
primly: "I held that it was unchristian for nations to cast off
their governors, and, much more, sovereigns who had the divine
right of inheritance." (The sovereigns in question were the
corrupt and worthless Bourbons, who had learned nothing from
the fate of their predecessors after 1789.) So great was Newman's
horror of the almost bloodless July Revolution, whose hero was
Lafayette, and by means of which the middle classes in France
drove the clericals and aristocrats from power, that three years
later, when passing through Paris, finding himself forced to remain there for twenty-four hours, he kept indoors the whole
time and refused even to walk the streets of so sinful a city.
When he saw the detested tricolor he averted his eyes.

Not only was Newman opposed to revolution, he was equally
set against reform. The Great Reform Bill of 1832, the prelude
to democracy in England, he considered the work of the devil.
"I had fierce thoughts against the Liberals," he wrote ingenuously
in 1833. It had been these same "Liberals," incidentally, who together with the Irish, had in 1829 forced Peel and Wellington to
concede Catholic emancipation. In view of Newman's later conversion to Catholicism, it is ironic that he should have led the
opposition to Peel at Oxford, partly to "discountenance the dangerous laxity of modern politics," and partly to punish him for
this defection from the ranks of the "two bottle orthodox."
Peel's change of front, he declared, reminded him of Sir Robert
Walpole, and encouraged bad men "to disparage the very idea
of public virtue."

Almost the sole contemporary political enthusiasm of Newman's life was that which he showed over the success of Disraeli's
jingoistic policy in the Near East in 1878. It appears that he
actually preferred infidel Moslems to orthodox schismatics. "It
is a grand idea," he wrote Lord Blachford, "that of hugging from
love the Turk to death, instead of the Russian bear, which, as
a poem or romance, finds a weak part in my imagination. And

then it opens such a view of England, great in the deeds of their forefathers, showing that they are not degenerate sons." His political ideas had always been as romantic as they were irresponsible.

Newman's fundamental sense of the unreality of the physical world was colored by another feeling, derived from his early Calvinist inheritance: a sense that the world was irredeemably depraved. "I look out of myself," he wrote in the *Apologia*, "and there I see a sight which fills me with unspeakable distress. The world seems simply to give the lie to that great truth, of which my whole being is so full; and the effect upon me is, in consequence, as a matter of necessity, as if it denied that I am in existence myself. . . . The sight of the world is nothing less than the prophet's scroll, full of 'lamentations, and mourning, and woe.' "

The contemporary world—the England of the nineteenth century, of the Industrial Revolution—impressed him as being more evil than any period in history with which he was acquainted. He recoiled in horror from what he termed "the multitudinous blasphemy of the day—its newspapers, its reviews, its magazines, its novels, its controversial pamphlets, its Parliamentary debates, its law proceedings, its platform speeches, its songs, its drama, its theatre, its enveloping, stifling atmosphere of death. All this," he exclaimed, "is a vision to dizzy and appall; and inflicts upon the mind the sense of a profound mystery, which is absolutely beyond human solution. What shall be said to this heart-piercing, reason-bewildering fact?"

Newman was a man of extreme sensibility—no man was less a coarse-grained Philistine—and he found existence insupportable when viewed in the cruel light of history without illusion. By an act of will, therefore, which was for him the supreme affirmation of life—an instance of Carlyle's yea-saying—he declared that the reality of recorded history, from which he did not flinch, *could* not be ultimate reality.

He therefore fell back upon a second line of defense, regarding reality not merely as an illusion, but condemning it as utterly evil. "It is because of the intensity of the evil which has possession of mankind, that a suitable antagonist has been provided against it; and the initial act of that divinely-commissioned power is of course to deliver her challenge and to defy the enemy." The primal evil was original sin; the power set against it, potent to vanquish it, was God's grace bestowed through the channel of the sacraments. "The human race," he wrote in an extraordinary sentence, "is implicated in some terrible aboriginal calamity. It is out of joint with the purposes of its creator. This is a fact," he asserted, "as true as the fact of its existence."

It was not, as with Bentham or Mill, by the use of analytical reason that Newman reduced the world to terms on which he could find it supportable, but by a decisive act of will, an energetic repulsion of the adversary through the aid of a superior power. Newman's distrust of purely rational processes is a leading theme of the *Apologia* and sounds again and again through its pages. "Rationalism," he said sharply, "is the great evil of the day."

There are truths, he insisted, to which no language can do justice, and to which the human mind is unequal. The Bible itself is a book—"but a book, after all, cannot make a stand against the wild, living intellect of man." "First principles of whatever kind," he maintained, were matters beyond the scope of human judgment; and of such first principles, "the most sacred and momentous are especially to be reckoned the truths of Revelation."

He attempted to draw a distinction between "right reason" (reason as it existed before the fall of Adam) and "reason as it acts in fact and concretely in fallen man." It was no doubt argumentation such as this which led T. H. Huxley on reading Newman to exclaim impatiently: "That man is the slipperiest sophist I have ever met with." Carlyle, more rudely, implied that Newman hadn't got the brains of a rabbit. The tendency of the unaided reason, Newman made clear in a significant admission, was "towards a simple unbelief in matters of religion. No truth, however sacred, can stand against it in the long-run." Even Samuel Taylor Coleridge, to whose philosophy he, like other conservatives, was much indebted, was a dangerous example of free inquiry, for the philosopher of Highgate Hill though "a very original thinker . . . indulged a liberty of speculation which no Christian can tolerate, and advocated conclusions which were often heathen rather than Christian."

Curiously enough, although he deprecated the influence of

reason, admitting that in his own case it was not logic that carried him on, yet at other times Newman imagined that in his movements toward Rome he was responding not to emotion but to argument. "I determined to be guided," he writes in the *Apologia*, "not by my imagination, but by my reason. And this I said over and over again in the years which followed, both in conversation and in private letters. Had it not been for this severe resolve, I should have been a Catholic sooner than I was." At times he even wondered whether the promptings of his heart did not proceed from Satan himself. Such considerations led him to preach most earnestly to others "against the danger of being swayed in religious inquiry by our sympathies rather than by our reason."

There were, in fact, two grounds on which Newman indicted reason: one was its inability to probe the nature of the reality lying beyond the visible world; the other, its inability to control the passions of men. Thus, in a beautiful passage in his *Discourses on the Scope and Nature of a University Education* (1852), Newman warned the Catholics of Dublin: "Quarry the granite rock with razors, or moor the vessel with a thread of silk; then may you hope with such keen and delicate instruments as human knowledge and human reason to contend against these giants, the passion and pride of man."

Yet, though too weak to prevail against instinct, reason was too strong to be trusted with liberty. In the interests of transcendental reality, it needed to be bridled and bitted. Hence the justification for authority, for dogma, for infallibility. Only the last-named, Newman wrote, was capable of "smiting hard and throwing back the immense energy of the aggressive, capricious, untrustworthy intellect"; only this could strike down the "pride of reason," and "rescue it from its own suicidal excesses."

In the *Apologia*, Newman gives us an affectionate portrait of his beloved friend of Oxford days, John Keble. "He had the purity and simplicity of a child." As so often, this portrait is, if unconsciously, a self-portrait. "Keble," wrote Newman, "was a man who guided himself and formed his judgments, not by processes of reason, by inquiry or by argument, but, to use the word in a broad sense, by authority. . . . It seemed to me as if he ever felt happier, when he coud speak or act under such primary or external sanction." Perhaps it was this very need for dependence in Keble which drew Newman to him so strongly.

The hero of Newman's autobiographical novel *Loss and Gain*, longs for someone to tell him: "This is true, this is not true." Newman's own compelling need to submit to authority, to find certitude in judgments consecrated by age and handed down by tradition, long antedated his conversion to Rome. One of the decisive moments of his life, Newman tells us in the *Apologia*, came "in the course of a walk, I think, round Christ Church meadow," about the year 1823, when the Reverend William James, then Fellow of Oriel, had taught him the doctrine of apostolical succession—i.e., that the bishops of the Church derived their spiritual power lineally from the Apostles, who had been consecrated by Christ himself. Of the days when he had been an Anglican, Newman once declared: "My own Bishop was my Pope; I knew no other; the successor of the Apostles, the Vicar of Christ." He had even gone out of his way to invite censure from his ecclesiastical superior, the Bishop of Oxford, for some of his *Tracts*, and he expressed an anticipatory pleasure in the prospect of being condemned. "I should feel a more lively pleasure," he informed the Bishop, "in knowing that I was submitting myself to your Lordship's expressed judgment in a matter of that kind, than I could have even in the widest circulation of the volumes in question."

"I am far from denying," he wrote, "that every article of the Christian Creed, whether as held by Catholics or by Protestants, is beset with intellectual difficulties; and it is a simple fact, that, for myself, I cannot answer those difficulties." The doctrine of the Trinity, he admitted, was incompatible with reason. "He has a deep distrust of the intellect," Dr. Fairbairn noted of Newman in 1885: the *Grammar of Assent* was "pervaded by the intensest philosophical scepticism." So fundamental a skepticism, like that of Dostoevsky, could only be kept in check by means of an unremitting assertion of faith resting on authority. His own brother-in-law, Reverend James B. Mozley, observed acutely how "Newman would not be alone and left to his own thoughts when he was neither studying, nor writing, nor praying. So, putting things together, we might say that he was always flying from a void, as well as from the temptation to rest." Behind him lurked always the shadow of unbelief. "It might be that having once caught sight of that spectre, and found it for a moment gaining upon him, he had resolved never once to abate the speed of his onward progress, never even to look behind."

This was likewise the view of the keenest thinker among the bishops in Victorian England. It was not primarily the historical element of Catholic tradition, thought Connop Thirlwall, or the sensuous elements in Catholic worship, that led Newman to Rome, but its unshakable confidence in its own authority.

No wonder that, once he had submitted to the authority of the most august religious institution in the Western world, Newman felt a supreme happiness and well-being. He had fulfilled the most urgent need of his emotional life. Almost twenty years later, he gratefully described how he had since then "no anxiety of heart whatever. I have been in perfect peace and contentment; I have never had one doubt. . . . it was like coming into port after a rough sea; and my happiness on that score remains to this day without interruption."

Viewed objectively, such a conversion may well have been what John Stuart Mill had in mind when he wrote in his *Autobiography:* "I have never been able to find any other explanation of this, than by attributing it to that timidity of conscience, combined with original sensitiveness of temperament, which has often driven highly gifted men into Romanism from the need of a firmer support than they could find in the independent conclusions of their own judgment."

The central difference in thought between Newman's *Apologia* and Mill's *Autobiography*—the reliance of the one upon dogma, of the other upon reason—can hardly be better illustrated than by juxtaposing two key passages from these works.

> Liberalism [wrote Newman] is the mistake of subjecting to human judgment those revealed doctrines which are in their nature beyond and independent of it, and of claiming to determine on intrinsic grounds the truth and value of propositions which rest for their value simply on the external authority of the Divine Word.

To which Mill answers:

> The notion that truths external to the mind may be known by intuition or consciousness, independently of observation and ex-

perience, is, I am persuaded, in these times, the great intellectual support of false doctrines and bad institutions. . . . There never was such an instrument devised for consecrating all deep-seated prejudices.

For Newman, to whom doubt was suspect and skepticism sinister, truth could be pronounced only by authority, and in the form of dogma. "I have changed in many things: in this I have not," he wrote when he was sixty-three. "From the age of fifteen, dogma has been the fundamental principle of my religion: I know no other religion: I cannot enter into the idea of any other sort of religion; religion, as a mere sentiment, is to me a dream and a mockery." As Geoffrey Faber vividly puts it, dogma was to Newman like the hard shell secreted by some sea creature in order to protect its otherwise naked sensitivity.

Now, it is an unfortunate fact, of which history furnishes many examples, that the more belief—whether political or religious—becomes dogmatic, the more it becomes intolerant. It is almost as though at the heart of dogmatic conviction there lies a secret unacknowledged doubt, the murmur of whose insistent questioning can only be stilled when the audible voices of other doubters are silenced too. Hence the paradox of a nature gentle as that of Newman justifying the persecution of others for the sake of enforcing uniformity of truth. Not content with enunciating this doctrine from the pulpit of St. Mary's, more than twenty years later he deliberately repeated his statement of it, word for word, in an often quoted passage of the *Apologia*. "I do not shrink from uttering my firm conviction," he declared, "that it would be a gain to this country were it vastly more superstitious, more bigoted, more gloomy, more fierce in its religion, than at present it shows itself to be." The only difference, wrote the liberal Catholic, Lord Acton, between Newman and St. Charles Borromeo, who condoned the Inquisition, was "a difference of times, not of persons."

In one of his *Tracts* Newman wrote that "an heresiarch (Wycliffe, Luther, Calvin, Zwingli) should meet with no mercy: he assumes the office of the Tempter. . . . To spare him is a false and dangerous pity. It is to endanger the souls of thousands, and it is uncharitable towards himself." "I cannot deny that this is a very fierce passage," Newman added reflectively, and proceeded to excuse himself: "It is only fair to myself to say that neither at this, nor at any other time of my life, not even when I was fiercest, could I have even cut off a Puritan's ears, and I think the sight of a Spanish *auto-da-fé* would have been the death of me." So, too, may have thought many an Inquisitor before he had gained practical experience of his art. The modern reader, moreover, my feel dismay at the casual reference to trimming a Puritan's ears.

An interesting comment on the lengths to which the dogmatic spirit will go is found in one of the letters of that remarkable Spaniard, Joseph Blanco White, a Catholic priest turned—to Newman's horror—Unitarian. In the days when the future cardinal had still been a Fellow of Oriel, he and White, both excellent musicians, used to play chamber music, especially Beethoven, together. An observer contrasted "Blanco White's excited and indeed agitated countenance with Newman's Sphinx-like immobility, as the latter drew long rich notes with a steady hand." Just before his own conversion to Rome, Newman meditated over Blanco White's defection from the Church. The sacrifice Newman was about to make of all that he held dear, was one, he realized, that had already been made by the Spaniard. "Here is Blanco White sincere and honest," he wrote in 1865. "He gives up his country, and then his second home—Spain, Oxford, Whately's family—all for an idea of truth, or rather for liberty of thought." When White became a Unitarian, Newman regretted that "the affectionate and mutual friendship between that excellent man and myself" must come to an end. For how could Newman any longer endure the friendship of one whom he now regarded as "doomed to eternal perdition"? "Such is the venomous character of orthodoxy," lamented White. "What mischief must it create in a bad heart and narrow mind, when it can work so effectually for evil, in one of the most benevolent of bosoms, and one of the ablest of minds, in the amiable, the intellectual, the refined John Henry Newman."

Through the *Apologia,* Newman recovered at one stroke, and as a Catholic, the unique position in the hearts of his fellow countrymen which he had held long before, as Anglican vicar of St. Mary's. New honors now awaited him. In 1878, Trinity, his old college at Oxford, made him an honorary fellow—"perhaps the greatest compliment I have ever received." And so at length, after thirty-two years of exile, he returned to "see once more, before I am taken away, what I never thought I should see again, the place where I began the battle of life, with my good angel at my side, a prospect almost too much for me to bear." Lord Bryce, who heard him speak on the occasion of this last visit to Oxford, remembered "the exquisite finish of his expressions, the beautiful clearness of his articulation and the sweetness of his voice . . . the voice so often heard in St. Mary's retaining, faint though it had grown, the sweet modulations Oxford knew so well, and the aged face worn deep with the lines of thought, struggle and sorrow. . . . What struck us most," Bryce recalled, "was the mixture of sadness and pleasure with which he came among us and recalled his early days."

The next year, his old enemy Pius IX having died, the Duke of Norfolk prevailed on the new pope, Leo XIII, to raise Newman to the purple. And so the world remembers as a cardinal, as a prince of the Church, one who in all humility preferred to be known, and was known for over thirty years, simply as plain Dr. Newman. When the Cardinal died in 1890, the Liberal statesman Lord Rosebery telegraphed to the Oratory to request that he, never having beheld Newman alive, might be allowed to see him dead. Permission was granted, and the great patrician stooped down to kiss the pale dead face.

For one whose basic philosophy of life was that there were "two only absolute and luminously self-evident beings, myself and my Creator," it is clear that an endless self-concern would be a marked feature of his character. Believing that he saw in them a direct providential dispensation, Newman took a deep interest in the smallest details of his daily life, and noted them down for the instruction of posterity. Besides the *Apologia*, he kept daily journals and composed various autobiographical sketches, the arrangement of which was one of the chief concerns of his last years.

Only by comparing the personality revealed—not without a good deal of perhaps unconscious selection and management of details—in the *Apologia* with that which emerges from the later autobiographical fragments can we measure the distance between the brilliant young fellow of Oriel and the obscure, middle-aged Oratorian of Birmingham. The former had been priggish, proud, ambitious, sometimes uncharitable, and not without revengeful feelings—all of which traits are candidly set down in the journals; the latter was gentle, humble, charitable, and submissive—though not without occasional flashes of fire, as the duel with Kingsley showed. Chastened by misfortune, pride humbled, ambition crushed, all passion spent, Newman impressed those who knew him toward the end of his life by his absolute selflessness and unaffected sweetness of nature. The frail old man emanated an extraordinary charm.

"What a world this is, and how piercing are its sorrows" is one of Newman's most characteristic utterances. Drawn by imagination to the loved places of his youth, he found to his surprise, on revisiting them in old age, not pleasure, only sadness. "My pain was most piercing. I had no pleasure," he wrote after visiting the scenes of his early life at Ham. "Yet, I am drawn to them. I cannot understand it." After the death of his sister Mary, in 1828, he wished that it "were possible for words to put down those indefinite, vague and withal subtle feelings which pierce the soul and make it sick. . . . What a veil and curtain this world of sense is! beautiful, but still a veil." Because he was capable of such feeling, Virgil was his favorite ancient poet, "his single words and phrases, his pathetic half-lines, giving utterance as the voice of Nature herself, to that pain and weariness, yet hope of better things, which is the experience of her children in every time."

"I several times heard him notice," wrote Thomas Mozley, "that the sounds of nature, the winds, the water, the poor beasts and even the birds, were all in the minor key as, too, age itself, in comparison with youth. Energy, contest, glory and triumph were in the major key." Animals always disquieted Newman: he never cared for pets. Like human beings, animals suffered, yet, since they had never sinned, from one point of view their sufferings were more perplexing even than those of mankind. More and more as life proceeded, the word "sadness" found expression in his writings. In the poem "Heavenly Leanings," in *Lyra Apostolica*, he thought of God as measuring out his days,

Willing me year by year, till I am found
A pilgrim pale, with Paul's sad girdle bound.

And in Newman's "Dream of Gerontius," the poem that solaced
Gordon in his last days at Khartoum, as Gerontius' soul goes
down to purgatory he cries out:

> There, motionless and happy in my pain,
> Lone, not forlorn—
> There will I sing my sad perpetual strain
> Until the morn.

Newman's evocative verse and subtly cadenced prose, rather
than his arguments, are the source of his appeal to our sympathies,
and the explanation of his power over us. "The world," wrote
Oscar Wilde in a graceful tribute not untouched with irony,
"will never weary of watching that troubled soul in its progress
from darkness to darkness. The lonely church at Littlemore,
where the breath of the morning is damp and the worshippers
are few, will always be dear to it, and whenever men see the yel-
low snapdragon blossoming on the walls of Trinity, they will
think of that gracious undergraduate."

Though the *Apologia* remains the crown of Newman's fame,
he is best known today, and throughout the world, by the hymn
he composed in 1833, "Lead, Kindly Light." Its appeal is universal, for among those in our own time who are said to have
called it their favorite hymn are Mahatma Gandhi, President
Eisenhower, Chiang Kai-shek, and Kwame Nkrumah. It was sung
at Gandhi's cremation at New Delhi in 1948, and it was the national anthem of Nkrumah's Ghana: an odd fortune for words that
sprang suddenly from the heart to comfort a homesick wanderer,
becalmed in the gathering dusk on an evening in 1833 in the
Strait of Bonifacio.

In twenty words of absolute simplicity, Newman succeeded
in compressing the essence of his life's lonely quest—the helpless-
ness of child or exile, and the redeeming faith:

> Lead, kindly Light, amid the encircling gloom;
>   Lead thou me on!
> The night is dark, and I am far from home;
>   Lead thou me on!

IV

Benjamin Disraeli

(1804-81)

BENJAMIN DISRAELI is a figure unique in the history of English politics. As one of his earliest biographers, James Anthony Froude, observed: "Disraeli had no personal interest in any of the great questions which divided English opinion. He owned no land; he was unconnected with trade; he had none of the hereditary prepossessions of a native Englishman. . . . In the teeth of prejudice, without support save his own force of character, without the advantage of being the representative of any popular cause which appealed to the imagination, he fought his way till the consent of Parliament and country raised him to the Premiership." A Jew by ancestry, a dandy in dress, an artist by temperament, the young Disraeli exaggerated these political handicaps and openly affronted the sensibilities of the majority of his countrymen. If he succeeded in the end, it was because he overcame their opposition and vanquished their bigotry, not because he relinquished one iota of his own personality. He forced friend and foe alike to accept him at his own valuation. He is the only major figure in the history of English politics to be also a successful novelist: indeed he may be said to have originated a new genre, the political novel.

He not only rejuvenated the old Tory party—"the stupid party," as Mill had termed it—but gave it a new lease of life, which has lasted into the twentieth century. "I had to educate—if it be not too arrogant a phrase," said Disraeli, "I had to educate our party." Though the other great party—that of Gladstone and Liberalism—has withered away, today Conservatives in England look back to Disraeli as the founder of the party, and comemorate the day of his death, April 19, as Primrose Day. "Of all British statesmen of the Victorian era," Cecil Roth remarks, "Disraeli is perhaps the only one who is still a living force, and whose opinions are still a pattern for the political party which he had not merely led, but created."

He transformed the Queen of the United Kingdom into the Empress of India, and was one of those who did most, for better or worse, to create the atmosphere and sentiment of modern British imperialism. By one of the most daring personal coups of the nineteenth century, he acquired for Britain a controlling interest in the Suez Canal, and thus launched her into the world of Near Eastern politics, from which, only now, a century later, is her influence finally receding. In old age, at the Congress of Berlin in 1878, he gained the admiration of Bismarck and with it his greatest diplomatic victory by defeating the designs of Russia and thwarting her plans for Balkan expansion. Four dukes welcomed him home on his triumphal arrival at Charing Cross, bringing, in his boastful phrase, "peace with honour."

By purchasing the Suez Canal shares, he extended British influence to Egypt, and thus, since the control of Palestine was of strategic importance in relation to the Suez Canal, indirectly paved the way for the Balfour Declaration of 1917, which led in turn to the state of Israel as it exists today. Hence Theodore Herzl, the founder of modern Zionism, came to regard Disraeli as one of "the leading exponents of the Zionist idea," while Jews throughout the West, like the young Viennese doctor Sigmund Freud, looked with gratitude to Disraeli as the supreme example of one who had overcome the prejudice and hostility of the gentile world to reach the highest public position achieved by any Jew in the history of European civilization.

One asks, therefore, what sort of man was this unique figure, by what means did he achieve his success, and what did that success mean to him?

Benjamin Disraeli was the second child and eldest son of a family of five. His ancestors were Sephardic Jews who had come to England from Venice in the eighteenth century, and who—he liked to think—had, at a still earlier time, been among those expelled from Spain by the Inquisition. Disraeli, like others, regarded the Sephardim as the aristocracy of Jewry, and he took an inordinate pride in his descent. He was, indeed, as Cecil Roth has shown, in this respect not above embellishing the record and falsifying the facts.

His father, Isaac d'Israeli, the son of an immigrant, was an easygoing man of letters who had gained a competency and made a reputation by his researches into English literature. His reading, curiously enough, had made him a Voltairean in philosophy and a Tory in politics. His *Commentaries on the Life and Reign of Charles I* had earned him an honorary degree at Oxford. He wanted to send his eldest son to Eton, but the project miscarried—fortunately for the sensitive and foreign-looking boy who no doubt at that period would have suffered cruelly at any English Public School. The result was that the boy was educated chiefly in his father's library, amidst a splendid collection of twenty-five thousand books. Like Bentham, Mill, and Newman in their youth, the young Disraeli read omnivorously—often for twelve hours a day. Having a retentive memory, he thus acquired a large stock of information, chiefly historical and literary, which was to be valuable to him in the world of politics.

This almost solitary childhood—shared though it was with his loved elder sister, Sarah, who till her death in 1859 was his closest confidante—predisposed the boy's romantic mind to dreams and reverie. His dreams were of individual greatness: Napoleon, William Pitt, and Byron were among his heroes. The French Emperor had dominated the Europe of his day; Pitt the Younger had been Prime Minister at twenty-four; Byron at twenty-one had waked one morning in London to find himself famous: Disraeli resolved that he would emulate all three. He was talented, high-spirited, ambitious, and had a marvelous fluency of language.

One obstacle stood in his path: his race. Though circumcized at birth, he had not been given an orthodox religious training. He was unable to read Hebrew, and knew nothing of Jewish rites or dietary laws. At the age of thirteen, he was baptized a Christian, and for the rest of his life fulfilled the outward observances of the Church of England. Nevertheless, in his inmost being he felt himself a Jew, nor was he allowed by his companions to forget that he was Jewish. He consciously identified himself with the pride and glory of Jewry as he knew them through history. When, later, at an election he found himself opposed by a member of the Duke of Devonshire's family, he proudly declared: "I am not disposed for a moment to admit that my pedigree is not as good, and even superior to that of the Cavendishes."

Beneath such brave words lay the awareness of a tremendous, indeed of an almost insuperable, handicap. No orthodox Jew could yet enter the House of Commons, be elevated to the peerage, or hold any high office of state. Shylock in the *Merchant of Venice*, Fagin in *Oliver Twist*, or the opprobrious cry "old clothes": these were the epithets at that time often used in England against Jews, and they were hurled at Disraeli when he first offered himself as a candidate for Parliament. In the face of such prejudice, two courses were open: to conciliate it, or to defy it. As a young man of boundless energy and self-confidence, Disraeli chose defiance.

He set himself to cultivate a personality that at every point affronted conventional standards and opinion, and showed himself insufferably conceited, arrogant, and egotistical. He boldly flaunted Pistol's saying in *The Merry Wives of Windsor*:

Why, then the world's mine oyster,
Which I with sword will open.

In his first novel, *Vivian Grey*, published in 1826, when he was twenty-one, a work in which the autobiographical element is transparent, he wrote: "It was one of the first principles of Mr. Vivian Grey that everything was possible. Men did fail in life to be sure . . . but still all these failures might be traced to a loss of physical or mental courage. . . . Now Vivian Grey was conscious that there was at least one person in the world who was no craven either in body or in mind, and so he had long come to the comfortable conclusion, that it was impossible that his career could be anything but the most brilliant." "Impertinent and flippant," said Vivian Grey, "I was universally hailed as an original and a wit. I became one of the most affected, conceited and intolerable atoms that ever peopled the sunbeam of society." Of his second novel, *Contarini Fleming*, written after his journey to the East in 1830, Disraeli allowed that he would "always consider this book as the perfection of English prose and as a *chef d'oeuvre*."

So far as affectation and insolence were concerned, his performances in real life matched those of his fictional heroes. Arriving at Gibraltar, on his Eastern tour, he boasted to his father how he had astonished society on the Rock. "I have had the fame of being the first who ever passed the Straits with two canes, a morning and an evening cane. I change my cane on the gunfire and hope to carry them both on to Cairo." From Malta he wrote home: "Affectation tells here better than wit. Yesterday at the racket court, sitting in the gallery among strangers, the ball entered, and lightly struck me and fell at my feet. I picked it up and observing a young rifleman excessively stiff, I humbly requested him to forward its passage into the court, as I really had never thrown a ball in my life. This incident has been the general subject of conversation at all the messes today!" The pleasure he took in shocking others remained with him all through life. On this early Eastern tour he left in his wake a ripple of outraged amazement which stretched from Gibraltar to Constantinople. It was later to agitate the cloisters of Westminster.

By dint of practice such affectation became second nature, and as Froude observes, "the stripling of seventeen was the same person as the statesman of seventy, with the difference only, that the affectation which was natural in the boy was itself affected in the matured politician, whom it served as a mask or as a suit of impenetrable armour."

His foible was omniscience, and he exploited his knowledge in a way that would have repelled serious students like Bentham or Mill, whose reading was so much more extensive than his own. "Vivian Grey was reputed in the world as having the most astonishing memory that ever existed; for there was scarcely a subject of discussion in which he did not gain the victory, by the great names he enlisted on his side of the argument."

As for insolence, Lady Dufferin tells a typical story of the young Disraeli at the table of her "insufferable brother-in-law, Mr. Norton." When Disraeli agreed that his host's wine was good, and Norton replied that he had wine "twenty times as good" in his cellar, "no doubt, no doubt," agreed Disraeli, looking around the table, "but, my dear fellow this is quite good enough for such *canaille* as you have got today."

The follies of his dress outran the follies of his speech, and in the dawn of Victorian respectability, the flamboyance of his attire matched the outrageousness of his conduct. We first see him in society, giving a recitation of his (bad) poetry at Mrs. Austin's: "There was something irresistibly comic in the young man dressed in the coxcombical costume that he then affected—velvet coat thrown wide open, ruffles on the sleeves, shirt collars turned down in Byronic fashion, an elaborate embroidered waistcoat from which issued voluminous folds of frill, shoes adorned with red rosettes, his black hair pomatumed and elaborately curled and his person redolent with perfume." At Lady Blessington's he appeared arranged in "the gorgeous gold flowers of a splendidly embroidered waistcoat. Patent leather pumps, a white stick with a black cord and tassel, and a quantity of chains about his neck and pockets. . . . A thick, heavy mass of jet black ringlets," wrote an American observer on that occasion, "falls on his left cheek almost to his collarless stock, which on the right temple is parted and put away with the smooth carefulness of a girl."

What is certain is not only that these sartorial extravagances provided abundant material for gossip, but that the young dandy who indulged them was the most brilliant talker and most arresting person in society. He never bored people, and if for no other reason than the sensation he provided, his company was eagerly sought after.

Disraeli cared little for the normal masculine interests. "I hate clubs," he wrote on one occasion, "not being fond of male society"; and on another: "There are many dreadful things in life, and a dinner of men is the worst of all." "Talk to women," he admonished himself in his journal, "talk to women as much as you can. This is the best school. . . . Nothing is of so much importance and of so much use to a young man entering life as to be well criticized by women."

Notwithstanding the success of his early novels, Disraeli quickly realized that literature alone would not enable him to live on the scale he desired. His father wanted him to be a barrister, and for three years he was articled to a lawyer, and ate dinners at Lincoln's Inn. "The Bar! pooh!" thought Vivian Grey. "Law and bad jokes till we are forty, and then with the most brilliant success the prospect of gout and a coronet. Besides, to succeed as an advocate I must be a great lawyer, and to be a great lawyer I must give up my chances of being a great man." "The 'services' in war time," he added, "are fit only for desperadoes (and that truly am I), and in peace are fit only for fools."

Besides, it was power chiefly that the young Disraeli craved—including no doubt that of avenging the numerous snubs and humiliations he had suffered. "I live for Power and the Affections," he once wrote, "and one may enjoy both without being bored and wearied with all the dull demands of conventional intercourse." But power was centered in the House of Commons, and so, despite the improbability of so exotic an outsider ever finding his way into the most exclusive club in England, Disraeli began to entertain a new ambition. One evening at Caroline Norton's house, he was introduced to Lord Melbourne. The Prime Minister was struck with his originality and wit and, possibly discerning a new recruit to the party, offered to help him. "Well, now, tell me, what do you want to be?" he asked. "I want to be Prime Minister," the young man coolly answered the slightly disconcerted statesman.

"When I was considered very conceited," Disraeli wrote in his diary, "I was nervous and had self-confidence only by fits. I intend in future to act entirely from my own impulse. I have an unerring instinct—I can read characters at a glance; few men can deceive me. . . . I am only truly great in action. If ever I am placed in a truly eminent position, I shall prove this. I could rule the House of Commons, although there would be a great prejudice against me at first."

When he attended debates in the House, even the most eminent leaders failed to impress him. "Mr. Peel," he noted patronizingly of his own future chief, "improves as a speaker, though like most of the rest, he is fluent without the least style. . . . I have heard Canning. He was a consummate rhetorician; but there seemed to be a dash of commonplace in all he said." Once he "heard Macaulay's best speech. . . . Macaulay admirable," he admitted to his sister, "but between ourselves I could floor them all. This *entre nous*. I was never more confident of anything than that I could carry everything before me in that House."

Not yet embarked on public life, with superb self-assurance he looked beyond the Commons to that preserve of aristocracy—the Lords. "A man may speak well in the House of Commons," said one of the characters in his novel *The Young Duke*, "and fail very completely in the House of Lords. There are two distinct styles requisite: I intend, in the course of my career, if I have time, to give a specimen of both." He was as good as his word.

In 1832 Disraeli offered himself as an independent candidate to the electors of High Wycombe. On this, as well as on two subsequent occasions, he was not only defeated, but came at the bottom of the poll. An eyewitness has left an unforgettable impression of the young Disraeli soliciting the popular vote.

> Never in my life have I been so struck by a face as I was by that of Disraeli. It was lividly pale, and from beneath two finely-arched eyebrows blazed out a pair of intensely black eyes. I never have seen such orbs in mortal sockets, either before or since. His physiognomy was strictly Jewish. Over a broad, high forehead were ringlets of coal-black, glossy hair which, combed away from his right temple, fell in luxuriant clusters or bunches over his left cheek and ear, which they entirely concealed from view. There was a sort of half-smile, half-sneer, playing about his beautifully-formed mouth, the upper lip of which was curved as we see it in the portraits of Byron. . . . He was very showily attired in a dark bottle-green frock coat, a waistcoat of the most extraordinary pattern, the front of which was almost covered with glittering chains, and in fancy pattern pantaloons. Altogether he was the most intellectual-looking exquisite I had ever seen.

Had anyone prophesied at this point that this flamboyant youth would one day be Prime Minister of England, he would have been thought out of his mind.

In these early electoral defeats, which he did not suffer to depress him, Disraeli's politics were hard to define: sometimes he seemed a Tory, sometimes a radical, at other times to be weary of the whole system of party politics. In one address, he invited the electors to "make an end of the factious slang of Whig and Tory, two names with one meaning, and only to delude the people," and to "unite in forming a national party." "I come before you," he announced, "to oppose this disgusting system of factions: I come before you wearing the badge of no party and the livery of no faction."

In *The Young Duke*, he cynically expressed his feelings about the party. "Am I a Whig or a Tory? I forget. As for the Tories, I admire antiquity, particularly a ruin; even the ruins of the

Temple of Intolerance have a charm. I think I am a Tory. But then the Whigs give such good dinners, and are the most amusing. I think I am a Whig; but then the Tories are so moral, and then morality is my forte; I must be a Tory. But the Whigs dress so much better, and an ill-dressed party, like an ill-dressed man, must be wrong. And yet. . . ."

In assessing his own motives he was astonishingly frank. "There is no doubt, gentlemen," he once admitted, "that all men who offer themselves as candidates for public favour have motives of some sort. I candidly acknowledge that I have, and I will tell you what they are: I love fame, I love public reputation; I love to live in the eyes of the country; and it is a glorious thing for a man to do who has had my difficulties to contend against." What he naturally did not tell the electors in 1837, when he joined the Tories, the party of protection, was that a few years earlier, in his *Voyage of Captain Popanilla*, he had effectively exposed and ridiculed the fallacies of protection. Perhaps he had already forgotten the book himself.

In 1837, after four unsuccessful attempts to enter Parliament, Disraeli at last got himself elected as Tory M.P. for Maidstone in Kent, and placed himself under the leadership of Sir Robert Peel. He likewise got himself elected to the Carlton Club. In thus allying his fortunes with those of the Tories, the party most steeped in prejudice and most opposed to Jewish emancipation, Disraeli might seem to have been lacking in scruple. Principle, however, sat as lightly upon him as seventy years later upon Lord Birkenhead, and each must have realized that, while in the Liberal party their talents might be eclipsed by those of brilliant rivals, in "the stupid party" brains, being scarcer, would be proportionately more valued; and indeed, from the moment of his first appearance as a Tory, Disraeli's progress was watched with almost fatherly solicitude by two of the most eminent elder Conservative statesmen—the Duke of Wellington, and the ex-Lord Chancellor, Lord Lyndhurst.

The maiden speech of any new member is necessarily an ordeal. Dressed in a bottle-green coat, with a white waistcoat covered with gold chains, Disraeli rose to deliver his carefully phrased and elaborately rehearsed address. Unfortunately for him, he had counted without Daniel O'Connell. In one of his unsuccessful campaigns at Wycombe, Disraeli had received some help from the Irish leader, but after turning Tory, he had denounced O'Connell as an "incendiary." Now the "Liberator" was well known for his foulmouthed scurrility, and Disraeli would have been wise not to provoke him. "The miscreant had the audacity to style me an incendiary," roared O'Connell. "He calls me a traitor; my answer to this is, he is a liar. His life is a living lie. He is the most degraded of his species and kind, and England is degraded in tolerating and having on the face of her society a miscreant of his abominable, foul and atrocious nature." Not content with this volley of abuse, O'Connell went on to allude to Disraeli's being a Jew, and concluded that he must be the heir-at-law of the impenitent thief on the cross. To this Disraeli retorted that he would "not be insulted even by a Yahoo without chastising him." He challenged first O'Connell himself, and then his son, to a duel. The upshot was that when Disraeli rose from the Opposition benches to deliver his maiden speech, the Irish members created such an uproar with derisive laughter, shouts, and catcalls that the speaker could not be heard. "I will sit down now," the victim called out loudly, "but the time will come when you will hear me." "D'Israeli made his first exhibition this night," reported Charles Greville, clerk of the council, "beginning with florid assurance, speedily degenerating into ludicrous absurdity, and being at last put down with inextinguishable shouts of laughter."

For the next four years, Disraeli served as a loyal and regular member of the Opposition; but when, in September 1841, Melbourne fell from power and was succeeded by Peel, Disraeli, to his intense chagrin, found himself omitted from the new administration. He thereupon wrote an urgent letter to Peel, begging to be saved "from an intolerable humiliation." "I have had to struggle," he told him, "against a storm of political hate and malice which few men ever experienced." That same evening, and without his knowledge, Disraeli's wife, (for he had married two years earlier) also wrote Sir Robert. "I beg you not to be angry with me for my intrusion," she pleaded, "but I am overwhelmed with anxiety. My husband's political career is for ever crushed, if you do not appreciate him." She concluded by begging him not to let "any human being know that I have written you this humble petition." The appeal was in vain, and Disraeli never forgave Peel the fancied injury. So deep was the mortification to his pride that in after years, with Peel long dead and himself Prime Minister, Disraeli denied ever having made such an application; nor were the facts finally established until 1899, in Charles Stuart Parker's *Life of Peel.*

Often in Disraeli's novels his heroes owed their success to the fact that as young men they formed attachments to fashionable women who were older and more mature. The author knew whereof he spoke. Between 1833 and 1836 he was involved in clandestine affairs with two older women—Henrietta, Lady Sykes, and Mrs. Clara Bolton. That discretion was required may be judged from the fact that Lady Sykes (the model for Disraeli's novel *Henrietta Temple*) was at the same time the mistress of Lord Lyndhurst. It appears that Lady Sykes even used her influence with Lyndhurst to promote Disraeli's political career. Sir Philip Rose, Disraeli's secretary in his last years, believed that the liaison was known to Peel and was the reason for the snub that Peel administered to Disraeli when the latter sought office in 1841. What is really extraordinary is that rumors of this scandal were not revived thirty years later to discredit Disraeli when he was Prime Minister.

By that time, however, Disraeli had long been a model husband, for in 1839 he had married a widow thirteen years his senior, with a fortune of £4,000 a year. At their first meeting, he had found her only "a pretty little woman—a flirt and a rattle." "I may commit many follies in life," he had written his sister, "but I never intend to marry for love, which I am sure is a guarantee for infelicity." He kept his resolve—he did not marry for love, but with each passing year affection grew between himself and Mary Anne, and they lived happily together till her death thirty-three years later.

During the eighteen-forties, Disraeli wrote two novels in quick succession—*Coningsby* (1844) and *Sybil* (1845). They combined the gifts of the poet and the historian with the ardor of the partisan and the smoothness of the propagandist. Though the poetry was tinsel and the history false, both books won immediate popular success in England and also in America. "Some serious creed," wrote Sir Leslie Stephen, "however misty and indefinite, is required to make the mere mocker into the genuine satirist." For Disraeli that creed was Young England—the belief that the working class could only be saved from exploitation at the hands of the manufacturers by the leadership of a chivalrous landed aristocracy.

The two books consist of a romantic exaltation of the Middle Ages, a scathing indictment of the Industrial Revolution, a Tory philosophy of history to offset the prevailing Whig version of Hallam, a spirited description of contemporary politics (in which well-known figures appear, sometimes under fictitious names), and a harrowing account (based on parliamentary "blue books") of contemporary social conditions. Thrown in for good measure are bitter attacks on political enemies, idealized accounts of the author and his friends, and a glorification of the Jewish "race."

When a novel contains so many diversified elements, it seems captious to complain that the plot is flimsy, the characters unreal, the sentiments shallow and insincere. The style is brisk and sparkles with epigrammatic wit: it is well suited to express that sentimental-ironic attitude to life in which Disraeli shows himself the precursor of later writers such as Oscar Wilde and Somerset Maugham. "Youth is a blunder; Manhood a struggle; Old Age a regret." Such a sentiment, expressed over a hundred years ago, has bred a numerous progeny.

Few politicians are able to avenge themselves on their enemy within the covers of a best-seller. However painful the injury, the fictional web in which the victim is caught deters him from defending himself, or if he seeks to do so, he runs the risk of inculpating himself more deeply. One may imagine Peel's feelings on reading that "there is no treason except voting against a Minister, who, though he may have changed all the policy which you have been elected to support, expects your vote and confidence all the same." This was transparently an allusion to Peel's abandonment of protection in 1846. In the obsequious party hacks, the Tapers and Tadpoles of *Coningsby*, whose names have passed into history, Disraeli excoriated the faithful followers of Peel, his own leader.

In a famous paragraph in *Sybil*, Disraeli described England as consisting of not one nation, but two—"two nations, between whom there is no intercourse and no sympathy; who are as ignorant of each other's habits, thoughts and feelings as if they were dwellers in different zones, or inhabitants of different planets; who are formed by a different breeding, are fed by a different food, are ordered by different manners, and are not governed by the same laws. . . . THE RICH AND THE POOR." The professed object of Young England was to put an end to this terrible dichotomy and to reconcile all classes under the benevolent rule of Crown and Aristocracy.

If one is, however, sufficiently indelicate to ask how far Disraeli's performance in Parliament matched the professions of his fictional heroes, the answer is disillusioning. For the rising politician, as his voting record in the forties shows, took little interest in the factory legislation and other reforms whose object was to alleviate the evils so graphically described in his novels: hence the harsh judgment of Marx on the Young England group—"those corrupt, heartless and genteel loafers." Even aristocrats of Young England regarded their champion with suspicion. "If I could be sure," wrote Lord John Manners, "that Disraeli believes all he says, I should feel happier. His historical views are my own, but does he believe in them?"

Not only in his novels but also on the floor of the House, Disraeli got his revenge on Peel for having been rejected in 1841. In the years that followed, he became in fact the most vehement and pertinacious critic of his own chief, "traducing with laborious virulence," as Goldwin Smith wrote sourly many years later, "the character and career of a statesman whom he knew to be doing right, on whom a little time before he had been lavishing his adulation, and to whom he had been a suitor for place." "A Conservative Government," Disraeli roundly stated, "is an organized hypocrisy."

The pages of Greville record the mounting bitterness of his attacks on Peel: from being "very clever . . . ingenious and amusing," they gradually become "more and more rabid." In January 1846 Greville heard Disraeli in person for the first time: ". . . an hour of gibes and bitterness, all against Peel personally, from D'Israeli, with some good hits, but much of it tiresome." Finally, in the great controversy over Corn Law Repeal, Disraeli launched his most deadly attack. He wound up the debate with a speech in which, according to Greville, "he hacked and mangled Peel with the most unsparing severity and positively tortured his victim. It was a miserable and degrading spectacle. The whole mass of the Protectionists cheered him with vociferous delight, making the roof ring again; and when Peel spoke, they screamed and hooted at him in the most brutal manner. When he vindicated himself and talked of honour and conscience, they assailed him with shouts of derision and gestures of contempt. . . . They hunt him like a fox," wrote Greville of the Young England group, "and they are eager to run him down and kill him in the open. . . . It is high time such a state of things should finish." Greville, himself, it must be remembered, was a political opponent of Peel. "It does not follow," wrote Froude blandly, forty years later, "that Disraeli believed all he said, but the object was to make Peel suffer, and in this he undoubtedly succeeded." The downfall of Peel paved the way for Disraeli's accession in 1848 to the leadership of the Conservative party in the House of Commons.

No sketch of Disraeli's life can omit to notice his ideas about the Jewish people. Baptized a Christian, it was through that fact alone that he was able to take part in the public life of England. He fulfilled the outward duties of a Christian, going to church regularly every Sunday, and taking the sacrament every Easter at his country home at Hughenden. Occasionally, he even went out of his way to pay homage to Christianity, yet he wore his religion with a difference—wryly, punctiliously, and ironically. Christianity he once described as "the most important portion of the Jewish religion." In his novel *Tancred* he asserted that "Christianity is Judaism for the multitude, but it is still Judaism." "It is no doubt to be deplored," he added gravely in his *Life of Lord George Bentinck*, "that several millions of the Jewish race should persist in believing only a part of their religion."

He took sardonic pleasure in reminding his nominal co-religionists of the origin of their faith. "Christianity may continue to persecute the Jews . . . but who can deny that Jesus of Nazareth, the Incarnate Son of the Most High God, is the eternal glory of the Jewish race?" As for the Incarnation, it was impossible to deny "that only one race could be deemed worthy of accomplishing it." The Blessed Virgin, the Apostles, and St. Paul were all Jews: "A Jewess is the queen of heaven and, . . . the flower of the Jewish race are [sic] even now sitting on the right hand of the Lord God of Sabaoth." Logic and audacity carried him yet further. "No one," he solemnly admonished his fellow Christians, "has ever been permitted to write under the inspiration of the Holy Spirit, except a Jew. . . . The Saxon, the Slav and the Celt . . . daily acknowledge on their knees, with reverent gratitude, that the only medium of communication between the Creator and themselves is a Jew."

Even the doctrine of Atonement was not spared his suave satire. "Persecute us!" cried Eva in *Tancred*. "Why, if you believed what you profess you should kneel to us! . . . We have saved the human race, and you persecute us for doing it!" And in the *Life of Lord George Bentinck*, Disraeli demanded: "If the Jews had not prevailed upon the Romans to crucify our Lord, what would have become of the Atonement? . . . Could that be a crime which secured for all mankind eternal joy—which vanquished Satan, and opened the gates of Paradise?"

Some of these thrusts must surely have gone home. Not everyone can have missed the irony or failed to hear the sardonic laughter. "He speaks of the mysteries of Christianity," wrote his admirer Froude, "in a tone which, if not sincere, is detestable." But was it sincere? The choleric Irish Catholic T. P. O'Connor, later "Father of the House," thought not. "Mr. Disraeli," he fumed, "actually claims credit for the Jews for committing that act which, in the eyes of the orthodox Christian, must always be regarded as an inexpiable crime."

Religion apart, Disraeli never doubted that the Jews were the salt of the earth. He called them "the human family that has contributed most to human happiness. . . . We hesitate not to say that there is no race at this present . . . . . . that so much delights, and fascinates, and elevates, and ennobles Europe, as the Jewish; . . . the most entrancing singers, graceful dancers, and exquisite musicians, are sons and daughters of Israel."

No one believed more fervently than Disraeli in the doctrine of race. "Race is the key to history," he proclaimed in *Endymion*. "There is only one thing that makes a race, and that is blood."

When Baron Lionel de Rothschild's son Leopold was born, Disraeli congratulated his friend: "I hope he will prove worthy of his pure and sacred race." Had not Jews produced Moses, the greatest of legislators, Solomon, the greatest of administrators, and Christ, the greatest of reformers? "What race, extinct or living," asked Disraeli, "can produce three such men as these?"

The longer Disraeli lived, the more obsessed about race did he become. He even devised his own brand of anthropology, according to which Aryans and Semites became branches of the Caucasian race. "The fact is," blandly explained the sapient Sidonia in Coningsby, "you cannot destroy a pure race of the Caucasian organization."

Addressing his English readers directly, Disraeli reminded them that "vast as are the obligations of the whole human family to the Hebrew race, there is no portion of the modern population so much indebted to them as the British people." He even warned that nations would fare well or ill at the hands of Providence, exactly according to the measure that they dealt well or ill with the Jews. Nor did he overlook the United States: "The great transatlantic republic is intensely Semitic, and has prospered accordingly." He warned the American people not to intermarry with Negroes. If they had, he prophesied, they would become "so deteriorated that their states would probably be reconquered and regained by the aborigines whom they have expelled, and who would be their superiors."

In the realm of practical politics, he fought wholeheartedly for Jewish emancipation. His friend Baron Lionel de Rothschild was in 1847 elected M.P. for the city of London, but was not allowed to take his seat. Eight times in the next ten years the question was raised, and on several occasions Rothschild was re-elected: but always the implacable Tories in the House of Lords, bristling with prejudice, barred the way. When victory was finally won in 1858, and Rothschild took his seat, it was due largely to Disraeli's tenacious leadership.

Curiously enough, Disraeli based his advocacy of Jewish emancipation not on grounds of general toleration, but on the basis of the privileged status due to a superior race; and for the benefit of his fellow Conservatives, he emphasized that the Jews "are a race essentially monarchical, deeply religious, and essentially Tories."

Their natural bias, he declared, was aristocratic. "They are a living and the most striking evidence of the falsity of that pernicious doctrine of modern times—the natural equality of man." But continued exclusion from civic rights, he hinted, might turn them all into communists and atheists.

It is doubtful whether Disraeli's political views were as sincere as his convictions about race. In 1851 Greville, who had closely observed his career, wrote that "D'Israeli has nothing but the cleverness of an adventurer. Nobody has any confidence in him, or supposes that he has any principles whatever." Now, Greville was reporting not only his own opinion—though by this time he knew Disraeli personally—but the sentiments of both sides of the House, since he himself had good friends in both parties. "Disraeli has been a perfect Will-o'-the Wisp," he wrote in 1852, "flitting about from one opinion to another, till his real opinions and intentions are become mere matter of guess and speculation," and in the following year, he added that the Conservative leader never seemed "to have a thought to any consideration of political morality, honesty or truth, in all that he said."

Despite Disraeli's position as leader of the Conservatives in the House of Commons for over twenty years, there was little accord between Disraeli and his followers on the one hand, or between himself and his chief, Lord Derby, on the other. Disraeli, said Derby, possessed "a capacity so great that he cannot be trusted." The antipathy was mutual, for Disraeli is reported as saying that he "disliked and despised Derby [and] had a great contempt for his party." As for the rank and file of the Tories, according to Greville in 1853, they "dread and hate him, for they know he in his heart has no sympathy for them, and that he has no truth or sincerity in his conduct or speeches, and would throw them over if he thought it his interest." It seems likely that there could never be much in common between the ex-dandy novelist-adventurer and the provincial-minded Tory squires. Seven years later, in one of the last entries of his famous diary, Greville reports: "The hatred and distrust of Disraeli is greater than ever in the Conservative ranks." Even his former patron, Lord Lyndhurst, now condemned Disraeli, saying that his "want of character was fatal to him and weighed down all his cleverness."

After 1848, twenty long years were to elapse before Disraeli at length succeeded to the premiership. In this period, the Conservatives accepted him as leader, partly because no other was available (this was more than ever true in the fifties, when Gladstone and most of the Peelites went over to the Liberals), and partly because he was unrivaled—as he had proved by his assault on Peel—as a guerrilla chieftain. He had as yet shown no capacity for constructive work, nor had he had any opportunity to do so. But he was a brilliant debater, a merciless opponent, and a large-sized thorn in the flesh of any Liberal government.

"The satire of Disraeli," wrote Froude, "is pleasant, laughing and good-natured." This might be true of his novels, but scarcely of his political attacks—witness the wounds inflicted upon Peel. "In all his life," Froude goes on to say, "he never hated anybody or anything, never bore a grudge, or remembered a libel against himself." As a young man, Lord Esher knew Disraeli in old age, and gave similar testimony: "He is without hatred, and never appears to bear malice." It may well have been that, unlike Gladstone, his great opponent in the years to come, Disraeli never cared deeply about anything except the conquest of power. A genuine cynic rarely cherishes hatreds. The Archbishop of Canterbury, on reading *Endymion*, observed that to its author politics appeared to be no more than "play and gambling."

To an opportunist in politics, the enemy of today may be the ally of tomorrow, and it is well to avoid irreconcilable feuds. In Disraeli's political career, the hounding of Peel is an exception to his general behavior; and if in the daily warfare of the House, he delighted his friends and galled his enemies by the bitterness of his attacks, there was in this verbal brilliance a certain pleasure in his own virtuosity, an element of play, a lack of absolute deadliness. Such characteristics were foreign to Gladstone, whose speeches bore the imprint of deep personal conviction.

Vehement Disraeli's attacks certainly were. Even when he was a young man, before he had entered Parliament, a visitor to Lady Blessington's salon noted that his "command of language was truly wonderful, his powers of sarcasm unsurpassed." Greville commented on "that sarcastic vituperation which is his great forte," and on another occasion reported how Disraeli's "eloquent tide of invective and sarcasm was received with frantic applause by his crew; they roared and hooted and converted the House of Commons into such a bear-garden as no one ever saw before." "While all around him are convulsed," wrote an eyewitness, "with merriment or excitement at some of his finely wrought sarcasms, he holds himself, seemingly, in total suspension, as though he had no existence for the ordinary feelings and passions of humanity; and the moment the shouts and confusion have subsided, the same calm, low, monotonous, but yet distinct and searching voice, is heard still pouring forth his ideas, while he is preparing to launch another sarcasm, hissing hot, into the soul of his victim."

During the years of seemingly endless opposition, Disraeli must sometimes have wondered whether, as a young man, he had not made a serious mistake in choosing to support the Tories rather than the Whigs. On three brief occasions, however, during these twenty years—in 1852, 1858, and 1867—the Conservatives found themselves in power, and Disraeli in office. Even his enemies admitted that his budget speech, as Chancellor of the Exchequer in 1852, was "a great performance," but it was based on a frank acceptance of the very principle of free trade for which he had denounced Peel in 1846. Now that the latter was dead, Disraeli gave "deep offence" to the protectionists within his party, by passing what Greville called "a frank, full and glowing Panegyrick" on Peel's free-trade measures, excepting only the repeal of the Corn Laws. Small wonder that simple-minded Tory gentlemen scarcely knew where they, or their party, stood—with a leader who was too clever by half.

In his second term of office in 1858, it was conceded that Disraeli "had raised himself immensely," and behaved "with a tact, judgment and ability of which he was not before thought capable." Yet only two months later, Greville reported: "The hatred and distrust of Disraeli is greater than ever in the Conservative ranks"; while Lord Clarendon added that Disraeli's own leader, Lord Derby, "was violently discontented" with him, and prepared to break off their relations. What with his own vanity and egotism on the one hand, and his party's prejudices on the other, the lot of a wayward, errant genius who deliberately allied himself with "the stupid party" was not an easy one.

Then came the second Great Reform Bill in 1867, when Disraeli shocked his friends and astonished his opponents by suddenly extending the franchise to that democracy which he had always professed to despise. He frankly avowed that in thus yielding to the storm whipped up by Bright and other radical orators, his main object was to stay in office; and he took special pride in the fact that he passed the bill against powerful opposition, some of which came from his own party, and as leader of a minority government. His position, in fact, was remarkably like that of Peel twenty years earlier—though in 1846 Peel had acted on principle rather than for self-serving reasons. Disraeli had once raised a laugh at Peel's expense by the taunt that the latter had been "stealing the Whigs' clothes while they were bathing." Now he exposed himself—but jauntily and with bravado—to the identical reproach of political tergiversation.

His colleague Lord Cranborne, later Lord Salisbury, termed Disraeli's reform act "a political betrayal which has no parallel in our annals," one that struck at the very root of parliamentary confidence (within ten years he was to be the firm ally of the man he was denouncing). The aged Lord Shaftesbury, most respected of Tory reformers, stigmatized the bill as "a gross hypocrisy," characteristic of "a sensual and self-seeking age." Lord Dalhousie observed that it proved that dishonesty was the best policy. The Whig Lord Clarendon remarked tartly that "a demoralized nation admires the audacity, the tricks and the success of the Jew." Thomas Carlyle, that well-known anti-Semite and foe of democracy, regarded the bill as "the suicide of the English nation," and in *Shooting Niagara* he denounced its author in terms of unmeasured abuse. "A superlative Hebrew conjuror," leading England by the nose, he called him in public; in private, "a fantastic ape" and "a cursed old Jew not worth his weight in cold bacon." The conservative poet Coventry Patmore designated 1867 as:

> . . . the year of the great crime,
> When the false English Nobles and their Jew,
> By God demented, slew
> The trust they stood twice pledged to keep from wrong.

Most of these attacks came from Conservatives. Disraeli shrugged his shoulders. "After all," he reflected, "politics is like war—roughish work; we should not be over-sensitive." The next year, on the retirement of Lord Derby, he found himself at the age of sixty-four in possession of the prize he had always coveted —the premiership. He could later afford to ignore, if ever he read it, the quiet judgment passed by John Stuart Mill in his *Autobiography*. "We are quite accustomed," wrote Mill, "to a minister continuing to profess unqualified hostility to an improvement almost to the very day when his conscience or his interest induces him to take it up as a public measure, and carry it."

Hardly did Disraeli find himself at home in Number Ten than he was rejected at the polls by the working-class electorate to whom he had just given the vote. In 1868 he had the chagrin of seeing his rival, William Ewart Gladstone, take his place on the front treasury bench. Thus began the most celebrated duel of Victorian politics, the opening shots of which had been fired long before. As far back as 1853 Greville had observed that Disraeli regarded Gladstone as his most dangerous opponent, and added that he had "the highest opinion of his ability."

No two men were more dissimilar in character and ideas than Gladstone and Disraeli. Each was the perfect foil for the other. The former was earnest, hard-working, solemn, humorless, and religious; the latter flippant, indolent, lighthearted, witty, and cynical. The youthful Beatrice Potter, later Mrs. Sidney Webb, spent hours listening to them in Parliament, "loathing Gladstone and losing my heart to Disraeli." For the one, politics was a most serious business, involving a lifetime's dedication; for the other, as one of his own characters declared, it was but "play and gambling." To Gladstone any event, from a dinner party to a massacre in Bulgaria, suggested a moral issue; he could not even enjoy a cup of tea, said one critic, until he had posed and resolved a moral dilemma in the drinking of it. To Disraeli, morality (especially when Gladstone had anything to do with it) was nine-tenths humbug. Both men were immense egotists, but they wore their egotism with a difference: in Gladstone, one might say, the superego had suffered hypertrophy; in Disraeli—save where Jews were concerned—it was a vestigial remnant. Both men loved power, but whereas to Gladstone its possession meant the triumph of principle, to Disraeli it meant the frank enjoyment of ambition finally achieved. Perhaps in this respect Disraeli was the more honest.

Revealing are the respective comments made by the two statesmen when each learned that he had achieved his highest ambition.
When, in 1868, Disraeli was congratulated by his friends on having at length become Prime Minister, he answered genially: "Yes!
I have climbed to the top of the greasy pole." Gladstone, when in
turn he triumphed, later that year, used his diary to take the Deity
into his confidence: "I ascend a steepening path, with a burden
ever gathering weight. The Almighty seems to sustain and spare
me for some purpose of His own, deeply unworthy as I know
myself to be. Glory be to His Name!"

One advantage over his rival that Disraeli possessed was the
artistic temperament, and the ironical wit that often accompanies
a mocking detachment from life. When the veneration that Gladstone inspired led his followers to call him the "G.O.M.," a single
derisive comment toppled the idol from its pedestal: "G.O.M."
said Disraeli, which the faithful interpreted as "Grand Old Man,"
could only mean "God's Only Mistake." The artistic temperament
likewise sets less value upon consistency of thought or conduct,
and allows more scope for individual whims and vagaries. Perhaps
it was such a whim that led Disraeli to become the half gallant,
half flippant supporter of women's suffrage (an unlikely recruit
to the cause nearest to Mill's heart), while Gladstone condemned
it on principle—in this case, the patriarchal principle.

The low regard in which each statesman held his opponent was
well known. At a fashionable banquet in Knightsbridge in 1878,
Disraeli, to the delight of his audience, added a gem to the treasury of political invective with his memorable characterization of
Gladstone as "a sophisticated rhetorician inebriated with the
exuberance of his own verbosity, and gifted with an egotistical
imagination that can at all times command an interminable and
inconsistent series of arguments to malign an opponent and to
glorify himself." In a letter to Lord Derby, the son of his old
leader, he savored the pleasure of flaying his enemy still further:
"Posterity will do justice to that unprincipled maniac, Gladstone
—extraordinary mixture of envy, vindictiveness, hypocrisy and su-
perstition; and with one commanding characteristic—whether
preaching, praying, speechifying or scribbling—never a gentleman!" "Tartuffe" was Disraeli's favorite nickname for his rival.

As for Gladstone, he realized from the first the great talents of his rival. "I would only pray that they might be well used," he had sententiously written in his journal in 1852. This pious hope diminished with the years. He came to believe that Disraeli was responsible for lowering the whole tone of public life, and for this he could never forgive him. Disraeli was personally responsible, said the Liberal leader in a speech at Oxford, for the fact that "the great name of England had been degraded and debased." "He was a very bad man," Gladstone confided to a friend. "He accused me of misrepresenting him when I could not trust myself to mention his name." The Liberal Lord Acton, one of Gladstone's close friends, thought Disraeli "the worst and most immoral minister since Castlereagh."

In 1879 Gladstone was installed as lord rector of Glasgow University, an office Disraeli had previously held. The latter, in his rectoral address, had held up to the students as an admirable principle of conduct the cynical maxim that "Nothing succeeds like success." Gladstone did not neglect the opportunity to put his predecessor in his place. "Effort, gentlemen," he sternly exhorted the undergraduates, "honest, manful, humble effort succeeds, by its reflected action upon character, especially in youth, better than success. . . . Work onwards and work upwards; and may the blessing of the Most High soothe your cares, clear your vision, and crown your labours with reward."

In the battle of wits which for a generation diverted the English public, Disraeli, besides denouncing Gladstone on the floor of the House, could also pillory him through the medium of fiction. And indeed, at the time of his death in 1881, Disraeli was engaged in the agreeable occupation of deriding a certain humorless middle-class politician, by name Joseph Toplady Falconet, who—with his endless loquacity and belief that he was in all his doings the agent of the Almighty—bore a striking resemblance to William Ewart Gladstone.

As we have seen, the urban electorate, to whom Disraeli had given the franchise by the Reform Bill of 1867, showed their gratitude—or perhaps one should say their appreciation of his real motives—by voting his rival into office next year. For the next seven years Gladstone was Prime Minister.

In this period of undesired leisure which was thrust upon him, Disraeli returned to the writing of novels, which he had abandoned for nearly a quarter of a century, and in 1870 published *Lothair*—"perhaps the first novel," says Froude, "ever written by a man who had previously been Prime Minister of England." Whatever its defects as literature, it was still a remarkable achievement for a man approaching seventy. For Disraeli it was as if, through all the years, time had been standing still. The old youthfulness and vigor were still there, the old playfulness of mind and coruscating flow of epigram, the identical preoccupation with the Jews and with the city that had never ceased to haunt his imagination—Jerusalem.

During his first premiership (1868–74), Gladstone accomplished an impressive amount of political, administrative, and legal reform. He was also the first English politician to approach "the Irish problem" in a humane and statesmanlike manner. The result was that he antagonized so many different interests—the Church, the landlords, the army, the lawyers, the Dissenters—as well as national pride (with regard to the payment of the *Alabama* compensation to the United States), that at the end of seven years he was as unceremoniously dismissed from office as the Conservatives had been in 1868. Hence, for the first time in his life, Disraeli found himself in command of a strong parliamentary majority, and premier in fact as well as in name. He was likewise able to count upon support from an august quarter—one that was presumed to be above politics.

Disraeli's friendship with the Queen was neither new nor fortuitous: for years, he had cultivated her regard and had devoted himself especially to consoling her in her grief for the death of her husband in 1861. The serious-minded, conscientious, hard-working Prince Consort had never liked Disraeli, whom he had once dismissed as not having "one single element of the gentleman in his composition." As for Victoria herself, not only did she follow her husband's lead in everything, she had reasons of her own for disliking Disraeli: she had never forgiven him for turning out of office her trusted friend and counselor Sir Robert Peel—the man who more than any other minister had appreciated Prince Albert. "The House of Commons," she wrote, in consoling Peel on that occasion, "ought to be ashamed for having such members as Ld G. Bentinck and that detestable Mr. D'Israeli."

The novelist-adventurer turned politician gauged the nature of the obstacle in his path, and set himself with all the resourceful-

ness at his command to circumvent it. He perceived the Queen's
naiveté and how easily governed she could be, if only the right
approach were used. No elaborate strategy was necessary to remove her prejudice against him: flattery would be sufficient.
Everyone likes flattery, Disraeli told Matthew Arnold, but when
you flatter royalty, you must lay it on with a trowel. The Prime
Minister used it skillfully—and often.

The key to the affections of the grief-stricken widow lay
in the memory of her adored husband. Despite the total lack of
rapport between himself and the late Prince, Disraeli now discovered that Prince Albert had been the only person he ever knew
who approached the ideal. "There was in him," he wrote the
Queen, "a union of the manly grace and sublime simplicity, of
chivalry with the intellectual splendour of the Attic Academe.
The only character in English History that could, in some respects, draw near to him was Sir Philip Sidney."

With practiced hand, Disraeli played on every weakness in
Victoria's nature and touched every chord in the afflicted royal
heart. Referring to the letters that necessarily passed between the
Prime Minister and the sovereign, he told her that "during a somewhat romantic and imaginative life, nothing has ever occurred to
him so interesting as this confidential correspondence with one so
exalted and so inspiring." In a manner calculated to hold the interest of one whose intellect was neither searching nor profound,
he daily reported the gossip of the House. His letters dealt with
personalities rather than with statistics or principles. Instead of the
stern homilies with which Gladstone wearied her, Disraeli entertained his royal mistress with amusing stories. "Mr. Disraeli (*alias*
Dizzy)," wrote the Queen herself, "writes very curious reports to
me of the House of Commons proceedings much in the style of
his books." "He spoke and wrote to the Queen," says Sir Philip
Magnus, "in what was virtually basic English."

The Queen had herself written books—*Leaves from a Journal
of Life in the Highlands* and *More Leaves from a Journal of Life
in the Highlands*—works of an incredible naiveté dealing with
picnics or churchgoing, and full of a childish petulance which
found everything from the Irish to the weather "so provoking." In
deference to these accomplishments, Disraeli would sometimes
include the Queen in his own literary success. "We authors,

Ma'am," he used to say, including her in some perhaps trenchant judgment on men and affairs. All was on so delightfully personal a basis that the difficulties of constitutional procedure seemed to vanish away. Disraeli even succeeded in persuading Victoria that the Queen's speech at the opening of Parliament, though written for her by others, was really her own: that it was the work of her ministers was "only a piece of Parliamentary gossip." Similarly in foreign affairs: having acquired for £4,000,000, through an audacious personal coup, a controlling interest in the Suez Canal, Disraeli presented it to the Queen as if it were a personal gift. "It is just settled; you have it, Madam. It is yours." He might have been handing her a piece of jewelry—or a toy.

Nearly thirty years earlier, one of his characters in *Tancred* had mentioned the Queen: "If she like, she shall have Alexandria as she now has Malta." The statesman made the prophecy of the novelist come true. Since Disraeli also gave Victoria to believe that the empire was her own, it is perhaps not surprising that she now embarrassed him by her determination to be styled an empress. In the end, the old conjuror yielded, and in 1876, by a unique display of political thaumaturgy, the Queen of the United Kingdom was transformed into the Empress of India. Her Majesty returned the compliment, and Disraeli found himself Earl of Beaconsfield—a title that, curiously enough, he had bestowed fifty years earlier upon a character in his first novel, *Vivian Grey*.

Sometimes in approaching Victoria, Disraeli, like Lewis Carroll dealing with an importunate admirer, blended truth and flattery in a delicious potpourri whose scent was as grateful as the savor of Gladstone's homilies was stale. If the Prime Minister received kindnesses in Berlin, it was "owing to the inspiration of one to whom he owes everything," and if he begged her not to exhaust herself with overwork, it was because "he lives only for Her, and works only for Her, and without Her, all is lost." With this opinion at least, Gladstone might have growled assent: "flunkeyism" was his term for Disraeli's assiduous cultivation of the Queen.

It seems beyond doubt that Victoria, while not abating any detail of the ritual and luxury of grief which for years she had lavished on her husband's memory, had fallen, without her even realizing that she was capable of so monstrous an act of infidelity, wholly in love with her widowed and elderly Prime Minister. On his death she found herself heartbroken.

The election of 1874 was Disraeli's greatest triumph at the polls. After that victory, wrote Lord Rosebery with barbed malice, "as at the sound of the sackbut, psaltery and dulcimer, the whole party fell down and worshipped." Disraeli's second ministry passed a number of important social reforms—a field which Gladstone had neglected—and some have seen in them the fulfillment of the ideas of Young England. These measures, however, were chiefly the work of Disraeli's able Home Secretary, Richard Cross, the Prime Minister taking little interest in such matters. Though he relished the gladiatorial encounters in the Commons, the actual work of legislation bored him. Whereas Gladstone scrutinized every line of every statute for punctuation and grammar as well as for sense, Disraeli took only the most perfunctory interests in the drafting of legislation. "No Prime Minister," wrote Gladstone's son, "took less part or showed less interest in the activities of his colleagues."

Foreign policy had always absorbed Disraeli more than home affairs, and the Orient in particular had always exerted over him a strong appeal. Ancestral origin and early travel alike gave him an abiding interest in the Near East—a concern reflected in many of his novels. It was in the Orient that he gained his chief diplomatic victories. The establishment of British control over the Suez Canal ranks as the outstanding achievement of Disraeli's whole career.

Then came the Balkan crisis of 1876–77, the acquisition of Cyprus, and the crowning triumph of the aged Beaconsfield at the Congress of Berlin. Ever since his visit as a young man to Constantinople, Disraeli had cherished a fondness for the Turks; no doubt he remembered how they had formerly given refuge to his people fleeing the Inquisition. As a young man he had taken readily to the hookah and the turban, and was not now going to get excited over stories of atrocities against Christians—"mere coffee-house babble," as he called them. His nominal Christianity did not include the passionate feelings that possessed Gladstone and summoned him from retirement. Beaconsfield's unpardonable flippancy over the atrocities committed by the Turks in Bulgaria removed any lingering doubts in Gladstone's mind about his essential immorality. To Beaconsfield, however, Gladstone's anger seemed not that of "a pious Christian," but of a "vindictive fiend." The old man had been carried away by his own ridiculous hyperbole: "There is not a criminal in a European gaol," Gladstone had written, "not a cannibal in the South Sea Islands, whose indignation would not rise at the recital of what had been done." Gladstone's pamphlet Disraeli found vindictive, absurd—and of course, ill written: in fact, an atrocity greater than those he was denouncing.

Apart from the wrongs to orthodox Christians, there was the menace of Russian control over the Balkans; and Lord Beaconsfield could rightly point out that whereas Gladstone's oratorical fervor would have brought the Russians to the Bosporus, his own cool, detached handling of affairs had kept the Balkans free from direct Russian control. No doubt many professing Christians would have agreed with the poet laureate: "I hate Dizzy and I love Gladstone," wrote Tennyson, "still I want Russia snubbed." When Beaconsfield returned to London in 1878, "bringing peace with honour" (plus Cyprus), he found himself at the pinnacle of fame and popularity. Unaided, he had conquered the people, always half alien to him, among whom he had been born. Now at length he could talk freely, and not a little disdainfully, about "you English."

When Disraeli left the Commons for the Upper House, a leading Liberal, Sir William Harcourt, paid him a handsome tribute: "Henceforth the game will be like a chessboard when the queen is gone—a petty struggle of pawns." And in taking his seat among the peers, Lord Beaconsfield in a graceful speech explained that he was not really dead, but only entering the Elysian fields.

Then, in 1880, he had the mortification of suffering defeat once more, being forced to witness Gladstone's greatest parliamentary triumph—his Midlothian victory. The retiring premier's last political action (foreshadowing Chamberlain's spitefulness to Churchill in 1940) was an abortive effort to cheat Gladstone out of the premiership by pressing upon the Queen the rival claim of Lord Hartington.

"The aim with which he started in life was to distinguish himself above all his contemporaries, and wild as such an ambition must have appeared, he had at least won the stake for which he played so bravely." With this tribute Froude took leave of his hero. But how did Lord Beaconsfield himself—aged, painted, gouty, and asthmatic—regard the stake that he had won? "I have known something of action in my life," he confided to a friend. "It is a life of baffled hopes and wasted energies." "Power! It has come to me too late," he sighed. "There were days when, on waking, I felt I could move dynasties and governments; but that has passed away. . . . I can only tell you the truth. . . . I am wearied to extinction and profoundly unhappy." When he rose to speak in the Lords, he needed drugs to keep him on his feet. In private, he reverted to memories of Byron and of his own youth—and of the Wandering Jew. After a life of almost superhuman effort, Disraeli found himself at last, in the words of Lytton Strachey, "old, hideous, battered, widowed, solitary, diseased, but Prime Minister of England."

The desire for power had been so long the moving force in Disraeli's life that when his ambition was gratified at length, little was left to take its place. With Disraeli, writing had for so long been an adjunct to politics that now, in his old age, literature for its own sake could neither console nor inspire. For, in any real sense, his mind had never been enriched by the profound study of any serious object. In religion, philosophy, and science, he saw only so many opportunities for the display of flippancy and wit. He ridiculed equally the Oxford movement and Utilitarianism, the claims of faith and the demands of reason. In 1864, at Oxford, undeterred by the fate which four years earlier had overwhelmed Bishop Wilberforce at the hands of Huxley, he attempted, like his episcopal predecessor, to extinguish evolution—"this tattle about science," as he called it—with a phrase. "Is man an ape or an angel?" he asked facetiously. The wily politician delighted his clerical audience by assuring them that he at least was on the side of the angels.

His only real faith was in himself, and in his own destiny. Years before, one of his heroes, Contarini Fleming, had written: "I believe in that Destiny before which the ancients bowed. Modern philosophy, with its superficial discoveries, has infused into the heart of man a spirit of scepticism. . . . Destiny is our will, and our will is our nature."

To the aged, disillusioned statesman who had garnered what rewards public life had to offer, only one thing could make life bearable—the presence of love. In 1872, after thirty-three years of conjugal happiness, his beloved Mary Anne had died. She was then eighty-one, Disraeli sixty-eight. They had both been outlandishly attired (a young French chargé once mistook Lady Beaconsfield for an aging rajah), two museum pieces surviving from an earlier age: in Andre Maurois' phrase, "a ridiculous and touching pair." In a sense it was true, as Mary Anne realized, that her husband, whatever the distractions of politics or society, had lived solely for her. No serious difference had ever cast a shadow on their quiet idyll.

Going through her papers after her death, Disraeli was moved to tears on finding that she had kept and cherished every scrap of paper on which he had scribbled a message. Every fortnight for thirty-three years, she had cut his hair, and now Disraeli found the clippings carefully preserved. He discovered also one last letter, kept secret for sixteen years:

> My own dear Husband—If I should depart this life before you, leave orders that we may be buried in the same grave at whatever distance you may die from England. And now God bless you, my kindest, dearest! You have been a perfect husband to me. Be put at my side in the same grave. And now, farewell, my dear Dizzy. Do not live alone, dearest. Someone I earnestly hope you may find as attached to you as your own devoted Mary Anne.

As she had realized, a woman confidante would always be a necessity in Disraeli's life; and since his exalted devotion to the Queen afforded no outlet for his own loneliness, the septuagenarian statesman now fell in love with two sisters simultaneously, both grandmothers, one a widow—Anne, Countess of Chesterfield, like himself aged sixty-eight, and her sister Selena, Countess of Bradford, who was a mere fifty-five. During the eight years of his life which remained, Disraeli wrote nearly two thousand letters to these sisters, two-thirds of them to Lady Bradford, all on black-edged writing paper, in token of mourning for his wife. He now lived solely, he declared, for "the delightful society of the two persons I love most in the world."

"To love as I love," he wrote Lady Bradford in 1874, "and rarely to see the beings one adores, whose constant society is absolutely necessary to my life; to be precluded even from the only shadowy compensation for such a torturing doom—the privilege of relieving my heart by expressing its affection—is a lot which I never could endure, and cannot." What he felt was simple "misery: that horrible desolation which the lonely alone can f l."

The impropriety of such declarations shocked the conventional Victorian lady with a dutiful husband and daughters of marriageable age, and several times Lady Bradford threatened to end their friendship. In despair, Disraeli proposed marriage to the widowed elder sister—hoping that he might thereby, without breach of decorum, see more of the younger. "To see you, or at least to hear from you, every day, is absolutely necessary to my existence," he had written the latter. Deeply involved in affairs of state, harassed by Gladstone and the Russians, he still found time to write Lady Bradford from Downing Street twice or even three times a day. "I can truly say," the Prime Minister told her, "that amid all this whirl, you are never, for a moment, absent from my thoughts and feelings." A little later, he bowed before the inevitable. "I fear our romance is over," he wrote, "if indeed it ever existed except in my imagination; but still I sometimes dreamed that the dream might last until I slumbered for ever."

Gladstone as septuagenarian was engaged in strenuous polemics against Huxley or the Vatican, and thick in quarrels—political, theological, or merely literary—yet always fighting, over Turkey or Ireland or Homer. From the aridity of such controversies, one turns almost with relief to the dependence of Disraeli on the single book of the affections. "The page of human life," he wrote, "is quickly read, and one does not care to dwell upon it, unless it touches the heart." Had he but followed this simple precept, he might never have been Prime Minister, but he might well have been a better writer.

When Lord Beaconsfield died in 1881, Gladstone as Prime Minister offered a national burial in Westminster Abbey; but the wishes of Mary Anne were not forgotten, and so the rootless Sephardic, the accomplished adventurer, the flamboyant cosmopolitan man, was laid to rest beside her in the little country churchyard of Hughenden in Buckinghamshire, among the primroses and violets beneath the beech trees, and by the clear chalk streams of that very English county.

V

William Ewart Gladstone

(1809-98)

VICTORIAN LIBERALISM, in its virtues and in its defects, was incarnate in one man—William Ewart Gladstone. More than any other person he was responsible for the series of reforms which, during the second half of the nineteenth century, rationalized the government of England and transferred its ultimate control from an aristocratic elite to the leaders of the new democracy. He it was who translated into fact many of the ideas for which Bentham and Mill had contended. A more unlikely champion than Gladstone of these Utilitarian ideas—rational, scientific, anti-historical, anti-metaphysical—can hardly be imagined. For Gladstone was deeply religious, imbued with deep reverence for the past and especially for its great surviving monuments—the Crown, the Church, and the Lords. Yet it was his fortune to antagonize all three, and to find himself the leader of a democracy whose religious beliefs were repugnant to him, and whose origins in English puritanism he detested. At the time of his death he had come to represent—perhaps more than any other man in English history—the conscience of the nation. His reputation abroad was as great as at home. As Sir Philip Magnus puts it, he had become "the most venerable and influential statesman in the world."

The fourth and youngest son of a rich Liverpool shipowner, whose wealth was largely derived from the slave trade, and who actually owned slaves in the West Indies down to the Abolition Act of 1833, Gladstone received in his youth the training of an ardent Conservative and Evangelical. At Eton and Oxford he received the finest classical education England had to offer. His career at Oxford was one of unique achievement and unlimited promise—for he not only gained a "double first" in classics and mathematics, but made in the Union Debating Society so devastating an assault on the Great Reform Bill of 1832—which, like Newman, he then regarded as the work of Antichrist—that this single speech, through the influence of an aristocratic friend, at once procured for him a seat in the House of Commons. Macaulay described Gladstone at twenty-nine as "the rising hope of the stern and unbending Tories," and at thirty-three Gladstone was already a Cabinet member under Peel in the ministry from which Disraeli had been rejected, and of which, apart from the Prime Minister himself, he was to be the chief success.

Sharing Peel's conversion to free trade, Gladstone bitterly resented Disraeli's fierce personal attacks upon their common leader. These invectives made him distrust Disraeli as a pure opportunist, and with every passing year this distrust deepened into detestation, until his rival (especially after his unscrupulous tactics in suddenly renouncing his principles in order to pass the Reform Act of 1867) came to typify for him all that was most questionable in political life. Whereas Disraeli had lightheartedly begun his public career as a radical independent and suddenly became a Tory, Gladstone, beginning as a Tory, slowly and painfully evolved over a period of years, first into a Liberal and then, perceiving how much the Liberal party was still dominated by Whig aristocrats like Palmerston and Hartington, into a radical—or as his opponents would have said, into a pure demagogue.

Perhaps no statesman in English history has ever had so broad an intellectual background as Gladstone. Aristotle, St. Augustine, Dante, and Bishop Butler were the great formative influences in the development of his thought. In consequence of this rigorous mental discipline, no one was less provincial than Gladstone in his approach to contemporary history. For him, Europe and European culture were living realities. Though a staunch member of the Church of England and—in a way that was unthinkable for Disraeli—a "true-born Englishman," yet he was also, in a way that was equally inconceivable to his great rival, a good European.

It was typical of Gladstone that his first self-questionings upon the subject of his inherited conservatism came not from any direct experience in English politics but from an emotional shock that he experienced on his visit to Naples in 1850. There he found still in control the same cruel and stupid tyranny that, half a century earlier, the guns of Nelson had sustained. In foul and fetid dungeons, Gladstone saw for himself some of the twenty thousand manacled and starving prisoners whose only crime had been to desire for their country the smallest part of those liberties that Englishmen enjoyed.

> It is the wholesale persecution of virtue. . . . It is the awful profanation of public religion. . . . It is the perfect prostitution of the judicial office. . . . It is the savage and cowardly system of moral as well as physical torture. . . . This is the negation of God erected into a system of Government.

The protest he printed in 1851 against tyranny in Naples made Gladstone at once "a national hero and a moral force in Europe."

In the months after his return, Gladstone was so obsessed by the horrors he had seen that in society he could talk of little else. To his indignation, he discovered that his own party was totally indifferent to the iniquities that he described. Even so humane a Conservative as Lord Aberdeen was indifferent about the subjection of peoples abroad. Little by little, Gladstone was forced to realize the intimate connection that existed between conservatism at home and the tolerance of tyranny in Europe.

The change of political allegiance that Disraeli had accomplished almost overnight took Gladstone—moving in the opposite direction—thirteen years of doubt and soul-searching. In 1859 he joined Lord Palmerston's Cabinet and consented at length to call himself a Liberal. It was, in fact, largely the repellent personality of Palmerston himself—cynical, boastful, jaunty, and aggressive—that had hitherto deterred Gladstone from openly declaring himself a Liberal; and when he finally did so, it was due to his strong desire to champion, within the Cabinet, the cause of Italian liberation from Austria. Five years after joining Palmerston's Cabinet, Gladstone astonished the House, as well as his own colleagues, by an unequivocal statement of his belief in political democracy. "I venture to say," he told the House, "that every man who is not presumably incapacitated by some consideration of personal unfitness or political danger, is morally entitled to come within the pale of the Constitution."

When, finally, after the death of Palmerston and the retirement of Lord John Russell, Gladstone in 1868 found himself Prime

Minister, he was nearly sixty years of age. Almost a quarter of a century had passed since his brilliant debut as a Cabinet minister under Peel. His extraordinary abilities as a parliamentarian had long been manifest; it seems probable, therefore, that the slowness with which he achieved the highest power was due to obstacles and scruples that he himself had interposed. This consideration, as J. L. Hammond has pointed out, effectually disposes of the charge of self-seeking opportunism so often urged against Gladstone by his enemies during his own lifetime.

Gladstone's ministry of 1868–74 was the most significant government of the Victorian era. It established universal elementary education; it did away with patronage in the civil service and threw open all posts, save in the Foreign Office, to competition based upon examinations; it abolished the purchase of army commissions; it removed the last religious tests at the universities; it introduced the secret ballot, which, among other results, at length enabled the Irish voter to vote without fear of his landlord; it abolished the last vestiges of corruption in parliamentary elections; and it brought system and order, on lines suggested by Bentham, into the complexities and confusion of common law and equity. The great Judicature Act of 1873 has been, ever since that date, the foundation of English justice. Though remaining a High Churchman, Gladstone more than any other statesman of the century had come to personify the ideas propounded by John Stuart Mill.

Gladstone also turned his attention to one other grievous problem, which Mill had analyzed, but which all other politicians, including Disraeli, had ignored—the problem of Ireland. In 1869 he freed the Irish Catholic peasantry from the necessity of supporting by taxation a church to which they did not belong; and in the following year he invoked the authority of the state to protect them from some of the more odious abuses of landlord tyranny. In his second ministry (1880–85), he destroyed forever the power of the Irish landlord to victimize his tenants and gave the franchise for the first time, in Ireland as in England, to the agricultural laborers. The third Reform Act, of 1884, which added two million voters to the electoral lists, thus completed, so far as the nineteenth century was concerned, the democratic process begun by the statutes of 1832 and 1867.

Most important of all, in 1886 Gladstone committed his reluctant party to Home Rule for Ireland. During his eight remaining years of public life, the Irish problem came to transcend all others in importance. Indeed it became an obsession with him, and though he twice suffered defeat over the Irish question (in 1886 and 1893), he displayed such superlative gifts of oratory and leadership that even his enemies were forced to admit that he was perhaps the greatest parliamentarian who had ever appeared in the House of Commons. The energy with which, at the age of eighty-three, he engaged in the struggle for the second Home Rule Bill far surpassed the performance, sixty years later, of Sir Winston Churchill at the same age.

In addition to his championship of Ireland, in the closing years of his life Gladstone became known as the enemy of imperialism, British or otherwise. As he had detested Palmerston's bullying of China and denounced the two infamous China wars (1838–40 and 1858–60) that Palmerston had waged, so now he condemned Disraeli's aggressions in the Transvaal and Afghanistan. Both on grounds of religion and of economy, Gladstone had always abhorred war. As he had once risked unpopularity by opposing the prolongation of the Crimean War, so now, after the defeat of Majuba (1881) and the death of Gordon (1885), he had the courage to oppose an inflamed public opinion, and twice refused to send punitive expeditions to avenge reverses suffered by British arms. Even the bombardment of Alexandria in 1882, and the sending of troops next year to Egypt, which appear as notable exceptions to the policy of nonaggression, scarcely justify the charges made by Marx and others that Gladstone was nothing but a hypocrite. The safe operation of the Suez Canal, not the annexation of Egypt, was his paramount consideration, and there is no reason to believe him insincere in regarding as temporary the occupation of that country. He would, in any case, have preferred to act in concert with other European powers, and had no wish to secure a selfish advantage for Britain alone. His policy in South Africa, and later in the Sudan, does not support the view that he was really a cunning Machiavellian; while those who knew him most intimately—for example Arthur Godley, later Lord Kilbracken, his private secretary for a number of years—were convinced of his personal and public integrity.

"I have no doubt," wrote Lord Grey, Britain's Foreign Secretary in 1914, that "taking force of character, energy and intellectual power combined, Gladstone was the greatest man in whose presence I have ever been." The Liberal Catholic historian Lord Acton—one not given to praising his own contemporaries—believed that Gladstone united in himself the highest qualities of Burke, Pitt, Fox, Canning, and Peel. More than any modern statesman, he believed, Gladstone personified "the three elements of greatness combined—the man, the power, and the result—character, genius, and success." Acton came finally to regard the Liberal leader as "the incarnation of a rational providence." If the extravagance of such eulogy puts one on guard, it is still true that only an extraordinary personality could have elicited such a tribute from so austere and critical a judge as Lord Acton.

One of Gladstone's chief opponents, Lord Salisbury, called him "the most brilliant intellect that has been applied to the service of the State since Parliamentary Government began." In our own time, Bertrand Russell—himself no respecter of persons—recalled Gladstone, whom he had known as a young man, as the most formidable person whom in the course of a long life he had ever met. The opinion of such observers was shared by half the nation in Gladstone's own lifetime. It is doubtful whether, before the year 1940, any English statesman ever aroused such fervor of popular support—at least in modern times. A Liberal candidate, said Walter Bagehot, if at a loss for words, had only to pronounce the magic name, "Gladstone." In the frenzied cheering that was evoked by the mere sound of that word, the candidate had ample leisure to collect his thoughts. Merely to see the old man pass along the street gave men the feeling that they had been in momentary contact with some more than human force. John Davidson, the dour and dogged Scottish poet who later—his verse ignored—drowned himself off Cornwall, remembered all his life how, on first coming to London, he had once seen Gladstone walking alone on a summer evening in Bond Street. "I had seen the most wonderful sight London had yet offered me. Black broadcloth, ordinary silk hat—it was yet to me as if a vision had passed." And when Ellen Terry invited Gladstone to attend her benefit performance at the Lyceum, "I should feel prouder of your presence," she wrote, "than that of any other Englishman." Since Gladstone's time, only Churchill has had the power to arouse in the nation similar feelings of hero worship.

Gladstone, unlike Disraeli, was incapable of talking down to people: his popularity was not earned by patronizing the public. He paid his audiences the compliment of supposing that they were on his own level of understanding and knowledge. Nor, any more than Mill, did he appeal to the material advantages they might hope to gain by voting for him. He dominated them by sheer force of conviction and personality.

Above all in the Midlothian campaign of 1880, by his denunciation of imperialism and the corrupting effects of power, Gladstone impressed his hearers with his own sense of the ethical basis of politics. These speeches angered the Queen and repelled Disraeli, who, great actor though he was, could not simulate a moral passion that he was incapable of feeling. "It is certainly a relief," wrote Disraeli contemptuously at the end of that campaign, "that this drenching rhetoric has ceased." The truth, as Francis Birrell has observed, is that Gladstone's Midlothian speeches, far from being demagogic, were closely reasoned, almost pedantic, analyses of foreign politics, "full of references to international law and European history." To read them now, as Birrell says, "fills one with disgust for the squalors of modern electioneering," and reminds us how far the level of public understanding today has fallen below that of the late-Victorian period.

But if Gladstone was idolized by many, there were many who loathed him. The most crushing blow that he received in the course of his political life was his rejection in 1865 as M.P. for Oxford. Having represented his own university for nearly twenty years, he was now defeated by the clerical vote, which he had alienated through his declared intention to disestablish the Protestant Church of Ireland.

About this time the Queen, who had always disliked Gladstone, no longer troubled to conceal it. In her letters she referred to him as "this half-crazy and really in many ways ridiculous old man."

So great was her personal aversion for him, and so completely had she succumbed to the insidious flattery of Disraeli, that finally she gave up even the pretense of being impartial in politics. Thus, referring to Gladstone's Midlothian campaign, she wrote: "The Queen is *utterly* disgusted with his *stump* oratory—so unworthy of his position—almost under her very nose"; and when Disraeli was defeated in that election, she declared indignantly: "The Queen cannot deny she (Liberal as she has ever been, but never Radical or democratic) thinks it a great calamity for the country" —the more so since Disraeli's mind was "so much greater, larger and his apprehension of things great and small so much quicker than that of Mr. Gladstone." She held the latter personally responsible for the death of Gordon at Khartoum, and privately regarded him as Gordon's murderer. "Mr. Gladstone and the Government *have*—the Queen *feels it dreadfully*—Gordon's innocent, noble, heroic blood on their consciences."

Not once during his fifty years of public service did she offer him her hand or allow him (even when he was over eighty) to be seated in her presence. This privilege was reserved for Disraeli. One may imagine the myopic distaste with which Victoria regarded "the shaking hand of an old, wild and incomprehensible man of 82½," and the profound relief she experienced when at last the painful infirmities of extreme old age put an end to Gladstone's public career. When she finally heard the news of his death, she dryly commented: "How can I say that I am sorry when I am not?"

Few things are more admirable in Gladstone's political life than the almost complete absence of rancor or recrimination in his attitude to the Queen. In his autobiography, Alfred North Whitehead mentions how one of Gladstone's ministers recalled the old man's custom of opening a Cabinet meeting by solemnly reading out some letter of vehement reproach from the Queen, and then proceeding to business without a single further reference to it. Once, it is true, in 1883, while walking in the garden at Hawarden with Lord Rosebery, Gladstone let a groan escape him: "The Queen alone is enough to kill any man."

Gladstone's conversion to Home Rule in 1886 provoked the most virulent personal diatribes. "He will ruin the country if he can," wrote the Queen on first hearing the news, "and how much mischief has he not done already." The typical view at court was expressed by Sir Dighton Probyn, later comptroller to Queen Alexandra: "Don't talk to me about Gladstone," exclaimed Sir Dighton irritably. "I pray to God that he may be shut up as a lunatic at once, and thus save the Empire from the destruction which he is leading her to. If he is not mad, he is a Traitor"; and when he heard that Gladstone had converted Lord Spencer to Home Rule, Sir Dighton began to feel the foundations of the world tremble beneath him. "A man of that sort advocating Communism," he declared, "shakes my belief in anything mortal."

Many Conservatives were of the opinion that Gladstone was out of his mind. In the Carlton Club (from which he soon resigned) the members spoke of him as unquestionably "insane." One Tory M.P. maintained that the only difference between Disraeli and Gladstone was that the former was an unprincipled scoundrel, the latter a dangerous lunatic. Rumors of madness were busily circulated in society. For years the story was told of how Gladstone had once entered a toy shop and ordered the whole contents to be sent to his house. Another version was that he had gone into a West End hat shop and ordered dozens of hats. (Mrs. Gladstone had actually done so—on behalf of an orphanage in which she was interested.) Some believed that he was a secret convert to Roman Catholicism; others that he was "a destructive and angular Jesuit." It was fashionable in Conservative circles to refer to him as "the Archfiend." He and his family were ostracized by large sections of society. In expensive prep schools, on the fifth of November—when the salvation of Protestant England from the Gunpowder Plot was commemorated—he was burned in effigy; in certain aristocratic houses there was a taboo on the very utterance of his name. Thus Lord Midleton's daughter recalls how, in reading aloud from the paper when she came upon a reference to Gladstone, she was taught to allude to him as "the man whose name we are not allowed to mention."

He used to receive hundreds of abusive anonymous letters, all of which he carefully preserved in a special box. He was systematically held up to ridicule, and on every possible score—from his table manners to the cut of his coat or the size of his boots. Duff Cooper remembered how when he was a child his mother had taken pains to impress upon him the fact that Mr.

Gladstone was "a very bad man but a very great one." And nearly forty years after the old man's death, Neville Chamberlain, in reading Garvin's life of his father, felt all the bitter antagonisms once more. "The wickedness of the old man," he recalled in 1933, "his cunning and treachery, and his determination to get his own way while he had time, are plain to see. I feel my old resentments burn up again as I read."

As for distinguished writers, Carlyle thought Gladstone nothing but a "poor phantasm" (Carlyle, of course, was known to pity the moon). The Prime Minister, he declared after meeting him, was "one of the contemptiblest men I ever looked on—incapable of seeing veritably any fact whatever." What Carlyle actually meant was that Gladstone had dared to disagree with him. Ruskin wrote publicly that he cared "no more for Mr. d'Israeli or Mr. Gladstone than for two old bagpipes with the drones going by steam," adding, "I hate Liberalism as I do Beelzebub, and with Carlyle I stand, we two alone now in England, for God and the Queen." As early as 1878, the poet Swinburne was longing for Gladstone's execution. "A genuinely reformed government," he wrote Lord Houghton, "would send the old man to the guillotine, whither God speed him! May I be there to see him sneeze in the bag à la Marat."

Disraeli, however repulsive or attractive he might seem, was incapable of arousing either the vehement hatred or the passionate love that Gladstone inspired in the hearts of his fellow countrymen. What was the nature, we may ask, of the man who could thus divide a nation as few had ever done before, and stir its feelings to their depths?

The personality of Gladstone was, in truth, extraordinary—in a sense, titanic. It was also deeply divided. Even casual observers were struck by the combination of shrewdness and feeling: Oxford on top, Liverpool below, according to one estimate; an ardent Italian in the custody of a Scot, according to another. The dual aspect, however, of Gladstone's nature went much deeper than this. Anyone who should undertake to write her husband's life, Mrs. Gladstone told John Morley in 1891, "must remember that he had two sides—one impetuous, impatient, irrestrainable, the other all self-control, able to dismiss all but the great central aim, able to put aside what is weakening or disturbing; that he achieved this self-mastery, and had succeeded in the struggle ever since he was three or four and twenty, first by the natural force of his character, and second by the incessant wrestling in prayer —prayer that had been abundantly answered."

The harmony that Gladstone succeeded in establishing between the two competing sides of his nature was facilitated by the happiness of his married life. In this single respect, if in no other— in the secure possession of a happy love—the fortunes of Gladstone and Disraeli were alike. In marrying, at the age of thirty-one, the beautiful Catherine Glynne, to whom he had proposed by moonlight in the Colosseum in Rome, Gladstone allied himself to an ancient and aristocratic family. Charming, wayward, and unconventional, Catherine Glynne had none the less a seriousness of mind which matched his own. Comparing the luxury in which her own class lived with the straits in which many churches found themselves, she had once asked William: "Do you think we can be justified in all these luxuries?" "I loved her for this question," Gladstone noted in his diary. His favorite quotation from Dante became the motto of their life together: *In fulfilling His will we find our peace.* Seven children were born to Catherine Gladstone. Through six decades her unfailing sympathy and understanding sustained her imperious and self-willed husband. She outlived him by two years only, and was buried with him in Westminster Abbey in a common grave.

Duality of nature is not uncommon. The uniqueness of Gladstone lies in the fact that the two sides of his nature were developed to an unusual intensity. The foundation of his being, as was later the case with Winston Churchill, was a superb vitality, and like Churchill, Gladstone inherited an almost inexhaustible fund of physical strength. Throughout his long life, he scarcely knew what it was to be ill. He kept himself fit by constant exercise and never indulged in the slightest dissipation. His physician, Sir Andrew Clark, once said that he had never seen so perfect a physical specimen as Gladstone. (In his last few months, this immense vitality was to cause him much suffering—another organism might perhaps have succumbed more readily to the cancer that came to ravage his body.)

The emotional and sensual elements of Gladstone's nature were, however, subject to the discipline of a powerful will and to the daily restraints imposed by an iron regimen of lifelong self-repression. The result was an extraordinary tension, which was reflected in all that he did, and which communicated itself to those with whom he came in contact. Lord Kilbracken remembered how Gladstone played a children's card game like Beggar-My-Neighbor with the same intensity that he devoted to politics or to Homer. Every quality that Gladstone possessed he possessed in excess—excess of energy, excess of feeling, excess of will, and excess of intellectual power (though this was not combined with originality). It was as though an extremely high-spirited horse were ridden closely bitted and bridled by a domineering rider—Gladstone himself being both horse and rider.

Lord Kilbracken records a remarkable instance of Gladstone's stern repression of feeling. "I have been told," he wrote, "that many years ago, when a great sorrow came upon him in the death of one of his children at a very early age, he was for some hours in a state of such violent grief as to cause positive alarm to those around him. Then, suddenly, his sense of duty got the upper hand; thence-forward he was perfectly calm, and returned in all respects to the demeanour and habits of everyday life."

Such self-control became almost as much second nature with him as affectation was with Disraeli. Lord Rendel, a close friend of his last years, was once granted a glimpse into the elemental strength of Gladstone's emotions. At the age of eighty-eight, the latter recalled an incident that had happened more than sixty years before in St. Peter's in Rome. He had there seen an Irish girl of such beauty that it "struck him with a physical force. 'It was a blow,' said the old man, striking his forehead." Though the most faithful of husbands, Gladstone, observed Lord Rendel, was extremely susceptible to the beauty of women. The restraints that Gladstone imposed upon his volcanic nature remind one irresistibly of a Titan bound in chains.

Passion—controlled passion—was the mainspring of Gladstone's character, "his stupendous driving power," as Lord Kilbracken called it. Whatever he did, he did with passion. His original entrance into politics had not been the result of his own volition (he had wished to enter the Church), but of filial obedience to his father's wishes. "His sense of duty," says Lord Kilbracken, "which in him was nothing less than a passion, impelled him to put his whole strength into the business, and he did so, with the result that we all know." When Peel offered him his initial post at the Board of Trade, Gladstone was at first disappointed. Until that moment his whole interest had centered in religion, and despite his father's being a businessman, he had "no general knowledge of trade whatever." "In a spirit of ignorant mortification," as he reminded himself many years later in an autobiographical note, "I said to myself at that moment: the science of politics deals with men, but I am set to govern packages." Soon, however, he discovered a principle on which to operate— the principle of economy; and as Francis Birrell well observes: "Economy was for him a passion, not, as for Peel, merely a form of good housekeeping." At the Board of Trade he soon discovered a second principle: free trade, which for him meant not merely commercial prosperity but, as with Cobden and Bright, the hope of international peace and the eventual brotherhood of man— the same idea that his friend Tennyson was just then clothing with the rhetorical verse of "Locksley Hall."

It was above all in his oratory that the vehemence of Gladstone's feelings was able to find expression. In December 1852, on the occasion of his first open clash with Disraeli, the betrayer of Peel, even though the question at issue was a financial one, one of those who heard him reported that "his utterance was choked with passion, and for once in his life he was unable to finish the sentence that he had begun." Forty years later, in extreme old age, Gladstone could still feel an occasional spasm of anger when he suddenly recalled Disraeli's "vicious" budget of 1852. For he could not understand how anyone "could treat with levity the gravest financial questions." Generally speaking, however, in later years his self-control was well-nigh perfect, and "only from time to time a few fiery sparks gave a reminder of the volcano within him." His self-control was also in evidence at home, where his son, Viscount Gladstone, never remembered his father as having once lost his temper with any of the family.

"This intense natural vehemence," says Lord Kilbracken, "thus effectively curbed and guided, was the secret of his ascendancy, and of the unbounded enthusiasm which he kindled in nearly all who knew him, and in many hundreds of thousands who had never seen his face or heard his voice." Such intensity of feeling was so great that occasionally it frightened those who knew him. "I sometimes think him rather mad," wrote the Queen's private secretary, Sir Henry Ponsonby, in 1873. He was referring not to Gladstone's ideas but to his headstrong nature. The vehemence of Gladstone's feelings appeared also in his writing. Thus his pamphlet on the Bulgarian atrocities in 1876 was written in a white heat of anger—which perhaps explains why two hundred thousand copies were sold within three weeks.

Gladstone could hardly have been unaware of the nature of the power that he possessed, whether in speech or in writing. "Good ends," he wrote, "can rarely be attained in politics without passion." Nor could he have failed to notice the effect of his sudden intervention in debate. "The new members," wrote Disraeli, "trembled and fluttered like small birds when a hawk is in the air." But though he appeared so dominant, his power was not always matched by a sense of inner assurance. Thus, after one speech, which Balfour said he never could forget because of its passion, Gladstone confessed that evening in his diary: "Never did I feel weaker or more wormlike."

By a strange irony, it was Gladstone's defeat at Oxford in 1865 which enabled him to realize for the first time—relatively late in life—his almost hypnotic power of swaying vast crowds. So reserved and conventional were the academic and clerical electors of Oxford that it was thought unseemly to solicit their votes save through the impersonal medium of print; but when Gladstone, to his intense chagrin, was rejected by the voters of Oxford and forced to exchange "that sweet city with her dreaming spires" for the wilderness of industrial England, he found himself on the platform facing, for the first time, huge masses of human beings. His effect upon them—in Lancashire, in London, and above all in Midlothian—was electrifying; and he in turn received from them—from their rapturous devotion and tumultuous applause—an accession of psychic strength such as he had never known before. Opinions differed as to the nature of these forensic triumphs. To unsympathetic observers they savored of pure demagoguery. Thus Beatrice Potter (later Mrs. Webb) observed in her diary the obvious pleasure that Gladstone took in "the heady emotion of feeling himself in accord with crude democracy and, owing to his superlative talent as a revivalist preacher, leading it."

Gladstone's own diary dramatically recorded his awareness of the change in his situation. On July 17, 1865, he sadly noted the arrival of the telegram "announcing my defeat at Oxford as virtually accomplished. A dear dream is dispelled. God's will be done." The very next day, however, he was immensely elated by his success in speaking first in the Free Trade Hall in Manchester to six thousand people, who "were in unbounded enthusiasm," and then to another meeting of five thousand in Liverpool, "if possible more enthusiastic than at Manchester." Still more significant, though perhaps at the moment its full import eluded him, was his famous declaration in the Free Trade Hall: "At last, my friends, I am come among you, and I am come among you unmuzzled." Thus by a curious chance did the citadel of Utilitarianism and laissez faire hear the ringing declaration of faith by one whose previous loyalty had been given wholly to "the God-fearing and God-sustaining University of Oxford."

In one sense at least the radicalism, which increased with age, was evidently sincere. Gladstone had always identified his own will with the will of the Almighty, and now it appeared that *vox populi* might also be *vox dei*. Had he not been exiled from Oxford, it is conceivable that "the People's William" would never have emerged as an irresistible popular symbol. In winning at Midlothian in 1880 a safe Tory seat from the Duke of Buccleugh, one of the greatest magnates in Scotland, and "the man who owned the whole county," Gladstone may have felt something of the emotions of the Crusaders on first entering the city of Jerusalem.

Gladstone's forensic triumphs could not have been gained without certain natural gifts—a superb physical presence, a majestic flashing eye, a voice of surpassing range and depth and beauty, as well as an immense emotional power over which, as over his voice, the orator had such perfect control that he could skillfully modulate it to command any effect that he desired. The impression the aged Gladstone made upon his hearers was ineffaceable—half eagle, half lion.

Professor Goldwin Smith, who knew Gladstone well, singled out as his most remarkable physical attribute the brightness of his eye. Maurice Baring, when a boy at Eton, heard Gladstone speak on Homer. Thirty years later he recalled his flashing glance and how his whole body seemed to expand as he warmed to the praise of Greek as an indispensable intellectual discipline. Various witnesses remarked upon the peculiarly disconcerting effect, above all when he was angry, of Gladstone's "glittering eye." If anything occurred in conversation, said Lord Rendel, that Gladstone thought questionable, "he would unconsciously throw into his eyes and whole face a sort of lion-like challenge— in fact, he pulled one up with a very formidable air." The Irish historian Lecky also commented upon Gladstone's "wonderful eye, a bird of prey eye—fierce, luminous and restless." Kitty O'Shea, Parnell's mistress, and for a time his intermediary with Gladstone, always remembered "how like a beautiful bird of prey the old man was, with the piercing, cruel eyes belying the tender, courteous smile, and how, relentless as an eagle, men like this had struck and torn their victims." To be sure, Mrs. O'Shea was not an unbiased observer.

In extreme old age, when Gladstone visited Oxford for the last time, though willing to talk freely about the past, he would not be drawn out on the subject of contemporary politics. At the mere hint of this, says the historian C. R. L. Fletcher, who was present, the tactless questioner would be "transfixed by a terrible eye." No doubt the home circle of Hawarden saw an entirely different man; and even when Gladstone was greatly moved in public, a sensitive observer like the American journalist George Smalley was struck by "a strange luminous softness in his eyes."

One contemporary, who previously had not been much impressed by Gladstone, happening to meet his eye, felt immediately "a sense of having been in that instant examined, commented upon, summed up and dismissed." A still more remarkable example of this power to intimidate with a glance is related by Sir Joseph Boehm, the sculptor, who chanced to be present when a dispute about Homer took place between Gladstone and John Stuart Blackie, then professor of Greek at Edinburgh. "The latter," says Boehm, "in his excitement, jumped out of his chair at one moment in order to contradict one of Gladstone's more extraordinary theories. Gladstone made no movement of any kind, but his outer eyelids expanded like those of a bird of prey when it is making ready to paralyze the nervous system of a prospective victim. That baleful glare was concentrated for a full moment upon Blackie, whose tongue stumbled. He flushed and looked confused and sank back speechless into his chair." The sculptor also recalled how he had once seen Sir Stafford Northcote, the Conservative leader in the Commons after Disraeli's retirement to the Upper House, become as if paralyzed on the front Opposition bench. He visibly "quailed beneath the eye of the Prime Minister."

It is possible that Gladstone realized the power of his glance, for in commenting upon the genius of Napoleon, he emphasized particularly the Emperor's "terrible" eye, as indicating immense will power. "Napoleon had no equal," he told his friend Lord Rendel, "and . . . he was justified in knowing and acting as though no man were his equal."

A curious paradox emerges from Gladstone's overwhelming success as a platform speaker. With the masses of detail which he employed, his elaborate argumentation, his strong sense of historical fact, his use of parallels and precedents, and the severely logical development of his ideas, no doubt he thought of himself as appealing primarily to the minds of his hearers. Unlike Disraeli, he rarely joked, and never condescended to amuse or entertain an audience. Yet the ascendancy he established over the crowds who came to hear him was other than intellectual. No doubt it was a real compliment to his hearers—many of whom did not even have the right to vote—to assume that they were educated and rational people, capable of following the thread of a complicated argument and of making up their own minds on difficult questions. But he also made it plain that he regarded them as moral beings, that the political questions they were discussing had an ethical basis, that politics and ethics were inseparable. It therefore followed that great consequences might hinge on the way each one of them would cast his vote; hence not merely the importance, but even the sacredness of the franchise.

Actually, however, deeper than the appeal either to reason or to morality was Gladstone's hold upon the emotions of his audience. It had been in the realm of feeling that Bentham and the Utilitarians had been deficient, and in persuading the public to accept the reforms they had urged, Gladstone overwhelmed his listeners with the conviction that these reforms were both rationally defensible and morally necessary. Eyewitnesses have told us how he used his physical gifts—the commanding presence, the powerful, resonant voice—to dominate his audience. With a single opening sentence, he could thrill his hearers. "Never shall I, an unenthusiastic non-party man," wrote one of them, "forget those tones; . . . it seemed to me as if someone had touched the stops of a mysterious organ, that searched us through and through. Two more sentences, and we were fairly launched upon a sea of passion. . . .In that torrent of emotion, the petty politics of the hour figured as huge first principles, and the opinions of the people became as the edicts of eternity."

At the age of eighty-three, half deaf, his eyes beclouded with cataracts, Gladstone was still spoiling for a fight. When in 1893 the House of Lords defeated his second Home Rule Bill, he finally made up his mind that the peerage must be abolished, but to his chagrin found his Cabinet—composed of men so much younger than he—too pusillanimous to fight. What he then wanted, as we learn from his last autobiographical notes, written at Hawarden after he had retired from politics, was "not a victory but a crushing and smashing victory."

The demonic energy of Gladstone found employment in a variety of ways. Thus, at the age of seventy, in addition to the premiership he took over the office of Chancellor of the Exchequer. Besides his career in politics, he also kept a lifelong interest in theology and in classical scholarship, and wrote voluminously on such subjects. Extremely complicated pieces of legislation, such as the Act to Reform the University of Oxford in 1854, or the Irish Land Act of 1881, he drafted personally, superintending almost every phase of their difficult passage through the House. In connection with the bill to reform Oxford, Gladstone wrote in his own hand three hundred and fifty letters in a single year. Sir Philip Magnus estimates that when in office, Gladstone, with the aid of secretaries, wrote about twenty-five thousand letters per annum. Lord Kilbracken made the almost incredible claim that his chief could dispose of correspondence at the astounding rate of over two hundred letters in a quarter of an hour, and described the system by which he accomplished it. His correspondence was worldwide, and included more than twelve thousand individuals. With the possible exception of Churchill, the bulk of Gladstone's papers is greater than that of any other Prime Minister in English history, filling seven hundred and fifty volumes in the British Museum today. There are two hundred thousand documents in the Gladstone papers, while fifty thousand more are preserved in his country house at Hawarden. Besides all this, from 1825 to 1896, Gladstone kept an almost daily diary running to twenty-five thousand separate entries in forty-one small volumes. The surplus energy which still remained after all these activities was devoted to felling trees, a favorite occupation. At Hawarden, his son tells us, he cut down literally thousands of trees, while planting others to take their place. Nor did he give up this strenuous occupation till he was eighty-one. "His amusements, like politics," wrote Lord Rosebery sardonically, "are constantly destructive. The forest laments in order that Mr. Gladstone may perspire."

Gladstone's restless and unremitting activity was such as to suggest a profound subconscious fear of ever being left alone with his own thoughts. He was as exact and economical with time as a miser is with money: not a single moment was left unaccounted for. While dressing and undressing, he read the Bible. A book was always in his pocket. Much of his reading was done on cross-country railway journeys, and in going to and from meetings. If he had time, he carefully examined the literature for sale at railway bookstalls. Once, during a long conversation on political and theological subjects, his host Dr. Döllinger, the teacher of Lord Acton, left the room for a moment to consult a book. On his return, he found Gladstone "deep in a volume he had drawn out of his pocket—true to his principle of never wasting time." Gladstone never ceased to exercise this compulsive vigilance over the expenditure of time. Thus, when walking in London (and he preferred always to walk), he would time himself to the minute, and sometimes on arriving at his host's for dinner would consult his watch to see precisely how long it had taken him to get there. Similarly with the details of his financial expenditure: Gladstone kept minute and accurate accounts of all his outlays. This did not mean, however, that he was parsimonious—he was, in fact, a very generous man; but he had a positive hatred of every kind of waste—of food left on plates or heeltaps in glasses—and a mania for minute economies. In a special drawer at Hawarden he kept what he called his "orts"— half-sheets of notepaper, neatly coiled pieces of string, the edgings of stamps, and such things.

His personality exhibited masochistic as well as aggressive elements. Thus, when in his last years cataracts in both eyes made reading difficult, he fell to drawing up lists of those who, at one time or another during his long public life, had judged him unfavorably. One list, in September 1894, included the names of Swinburne, Carlyle, Froude, Clerk Maxwell, Lord Shaftesbury, Professor Goldwin Smith, Sir Francis Doyle, and Lord Grey. "I do not know," he reflected, "if it has happened to any other man to be so contemptuously or so severely censured as myself, by such a number of persons, undoubtedly able, conspicuous and distinguished." The following year, he repeated this painstaking and peculiar performance, adding to the list of his critics the names of Pius IX, the historian Lecky, John Ruskin, Dean Hook, and Archbishop Magee. "Nothing, I would incline to say, could have united such a body of independent witnesses on this, except that what they said was the truth." (Conspicuously absent from either list is the name of his real rival, Disraeli, who had probably caused him more hurt than any other man). Perhaps the source for these penitential compilations was not so much a feeling of guilt as the memory of outraged pride.

Gladstone likewise proceeded to reproach himself about the self-styled "blunders" of his political life, blunders that he classified as "certain," "doubtful," and "suppositious." He enumerated six, most of them about relatively trifling matters, and only one— the premature recognition of Jefferson Davis in 1862—involving a really serious error of judgment. Some of these "blunders" he discussed in conversation with friends like Lord Rendel. Interestingly enough, none of the major mistakes of his political life were even mentioned. Neither the bombardment of Alexandria in 1882, nor the death of Gordon in 1885, occurred to him for inclusion in this catalogue of self-reproach. It would appear that Gladstone's soul-searching was neither searching nor deep.

One of the most curious aspects of Gladstone's innumerable activities was his lifelong concern for the condition of the prostitutes with whom the streets of London then abounded. The official biography by Lord Morley in 1903 naturally avoided this subject altogether, yet in any estimate of Gladstone's character, it cannot be dismissed as merely incidental. Among other things, it was used against him as a weapon by his political enemies, by the Queen herself as well as by Disraeli, and in any other man such indiscreet behavior would have led to almost certain ruin.

To quote Sir Philip Magnus' penetrating study:

> Gladstone's method was to walk the streets by night, alone, on at least one evening a week, armed with a stout stick for protection when he wandered into unfrequented districts. At first, he liked to wait for prostitutes to accost him, and he would then reply with courtesy, simplicity and charm. But he would often accost women himself, and suggest that they should accompany him home, where he told them that they would be treated with respect by his wife and by himself, and that they would be given food and shelter.
>
> He kept a record of every case, but he was scrupulous to treat the women as human beings and not as cases. He spent large sums of money supporting rescue homes, and smaller sums in personal gifts. He felt that he was making a personal contribution towards righting an infamous wrong. He was never unctuous. He did not demand penitence. He looked always to the future. His object was to enable the women to escape from their profession, and, in the Victorian phrase, to assist them to redeem themselves. If, after their health had been restored by a spell by the seaside, the women, as often happened, resumed their former occupation, Gladstone never scolded them. He often blamed himself for want of zeal, tact, or charity. He would go after them again and again, and he did not hesitate to pursue them into brothels, preferably in the daytime, but with a supreme, and almost perverse, disregard of worldly considerations.

It has been estimated that Gladstone spent £83,500 on such relief work. He marked out for himself a special area in the West End, bounded by Piccadilly, Soho, and the Thames embankment, as the theater of his operations. When blackmailers occasionally tried to take advantage of him, he immediately turned them over to the police. His opponents naturally dined out upon such stories, and the clubs were full of malicious gossip. There was also the ever-present risk of scandal appearing in the press. During the Home Rule crisis his enemies set spies upon him at night to dog his footsteps through the streets. Yet not even when he was Prime Minister did Gladstone cease from such activities: after a long evening at the House, he might be observed in Whitehall or on the Duke of York's steps engaged in earnest conversation with a prostitute.

As Sir Philip Magnus rightly observed: "It is an unparalleled tribute to the radiant integrity of Gladstone's character that the inevitable effort made during his life-time, and after his death, to cast doubt upon the purity of his motives should have been at once so feeble and so ineffectual." It is nevertheless evident that the motive power behind this work was a pressure, perhaps not admitted to consciousness in Gladstone's mind, far stronger than mere philanthropy. Thus it is significant that his interest in prostitutes coincided with periods of special vitality in his life; nor, despite all the entreaties of his friends, would he renounce that interest till he was nearly eighty. By such means did a subtle mind, a religious spirit, and a resolute will sublimate clamorous instinctual demands that appear to have been far more urgent than the average. The depth of his repression may be gauged from the fact that, unlike the equally austere Peel, Gladstone was intolerant of risqué stories.

The vehicle of Gladstone's sublimation was his strong religious feeling. From earliest childhood, he had been brought up by his father as a strict Evangelical, one to whom rationalism and Catholicism were equally abhorrent. On Sundays he read only religious books. Like Newman at a similar period of his life, in early manhood Gladstone had an overwhelming consciousness of guilt and regarded the world as irretrievably wicked. When the Cabinet minister, William Huskisson was run over and killed by a train at the opening of the Liverpool-Manchester railway in 1830, the young Gladstone, who had nothing whatever to do with it, for some extraordinary reason held himself responsible. "While the Minister, poor man, was in his last agonies—I was playing cards on Wednesday night. When shall we learn wisdom?" No other religion but Christianity, he said, had a proper sense of sin, of "the intensity and virulence of sin." Improvement of social conditions would not abolish sin, for the worst evil was found in the most favored classes. His own earnest desire was to enter the Church. How otherwise, he asked himself, could he live in the world "while every day my fellow-creatures, to whom I am bound by every tie of human sympathies, of a common sinfulness and a common redemption, day after day are sinking into death?" His point of view was exactly that of Newman in the *Apologia;* and in old age, Gladstone, too, confessed that as a young man he had seen "an element of anti-Christ in the Reform Act."

But Sir John Gladstone, for all his evangelical piety, wanted his brilliant son—the prodigy of Eton and Oxford—to make his career in secular life. Regretfully, the boy complied with his father's wishes, while never losing his interest in theology or in the Church. At Oxford, he had once surprised his examiners by his eagerness to continue discussing a point in theology after they had tired of it. He never ceased to regard politics as a means of achieving, if indirectly and at a lower level, the aims of a churchman. His first book, *The State in Its Relations with the Church* (1838), was a statement about religion similar to that of Coleridge in which John Stuart Mill had recognized an ideal conservatism. It was the duty of the state, Gladstone maintained, to distinguish truth from error and to support true religion. "That young man," said Sir Robert Peel acidly, "will ruin his fine political career if he persists in writing trash like this." High Churchmen, however, like Newman's brother-in-law, welcomed the book in spite of the still-lingering Protestant bias of the writer. "It is a very noble book," wrote the Reverend James B. Mozley, "and has damaged if not destroyed, his prospects with the Conservatives. People are saying now, 'Poor fellow,' and so on."

Gladstone's first visit to Rome, in 1832, when he was over-whelmed by the grandeur of St. Peter's, gave him a new sense of the apostolic character of the Church, and marked the begin-ning of his sympathy with the Anglo-Catholic party, whose most illustrious lay member he was to become. "I had previously taken a great deal of teaching direct from the Bible, as best I could," he wrote, "but now the feeling of the Church rose before me as a teacher too, and I gradually found in how incomplete and fragmentary a manner I had drawn divine truth from the sacred volume." With sympathy he watched the growth of the Oxford movement, and though regretting Newman's secession to Rome, always preserved a strong feeling of devotion to the ex-

vicar of St. Mary's. "It is enough to make the heart burst," he
wrote of Oxford's condemnation of Newman, whom, he said,
the dons had treated "worse than a dog." Against rationalism, on
the other hand, he cherished an undiminished prejudice. "Contempt for Locke is the beginning of wisdom" was an aphorism
attributed to him.

There was about Gladstone something of the clergyman
manqué, nor did he ever quite overcome a feeling of guilt at
not having been ordained. Hence he was delighted when his
daughter Mary married the penniless curate of Hawarden. Gladstone's "true interests were outside politics," says Sir Philip Magnus, "and as he grew older politics disgusted him more and more."
Some considered him to be the most learned lay theologian in
England. For the use of his family he wrote out two hundred
sermons, and when abroad, it was his custom to make a summary
of every sermon he heard. If he came home exhausted, it was
said of him that he wanted to go not to bed, but to church; and
in engaging a cook, he was more concerned about her religious
opinions than about her culinary abilities.

One result of Gladstone's religious obsession, which Disraeli
for one found exasperating was the frequent identification of his
own will with the will of God—which left little doubt as to
whence he thought his opponents derived their inspiration. After
his defeat at Oxford in 1865, he noted in his diary: "Always in
straits, the Bible supplies my needs. Today it was in the first
lesson, Jer. i. 19. 'And they shall fight against thee, but they
shall not prevail against thee, for I am with thee, saith the Lord,
to deliver thee.'" After the great Midlothian victory in 1880, he
spoke in the accents of Cromwell. "It seemed as if the arm of the
Lord bared itself for work that He has made its own." A little
later that same year, when a Greco-Turkish crisis seemed imminent: "One way or another," Gladstone pontificated, "I believe
the Almighty will work it out." It was, however, in the struggle for Home Rule that he saw himself as the special instrument
of righteousness. Thus, following a huge meeting at Liverpool in
1886, just after he had been savagely attacked by Lord Randolph
Churchill and the *Times,* he confided to his diary: "I went in
bitterness, in the heat of my spirit, but the hand of the Lord
was upon me."

If opportunism seemed to many the chief characteristic of Disraeli's political conduct, Gladstone prided himself that his own change of front—from the fervent Toryism of his youth to the ardent Liberalism of his middle age—was the result of genuine conviction. "Conviction," he once declared, "in spite of early associations and long-cherished prepossessions—strong conviction and an over-powering sense of public interests operating for many, many years before full effect was given to it—placed me in the ranks of the Liberal Party." And on another occasion he told his followers: "I came among you an outcast from those with whom I associated, driven from them, I admit, by no arbitrary act, but by the slow and resistless forces of conviction."

It was frequently charged against Gladstone that he invoked principle to cover expediency, that his changes of front were usually to his own advantage, and that he was in fact little more than a hypocrite. There were, however, a number of occasions when his conduct ran directly counter to his interests and to those of his party. The damage he did to his political prospects in 1838 by the publication of his views on church and state has already been mentioned. Seven years later, after he had been conspicuously successful at the Board of Trade, he mystified Peel by resigning over a measure—an increased grant to the Catholic seminary of Maynooth in Ireland—with which he happened to be in complete agreement. This was a subject, however, on which he had changed his mind since his book had appeared in 1838, and because that book had then condemned what Peel now proposed, he felt himself in honor bound to resign. Such a course of action may have been overpunctilious, but it was certainly the reverse of unscrupulous. "Everybody," wrote Greville, "said that his resignation was quite uncalled for."

In 1847, although he had previously opposed such a measure, Gladstone supported the bill to allow Jews to hold public office and sit in the House of Commons. By so doing, he outraged his father and jeopardized his seat at Oxford. The High Churchman Dr. Pusey denounced it as a prelude to the coming of Antichrist. Again, in 1850, by opposing Lord John Russell's Ecclesiastical Titles Bill, Gladstone offended the hidebound Oxonian electors. His courage on this occasion, in resisting the last hysterical cry of "No Popery" in England, was conspicuous. It brought him, for the first time, to the favorable attention of liberals abroad; de Tocqueville in particular praised his conduct. Nearly a quarter of a century later, however, shocked like his friend Lord Acton by the Vatican's claim to infallibility, Gladstone did not hesitate to publish a scathing denunciation of the papacy—"she has equally repudiated modern thought and ancient history"—yet he must have known that this would offend the Irish Catholics who controlled many seats in the House of Commons on which he depended for support.

On numerous occasions before 1877, when he was actually booed in the streets of London and had his windows broken for challenging Disraeli's jingoism over the "Eastern question," Gladstone had opposed popular moods of bellicosity. Thus he had voted against the two China wars waged by Lord Palmerston as being "at variance both with justice and with religion," and had condemned Pam's bullying tactics, applauded as they were by the public, in the case of Don Pacifico.[1] "The worst and most demoralizing Prime Minister for this country," Gladstone later called Palmerston, "that our day has known. He lives and thrives upon the bad parts of its character, and laughs the good ones to scorn, or passes them by with contempt." "Old Pam" had naturally retorted by impugning the patriotism of his critic.

The ability publicly to admit error is an unusual form of political courage; and if Gladstone in 1862 committed an egregious piece of folly in saluting Jefferson Davis as the maker of a nation, he did much to atone for it by the amplitude of his apology. This mistake continued to haunt him for the rest of his life, and even after he had retired from politics. "My offence indeed was not only inexcusable," he wrote in 1896, "but one of incredible grossness." In honoring the Geneva award made to the United States over the *Alabama* claims in 1872, Gladstone proved his sincerity and made amends for his indiscretion—for by so doing, he invited the obvious charge that he had truckled to a foreign power. This accusation was, in fact, one of the reasons for his defeat at the polls not many months later.

[1] In 1850 Palmerston had brought England close to war with France and Greece by belligerently defending Don Pacifico, a Jewish merchant from Malta who was also a British subject and who had become involved in a dispute with some Athenian merchants who had attacked his property.

Perhaps the most conspicuous example, however, of Gladstone's willingness to court unpopularity for the sake of conviction was his championship of Charles Bradlaugh's right to sit in the House of Commons. As an avowed atheist and open advocate of birth control, Bradlaugh was doubly repugnant to the Prime Minister as well as to the nation; but he had been duly chosen by the electors of Northampton, and when the Commons in 1880 refused to let him take his seat, Gladstone believed that a fundamental issue affecting civil liberty was at stake. Notwithstanding the extreme urgency at that moment of Irish and Egyptian affairs, he devoted much time and energy to the thankless task of defending, chiefly against the scurrilous attacks of Lord Randolph Churchill, an unpopular cause and an unpopular person. By so doing, he was also jeopardizing the good relations he was then seeking to establish with the Catholic Home Rulers. The Bradlaugh case actually occasioned what Francis Birrell called "some of the most magnificent of all his speeches." In the end, but not till five years had passed, Gladstone's courage was to be vindicated.

Important as was the principle involved, the Bradlaugh case was only an isolated episode in nineteenth-century politics. It was far otherwise with the great issue to which Gladstone next devoted his energies—Irish Home Rule. Even here, it has been alleged that his motives were disreputable and that under cover of a principle, he was really seeking to secure the support of Parnell's eighty Irish votes: an odd accusation, since the first Home Rule Bill (1886) provided for the elimination of those very Irish members from the Commons. What is certain is that no issue in Gladstone's sixty years of public life more thoroughly engaged his energies or more completely appealed to his idealism. On this question he was prepared to hazard everything—if necessary, to destroy his own party and terminate his own political career.

"Ireland! Ireland!" Gladstone had written to his wife forty years earlier. "That cloud in the West, that coming storm, the minister of God's retribution upon cruel and inveterate and but half-atoned injustice." Now he reproached himself for his own supineness and lack of imagination in not grappling earlier with the Irish problem. It had taken the criminal outrages and the desperate heroism of the Fenians to awaken him to the urgent need for action. Hence those solemnly spoken first words on hearing in 1868 that he was at last to be Prime Minister: "My mission is to pacify Ireland."

What now gave added joy to the conflict was the sense of fighting almost alone and against tremendous odds, since the majority of his followers were lukewarm, and the bulk of the electorate indifferent, if not actually hostile, to Home Rule. The Queen and the court, the aristocracy and the Church, and the country gentlemen of England were, of course, ranged solidly against him. Even the intellectual elite, who had once supported the cause of the American Union, were almost unanimous against Home Rule. Among those who now condemned Gladstone, often in unmeasured terms, were scientists like Huxley and Tyndall; writers like Tennyson, Browning, Swinburne, Matthew Arnold, and Harriet Martineau; historians like Lecky, Seeley, Froude, and Goldwin Smith; philosophers like Herbert Spencer; scholars like Benjamin Jowett; painters like Millais and Leighton; even Nonconformist preachers like Spurgeon, Allen, and Dale. Perhaps what affected Gladstone most was the news that in Germany his revered friend Dr. Döllinger, too, had pronounced against Home Rule.

Forty years earlier, Disraeli had taunted Peel for his failure to solve the Irish problem and advised the Irish members to distrust a man "whose bleak shade had fallen on the sunshine of their hopes for a quarter of a century." But when Disraeli himself came to power, though Ireland still possessed what he had once stigmatized as "a starving population, an absentee aristocracy and an alien Church," he did nothing whatever to redress the wrongs of Ireland. Not once in his whole life did this accomplished traveler ever cross the Irish Sea to see for himself the condition of "the most distressful country." All that his devoted biographer Froude can say for Disraeli in this connection is that "he left Ireland to simmer in confusion." When Gladstone, by his first Land Act, in 1870, sought to give the Irish peasant some small measure of protection against his landlord, Disraeli charged him with "consecrating sacrilege, condoning treason . . . and sowing seeds of Civil War," and in 1880 he denounced Home

Rule as a menace "scarcely less disastrous than pestilence and famine."

By 1886, however, Disraeli was dead, and the leadership had fallen upon Lord Salisbury, who, on one occasion, classified the Irish along with Hindus and Hottentots as being alike unfit for self-government. "I have not the slightest desire," proclaimed Salisbury as Prime Minister, "to satisfy the national aspirations of Ireland." Gladstone's second Home Rule Bill, of 1893, he stigmatized as "this atrocious, this mean, this treacherous revolution."

The most outrageous onslaught of all was made by Lord Randolph Churchill. "Mr. Gladstone has reserved for his closing days," he told the electors of South Paddington,

> a conspiracy against the honour of Britain and the welfare of Ireland more startlingly base and nefarious than any of those other numerous designs and plots which, during the last quarter of a century, have occupied his imagination. This design for the separation of Ireland from Britain . . . this monstrous mixture of imbecillity, extravagance, and political hysterics, is furnished by its author with the most splendid attributes, and clothed in the loftiest language. . . . all useful and desired reforms are to be indefinitely postponed, the British constitution is to be torn up, the Liberal party shivered into fragments.
>
> And why? For this reason and no other: To gratify the ambition of an old man in a hurry.

This brutal and inflammatory language is a vivid reminder of the atmosphere in which Home Rule was debated as well as a gauge of the extreme bitterness of the attacks that were made on Gladstone. He was widely compared with Judas and accused, as Herbert Paul wrote, of "betraying his followers, insulting his Sovereign, selling his country, compounding with crime." More than ever current during this period was the envenomed gossip about Gladstone's private life and his relations with prostitutes— of which the worst was imagined, and hoped. The old man was nothing but a hypocrite, a Jesuit in disguise, an imbecile, a moral leper. Once at this time, when he attended the Savoy Chapel and was kneeling at the communion rail, a well-dressed lady kneeling next to him, suddenly recognizing her neighbor, got up at once and left the church. (It was the Hon. Mrs. Charles Grey, a beauty whom Gladstone as a young man had admired.) A daring Orangeman even conceived a plot to kidnap the Grand Old

Man and maroon him on some Pacific island with Homer, the Bible, and an ax.

Though Home Rule was finally defeated—through the monolithic resistance of the House of Lords—the debates on the two bills afforded the greatest personal triumph of Gladstone's long parliamentary career. The physical exertions, the moral courage, the gifts of leadership, the power of sustained oratory that he now displayed—these things would have been remarkable in any man, but in a man of eighty-three (as Gladstone was when he steered the second Home Rule Bill through the Commons), they were almost incredible. On the first occasion, he spoke for three and a half hours, for two and a half on the second, "and not for a moment," in the words of Erich Eyck, "did the concentrated attention of a single listener in the House relax. Friend and foe were equally swept off their feet by this marvelous display of physical and intellectual energy, which seemed to defy all the laws to which human power is subject."

"After the disillusions of more than thirty years," wrote the irreconcilable Home Ruler William O'Brien in 1920, "the memory of the scene comes back in a more mountainous bulk and in a more sacred light than ever. The night which was to have been the grave of his greatness as a statesman will, perhaps, be remembered in the coming ages as the occasion of the most sublime message to humanity to be found in his long life."

The doctrine of self-determination which he sought to apply to Ireland was also, anticipating Woodrow Wilson by half a century, the basis of Gladstone's foreign policy in Europe. In 1871, he sought to restrain Bismarck from seizing Alsace-Lorraine, an act "repulsive to the sense of modern civilization." Gladstone was the champion of Italian, Greek, and Balkan independence. Disraeli's acquisition of Cyprus in 1878 he termed "an act of duplicity not surpassed and rarely equalled in the history of nations . . . a gross and open breach, or rather a gross and manifest breach, of the public law of Europe." On coming into office in 1880, he wished to cede the island to Greece, but was overborne by his own Foreign Secretary, the Cabinet, and public opinion. Had Gladstone prevailed, how much future bloodshed would have been averted.

Widely current in Victorian England was the story of the Greek who arrived knowing only two words of the language—"Gladstone" and "England." Notwithstanding the severe fighting in Athens in 1944, Gladstone's statue still graces one of the chief streets of the city—along with those of Byron and Canning. Thirty years after his father's death, when Viscount Gladstone went to Bulgaria, he found the old man's portrait in every school, alongside that of the King. When the architect of the Oxford schools, Sir Thomas Graham Jackson, traveled in Montenegro he found that everyone he met in that barren little mountain country pronounced the name of Gladstone "with admiration and gratitude." The well-known traveler Harry de Windt, passing through the Balkans in the years just preceding the First World War, found that Gladstone's name was remembered in every country he visited. Nor was Europe alone in recognizing the greatness of Gladstone, for, as the old man gratefully remembered, his admirers in America were legion. "The United States," he wrote, "has been that country in the world in which the most signal marks of honour have been paid me, and in which my name has been the most popular, the only parallels being Italy, Greece and the Balkan Peninsula."

In addition to his championship of the rights of small nations, Gladstone, more than any other English statesman, believed in a European policy to which the national interest of England, like that of every other state, ought to be subject. The basis of British foreign policy, he wrote in 1869, should be "to develop and mature the action of a common or public or European opinion, as the best standing bulwark against wrong." Free trade he believed to be one of the most valuable ties that could hold together a European community of nations. The commercial treaty with France in 1860, which Cobden had negotiated and which he himself had enacted into law, he regarded as one of the most important events of his public life. Charles Greville called Gladstone's speech on this occasion "one of the greatest triumphs that the House of Commons ever witnessed."

It was fitting that the last speeches of Gladstone's public life, delivered in 1896 at Liverpool after his retirement from politics, again concerned the cause of freedom—this time that of the Armenian people, now threatened with annihilation by Turkey, Gladstone's old enemy of twenty years before. Now as then he urged decisive action. "Indignation without action is froth," he had written at the time of the Bulgarian Massacres. "The ground on which we stand," he now proclaimed, "is not British, nor European, it is human."

All his life he had striven for peace, and now, in his last years, he saw the growth of an aggressive British imperialism and the beginning of the armaments race among the powers of Europe. The new imperialist policy of Joseph Chamberlain he denounced in 1897 as "a vulgar road to popularity and power." Years before, he had turned on one occasion to his private secretary, Sir Edward Hamilton, and told him "solemnly in a low voice which vibrated with intensity," that what he feared above all was—"the *men* of the future, personalities of the stamp of Randolph Churchill, and Chamberlain!" At the opening of the Kiel Canal, which he attended in 1895, his only comment was: "This means war." An arms race in Europe, he prophesied, "would end in a race towards bankruptcy by all the powers of Europe." It was singularly appropriate that the last fight of his long parliamentary career was against a proposal to increase naval spending. In urging the rejection of this proposal, the old man was "glowing with indignation and deeply stirred." In vivid language he pictured to Lord Rendel "the ghosts of our old statesmen rising from their graves at this portent and going to and fro on the earth gibbering out their vain protests." Defeated in his own Cabinet, Gladstone laid down his fourth and last premiership. He was then eighty-four, and had a little over four more years to live.

If as a statesman Gladstone towered above his contemporaries in the nineteenth century, much as did Churchill in the twentieth, his faults, like those of Churchill, were commensurate with his virtues. Unlike Disraeli, he was a poor judge of men, and hence unskillful in handling them. He was, for example, unable to understand such a colleague as the thrusting, aggressive radical Joseph Chamberlain, nearly thirty years his junior. A man of this sort was a new phenomenon in politics, a phenomenon that Gladstone disliked intensely. All through his second ministry, he gravely mismanaged his relations with Chamberlain. It seems possible that had the latter been more tactfully handled by

Bentham as a student at Oxford (he was then about fourteen)

Bentham about the age of sixty, at the period when he was beginning to acquire distinguished disciples such as Broagham and James Mill

Courtesy The New York Public Library

J. S. Mill about the age of thirty (he went prematurely bald). This was his appearance at the time he became acquainted with Harriet Taylor.

Courtesy Brown Brothers

Daguerreotype of J. S. Mill in the period after his wife's death. He was then sixty years of age.

Harriet Taylor at thirty, when she first made the acquaintance of J. S. Mill

From an oil portrait in the possession of Professor F. A. Hayek

Newman in 1844, on the eve of his leaving the Church of England

Disraeli at thirty-six (portrait by A. E. Chalon)

Newman in his sixties—still Father Newman (about the period of the *Apologia* in 1864)

Photograph of Disraeli in 1873. He was then sixty-nine.

Courtesy Culver Pictures, Inc.

(left) Gladstone as president of the Oxford Union at twenty-one (drawing by F. J. Meyer)

(bottom left) Gladstone in 1854, aged forty-five

Courtesy The Bettmann Archive

(bottom right) Gladstone nearing seventy—the formidable look which made Professor Blackie quail

Courtesy The New York Public Library

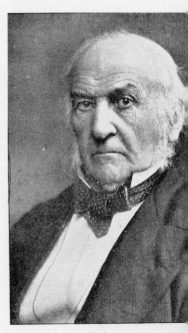

Sidney and Beatrice Webb in the 1890s—during the early days of their marriage

Sidney and Beatrice Webb in the early 1920s. They were then in their early sixties, and at the height of their influence since he was in the Labour Government in 1924.

Lloyd George in 1879—at the age of sixteen before he had ever left Wales. One sees, perhaps, a look of determination like that which appears on the face of Winston Churchill as a youth.

Courtesy Brown Brothers

Lloyd George in his first year as Premier. He was then fifty-four.

Lloyd George on his eightieth birthday—still the fighter

Churchill as a boy. Is it imagination only that suggests a look of defiance, hinting an obstinacy already well developed?

Churchill at the time of his first entrance into Parliament. He was then twenty-six.

Churchill as First Lord of the Admiralty, just before the war of 1914. He was then approaching forty—one of the youngest First Lords ever to hold that position.

Churchill on V-E Day, 1945, with
George VI

Churchill in New York, arriving
in America for his famous "Iron
Curtain" speech at Fulton, Missouri, in 1946

Courtesy Culver Pictures, Inc.

Gladstone, he might have remained loyal to the party. Similarly with Lord Rosebery, whose appointment as Foreign Secretary in 1892 Gladstone bitterly regretted—one of the biggest blunders of his life, he called it. Then there was General Gordon: no one, perhaps, could have controlled such a fanatic, but Gladstone took full responsibility for the series of errors, not all of them due to his own fault, which led to Gordon's death. As for the Queen, it was a waste of time and energy to argue with her, let alone, as on one occasion, to take the trouble of refuting her objections under six main headings, and then, when she indignantly protested, repeating the process—under five new headings. Humor was not Gladstone's forte.

"The average man," as Lord Kilbracken says, "*l'homme moyen sensuel*, was a creature whom Gladstone did not in the least understand, and in whose existence he was inclined to disbelieve, except when the truth was absolutely forced upon him." Like Bentham, Gladstone assumed that everyone resembled himself and was dominated by the same idealism. He habitually overestimated the power of abstract ideas, and undervalued the need for personal contact with others. Thus Lord Acton speaks of his "lofty unfitness to deal with sordid motives," and "his inability to sway certain kinds of men."

But it is also true that—serious defect in a politician—Gladstone was not really much interested in human beings as such. Though he might never have expressed it so plainly, he shared to some degree Newman's conviction that there were in the world only two ultimate realities: himself and his Creator.

Nothing bored him more than the mediocrities of both parties who abounded in Parliament. He stayed aloof from his followers and was seldom seen in the smoking room. When they were thinking of the Derby or the stock market, his mind was on Homer or the Pentateuch. "Free from the lower forms of self-seeking," wrote Lord Selborne, "he was too much occupied with his own thoughts to give much attention to those of other people." "With all his magnificent gifts," one of his secretaries admitted, "Mr. Gladstone was not a good party leader, mainly because he was so utterly unlike the colleagues with whom he had to work, and the supporters in Parliament on whom he had to rely."

Of all his colleagues in later years, only Lord Granville, his

Foreign Secretary, dared to address him as "Gladstone." Seeing how much he gave offense to his followers by not associating with them, Granville once begged him to take a certain M.P. into a corner and talk to him—no matter about what, so long as he talked to him: "tell him that he is a fool, that he smells disagreeably or any other not very secret fact."

The passage of years gradually raised still another barrier between Gladstone and his younger contemporaries. Old age also intensified his faults: his egomania; his casuistical use of reason to deceive himself by justifying departures from what he had previously maintained; his impatience of contradiction; his pursuit of an *idée fixe;* his belief that he was responsible to God alone; his increasing tendency to self-deification. Döllinger once remarked of Gladstone that it was extremely "hard to convince him, for he is clad in triple steel." More and more he came to pass moral judgments on others for daring to differ with him. "He found it very difficult," says Lord Kilbracken, "to realize that an opinion, contrary to his own, could be held without some slight tinge of moral obliquity." More and more, matters of expediency were transformed for him into questions of principle, and as Goldwin Smith noted, when his pugnacity and aggressiveness were roused he thought of little else save how to win.

A sense of proportion Gladstone had always lacked. To the smallest matters he brought the same intensity and the same ponderousness with which he approached the problems of the universe. Arthur Balfour has amusingly described how Gladstone would debate some trifle of daily life, gravely weighing the pros and cons, as if it were a serious affair of state. Joined to this lack of perspective was a constitutional lack of humor, although at home at Hawarden he was often full of gaiety and fun, especially with his children and grandchildren.

Occasionally he made himself absurd, as once at Chequers when he became the victim of a practical joke. There he "came upon a parrot who spoke modern Greek. Gladstone, all enthusiasm, responded with a long quotation from Homer, and could not hide his disappointment when the bird failed to reply." A lively passage in a letter from Emily Eden to Lord Clarendon throws some light upon Gladstone's difficulties in communicating with others:

He is always above me, and then he does not converse, he harangues, and the more he says the more I don't understand. Then there is something about high-church people that I can't define, but I feel it when I am with them—something Jesuitical—but they never let themselves go—and to complete my list of things, there is some degree of Parvenuism about him as there was about Sir Robert Peel, something in his tone of voice and his way of coming into the room, that is not aristocratic. In short, he is not frivolous enough for me. If he were soaked in boiling water and rinsed till he was twisted into a rope, I do not suppose a drop of fun would ooze out.

Another defect which grew on Gladstone with age was the tendency to verbosity—a weakness for which Disraeli had pilloried him effectively. Abundance of words Gladstone had always possessed. Already at Eton and in the Oxford Union his fluency had astonished and nonplused his contemporaries. But as early as 1846, Peel had complained to Sir James Graham: "I really have great difficulties sometimes in comprehending what Gladstone means"—a statement in which Graham had at once concurred. "It is always difficult," Sir James agreed, "through the haze of words to catch a distant glimpse of Gladstone's meaning." After a long conversation with him at Brantwood, Ruskin put it more bluntly. "Mr. Gladstone is an old wind-bag. . . . When he makes what is called 'a great speech,' in nine cases out of ten, he uses his splendid gifts of oratory not for the elucidation of his subject, but for its vaporization in a cloud of words."

By the time of his last pathetic visit to Oxford in 1890, of which C. R. L. Fletcher has left a vivid account, Gladstone's love of talk had degenerated into logorrhea. He talked incessantly, and at the end was literally exhausted by his own monologue. For half an hour he held forth in a continuous stream, without giving anyone else a chance to utter a word. On another occasion, he argued for hours with Mrs. Humphry Ward about her novel *Robert Elsmere,* and got "stern and angry and white to a degree." He dismissed her opinions as "trumpery objections," she complained, quite "in his most House of Commons manner." It had always been one of Gladstone's characteristics that he was more interested in what he was saying than in the person to whom he was saying it. He would have considered it unworthy of him to adjust his conversation to the personality or the level of intelligence of any particular hearer.

His tendency to verbosity limited the appeal of Gladstone to his own contemporaries. More serious still were the deficiencies of thought and imagination by which he cut himself off from the possibility of influencing the future. Though his intelligence was far-ranging and his interests wide, he lacked originality and depth of mind. All through life Gladstone, in a manner that puzzled observers like Lord Bryce, chose to remain ignorant of science and was suspicious of scientific developments, exhibiting, like Newman, an almost instinctive fear and ignorance. His compulsive need to fill every moment with reading was tantamount to fear of thought itself.

The most serious intellectual failing of Gladstone's old age was his indifference to new ideas. Marvelous as was his physical vitality, he lacked the mental youthfulness and flexibility which always characterized such a man as John Stuart Mill, and which finally led Mill to abandon the laissez faire by which he had been raised in favor of the socialism which his conscience told him was necessary to correct the inequities of laissez faire. Gladstone seems never to have realized that the end result of unlimited competition might be monopoly, or that the protection of the dispossessed equally with the security of the rich might be the proper function of the state. He never considered the relief of unemployment to be the responsibility of society. The social question, in fact, never interested him at all, for he had always conceived of government in terms simply of a business proposition. The use of taxation to redress social inequities seemed to him almost immoral. Nor did it ever occur to him that workingmen might break away from the Liberal party and develop a new leadership—their own.

"After 1880," wrote Beatrice Webb in her diary, Gladstone

> was out of sympathy with the collectivist trend of the newer democracy of town workmen, and became a reactionary, appealing pathetically to the Nonconformist middle-class in terror of the new creed and hating the new apostles. His soul was wrapped up in his own principles—religious and economic—each set in a watertight compartment, he never realized the new order of ideas. Moreover, he was socially an aristocrat and disliked the *parvenu* in riches and political power—such as Chamberlain.

"For me socialism has no attractions," Gladstone declared in

1890. "Nothing but disappointment awaits the working classes if they yield to the exaggerated anticipations which are held out to them by the Labour party." Hence, on account of the great posthumous influence of his unrivaled name and reputation, he must bear some responsibility for the almost complete destruction of his party within a quarter of a century of his death.

Yet in surveying the wreck of the once great Liberal party, the historian of today may still feel respect and gratitude for the statesman who sought to infuse politics with his own moral earnestness and raise them to the level of his own intellectuality, who saw England always in terms of Europe and seldom put the interests of his own country before what he conceived to be the welfare of mankind. Even those who completely rejected Gladstone's politics—Socialist hotheads like David Kirkwood from Clydeside, or Robert Smillie, the Northumberland miners' leader —could hold his name in high esteem, and remember him as the greatest man they had ever known. "We believe in no man's infallibility," once said Spurgeon, the Nonconformist preacher, "but it is restful to be sure of one man's integrity."

Idealism is not so commonplace a feature of the politics of the twentieth century that we can afford either to ignore or to patronize the memory of Gladstone, the outstanding representative of the political life of Victorian England.

VI

Beatrice & Sidney Webb

(1858–1943 and 1859–1947)

THE ROLE of the Fabians in England at the opening of the twentieth century was similar to that of the Utilitarians at the beginning of the nineteenth. In each case, a small group of social philosophers provided the intellectual basis for a radical movement in politics, thereby bringing about a profound transformation in the political and social life of the country. Among the thinkers who were influential in the Fabian Society, none were more significant or more devoted than Beatrice and Sidney Webb, the latter of whom served on the Fabian executive from 1886 to 1935. "Their effect," says Kingsley Martin, "upon social evolution in the twentieth century was as powerful as Bentham's had been in the nineteenth."

Despite the fact that the Utilitarians were arch-individualists believing in laissez faire, whereas the Fabians were collectivists advocating socialism, both groups had certain important things in common: above all, a similar ethical outlook and a devotion to the same social goal—the greatest happiness of the greatest number. This ideal, however, was interpreted by the Fabians not in the narrow, doctrinaire manner of Bentham, but in the richer and more humane fashion of Mill. "With John Stuart Mill," wrote Beatrice Webb, "I am inclined to think that the exercise of intellect—perhaps suffused with love—is the highest happiness of which we poor mortals are capable." "Love, truth, beauty and humour," she believed, had been omitted from Bentham's calculus of pleasure. Mill's *Autobiography*, as we have noticed, marks one of the earliest transitions from laissez faire to socialism.

In the opinion of Bernard Shaw, Mill's two most prominent

converts to socialism were William Morris and Sidney Webb (had he been thinking of America, he might have added Henry George, who had first read Mill in the Philadelphia public library). In the phrase of Max Beer, the distinguished historian of British socialism, "Webb stands on the shoulders of John Stuart Mill."

In character and personality, however, Sidney Webb was more akin to Bentham than to Mill. So close, indeed, was the resemblance that one might almost think him a reincarnation of the hermit of Queen Street Place. For both thinkers the touchstone of all things was their utility. Not only did Webb share Bentham's scientific and empirical approach to all problems—moral, social, economic, and pyschological—he was also very much like him in his disinterested devotion to truth, in his selflessness, in his remoteness from many normal emotions, and in his indifference to religion, art, and literature. Whatever Webb's deficiencies in feeling, they were compensated for by the highly emotional temperament of his wife. In the long and fruitful partnership of the Webbs it is almost as if in some mysterious fashion the personalities of Bentham and Mill had fused.

No two human beings did more than the Webbs to create the climate of opinion which fostered the growth of the welfare state in England. "Britain today," wrote Lord Beveridge, "would have been very different from what it is if there had been no Sidney and Beatrice Webb. For more than fifty years they were a ferment in society, bringing new ideas to men's minds, bringing new organizations and institutions to birth. . . . They did this, almost wholly without official position or power." Few people have lived to see so completely realized during their own lifetime the ideals to which they had devoted themselves.

The famous Minority Report on the Poor Law, which Beatrice Webb drew up in 1909, became a sort of blueprint for the social legislation of the Labour government in 1945. The achievement of the minimum wage, the adoption of humane standards of health in industry, the abolition of the Poor Law and the workhouses, the wide extension of the social services, the redistribution of the national income so that the burdens of society might be more equally shared, the ownership by the community of certain basic means of production—these proposals held in abhorrence at the turn of the century by Gladstonian Liberals as well as by Conservatives—Sidney Webb lived to see enacted into law, knowing that he and his wife were largely responsible for their enactment. Through their work, as Shaw said, socialism in England "became constitutional, respectable and practical," while their monumental history of trade unionism "made organized labour in England class-conscious, for the first time."

In addition to this, Britain today is indebted chiefly to the Webbs for such notable institutions as the London School of Economics, founded in 1895, and *The New Statesman*, begun in 1913. The London School fulfilled a dream of seventy-year-old Thomas Henry Huxley. It established as an inductive science the study of sociology, while at the same time training the future civil servants needed to administer the welfare state that was about to come into existence. In the field of modern journalism *The New Statesman* has built up a reputation of such excellence in social and literary criticism that today, with a circulation of over eighty thousand, it is the most successful magazine of its kind in English. According to the present editor, Kingsley Martin, the Webbs, Shaws, and other Fabians must have lost £100,000 before *The New Statesman* finally became a paying proposition.

After a lifetime of patient dedication to the ideals that they had embraced when young, the Webbs emerged as figures of such national repute that the recognition of their services transcended party lines. It was Churchill who, in 1944, bestowed on Sidney Webb the highest civil distinction of English life—the Order of Merit. In 1947 with the approval of the nation his ashes and those of his wife were buried in Westminster Abbey.

What was the nature of this unique combination of talents, of this lifelong partnership almost unparalleled in English history? The gifts possessed by Sidney and Beatrice Webb complemented one another so perfectly, and their interests coincided so completely, that most people who knew them shared the impression of Professor R. H. Tawney. In listening to them, he wrote, one had the impression of "one complex personality communing with itself rather than of two debating with each other." This effect was enhanced by their habit of saying in conversation, "*we* think" or "*we* feel." Yet in spite of the identity of their views, one was always aware of two distinct personalities. As their good friend Mary Agnes Hamilton observed: "Sidney was a born bureaucrat; Beatrice a born aristocrat."

With a modesty equal to that of Mill himself, Beatrice Potter wrote on the eve of her marriage: "We are both of us second-rate minds, but we are curiously combined. I am the investigator and he the executant. . . . A considerable work should result if we should use our combined talents with deliberate and persistent purpose." And indeed, their life's work was to comprise more than twenty-five volumes, including the epoch-making *History of Trade Unionism* (1894); the original studies in *English Local Government*, which stretched over a period of thirty years (1899–1929); and the large-scale study of *Soviet Communism* (1935), which Bernard Shaw termed "the first really scientific analysis of the Soviet State."

In their joint work, Beatrice, according to their secretary, was largely responsible for architectural design, "while all the actual construction was done by Sidney." The writing itself was apparently a mutual endeavor, each revising and amending the whole. Sidney possessed a greater knowledge of facts and had more energy and persistence, but some of the most illuminating insights came from Beatrice. Like Thoreau, she was more concerned with conceiving ideas than with carrying them out. Their work involved not only the examination of countless written records, but the interviewing in provincial cities, in trade unions, and in cooperative societies, of innumerable witnesses. "In dealing with documents," explained Mrs. Webb in *Our Partnership*, "he is far more efficient than I; but, in the manipulation of witnesses with a view of extra-confidential information, his shyness and scepticism of the use of it give me the advantage. And I am more ruthless in the exercise of my craft when he is not there to observe and perchance disapprove of my little tricks of the trade."

Much light is thrown upon the workings of their partnership by a passage from Mill's *Autobiography* in which Mill attempted to estimate the significance of the contributions made respectively by Harriet Taylor and by himself:

When two persons have their thoughts and speculations completely in common; when all subjects of intellectual or moral interest are discussed between them in daily life . . . when they set out from the same principles and arrive at their conclusions by processes pursued jointly, it is of little consequence in respect to the question of originality which of them holds the pen; the one who contributes least to the composition may contribute most to the thought; the writings which result are the joint product of both and it must often be impossible to disentangle their respective parts and affirm that this belongs to one and that to the other.

It is perhaps worth mentioning that when this passage was shown to him, Sidney Webb, despite his reluctance to speak of personal matters, did not demur to the suggestion that he and his wife had worked together in just that fashion.

Informed that Beatrice Potter and Sidney Webb were going to be married, John Burns, the labor leader, is said to have commented that the result would be not children but "another great Blue Book." What is certain is that over a period of forty years, every joint production was a labor of love. Beatrice had inherited an income of £1,000 a year, on which they were able to live comfortably without Sidney ever having to seek employment; and it is a tribute to his total lack of vanity and freedom from *amour-propre* that living on his wife's income—a situation that the average man would have found galling to his pride—never for a moment troubled him. Both of them regarded the money as a sort of trust to be used for the public good: it was a matter of pure chance which one had happened to inherit it.

"We have been fortunate," wrote Beatrice in her diary, "to do the work we believed in, blessed with a loving comradeship and endowed with sufficient means to do it without financial strain." This mood of quiet happiness, based on mutual affection, and beyond that, upon a sense of purpose shared and shared accomplishment, was constant throughout their lives. "Fortunately," wrote Beatrice after ten years of marriage, "we enjoy the incomparable luxury of freedom from all care for ourselves. We are secure in our love for one another and we are absolutely content with our present daily life, as far as our own interest and happiness is concerned. Well may we be! I have a constant wonder whether we are earning our maintenance." Nearly thirty years later, her mood was still the same: only time had changed, so that now the glance was retrospective, and the tense not present, but past. "An extraordinarily peaceful and interested life," she reflected at the age of sixty, "one long day of loving companionship and joint intellectual endeavor—no anxiety about ways and means, no serious illness or prolonged ill-health, always free and able to do what we thought best. 'We *have* been fortunate,' Sidney often says."

In their intense devotion to work, the Webbs were typical Victorians. While neither seems to have been directly influenced by Carlyle, no one practiced more arduously than they the gospel of work which he had preached. "Sidney is at it," wrote Beatrice, "from nine o'clock in the morning continuously until seven thirty, and once or twice a week lectures in the evening as well. For myself I peg along every morning at the book for three or four hours, some times putting in half an hour in the afternoon. But, generally, I find it pays better to do nothing in the afternoons except take exercise, especially as almost every day we have someone to lunch or to dine to talk shop." After a long morning's work Sidney usually spent the afternoons attending to the business of the London County Council, of which from 1891 to 1909 he was proud to be a member. Then, for another fifteen years (1912–27), he was professor of public administration at the London School of Economics—his "dearest child," he called it, in a phrase reminiscent of Bentham. Often, moreover, he and Beatrice spent the mornings working in the reading room of the British Museum. Even on vacation, they took their books along with them. Thus when staying with Lord Haldane in his Scottish home at Cloan, they dismayed his sister Elizabeth by their stern application to their self-imposed task. The mere sight of them, she wrote, working from morning till night, made one feel ashamed of oneself.

Their work at home, seated together at the table in the dining room of No. 41 Grosvenor Road, was no less exhausting. Thus Beatrice remembered "the intolerable toil of thought involved in working out a history of trade unionism consistent with the facts we had observed and the hypotheses we believed we had verified."

Her diaries record the mental and physical strain involved in such labor. "Not getting on with our book," she writes on July 10, 1894. "It is a horrid grind, this analysis—one sentence is

exactly like another, the same words, the same construction—
no relief in narrative. . . . I sometimes despair of getting on with
the book—I feel horribly vexed with myself for loitering and
idling as I do morning after morning; looking on while poor
Sidney drudges along." Occasionally—perhaps when under strain
or overworked—she doubted her own powers and was frightened
by her "sheer incapacity to grapple with a hard bit of complicated analysis."

Such moods of self-distrust were brief. "After nearly twenty
years of adult life," runs a later entry in her diary,

> I am still living the same daily life, still using my whole energy in
> unravelling ideas and attempting to clear issues. . . . There is an inex-
> pressible delight in this consciousness of continuity, in feeling that
> those hours of lonely and painful study are linked on to the settled
> occupation—perhaps one might almost say the settled profession—
> of a productive brainworker. If only one could have foreseen that
> this daily intellectual effort would one day be set in a frame of
> loving companionship and constant sympathy, one would have been
> less restless and morbidly self-conscious; . . . the old fervour for
> work has returned without the old restlessness.

Before becoming a scholar, Beatrice had been a social worker,
diligently investigating the actual conditions under which people
lived and worked. For her, research and life were never divorced
from one another. Where thirty years before Florence Nightingale had found an outlet for her frustrated idealism in the Crimean
War, Beatrice Potter found an outlet for hers in the slums of the
East End. At the age of twenty-seven she had taken over the
management of a tenement building near the London docks. It
was her first experience as a social investigator, and she was
appalled by what she saw of the daily life of that "constantly
decomposing mass of human beings" in Whitechapel. Nor was she
impressed by the spiritual release afforded by religious meetings in
Victoria Park, where on Sundays city clerks, "spotty, seedy and
smelly," sang "loudly of the blood of Jesus." Physically exhausted
and depressed in spirit, haunted by the "low, cunning, brutal
faces of loafers and cadgers," she had to retire from time to
time to her father's house in the Wye valley not only to record
her impressions but to restore her health. An article entitled
"Dock Life in the East End of London" marked her first appearance in print.

Her next project was to help her cousin Charles Booth, the shipowner and philanthropist, in the searching inquiry that produced his large-scale *Life and Labour of the People in London*— a survey that shocked the nation by demonstrating that almost a third of the population of London, the capital city of the greatest empire in the world, was living on or near the level of destitution. As an investigator of "sweated labour" in the East End tailoring trade, Beatrice actually worked for a time as a "plain trouser hand." She must have been shocked by a number of things for which her own sheltered education had not prepared her. When she published in a respectable magazine her "Pages from a Work Girl's Diary" in 1888, she had to omit all reference to the prevalence of incest among those living in one-room tenements.

For her, people were never merely ciphers or statistics—as perhaps they tended to be for her husband. It was her awareness of the human element that gave vitality to the great works on local government; and but for this, whatever their value from a historical point of view, they would have remained largely unreadable. "Constantly, as I walk in one of the crowded streets of London," she had written in her diary at the age of twenty-five, "and watch the faces of the men and women who push past me, lined, furrowed and sometimes contorted by work, struggle and passion; and think that all this desire and pain, this manifold feeling and thought is but a condition of thought and matter, phantom-like forms built-up to be destroyed, a hopelessness overtakes me, paralyzing all power of wishing and doing." In such a passage one sees already at work that combination of acute observation and quick sympathy, together with that passionate search for purpose, which underlay her strongly religious sense of life. Like Robert Owen before her, she was convinced of the all-powerful force of environment in shaping human destinies and was imbued with the belief that in learning through planning to control circumstance, man might develop a greater degree of freedom and individuality than he had ever known before. "As I hurry down Tottenham Court Road," she wrote, "and jostle up against the men and women of the people, with their various expressions of determined struggle, weak self-indulgence, and discontented effort, the conviction that the fate of each individual is governed by conditions born of 'the distant past' is irresistibly forced upon me."

The culmination of her practical experience was her work as a member of the Royal Commission on the Poor Law, to which her friend Arthur Balfour, the retiring Prime Minister, appointed her in 1905. The famous Minority Report, published in 1909, though signed by only four of the twenty-four members, proved in the end to be more influential than the report of the majority and indicated the direction that for the next forty years social legislation in England was to follow. Though drafted by Sidney, the Minority Report was really the work of Beatrice. It demonstrated the inadequacy of existing charitable organizations for the relief of distress and envisaged, through radical changes in taxation and legislation, not simply the alleviation but the elimination of poverty. Above all it urged the destruction of the existing Poor Law and the sweeping away of the workhouse system, with its cruel stigma upon poverty and its harsh treatment of the pauper. The Beveridge Report of 1944 followed the lines indicated by the Webbs in 1909.

To her work on the Poor Law Commission, Beatrice Webb gave five and a half years of her life—years taken away from the scholarly and historical work that temperamentally suited her best. At the end of that period, she found herself "in a state of abject exhaustion." From the beginning, at a time when few males recognized the right of women to take part in public life at all, she foresaw the difficulty of her position as the only woman sitting with a group of twenty-three men. She realized it would demand the greatest possible amount of tact, patience, and discretion, but she was also resolved to be firm. She would not be bullied or browbeaten. "It is a new experience for me," she wrote in her diary in 1906, "to *have* to make myself disagreeable in order to attain my ends. In private life one can only get one's way by being unusually pleasant. In official life—at least as the most insignificant member of a Commission overwhelmingly against me in opinion—I shall only get my share of control by quietly and persistently standing on my rights as an individual commissioner and refusing altogether to be overawed by great personages who would like to pooh-pooh a woman who attempts to share in the control of affairs."

Frequently she went into St. Paul's Cathedral to find refreshment of mind and spirit. "The beauty of the music and the old-world charm of the words, the great space of the dome, are always the best recreation when I am weary of straining my poor little mind. I prayed for strength to order my effort rightly and keep my motives pure, to preserve the patience and persistency of purpose needed to carry through our intentions. These next three years," she reflected, "are going to try my strength of body, intellect and character: I sometimes wonder whether I shall keep going, or whether some day I may not find that I have stopped for repair." Sometimes she was provoked by what seemed to her the obtuseness or lack of imagination shown by some of her colleagues. On one occasion, one of them lost his temper with her and "got white with rage." Admitting that the chairman, Lord George Hamilton, an aristocratic Conservative, had "personal charm and social tact," she could not help but realize that he had no knowledge of the subject and no experience in research. Sometimes he got into a fury with her; and in the end was reduced to such a state that, according to her, he "foamed at the mouth" at the mention of her name.

After the Poor Law Commission had completed its hearings, and the report of the Conservative majority had been adopted, Mrs. Webb engaged in a strenuous program of public education. For two years she traveled through England campaigning for the abolition of the Poor Law, lecturing in widely separated places, and sometimes speaking several times a week. This was the busiest and most exhausting period of her life.

For the furtherance of their political ends, the Webbs made use of the wide and varied range of social acquaintances which resulted from Beatrice's family connections. "It is a tiresome fact," she candidly confessed, "that to get things done in what one considers the best way, entails so much—to speak plainly—of intrigue. There is no such thing as spontaneous public opinion; it all has to be manufactured from a centre of conviction and energy radiating through persons, sometimes losing itself in an unsympathetic medium, at other times gaining additional force in such an agent as the Bishop of Stepney (Dr. Cosmo Lang, later Archbishop of Canterbury), or the *Daily Mail*." People were invited to lunch or dine, not for reasons of personal friendship, but according to their potential usefulness in helping to promote the Webbs' ideas. "It is an extraordinarily varied and stimulating society," wrote Beatrice. "The dominant note in our intercourse with these people is *social reconstruction*—in all the little dinners at Grosvenor Road and the *tête-à-tête* talk at other people's dinners—it is always round some project that the conversation ranges."

It was in this sense that the French historian Elie Halévy called them "disinterested Machiavellians," and that Leonard Woolf commented on "their integrity and unscrupulousness, the clearness with which they saw their limited objectives, and the pertinacity or even ruthlessness with which they pursued them." "They were so certain," he says, "of the rightness of the ends which they were pursuing that they did not worry very much about the means which they used to attain them." Beatrice herself realized the questionable nature of this aspect of their work. "London life," she noted in her diary, "with its constant clash of personalities—its attractions and repulsions, its manipulation and wire-pulling—is distracting and somewhat unwholesome." Twenty years later, as she reread her old diaries, she made the disarming admission that "reading of all our intrigues over the Education Bill was a shock to me, not so much the intrigues themselves as our evident pleasure in them! How far is intrigue possible?" she wondered.

What sort of individuals were these two indefatigable idealists, of whom their friend Bernard Shaw once declared that "only England could have produced them"? Beatrice Potter came from a wealthy middle-class family and was the youngest but one of nine sisters, all of whom married before her. Her father was a prosperous capitalist, a director of the Great Western Railway. Formerly a radical and a Unitarian, he had become a Tory and an Episcopalian. He was a cultivated man who appreciated a wide range of writers—among them figures as varied as Plato, Dante, Shakespeare, Burke, Carlyle, and Newman. Beatrice—his "little Bee"—had scant formal schooling: a fact for which in later years she felt grateful, since otherwise she might well have become a woman don. She had the usual social training of the Victorian girl of good family, and at the age of seventeen "came out" in society, taking part in the "London season" of 1876. Six years later, her mother having died, and all her sisters being married, she became her father's secretary and hostess and took over the supervision of his large household. It was, she used to say, her first training in social organization.

Her early life had been unhappy, since not even her father's affection could compensate for her mother's neglect and contempt. Notwithstanding Margaret Cole's brisk comment that there is "nothing for Freudians to lay hold on" in Beatrice Potter's life, her childhood would appear to be as perfect an example of what Jung called the Electra complex as even Victorian England could produce. The child was starved for affection, suffered from ill-health, and felt generally moody and resentful. Her loneliness, she later recalled, "was absolute."

As late as 1886, when she was twenty-eight, Beatrice Potter could write in her diary at Bournemouth: "I look out tonight on that hateful grey sea, the breaking and the vanishing of the surf on the shore; the waves break and vanish like my spasms of feeling; but they return again and again and behind them is the bottomless ocean of despair. Eight and twenty, and living without hope! Now and again deceived by a movement of physical energy, and then falling back on the monotony of despair. No future but a vain repetition of the breaking waves of feeling."

Besides these moods of melancholy, however, Beatrice Potter's early diary reveals an unusual precocity and a mature critical awareness. Over the life that flowed around her she cast a cold eye. Her respect for her father did not prevent her from seeing how aggressive, even unscrupulous, he could be where business was concerned: wealth was valued in his world chiefly as the basis for attaining power over others—"this degraded and coarsening scale of values," the young girl called it. Her exposure to the marriage market had disgusted her. "Dancing men in my time were chiefly fools," she tersely remarked. In later life she even quoted Proust on the insincerities of society.

Intensely introspective, for sixty years she kept an intimate diary of her thoughts and opinions. The portions of it which she published in 1926 show a ruthless self-honesty, together with a recognition of a tendency to vanity as her besetting weakness. She detected in herself a certain priggishness as well as an undue desire to impress others: such a desire, she realized acutely, as would prevent her receiving an accurate impression of them. At fourteen she was already reproaching herself: "Ah, vanity! vanity! Unfortunately for me my ruling passion. . . . Vanity, all is vanity. I feel that I have transgressed deeply, that I have trifled with the Lord. I feel that if I continue thus I shall become a frivolous, silly, unbelieving woman, and yet every morning when I wake I have the same giddy confident feeling and every night I am miserable."

From an early age she had been troubled by religious doubts. The Christian doctrine of atonement she felt to be morally repulsive. A country neighbor, Brian Hodgkin, an ex-Indian civil servant and Sanskrit scholar, interested her in Buddhism, which she found ethically superior to Christianity. The idea that each individual should devote himself to working out his own salvation she thought extremely selfish. Once, in Rome, at the age of twenty-two, she felt moved by the Catholic liturgy and experienced a strong temptation to commit what she called "intellectual (and perhaps moral) suicide"—i.e., to join the Church of Rome. Though she was later to label herself "an avowed agnostic," she wrote in 1881: "It is impossible for a woman to live in agnosticism." All her life she found consolation in prayer.

Intellectual emancipation came through her friendship with her father's friend the philosopher Herbert Spencer, whom in his last illness she nursed devotedly. Though she found repugnant the doctrine of uncompromising individualism which he preached, she learned from him the value of mental integrity and self-reliance, and the therapeutic power of work. He was also the first to urge her to publish her impressions of social conditions in England.

Early photographs of Beatrice Potter show a clear-eyed, handsome girl whose glance was candid and direct. From a Jewish grandmother she inherited a finely cut aquiline nose, and according to Consuelo Vanderbilt, later Duchess of Marlborough, she had "the beauty of an eagle." She walked and moved with the assurance of an aristocrat. Despite her formidable intellect, men found her attractive—at least on first acquaintance. Sir Robert Ensor, the Oxford historian, recalls her "almost unique combination of rare beauty and charm, with a piercing intellectual capacity." The Bloomsbury litterateur Sir Desmond MacCarthy, who knew her only after her marriage, recalled his first meeting with her, at a time when she was not yet famous. "I just thought her a fascinating woman," he wrote. "With her pale emphatic face, her dark-silver hair, aquiline features, fine eyebrows and bright brown eyes, she looked rather like a benevolent hawk, if you can imagine such a bird. Her voice also was extremely agreeable to my ear."

From her diaries it is evident that for years there existed a mutual attraction between herself and Arthur James Balfour, that dedicated bachelor and accomplished philanderer. Her charm was also felt by one who was as unlike Balfour as it is possible to imagine—Joseph Chamberlain. Both the languid and supercilious patrician and the hard, aggressive politician felt the magnetism of her personality. In 1883 Chamberlain, already twice a widower, was again set on marriage. Not until more than seventy years later did the world learn from Beatrice's diary the story of this curious episode.

In order that he might make known his intentions, the Potters invited Chamberlain to a house party. "At dinner, after some shyness," wrote Beatrice, "we plunge into essentials, and he begins delicately to hint his requirements. That evening and the next morning till after lunch we are on 'susceptible terms.' A dispute over state education breaks the charm." She had dared to controvert the great man's opinions.

As Miss Potter expressed her views, she could not help noticing how every minute Chamberlain's expression became

> . . . more gloomy and determined. . . . Not a suspicion of feeling did he show towards me. He was simply determined to assert his convictions. If I remained silent he watched my expression narrowly. I felt his curious scrutinizing eyes noting each movement as if he were anxious to ascertain whether I yielded to his absolute supremacy. If I objected to or ventured to qualify his theories or statements, he smashed objection and qualification by an absolute denial and continued his assertion. He remarked as we came in, that he felt as if he had been making a speech. I felt utterly exhausted; we hardly spoke to each other the rest of the day.

It is interesting to speculate upon what might have been the future both of Conservatism and of Fabianism had Beatrice Potter married Joseph Chamberlain in 1884; and it is curious to reflect that had this happened, she would have become the step-mother of Neville Chamberlain of Munich ill-fame.

When, in 1892, at the age of thirty-four, Beatrice Potter announced her intention of marrying Sidney Webb, whom she had known for two years, the sensation was immense. She had never dared to tell her father of her interest in Sidney. But within a week of her father's death, the engagement was announced. Six months later the marriage took place. Most of her relatives, including all but one of her married sisters, showed their disapproval. Her cousin Charles Booth, for whose great social survey she had worked, removed her from his list of acquaintances; Herbert Spencer dropped her as his literary executor. "It would not do for my reputation," he told her pompously, "that I should be openly connected with an avowed and prominent Socialist—that is impossible."

From a conventional point of view, Sidney Webb seemed to unite in his own person every conceivable handicap so far as marriage with a handsome heiress was concerned. In appearance he was small, insignificant, foreign-looking, and devoid of grace or charm. The son of an accountant, himself an obscure clerk in the civil service, he had neither social status nor money. His income not being sufficient to marry on, it was clear that he would be living on his wife's patrimony. He was a socialist and a cockney. His proletarian accent grated on patrician ears. "A grite wiste of spice" was how, according to Lady Cynthia Asquith, he once described Hampton Court. In addition to his other disadvantages, he was eighteen months younger than his bride. It is not surprising Beatrice Potter forbore to reveal her intentions to her father—that father whom now, perhaps, from a Freudian point of view, she was about to marry.

Being a clear-sighted person, Beatrice Webb was aware that her Sidney was no Adonis. In her journal, without finding them in the least embarrassing, she catalogued his physical oddities: the large head set on a tiny rotund body; the short tapering legs and little hands and feet; the slightly lisping speech; the unkempt black hair and shiny black suit the worse for wear. (In the portrait of the Webbs that Sir William Nicholson painted for the London School of Economics, Sidney's legs have been tactfully lengthened.)

Beauty, we know, is in the eye of the beholder, and Beatrice found "the little figure with a big head" the most romantic person in the world. Where others saw only someone "looking absurdly like a cockatoo, perched on a chair with his tiny feet scarcely reaching the ground and a high feather of hair standing up on his huge head," she beheld a combination of moral and intellectual gifts which she had never seen united in any other man, least of all in so autocratic and domineering a personage as Joseph Chamberlain.

> Sidney has no vanity or personal ambition, he never feels that he is not getting his deserts: his reward is perfect peace of mind and always-present consciousness of "good fortune"; he sits at his work, day in day out, doing every job as it comes along, leaving the result, as he often says, "in the lap of the gods."

For "the Other One," as she called him, was modest, kindly, and unselfish. Shy and unassuming, yet confident of his own powers, Sidney never boasted to others or got angry with them. He had an extremely clear mind, an immense store of knowledge, an extraordinary memory, and a boundless capacity for work. He used his gifts not for his own advancement, but to help mankind. He was calm and equable, free from snobbery, envy, and uncharitableness. He lacked all those faults of temperament which had beset Beatrice from childhood. He was, in fact, the incarnation of reason, and his lack of sensuality was congenial to the ingrained puritanism of her nature.

Nor was she mistaken in her estimate of her husband. Everyone who knew him concurred in it. Edward Pease, the secretary of the Fabian Society, who knew him for sixty years, affirmed that Sidney had not faults or weaknesses, only limitations—he lacked both a sense of humor and an aesthetic sense. Pease also found him free from snobbery. "He never talked in my hearing," says Pease, "about Rosebery or Balfour or any of the other important people who consulted him; he never laid claim to be the founder of British Socialism; . . . he liked to do things and write things, and did not care who got the credit . . . he never wrote to *The Times*." Thirty years later, when Sidney was in the Cabinet, he was the same person still. "The first impression he made on us," said Sir Drummond Shiels, who later worked under him at the Board of Trade, "was his great personal modesty; and then, quickly, we learned to respect his gift for analysis and the speed and thoroughness with which he got through a mass of hard work." "I never heard him speak an angry word," wrote F. W. Galton, for a number of years his secretary, "and he was a model of courtesy and kindness to all with whom he came in contact regardless of rank or position." "His triumphs left no sting," recalls Sir Robert Ensor. "If he proved you completely wrong, you never felt that it had been done to score off you." This last remark helps to explain Sidney's unrivaled success as a committee-man: he had not only superior knowledge, but an unobtrusive tact of persuasiveness as well. He had infinite patience; he never scolded or grumbled; and he was fertile in discovering the exact formula necessary to reconcile conflicting points of view.

His wife apart, no one knew Sidney better than Bernard Shaw, who in old age dashed off a lighthearted sketch of his lifelong friend and fellow worker. "The unassuming young cockney was in fact a prodigy. He could read a book as fast as he could turn the leaves, and remember everything worth remembering in it. Whatever country he was in, he always spoke the language with equal facility, though always in the English manner. He had gone through his teens gathering scholarships and exhibitions as a child gathers daisies."

According to Pease, Sidney had once read through the *Encyclopaedia Britannica* for a prize offered by the proprietors. Margaret Cole declares that his favorite reading was *Kelly's Directory* and the classified index to the London telephone book. When he went for a week's holiday by the seaside at Lyme Regis, he took along twenty books to pass the time; during a month at Cromer, according to his wife's reckoning, he "must have devoured some fifty or sixty books." Bernard Shaw recalls that Sidney once got through the first volume of Marx's *Das Kapital* in an hour, "for he was a miraculously quick reader. When I said, 'Well?' he replied, 'Scotland stands where it did,' the only time I ever heard him quote Shakespeare." Such a one naturally became a legend during his own lifetime. It was said that he could read and remember two hundred pages an hour, and that he had once got through *Chambers' Encyclopaedia* in the train between London and Edinburgh.

To expect humor from a "book in breeches" would be unreasonable. What Beatrice calls Sidney's "first token of personal regard" had been a pamphlet on the rate of interest. When shown a row of sweet peas he asked if they were the kind one ate. On one occasion his friend Emil Davies was surprised to hear that he had enjoyed a performance of *Parsifal*. "Our seats," Sidney explained, "were just behind Herbert Samuel's and during the interval we had a very interesting discussion on the incidence of sickness during pregnancy." Of course Beatrice knew that "the Other One" was absurd, but she loved him none the less—as she had always done since that memorable sunset long ago when they had walked the crowded streets of Glasgow together, "knocking up against drunken Scots," and had pledged their troth "with glory in the sky and hideous bestiality on the earth." For Sidney was her shield and protection against all that.

Sidney was in effect a thinking machine. He once told Kingsley Martin that he "had 'no inside'; he had never had a headache, never an attack of physical or spiritual indigestion." Beatrice herself rejoiced that he had "thank the Lord! no 'subconscious self' [!]: when not at work, or asleep, or talking, he reads-reads-reads—always ready for a loving word, given or taken. 'I am frightened at my own happiness,' he often says." Fortunately, her limitations, like her virtues, matched those of her husband. Just as his idea of a "rollicking good time" was to put in long hours on the Sankey Commission on the coal industry, so her notion of "a great lark" was to draft a *Constitution for the Socialist Commonwealth of Great Britain*. "The Other One" was always—to use her own phrase—"ridiculously happy," and she was happy because he was so. "One reason for my happiness with Sidney," she reflected after thirty-three years of marriage, "is that *he* does not seem to have any evil impulses; he does not want to get the best of every bargain; he has an instinctive liking for equality and a definite impulse towards inconspicuous and unrewarded service. But then as he is always saying," she added artlessly, "he has got my love and what does he want more?"

They were no doubt the oddest couple imaginable, and perhaps their friend Shaw was right in thinking that only England, that home of eccentricity, could have produced them. As Kingsley Martin suggests, Shaw may well have regarded them "in their old age as the nearest human equivalent . . . to the ancients in the last act of *Back to Methuselah*." Stories were current about "love among the Blue Books," and how the study of statistical abstracts would end in showers of kisses. Mrs. Webb's own diary provides ample illustration of such scenes of domesticity. "By nature and training economical in personal expenditure," she wrote of her husband after nearly twenty years of marriage, "abstemious without being faddy, untroubled by vanity or large appetite, he goes on his way of sane temperance, without temptation or scruple, and with one settled opinion that he wants *me* to indulge myself to the top of my bent! He is the most perfect of lovers, by night and by day, in work and in play, in health and in sickness!"

Fifteen years later nothing had changed. "On the twenty-third of June thirty-four years ago," she noted in 1926, "we were married and yesterday we celebrated it by spending the whole day together like two young lovers. . . . The Other One is extraordinarily well and happy." "One perpetual honeymoon, day after day, year after year," she called their life together, as old age began to press upon them. "Alas! in the course of nature, one will be left to struggle through the last days of life alone. The thought of the iminence of separation [she had yet fifteen years to live] adds a certain intensity to our love-making. 'Ridiculous old souls,' we say to one another as I curl up on his knees in the firelight."

Their dependence upon each other was well-nigh absolute. "I have been horribly depressed all this week," wrote Sidney during one of their brief separations, "with the *loneliness* of life except when you are there. I can't bear to think what it would be like if there were an accident to your train, or when you were bicycling, which left me really alone. I get thoroughly nervous and depressed and am miserable; unable to work, or read in the evenings, and wanting my colleague and companion, my helpmate and playmate." When he had an unexpected breakdown in 1922—even machines wear out—she worried about what would happen to him should anything happen to her. "What would Sidney do without me if he became an invalid? . . . There is no one to look after him, and he is so absurdly dependent on me. However, the Lord will provide." Her own health was never robust: she was troubled constantly by dyspepsia and insomnia. After periods of overwork, as during the sittings of the Poor Law Commission, she collapsed from exhaustion. "If it were not for my reliance on Sidney's strength," she wrote, "I should almost retire from business. I tremble to think how utterly dependent I am on him—both on his love and on his unrivalled capacity for 'putting things through.' When he is late, I get into a panic of fear lest some mishap has befallen him. This fear of losing each other is always present—more with me, I think, than with him."

Though history will undoubtedly identify the Webbs with the British Labour party, for many years they stood aloof from that party and were regarded by its leaders with distrust. Like other Fabians, they were willing to work for collectivism with any allies whose support might seem promising—with Chamberlain and Balfour, for example, among the Conservatives, or with Haldane, Lloyd George, or Churchill among the Liberals. Beatrice Webb, in particular, an intellectual and wellborn, was under no illusions as to the character of the working classes. Her view of them, unlike that of many socialist intellectuals, was realistic and unsentimental.

Meeting a number of miners at Chesterfield in 1895 she described them as "a stupid, stolid lot of men characterized by fairmindedness and kindliness—but oh! how dense. . . . How can one fear anything but Conservatism from the English Democracy? . . . They will depend exclusively on middle-class leadership for years to come." Seventeen years later, at the Newport Trades Union Congress, she saw no need to change her mind. "The bulk of the delegates," she commented, "are the same stolid stupid folk they have always been, mainly occupied with their Trade Union work, their own eating, drinking and smoking, and their family happenings: they take a placid, good-humoured and somewhat contemptuous interest in this or that 'new talk'—very much as a city man discusses the new toys that are sold on the pavement." During the First World War, her opinion remained unchanged. "There is very little that is sinister or actually corrupt," she wrote, "in the British Trade Union Movement, but there is appalling slackness, moral, intellectual and practical. . . . Will the British Labour Movement ever succeed in making use of middle-class brains?"

She was one of the first to sense another danger, which during the years to come was to loom larger and larger upon the horizon of labour. "The Trade Union Movement has become, like the hereditary peerage," she wrote in 1917, "an avenue to political power through which stupid untrained persons may pass up to the highest office if only they have secured the suffrages of the members of a large union. One wonders when able rascals will discover this open door to remunerative power." "The position of privilege, irrespective of capacity—a position occupied by many Trade Union officials," she declared a year later, "is becoming the most scandalous circumstance of the Labour Movement. It makes one despair of the Labour Party as an organ of Government. These men are not only incapable of doing the work themselves; they are not fit judges of other men's capacity. It is a mere lucky chance that they have Sidney at their disposal."

With the syndicalist movement the Webbs had even less sympathy than with trade unionism. Beatrice Webb, at least, appears never to have read Georges Sorel's famous *Reflections on Violence*. She abhorred alike the creed and the practitioners of the new gospel. "Syndicalism," she wrote in 1912, "has taken the place of the old-fashioned Marxism. The angry youth, with bad complexion, frowning brow and weedy figure, is now always a Syndicalist." Nor did the new movement in its English guise of guild socialism, as propounded by G. D. H. Cole and many of the younger Fabians, impress her much more favorably. Their philosophy, she judged, was one "which had its foundation in a contempt for intellect and an almost equal contempt for 'conduct.' It relied on impulse, more especially the impulse to violence."

As for the Labour party, it was "a poor thing, but our own," she commented wryly in 1912. "The Labour M.P.s are stupid, suspicious and timid," she wrote about this time, "and we have to work with them." "The Parliamentary Labour Party has not justified its existence either by character or by intelligence. . . . The cold truth is that the Labour members have utterly failed to impress the House of Commons and the constituencies as a live force, and have lost confidence in themselves." As a level-headed Fabian she even felt distaste for "the somewhat neurotic intellectuals of the Independent Labour Party."

Toward the end of the First World War, she viewed the labour movement as "a great lumbering mass moving forward towards the equalitarian state, slowly and irregularly, lurching now on one side, now on the other." It was at this point, nevertheless, that the Webbs linked their fortunes permanently with those of Labour; and through their manifesto *Labour and the New Social Order,* written in 1918, they committed that party finally to socialism. Already in the previous year, Beatrice had noted in her diary that Sidney had become "the intellectual leader of the Labour Party." "If he is not liked by the I.L.P.," she admitted, "they have confidence in his essential friendliness. And he is too old to excite jealousy in the young men."

With the two older parties they had now become completely disillusioned, and saw no hope of fruitful cooperation with either of them: on the one hand, there were "the hard-faced members who looked as if they had done well out of the war," and who, after the "Victory election" of 1918, overflowed the Conservative benches in the Commons; on the other, there were the coalition Liberals, now dominated by the unscrupulous opportunism of Lloyd George.

"Sidney and I are becoming every day more philosophical," wrote Beatrice in 1922. "We do not want a Labour Government before the Labour Movement has found its soul." Nor did she want Labour to come into office "by some fluke—some exceptionally advantageous combination of circumstances. I have no desire," she wrote, "for a fallacious and insincere acquiescence in Socialist doctrine." When, however, in 1923, for the first time in English history, Labour assumed office, the Webbs decided to support it. Yet, realizing as they did that Ramsay MacDonald's administration failed to fulfill the conditions that they had just laid down, their decision could not have been made without misgivings. Beatrice saw Labour in office as "a scouting expedition in the world of administration." "For Labour to accept the responsibilities of government," she wrote, "is a big risk: it may lead to immediate disaster." But she saw it also as an opportunity primarily for an "education in the realities of *political life,*" and in the assumption of political responsibility. Less than two years later, she frankly admitted her mistake.

About the new Prime Minister, whom they had known for more than twenty years, the Webbs had no illusions. Already in

1912, they had concluded that, whatever he might have been in his youth, Ramsay MacDonald had ceased to be a socialist. "I think he would welcome a really conclusive reason for joining the Liberal Party," wrote Beatrice just before the First World War. "He is bored with his Labour colleagues," she observed prophetically, "and attracted to Front Bench Liberals." Soon after the war, she heard MacDonald on one occasion angrily abusing the party, and suggesting that someone ought to "smash" it. At the Scarborough Conference of 1920, she saw him wandering about, "a restless and uneasy spirit," "bitterly malicious" to Tawney, Cole, and the younger intellectuals of the party.

Glaring as were MacDonald's defects, the Webbs saw no one else to take his place. Arthur Henderson, whom they genuinely respected and admired, was dull and prosy, completely lacking in personal magnetism. MacDonald was handsome in appearance, distinguished in bearing, and an accomplished orator. As in the case of Kitchener, he looked like a great leader even if he was not one. Beatrice, as we have seen, was not without personal preferences. "MacDonald," she wrote in 1914, "with his romantic figure, charming voice and clever dialectics, is more than a match for all those under-bred and under-trained workmen who surround him on the platform and face him in the audience. So long as he chooses to remain the leader of the Labour Party he will do so. . . . Owing to his personal distinction and middle-class equipment he is superior to all his would-be competitors." Partly for such reasons, the Webbs somewhat reluctantly accepted MacDonald's leadership in 1923; but in her diary, Beatrice noted acutely that it remained to be seen whether he was "a big enough man to rise superior to his personal hatreds and personal vanities."

Labour's assumption of office in 1923 revolutionized the private life of the Webbs, for Sidney, who the previous year had been elected to Parliament, now found himself at sixty-three a member of the Cabinet. Had he wished, he could almost certainly have got into the House before this. In 1899, Herbert Gladstone and Lord Haldane had urged him to stand as a Liberal for Deptford, "all expenses to be paid by the party." But Beatrice, partly for selfish reasons, which she recognized, had resisted the idea.

Now that the moment for self-sacrifice had arrived, to his wife's surprise Sidney found that he was enjoying himself immensely. Beatrice was a little taken aback by "his almost boyish pleasure." "I really believe," she added almost incredulously, "he is going to enjoy Parliament. . . . He is amazingly young for his age." Her own doubts were substantial. "To enter Parliament for the first time at sixty-three years of age," she reflected, "is a risky adventure from the standpoint alike of health and reputation. It would be a foolhardy risk if the need within the Parliamentary Labour Party for steady-going intellectuals were not so great." Somehow she was not quite pleased at this unexpected turn of events. "Sidney is like a boy going for his first term at a public school!" she exclaimed. "This light-heartedness, odd for a man of sixty-three, is due to the youthfulness of the party"— a palpable rationalization. "How long this phase of youthful keenness will continue, when exactly it will give way to physical fatigue and mental nausea," she added dubiously, it "is difficult to foresee." A year later, when Sidney was a member of the Cabinet, she admitted rather grudgingly that he was "still in the humour of a schoolboy: last year it was before his first term at a public school: today it is looking forward to acting for the first time as 'prefect.' He is excited, naively excited, really enjoying his life hugely in a simple sort of way, but he has no kind of self-importance or self-consciousness, and very little anxiety or diffidence." "What a joke, what an unexpected and slightly ludicrous adventure," was Sidney's description of his experience.

Unfortunately, "the Other One" was not a success either in Parliament or in the Cabinet. Neither as a speaker nor as a debater did he distinguish himself. His voice was thin, and in his nervousness he tended to gabble. Looking down from the ladies' gallery, Beatrice watched her husband's performance with apprehension and "with a sort of motherly interest." "He was nervous," she reported, "and the jeers of the Tory back benches . . . threw him off his subject—he repeated himself and failed to make all his points; and sat down without making his last words intelligible to the reporter for Hansard. . . . But it was a sincere utterance and based on thought and knowledge, and he was simple and humble in his recognition of partial failure."

Sidney's performance in Parliament was not unlike that of John

Stuart Mill nearly sixty years earlier. Certain Tories, "flown with wine and insolence," coming into the House after dinner, found something irresistibly comical in the appearance on the front Opposition bench of the odd little figure with the large head and the goatee, and to Beatrice's helpless indignation greeted him with cries of "Nannie." Once she heard him speak for one and a half hours on the Local Government Bill. "To me it is a nerve wracking ordeal," she confessed.

> I am far more agitated than if I were speaking myself. Any little imperfection in delivery or in the arrangement of his subject matter —any little slip in tact or unnecessary repetition of phrases—makes me wince as if my nerves were being cut one by one.

The very qualities that made Sidney a model civil servant militated against his success in the Cabinet. He was expert in providing accurate information and in giving advice, but not in assuming executive responsibility. The role he preferred was that of the *éminence grise;* and, as his wife had long remarked, he always had "a rooted antipathy to leadership." Watching him in the Cabinet, she observed that "in his heart of hearts," he remained "essentially a detached observer without any keenness for one way over another, or to his own continued participation in the exercise of power."

In the second Labour government of 1929, as Secretary of State for the Colonies, Sidney found himself elevated to the peerage as Baron Passfield and confronted with complicated problems in faraway places such as Palestine and Kenya. Since, like Bentham, he had not the slightest understanding of group emotion or of the feeling of the herd, it is not surprising that he was a total failure. It was small consolation to reflect that the Colonial Office had been the grave of more than one reputation— and Sidney was not, in any case, the man to find comfort in invidious comparisons.

The transformation, at the royal touch, of the erstwhile "socialist agitator" into a peer was something that could scarcely have happened anywhere but in England. Yet, though Sidney had thus surprisingly been metamorphosed into Baron Passfield, his wife obstinately refused to claim either the title or the privileges of peerage. She was resolved to remain plain Mrs. Sidney

Webb. "The Conservatives," she reported with some glee, "are furious with my refusal of the title, and regard it as a mischievous attack on the prestige of titles or an insult to the 'fountain of honour.'" Ramsay MacDonald took her action almost as a personal affront. Mrs. Webb, however, in what she called "this little attack on the social prestige of the House of Lords," was being more than just mischievous. "By merely passing over my right to use a title," she remarked, "I help to undermine the foundations of British snobbishness. . . . An honour ignored is an honour deflated." The affair, however, was a nine-day's wonder, for as soon as he left office, Lord Passfield became Sidney Webb once more.

Even before this, the problem of etiquette had arisen, for the wives of Cabinet members were expected to attend royal levées and to curtsey to royalty. But Mrs. Webb had never been impressed by the court and she felt in no mood now, as she put it, "to cringe before these admirable automatons." "That mark of servility—the curtsey!" she snapped. "It is all very ludicrous; though not altogether unimportant."

Like Walter Bagehot, she had come to consider the monarchy "an anachronism but a useful anachronism," but she had no wish to be presented at court, finding "the rather absurd background of the Royal Robots . . . as unreal as the Beggar's Opera." She regretted, however, to hear from Ethel Snowden, the wife of the Chancellor of the Exchequer and herself a notorious social climber, that the King and Queen were "seriously annoyed" at her refusal "in spite of seven years of invitations," to present herself at Buckingham Palace. To make amends for seeming rudeness, in 1930 she consented to appear at dinner at the palace as "the Lady Passfield," wearing "a high-necked, long-sleeved grey chiffon velvet which I have been wearing," she emphasized in her diary, "for six months at every dinner I have attended." She even had "two or three minutes perfunctory talk" with Queen Mary, "a fine figure of a woman," though what they discussed is not recorded. "How I loathe London Society in all its aspects," she concluded.

The only aspect of her husband's parliamentary career that Beatrice enjoyed was the opportunity to become acquainted with the voters of Seaham Harbour, the Durham mining constituency that Sidney represented in the House from 1922 to 1929. (Members of Parliament do not have to reside in their constituencies.) "There is a strange irony," she wrote with some pride, "in these simple-minded miners, living in a remote backwater, seeking out and persistently pressing into the service the most astute and subtle—and, be it added, the least popular leader of the Labour and Socialist Movement. The explanation is that these leading men in these isolated pit villages are readers of books and not hearers of revivalist speeches and propagandist lectures."

Seaham Harbour was described by their close friend Susan Lawrence as being "a town on a beautiful coast,"

> and all defiled with soot in the air, old boots, dirty paper and broken tins on the ground; romantic ravines looking like newly-made railway cuttings, no music, no public library, no hospital; the large unkempt picture palace in a back street, and suspicious smells pervading back courts and closed-up corners—railway lines and coal trucks everywhere. The only civilized buildings are the schools —Hail to the Education Act—the Saviour of the industrial districts.

Beatrice herself found "most depressing of all . . . those little groups of spindle-legged and pale-faced boys with vacant expressions loitering round public-houses and at street corners at all times, day and night. . . . All the same," she thought, "the very dreariness of these pit villages, the absence of any vitalizing ferments, makes our task as representatives easier to fulfil and richer in result than it would be in a more civilized constituency." "The women have no leisure and not much sleep," she observed on her first visit, "with the three, sometimes four, shift system and the perpetual coal dust to grapple with. In consequence, every woman is short and pale. There is a lot of money flying about, and much spent in alcohol and betting. The life seems, in fact, to be completely materialistic, though fairly respectable. There are groups of fervent chapel folk. Here and there," she noticed with pleasure, "is a bookish miner, usually a secularist, with quite a large bookcase filled with the well-known poets and classics—a little philosophy and more economics."

Sidney lectured on politics and economics to receptive audiences in the pit villages outside the collieries. "These simple-minded miners listen to his words," wrote Beatrice, "as the words not of a politician but of a teacher." In one village, "the miners' hall was packed   men and boys were standing outside. There   something infinitely pathetic in the dead silence and intense   they listened to his long and carefully   of the causes of paralysed trade." When   in Parliament over a year, she reported: "The miners have become genuinely attached to their member: they are proud of him; they trust him and they feel that he is 'their man'—that they have put him into Parliament."

Beatrice, too, lectured in the villages to respectful and attentive audiences. At the end of an hour's talk, she would be questioned closely about such things as "our present relations to Russia, the character of the Soviet Government, the capital levy, the Treaty of Versailles, the cure for unemployment, the possibilities of prospective tariffs, the state of education. I answered to the best of my ability exactly as I should have done at the School of Economics." "One thing is certain," wrote a Durham miner (though one would never guess the fact from Beatrice herself), "it was that Mrs. Webb gripped the women much more than he ever did. There was the real stuff of the north when she addressed meetings, and she left a memory which will never be forgotten by those now living."

She started a monthly letter dealing with current problems, which proved to be a great success among the miners' wives; and she established a free circulating library of some two hundred books. "There is something very touching," she wrote, "in these few hundred miners' wives, with here and there a professional woman, gathering round me with a sort of hero-worship." The Webbs took lodgings in the town and stayed there from time to time, feeling quite at home between the peaceful view of the North Sea and "the twinkling lights of the collieries on the horizon of the hills surrounding us."

The chief task to which Beatrice devoted her later years was the preparation for posthumous publication of the diaries in which she had laid bare her inmost thoughts, yearnings, and wrestlings with the spirit. For there were depths within her, and depths within depths, to which Sidney, with all his loving companionship, could never penetrate. Each of us is indeed alone: it was a truth of which Beatrice was more poignantly aware than her husband. For more than forty years she had been accustomed to use her diary as a safety valve for her emotions. "It is during sleepless hours in the night," she wrote in 1926, "that I get things down in my diary; during the day I am either at work, or reading newspapers. . . . I have no inclination to write. But in the loneliness and silence of the night, impressions and thoughts begin to fly through my brain and if I refuse to express them, I begin to worry. Also to begin to write is an excuse for a cup of tea!"

In 1926, under the title of *My Apprenticeship*, she published the first installment of what was really her spiritual autobiography. Though Sidney was apprehensive about the advisability of such intimate revelations, the book had an immediate success.

Just as André Gide will probably be better known for the self-revelation of his journals than for his novels, so Beatrice Webb is likely to be remembered by posterity more for her diaries than for the sociological works to which she and her husband devoted their lives. As a young woman she had once expressed the desire to be a novelist. Her diaries show that she was splendidly equipped with at least one talent necessary to the writer: the faculty of subtle and penetrating characterization involving a wide range of human beings.

Her gift for epigram was as keen as her power of observation. "To have unpopular convictions," she wrote, "is bad enough: to run away from them is fatal." At the Trade Union Congress of 1926, she observed acutely, "G. D. H. Cole, A. J. Cook, J. R. MacDonald, the intellectual fanatic, the inspired idiot and the accomplished substitute for a leader, are singularly antagonistic to each other." Her impression of the congress itself was one of "apathy tempered by pessimism." At the Labour party headquarters in London, her observant eye fell on "the little dwarf-like Gillies—an honest, over-sensitive and obstinate-minded but well-informed little Glasgow Fabian." When Lord Granville, Gladstone's Foreign Secretary, who had mistrusted her as a socialist, approached her at a party because she happened to be wearing "a pretty black gown," but could make nothing of her talk of labor questions, she commented acidly: "Mental insignificance, joined to great political position, is irritating to a democratic mind." Pomposity, when encountered in such a one as Viscount Long of Wraxall, she demolished with a single stroke: "Long is a loud-voiced persistent creature, who talks his colleagues down at Cabinet and committee meetings and is in touch with the commoner kind of obscurant Tory." Her observations could be trenchant, as when she reported of the Manchester Town Council: "The abler administrators have no pretension to ideas, hardly any to grammar: they are merely hardheaded shop-keepers."

Though interested primarily in social types, she never lost sight of the single individual; and here her intuition was quick to divine inner resemblances between the physical and the moral nature, between the outer and the inner aspect of those whom she met. This insight is the more curious since in her formal reading in literature—for example, in the eighteenth-century novel—she was more concerned with sociological significance than with the characters themselves.

Her own diaries are memorable for their richness and variety of human portraiture. They constitute, in fact, a wonderful picture gallery of all sorts and conditions of people in Victorian, Edwardian, and Georgian England. They cover the whole range of society from Buckingham Palace to the dreary provincial cities and the mining villages crouched beneath the slag heaps. They are, in the phrase of H. L. Beales, "pure gold to the historian." Among her most notable portrayals are the incisive and masterly sketches of such well-known figures as John Burns, Graham Wallas, Lord Rosebery, Lord Haldane, Edward VII, Lord Morley, Herbert Spencer, Bertrand Russell, the Irish poet A.E., Logan Pearsall Smith, Rabindranath Tagore, Lord Balfour, Lloyd George, Kerensky, Bishop Creighton, Lord Milner, Winston Churchill, Leonid Krassin, Ramsay MacDonald, "Jimmy" Thomas, A. J. Cook, Sir Walter Citrine, and Sir Stafford Cripps. Such a list of names, incidentally, reveals the astonishing range of her acquaintance.

It was a familiar saying of the Webbs that people could be divided into two categories: the A's and the B's. The former were aristocratic, anarchistic, and artistic; the latter were bourgeois, bureaucratic, and benevolent. Strangely enough, though the Webbs were a formidable example of the B's, whom they naturally preferred to the A's as more useful to society, Beatrice herself was by temperament an aristocrat.

When on one occasion they dined at the Asquiths, and there met the Earl and Countess of Lytton, Beatrice found them "a charming young couple with the delightful gracious deference of the well-bred aristocrat." According to Desmond MacCarthy, she was partial to the phrase "well-bred." The youthful Algernon Cecil, grandson of the Marquess of Salisbury, charmed her by "that delightful modesty of manner and easy deference which robbed the creed of any *appearance* of class insolence or religious intolerance." She was, in fact, as well aware as Henry James (whom she "heartily disliked," a dislike that was reciprocated) of the difference between the classes and the masses, between the social distinction of conservatism and the lack of manners of dissent. "What makes one despair," she wrote, "is the atmosphere in which these leaders live. Their lives are so rounded off by culture and charm, comfort and power, that the misery of the destitute is as far off as the savagery of central Africa." At times this awareness made her ruthless. Thus, when she dined with Lord Lucas "in his great mansion in St. James's Square," she found him "an attractive creature, dreamy and vague, with a charming veracity and gentleness of nature." "But, from our point of view," she added, "he is no good. He is steeped in his father's individualist philosophy. . . . Moreover, he has no notion of work. I fear that he must be written off," she concluded, "as useless though not dangerous." One can almost hear the ax fall.

It was the aristocrat as much as the Fabian in Mrs. Webb who was ashamed of British Socialists when she saw them *en masse*—"the callow youths and maidens of the I.L.P. and the S.D.F.," as she scornfully termed them. We have already seen what a cold eye she cast upon the flower of syndicalist youth, and when she met her first proletarian socialists, she was disgusted "with the dirty personalities with which they pelt each other; with their envy and malice against any leader, and with their ignorance, one might almost say their hatred and contempt of facts."

In her strictures upon the middle classes and the workers, and particularly in her distaste for certain Nonconformist types, one is reminded of Matthew Arnold. Her criticisms of English society recall in 1900 those of *Culture and Anarchy* a generation before. "To us public affairs seem gloomy; the middle classes are materialistic, and the working class stupid, and in large sections sottish, with no interest except in racing odds, while the Government of the country is firmly in the hands of little cliques of landlords and great capitalists, and their hangers-on." When she attended a women's conference in Manchester in 1897, the people she liked best were the bishops' wives, and she regretted "parting company with them. In spite of their party they are large-minded—take broad views, and have the pleasant manners of the great world . . . very different from the narrow, intriguing, fanatical little Nonconformists." Perhaps it was "the predominance of the Lyttelton family," she thought, that gave "the governing body of the conference its sweet and wholesome flavour."

For her as for Arnold, "Philistine" and "materialist" were two of the strongest terms of reprobation. "The lie of materialism," she wrote, was "far more pernicious and more utterly false than the untruths which seem to me to constitute the Christian formula of religion." Arnold himself could not have done a neater job of dissection on a Philistine than that she did on Sir Robert Perks, an engineer—and Methodist. "Imperial Perks" was the agent of Lord Rosebery, a patrician whom Mrs. Webb distrusted, while recognizing his "personal distinction, originality and charm." But Perks!—"a repulsive being—hard, pushing, commonplace, with no enthusiasms except a desire to have his 'knife into the Church'—a blank materialist although a pious Protestant, who recognizes no principle beyond self-interest; . . . how could we work with such a loathsome person!" She shuddered "to think of Perks as an English Cabinet Minister: Ugh! The very notion of it degrades political life. . . . Perks is an unclean beast."

Yet when she observed the nobility at close quarters, like Arnold she was compelled to admit that though it might have sweetness, it had precious little light. In the early days of their marriage, the group of youthful aristocrats known as the "Souls"

—"the brilliant but silly 'Souls,' " as Beatrice called them—had shown a passing interest in the Webbs. Among the "Souls," the men were noted for their independence and wit, and the women for their beauty. " 'Souls' good to look at," wrote Beatrice in her diary,

> gushing and anxious to strike up acquaintanceship with an unconventional couple. A charming pair—the Alfred Lytteltons—graceful, modest, intelligent, and with the exquisite deference and ease which constitutes good breeding. But to me the 'Souls' would not bring "the peace that passeth understanding," but a vain restlessness of tickled vanity. One would become quickly satiated.

Seated next to Sidney once at luncheon, the handsome Lady Desborough, a leading member of the "Souls," exerted herself to charm him. But if Beatrice found Lady Desborough charming, her husband did not. In fact, he thought her definitely "unpleasing with her artificial and insincere talk and silly trick of shutting her eyes at you." Years later, the Webbs met the Desboroughs at a "superlatively good dinner" given by the Asquiths, complete with "flunkeys" and "Second Empire" atmosphere. "Lady Desborough, Margot, Mrs. Lester and Lady Dickson Poynder," wrote Beatrice, "were all very *decolletée* and highly adorned with jewels. The conversation aimed at brilliancy . . . we might all have been characters brought on to illustrate the ways of modern society—a twentieth-century Sheridan's play. . . . We came away feeling half-flattered that we had been asked, half-contemptuous of ourselves for having gone. And not pleased with the entourage of a democratic Minister."

What Mrs. Webb admired was the idea of nobility more than its physical embodiments. In thinking of an aristocratic order, like Burke she stressed its responsibilities more than its privileges, its duties more than its rights. *Noblesse oblige* was to her the only conceivable justification for social privilege. "Hardly anything," says Desmond MacCarthy, "not even fundamental economic injustices, roused her indignation more than the bad manners of the rich towards the poor, of those who gave orders towards those who took them." The word of most "violent abhorrence in her vocabulary" was the word "insolence," especially when it referred to the bad manners of the upper classes.

The Webbs' position in society was singular: their friends included all classes, from peers to workingmen. Above all they prized their own independence. "I suppose it is well to be on terms with these people," wrote Beatrice in 1903 on returning from a dinner at the Asquiths, where they had met among others the Lyttons, the Birrells, and Lord Hugh Cecil, "but I came back from their society to our shabby little home and regular hard work with a deep sigh of gratitude that I am an outsider, and have not the time or energy to become one of them, even if they opened wide their doors."

Their close friends were limited in number, and they could not easily be defined in class terms. "Our small circle of acquaintances," wrote Beatrice in the early days of their marriage, "is pleasant enough: easy-going, unconventional and somewhat distinguished. We are sought but do not seek—the most agreeable way of seeing people. Not that 'society' pays us continuous attention: we are only casually found out by persons belonging to the great world—we live in a pleasant back-water of our own. But our social status, such as it is, is distinctly advantageous to the local government enquiry: it enables us to see any official from whom we want information." Their wide range of social contacts and their emancipation from social prejudice meant that they were free from the vice of snobbery. Sidney had no class sense whatever, whereas Beatrice could recognize quality wherever she encountered it—whether in a miner's wife or in a countess. Mrs. J. R. Clynes, the unassuming wife of the Labour politician, delighted her by her natural good sense. "A woman of strong character and good intelligence," wrote Beatrice. "She dresses immaculately: looks a duchess!"

Once, just after a weekend spent with Arthur Balfour in his country home, they left "the glamour and charm of Whittinghame" and cycled over to Berwick-on-Tweed. There they lived in "dirty stuffy lodgings," and spent "seven hours a day working at records in a cellar without windows and lit only by three gas jets. . . . But the hours in the cellar," wrote Beatrice, "passed rapidly in the fascinating pursuit of tearing the facts out of volume after volume of MS. minutes." From Berwick they went on to Alnwick, where they again "reposed in dirt—this time at the inn," and studied the records of the borough. Their social investigation at Alnwick, however, was not confined to the past.

One day they lunched with the Duke of Northumberland, the embattled walls of whose castle towered above the little town. In the feudal home of the Percys, Beatrice sensed "the atmosphere of a tomb in which several worthy and one distinguished soul (the poor Duchess) were shrinking up, day by day, into puppets walking their respective parts in the ducal establishment, with a strange combination of grandiose self-complacency and dull melancholy." "The stupid stiff Duke" was afraid of these unwanted socialist guests and sought to keep them at a distance. The castle officials, Beatrice observed, behaved in different ways to the townspeople, the superior ones being insolent, the inferior ones obsequious. "There is a heavy atmosphere of snobbishness," she noticed, "all folk having their eyes fixed on the castle, fearful of its displeasure and anxious for the slightest sign of its approval . . . the Duke, who is seated on a pinnacle, is just a stupid, commonplace Englishman—made stupider and more commonplace by his lifelong entombment in the magnificence of the Percys of Northumberland."

Beatrice Webb, as Kingsley Martin acutely observed, was "a complex mixture of aristocratic superiority, intellectual impatience and puritanical morals." That she was prudish in matters of sex is evident throughout the diary. "We have little faith in the average sensual man." In one form or another this idea occurs often in her writings. Another of her favorite sayings, sometimes repeated by Sidney, was that "marriage is the wastepaper basket of the emotions." When he heard her say this, Lowes Dickinson, the Cambridge philosopher, at once decided not to become a Fabian. In love, as in everything else, the Webbs believed in planning, and in "the inevitability of gradualism." No one could have disagreed more strongly than they with Bertrand Russell's dictum that freedom to follow impulse is a large part of human happiness.

The Webbs were repelled by modern novelists like Aldous Huxley and D. H. Lawrence. "There is a preference," Beatrice wrote, "for men and women who combine a clever intellect with unrestrained animal impulses. Analytic descriptions of these lascivious and greedy creatures, with their wit and clever dialectics . . . abound in the modern novel." The promiscuity of H. G. Wells was by no means to their taste, and though they

were too intelligent and too well-bred to be censorious in matters of private morality, their disapproval of Wells's personal
habits no doubt played a part in the notorious quarrel that led
to his leaving the Fabian Society.

In his novel *The New Machiavelli* (1911), Wells took a malicious revenge by making Altiora and Oscar Bailey (Beatrice and
Sidney Webb) and their "horrid little house" not only ridiculous
but hateful as well. They were represented as misers with a
horror of spending, Philistines with a horror of beauty, and
puritans with a horror of sex. Beings without lust, their ideal
was a state of anemia. With regard to the love affairs of others,
they were "malicious, spying and censorious." Altiora Bailey had
dark eyes without depth, a clear hard voice, and talked in a
high tenor. "Her soul was bony, and at the base of her was
a vanity gaunt and greedy." It says much for the charity and
self-assurance of the Webbs that they appear to have borne no
grudge against Wells for this caricature in which there was
sufficient truth to make it wounding.

Strange as it may seem, Mrs. Webb's puritanism was one of
the chief reasons for that admiration for Soviet Russia which
grew on her late in life. Unlike the rank and file of the working
class in England, the Webbs had not greeted the Russian Revolution of 1917 with fervor; on the contrary, they had regarded it
with suspicion. On meeting Litvinov, the first Bolshevik ambassador to London, they treated him patronizingly. "He is not a
bad sort," wrote Beatrice, "a crude Marxist in his views, without
experience in administration or knowledge of political or economic facts." How could a communist, one wonders, have had
"experience in administration" before 1917, when the inside of
a prison was all that he was likely to have seen of any government building? At this time Mrs. Webb was wont to refer to
communists as "simple-minded advocates of physical force," or
as "the Proletarian Fanatics at Moscow." Communist philosophy
was based on "a contempt for intellect and an almost equal contempt for 'conduct.'" Russia was nothing but "a servile state run
by fanatics." The Webbs declined an invitation to go and see for
themselves what was happening, lest they be held there as hos-
tages. They went, however, in 1920 to the Geneva conference of

the Second Socialist International and were gratified to hear "a defiant repudiation of the Russian Soviet system and the dictatorship of the Communist Party."

The British Communist party—"these little wrecking bands of Communists"—exasperated the Webbs even more than did the Bolsheviks in Russia—perhaps because it was so much nearer home. The Webbs ridiculed extreme left-wing leaders, such as the "impossible" Tom Mann, or the "hysterical" A. J. Cook. The latter, who was spokesman for the coal miners, they believed was "bound to become the tool of the Communist Party." They strongly urged the labour movement to purge itself of any Soviet taint. "The Communist gang should be once more discredited—the blister pricked—even at the cost of risking loss of blood." They equated Bolshevism and Fascism—the two "creed-autocracies," "two sides of the worship of force and the practice of cruel intolerance"—and hoped that Britain would steer an even course between the two. "*We* regard Soviet Russia and Fascist Italy," wrote Beatrice pontifically in 1926, "as belonging to one and the same species of government."

As early as 1925, they had foreseen the possibility that China might one day go communist. "The Gospel of Karl Marx," wrote Beatrice that year, "with its complete materialism translated by the Russians into an autocratic Government may yield a basis for orderly life among the millions of China." In 1932, she was greatly impressed by Pearl Buck's novel *The Good Earth*, "the finest piece of sociological fiction that I have read since *An American Tragedy*." It confirmed her impression of China, which she had briefly visited in 1911, as a completely "dead civilization—a wasted land, devastated by floods or droughts, where man is cruel and nature uncontrolled; where 'women are for use and boys for pleasure'; where . . . religious emotion is non-existent; where war, pestilence and famine rage. What the Chinese need," she concluded, "is a new culture—that would inspire an altruistic code of conduct and a passion for applying knowledge to life. Russian Communism is the only hope for China."

China, however, was one thing and Britain another. At the very time she was writing thus about the future of China, she was repelling more vigorously than ever the idea that Britain might find a solution to her problems in communism. "Compared to the pecuniary dishonesty of the U.S.A. political world and the fanatical brutality of Russian Communism," she wrote as late as 1931, "the Labour Party and, I think, the Liberal and Conservative party organizations are Angels of Light."

What, then, happened within a single year to make the Webbs change their minds so completely, to predispose them in favor of Russia, and above all, to make them so anxious to see that country for themselves? In 1932, not realizing that she was on the eve of the greatest adventure of her life, Beatrice Webb, then an old lady of seventy-four, was convinced that her days were over.

> Our personal life flows smoothly to its end with a settled conviction, on my part, that for me the end is not far off. Every night when I embrace my boy and give him my blessing before I retire to my room there is sadness in my heart at the thought that some day—and a day that cannot be far off—it will be our last embrace and that one or other of us will have to live for days, months, possibly a decade of years, alone, bereft of our comrade in work, thought and happiness.

She felt unusually old and tired. "For it seems to me," she confided to her diary in 1925, "that I may be sinking into the dim twilight of old age." Worse than this, for the first time in her life she was beginning to doubt herself. "Have I any longer any convictions?" she wondered. "Am I becoming a mere shadow of an intellect?" Questions such as these had never occurred to her before. "My one and only trouble," she complained in 1931, "is that I am *always* physically and mentally tired." Such moods as these, however, were transient, and her resiliency was great. "We must not allow ourselves to become depressed," she wrote on another occasion,

> because our careers are behind us: when you are nearing seventy that is inevitable. The bitter fate is to feel baulked when you are young or in the prime of life: we have had our cake and we have thoroughly enjoyed eating it. Now we must be content to help others to do likewise.

Ever since the First World War, she had feared for the stability of European culture. "I have lost my day-dreams, I have only the nightmare left," she lamented in 1926, "the same sort of nightmare I had during the Great War—that European civilization is in the course of dissolution." The world economic depression of the early thirties confirmed such fears. "It is the catastrophic failure of the motive of pecuniary self-interest today," she wrote on the eve of setting out for the U.S.S.R., "*the suicide of profit-making capitalism* as manifested by the world *depression,* that turns men's thoughts to Russia."

At home, the rout of the Labour party in the general election of 1931, and its betrayal by its own leader, Ramsay MacDonald, completed her disillusionment with English politics. Even before that crisis she had reflected: "Our usefulness to the Labour Party is exhausted; all that remains to be done is to retire gracefully and graciously without taking sides in the coming struggle between the discredited Right and the inflated Left. . . . *We* are too old and tired to be of use. My sympathies incline towards the Left, but I know too little about what is going on to have any opinion worth having." In her mood of general despondency, she had even come to question that cherished creed of a lifetime—"the inevitability of gradualness." As Margaret Cole remarks, she had in effect ceased to care "whether the British Labour Party lived or died."

The Webbs' sympathetic interest in the Soviet Union had first been awakened in 1930 by "two first-rate books by Americans"—*Humanity Uprooted* by Maurice Hindus, and *Soviet Russia* by W. H. Chamberlin. In this year also, Sidney, as a member of the Labour government, showed his wife "a remarkable report" from Sir Esmond Ovey, then British ambassador to Moscow. Reading carefully through this document, Beatrice felt how "clearly this acute diplomatist—a professional diplomatist—has been converted to the general outlook of Russian Communism as a practical creed and one the rest of the world will have to tolerate if not to adopt." Then came the return from Russia of their close friend Bernard Shaw—an enthusiastic convert to communism. Unable to resist his own gift for paradox, the "supreme charmer," as Beatrice called him (and all her life she was perhaps half in love with that half-human "sprite"), who had found in Joan of Arc the first Protestant, now discovered in Russia that Stalin had "recognized the inevitability of gradualness." [!] Ten days later the Webbs were defending the Soviet Union against the Snowdens' accusations (which they themselves had hitherto believed) that it was nothing but "a cruel slave state."

Before they went to Russia in 1932, the Webbs were already emotionally converted. For Beatrice had found at last what she had been always seeking—a new creed and a new puritanism, combined in one religion.

The idea of communism as a religion was quite explicit in her mind. "This Spiritual Power knows no boundaries," she declared. "It claims, like the Roman Church, to be a world-power and opens its arms to all peoples who subscribe to its creed and accept its discipline. Almost without intention on the part of its founders, the Communist Party has taken on the characteristic features of a religious order; it has its Holy Writ, its prophets and its canonized saints; it has its Pope, yesterday Lenin and today Stalin; it has its code of conduct and its discipline; it has its creed and its inquisition. As yet it has no rites or modes of worship. Will it develop ritual as did the followers of Auguste Comte?"

In May 1932 the Webbs arrived in Leningrad, and stayed in Russia for about sixty days, traveling as far as Stalingrad. Beatrice, especially, was in a lighthearted mood, happier at seventy-four than she had been for years. "What does it matter what two old 'Over Seventies' think, say or do," she asked, "so long as they do not whine about getting old and go merrily on, hand in hand, to the end of the road?" In Russia, though they went at their own expense, they were treated as honored guests and discovered, as Margaret Cole says, that their name had "an almost mythical prestige." Their previous attacks on communism were overlooked by the Soviet leaders, who preferred instead to remember that Lenin, in his Siberian exile, had translated into Russian their *History of Trade Unionism.*

Three years after their return to England, in what proved to be the most popular work they ever wrote, the Webbs published their conclusions about Russia. Both in England and in the United States, their book *Soviet Communism: A New Civilization?* exerted considerable influence. In the judgment of Bernard Shaw, "it was the first really scientific analysis of the Soviet State" that had yet been made. Certainly the organization and structure of Russian society and industry were studied by the Webbs more minutely and more comprehensively than they had ever been by foreigners before. Aspects of Soviet social planning and scientific achievement which had been little known in the West were now described and defended. To many who had been conditioned by propaganda to regard Russia as nothing more than a gigantic slave state, the antithesis of civilized society, the book came as a revelation. Its success was due in part to the previous excesses of anti-Soviet propaganda in the capitalist press. More than a quarter of a century later, it is difficult even to conceive the novelty and audacity of the challenge flung down by the Webbs—that Russia had actually created a new civilization, one such as the world had never seen before.

The limitations of the book are today as obvious as its merits and should have been so even at the time when it first appeared. While it purported to be a purely scientific study, it was also a piece of special pleading. Its value as an example of the inductive method applied to the study of society was partly vitiated by certain preconceptions held, as we have seen, by the Webbs before they even left England. The work was, in fact, propaganda on a massive scale, clothed in academic dress.

Apart from the basic fact that their minds were made up in advance, the Webbs suffered from certain defects as observers of a strange society. They were poor judges of human beings *en masse* and insensitive to group emotions. They were more interested in facts and statistics than in the feelings of what Beatrice dismissed as "the average sensual man." Only such insensibility can explain her belief that Russia was a real political democracy, and that Stalin was like "any other Prime Minister ultimately dependent on the votes of the people." The dictator, she declared emphatically, was not a dictator. The sycophantic worship of Stalin which so disgusted André Gide a few years later, and which perhaps did more than anything else to disillusion him about communism, passed unnoticed by the Webbs. "The idolization of Stalin," Mrs. Webb declared in 1942, "has largely ceased to exist in the Soviet Union of today."

In their two months in Russia, like most visitors the Webbs saw nothing of Soviet agriculture, village life, or rural conditions. To the end of their lives they seem to have been unaware of the liquidation of the kulaks, and of the terrible toll in human suffering taken by the collectivization of agriculture.

The extremes to which the Webbs were prepared to go in justifying communism are best illustrated from their final defense of that country, *The Truth about Soviet Russia*, written in 1942. Their intellectual ancestor, Jeremy Bentham, author of that masterpiece *The Book of Fallacies*, would have been shocked could he have observed the casuistical reasoning with which, in many instances, his spiritual progeny supported their arguments. When confronted with unmistakable defects in Russian society, they either denied them altogether or justified them by saying that similar abuses existed in capitalist countries as well.

Thus the Webbs defended the Russian one-party system by pointing out that certain observers did not regard the American two-party system as "a satisfactory example of political democracy." The banning of political opposition in Russia was justified by citing the case of Switzerland, which was certainly a political democracy, although neither Jesuits nor communists were allowed in that country. Lenin's concept of the "infantile diseases" of a new society was also invoked to condone the dictatorship of the Party and the total suppression of unorthodox political opinion. In refutation of the last charge, the Webbs pointed gravely to the fact that David Ricardo's works had just been translated into Russian by order of the Soviet government. In extenuation, moreover, of admitted flaws in the communist system, they emphasized that there was in Russia a greater degree of racial equality than existed in many parts of the British Commonwealth or in the Southern states of the U.S.A.

With regard to the shocking purges of 1936–38, the Webbs accepted at face value Stalin's charges that the old Bolsheviks had been traitors to the Revolution, and that the Russian General Staff had been involved in a Trotskyite conspiracy with the Germans. They even saw a parallel in the fact that Britain under stress of actual war had arrested (but not shot) Sir Oswald Mosley. "Have we not imprisoned two M.P.'s," they asked, "and a distinuished ex-Cabinet Minister, and some thousand other fellow-citizens? Have we not interned thousands of well-conducted and even distinguished foreigners?" Such reasoning was the result not, as some supposed, of senility, but of blind devotion to a cause.

Apart from such rationalizations, two aspects of Soviet society made a deep personal appeal to Beatrice Webb: the almost religious dedication of the Communist party, and the austere personal morality that she believed animated it. "Within the Communist Party," she wrote, "and among the five million Comsomols (the youth organization) sexual promiscuity, like all forms of self-indulgence, has come to be thought definitely contrary to Communist ethics, on the grounds enumerated by Lenin: 'it is a frequent cause of disease; it impairs the productivity of labour; it is disturbing to accurate judgment and inimical to intellectual acquisition and scientific discovery, besides frequently involving cruelty to individual sufferers.' " One sometimes gets the notion that, subconsciously at least, Mrs. Webb thought all who enjoyed sex were "sufferers"; at any rate, it was with satisfaction that she observed that there was no "spooning" in the Parks of Culture in Moscow.

Perhaps the most extraordinary gap in the Webbs' knowledge of Russia was their apparent unawareness that wholesale political terror existed in that country, that political freedom had been not merely curtailed but abolished, and that the victims of this unprecedented tyranny were numbered by the million. As Halévy once observed, the Webbs "had never felt anything but contempt for every formula of Liberalism and free trade." At heart they had always been not democrats but collectivists. Their admiration of Soviet society was not so much an aberration but, as with Shaw, rather the logical conclusion of the ideas of a lifetime.

On her return to England, Mrs. Webb appeared to former friends to have undergone a definite "conversion." Visiting Passfield in 1933, Thomas Jones (the ex-secretary of Baldwin and Lloyd George) listened with the Webbs to the "Internationale" broadcast over the Moscow radio, while Beatrice "beat time with her right foot," which was, he thought "as great a miracle as the wireless itself." Sir Desmond MacCarthy remembered how, on another occasion, when he criticized Russia, "she suddenly flew at him with a violence" that astonished Shaw. Kingsley Martin recalls that she would become "furiously angry" with anyone who ventured to cast doubt upon the idealism of the Communist leaders. "Her new faith," Sir Desmond says, "was fanatical." As Count Karolyi of Hungary, hearing her passionate defense of the Soviet system, murmured with gentle irony: "Fabianism adapted to Asia."

If Sidney was simple and uncomplex, without emotional depth or intensity and without need for solace in art or religion, Beatrice, as we have seen, was deeply religious, emotionally troubled, and intellectually perplexed. If she was rational in her outlook upon life, it was not, as with Sidney, due to a happy dispensation of nature but rather to an unending struggle for knowledge. The gift of happiness was not for her by any means an "unbought grace of life." Now, in old age, she had found at last the faith she had always craved.

At the time of her visit to Russia, the consciousness of age was constantly present in Beatrice's mind. Now she met this final challenge with the same gallantry and good humor that she had shown in all the other circumstances of life. No one could have accepted the coming of age more gracefully. "What we old people have to be continually recalling to our minds," she wrote at sixty-six,

> is that however desirable it may be to go on working we have to resign ourselves to becoming nobodies, we have to take our lives lightly, as if one's continued existence was of little consequence to ourselves or to anyone else. It is silly to worry because one can't work as one used to: obviously it is only a question of a few years before one will be tumbling out of life, in one way or another, and the only thing to be done is to tumble out of it as gracefully as possible, without making oneself a nuisance to younger folk.

Self-mockery and an unaffected interest in the young were her antidotes against the onset of old age. "Old and learned persons like ourselves," she wrote, "are treated with great kindness and with some deference, even by Rebels. . . . Old people are horribly troublesome when they lay their trembling old hands on the ways of the young. It is a chronic fear that Sidney and I may be doing it without knowing it, in one or other of our activities."

The great success of their book on Soviet Russia did not inflate the Webbs' literary vanity or disturb their quiet way of life. They had never wished to be lionized.

At Passfield in Hampshire, they spent their last twenty years in quiet retirement. Considerable merriment was caused in 1923 by an advertisement that they inserted in the press, indicating their desire for a building site which "must be relatively high; with a pretty view, and above all completely isolated from houses harbouring cocks or dogs." It was a country of open heath and hedgerow, where heather and gorse grew in wild abundance. Lavender bloomed outside the house. Beatrice, if not Sidney, had always loved nature. "The beauty of spring has arrived," she wrote on the first of May, "with the birds singing from early morning to late in the evening." In Grosvenor Road one could never hear the nightingales. At other seasons of the year she relished the absolute silence and found it, after London, "weirdly attractive." The winter, too, was beautiful "with the hoar frost on the forest trees, the warm tints of heather and the golden leaves of the birch trees and the russet coloured bracken." Before her study window was an ash tree which she "loved to look at, in its leafless winter tracing." Not anticipating Westminster Abbey, she hoped that their ashes might be buried under its roots.

"To make a new home when one is nearing seventy," she wrote, "seems, in some moods, a melancholy task: one is haunted by a vision of the funeral procession wending its way down the new drive, a few years hence, perhaps a few months hence, of one of us, leaving the other desolate and alone." At the time she wrote these words, nearly twenty years remained—including the most exciting adventure of all, the journey to Russia.

She looked forward to a little more work, "and then—our passage through the twilight into the Unknown reservoir of life—let us hope with not too long an interval of loneliness for one of us. . . . Our good fortune has followed us into old age, and when we begin to sink into weakness and perhaps into pain, we must remember with gratitude our past blessings. I doubt whether one would long survive the other one—we have grown together." She lived through the fiery ordeal of the "blitz," and heard the bells ring out for Alamein, but did not see the hour of victory. Beatrice died on April 30, 1943, and Sidney four years later, on October 13, 1947. The welfare state was by then a firmly established fact of British life.

VII

David Lloyd George

(1863–1945)

DAVID LLOYD GEORGE and Winston Churchill stand out as the two greatest Prime Ministers of Britain in the twentieth century. Each was the incarnation of the will to victory, the former in the First World War, the latter in the Second. Lloyd George was probably the only figure in English political life whom Churchill regarded as his peer. Both were colleagues in the great Liberal government of 1906–14 which gave Britain her first experience of what is now known as the welfare state. They remained lifelong friends.

In many ways, they were remarkably alike. Both were dominant personalities; both possessed great personal magnetism; both were practiced orators, capable of swaying immense crowds. Even after hearing Churchill's heroic speeches in the year of Dunkirk, Field Marshal Smuts of South Africa still believed Lloyd George's "stormy eloquence" to be the most effective he had ever heard: not till 1943 did he count Churchill as the forensic equal of his predecessor. Both were men of restless energy and inexhaustible vitality, of unshakable optimism and indomitable will. Both inspired the nation through a period of evil fortune and disaster. Neither would ever concede the possibility of defeat.

"The two great demagogues," as the French historian Elie Halévy calls them, resembled each other also in their faults. Both were immense egotists, arrogant to their colleagues, ruthless with their competitors and contemptuous of mediocrity. Both made numerous enemies and had few friends. Both were cynical about mankind in general, each believing only in his own genius. Both were headstrong, domineering, and almost incapable of admitting that they had ever been mistaken.

In their social origins, however, and in the development of their careers, the two were totally dissimilar. For Lloyd George had been born in a small Welsh cottage and educated by a cobbler, while Churchill had been born in a palace and educated at one of the best schools in England. The former, therefore, was in politics a democrat and a radical, hating landlords and the Church, while the other—whatever his changes of party—remained all his life an aristocrat and imperialist. Despite the fact that Lloyd George was an outsider and a Welshman (almost a foreigner in the opinion of *The Times*, which once declared that even Disraeli had been more English), the little Welshman achieved supreme power at the age of fifty-three. The highest prize eluded Churchill till he was sixty-five.

Victory in war brought very different results to the personal fortunes of the two statesmen, for whereas in 1918 Lloyd George gained the most brilliant triumph of his whole career—indeed the greatest single victory that any individual had ever won in a parliamentary contest in Britain—in 1945, Churchill, on the contrary, in what he regarded as an act of unparalleled political ingratitude, was thrust abruptly out of office, and forced to witness a social transformation that he detested, but opposed in vain.

Four years after his victory in 1918, Lloyd George was ignominiously defeated and thereafter, though he had more than twenty years of life remaining, never once held office again. His eclipse was total. Churchill, on the contrary, beaten in 1945, returned to power six years later and, to the delight of the nation, crowned his long career by being Prime Minister during the Queen's coronation in 1953.

If Churchill had died before the outbreak of the Second World War, like his father before him he would be remembered only as a brilliant and erratic politician whose early promise never had been fulfilled; whereas had Lloyd George died before the First World War, his name would still have gone down in history as that of the man who had finally broken the power of the House of Lords.

A resentment of authority in church and state, a passionate

feeling of Welsh nationalism, and a burning indignation against all forms of social injustice—these were the emotional roots of Lloyd George's early radicalism. As a Welshman, in his early life he was prone to identify himself with national feeling anywhere it might be oppressed by British power. Thus he supported Irish Home Rule, sympathized with Arabi Pasha's revolt in Egypt in 1883, and when the South African War broke out in 1899, became the outstanding champion of the Boers in England.

Having lost his father while still an infant, Lloyd George had been brought up by his mother and her brother, Richard Lloyd, in a strict Nonconformist atmosphere. His childhood reading was chiefly in books like the Bible and Bunyan's *Holy War*. The most exciting moments of his youth were those spent in listening to, and comparing the merits of, revivalist preachers. He envied alike their eloquence and the spell they cast over their hearers, and thought seriously of becoming a preacher himself. Baptized at twelve in a mountain stream, he was brought up in a sect called the Disciples of Christ—an offshoot of the Baptists. Even when a national figure, Lloyd George sometimes regretted not having followed the preacher's vocation. To the end of his life hymn singing and sermon-tasting were among his chief recreations. But when, at eighteen, he visited London and sat in the gallery of the House of Commons, looking down upon the members he felt like William the Conqueror surveying his future domain. The triumphs of the pulpit, he concluded, were too limited in scale.

Precocious in school, he was articled to a solicitor, and being a fluent and persuasive speaker both in Welsh and English, got elected to Parliament for Carnarvon in 1890. For the rest of his public life he was to retain this seat—through twelve elections and for fifty-five years, by which time he had become the "Father of the House." No matter how unpopular he might become in England—"with his large Welsh images and his little Welsh impertinences," as George Dangerfield puts it—so long as he preserved his hold upon the electors of Carnarvon he was safe; and the more he was vilified in England—as at the time of the Boer War—the more he was idolized in Wales. When he was returned in 1900, narrowly having escaped being lynched in Chamberlain's stronghold of Birmingham, he was perhaps the greatest Welsh hero since the fifteenth century—"Owen Glendower in a bowler hat," according to *The Times*.

In 1888, he married Margaret Owen, daughter of a prosperous neighboring farmer from Criccieth, the match being regarded by her family as a misalliance. For many years, Dame Margaret Lloyd George—to use her later title—provided the domestic security that sheltered her husband during his stormy public life. In the past, Mary Anne Disraeli and Catherine Gladstone had played this role, as Clementine Churchill was to do in the future. Unobtrusive and dependable, retiring and modest, Dame Margaret gave her husband absolute loyalty and supported him —as long as he needed her. She bore him five children; and when he was "petulant and irascible," she mothered him like a spoiled child. She also bore with resignation a long series of infidelities, any one of which might well have ruined him had she not stood by him in public.

After World War I, when Lloyd George bought a country estate at Churt in Surrey, and set up not only as a country gentleman but as a sultan with a harem, he and his wife separated at last. Dame Margaret returned to Criccieth to live "among her own people," and there she died—alone.

By 1906, Lloyd George had already made such a name for himself in the House of Commons that, after the great Liberal landslide of that year, he was offered a seat in the Cabinet—as president of the Board of Trade. He was then forty-three years of age. Like Churchill after him, such was his energy and competence that Lloyd George had the gift—not appreciated by his colleagues—of making whatever post he held seem the most important in the Cabinet. His outstanding achievement at the Board of Trade was the creation—out of a chaos of private companies— of a single unified control for the world's greatest port: the Port of London Authority. When, in 1908, Henry Herbert Asquith became Prime Minister, Lloyd George was invited to succeed him as Chancellor of the Exchequer. In this post, he prepared his famous budget of 1909, which made use of taxation to redress social inequality—a Fabian idea, but one that would have shocked Lloyd George's early idol Gladstone. The budget initiated a constitutional crisis of the first order.

It was one in which, to his intense delight, the new Chancellor found himself the defender of the poor against the rich, the champion of democratic equality against aristocratic privilege. For by rejecting the budget of 1909, which they regarded as an attack upon their rights, the Lords unwisely broke a constitutional precedent that was more than two centuries old. The peers thereby afforded Lloyd George just the battle he was seeking, and on ground of his own choice. With an ardor derived partly at least from the memory of youthful humiliations suffered as poacher and trespasser at the hands of local landlords, he threw himself into the fray. In a few months, adored by many and detested by as many more—had not Chamberlain once said that "every Englishman dearly loves a lord"?—Lloyd George found himself the central figure of a controversy that split the nation in two and produced the chief political crisis since the Reform Bill of 1832.

The Chancellor now paid off many an old score. *The Times* called his budget speech "a chaotic welter of half-ascertained facts, half-thought-out arguments and half-sincere sentimentalism," but among the working classes whom he now addressed all over the country, the Chancellor found more appreciative hearers. In July 1909, at Limehouse in the East End of London, amid sweltering heat, he delivered the famous speech in which, among other enormities, he was held to have personally insulted the Duke of Westminster. He showed, at any rate, that through the growth of London docks, landlords had made the most fantastic profits: land that had once rented at £3 an acre was now worth £8,000 an acre. The Duke of Northumberland owned property in the East End. For purposes of local taxation this had been rated at 30/— an acre, but when it was needed for a school site, His Grace valued it at £900 an acre.

At Newcastle-on-Tyne in October 1909, the Welsh wizard took on the whole ducal bench. Accused of having depressed the stock market by his demagogic outbursts, he retorted mischievously that the only sign of depression he'd noticed had been "a great slump in dukes." "One fully equipped duke," he calculated aloud to the vociferous delight of his audience, "costs as much as two dreadnoughts." Such noblemen were "just as great a terror as battleships and lasted much longer." The Upper

House he termed a body of five hundred men "chosen acci-
dentally from among the unemployed." All the same, he gravely
conceded, so long as the peers "preserved that stately silence
which befitted their rank and their intelligence," he for one
would not complain. Who could possibly have imagined at that
moment that the day would come when the gadfly from Wales
would one day be enrolled among them as a belted earl?

Edward VII was shocked by Lloyd George's witticisms. The
royal reproof was duly conveyed to the irrepressible minister—
without much visible effect. For the latter was soon demonstrating that three peers alone—the Earls of Derby and Sefton, and
the Marquess of Salisbury—drew £345,000 a year in ground rents
from the city of Liverpool, to which in return they contributed
absolutely nothing. As for the origin of such riches, when Lord
Robert and Lord Hugh Cecil resisted Lloyd George's demands
for the establishment of the Anglican Church in Wales, he
taunted them with a reminder of the source from which, during
the Reformation, their wealth had originally come—the lands
of the Church. With relish he referred to their noble forebears in
the sixteenth century, their hands "dripping with the fat of
sacrilege." And when the pompous Lord Curzon declared that
the world owed everything to aristocracies, the impish Baptist
wondered why in that case the founder of Christianity had
chosen as his apostles twelve fishermen and not twelve dukes.

Remarks like this were regarded by many as being in the
worst possible taste: Gladstone, for all his radicalism, had never
stooped so low. *The Times*, of course, deplored such "methods
of self-advertisement." "Mr. Lloyd George," it warned him
stiffly, "should no longer use tactics worthy of his own distant
past, and of Mr. Winston Churchill's present."

Not only were the Lords defeated over the budget, but the
Parliament Act of 1911 put an effective end to their power of
interfering with the will of the nation as expressed through the
House of Commons. Lloyd George was also responsible for the
first Old Age Pensions Act in English history (1908), for the
compulsory Accident and Sickness Insurance of workers (1909),
and for the first Unemployment Insurance Act (1911). Steering
the latter through Parliament cost him fifteen or sixteen hours
a day, working six days a week. "Even his enemies," says his

biographer Frank Owen, "paid tribute to his genius. He had never appeared so great." In providing for the first public medical care for the working class—it was a measure of limited scope, to which the workmen themselves contributed part of the cost out of their wages—Lloyd George met and defeated an opposition as vocal and as bitter as that of the Lords: that of the medical profession. He thereby provided a precedent for Aneurin Bevin nearly forty years later.

In this struggle to institute the first measures of the welfare state, Lloyd George's chief ally in the Cabinet was young Winston Churchill, who, only a few years earlier, had left the Conservatives and joined the Liberals—a desertion for which the former had not forgiven him. Not unnaturally, this infamous combination of the aspiring demagogue and the renegade aristocrat reminded Tories with a classical education of Cleon and Alcibiades. Lloyd George and Churchill were not only the two youngest, but also the two most resolute and courageous members of the Cabinet. In some instances, by sheer force of character they imposed their will on senior colleagues and upon the premier himself. "Nineteen rag pickers round a 'eap of muck,'" was how John Burns described Asquith's Cabinet considering the controversial budget of 1909. Lloyd George and Churchill galvanized the rag pickers into action. At one Cabinet meeting, Churchill scribbled a note to his senior colleague. "I am attached to you," he declared, "and have followed your instructions and guidance for nearly ten years." It was a tribute that Churchill paid to no other man.

The Fabians, in looking for possible allies, had never paid much attention to the intemperate little Welshman: neither his pacifism nor his nonconformity had accorded with their basic idea of the collective authority of the state. During the South African War, much as they disliked Chamberlain, the Fabians had believed British imperialism to be preferable to the absurd anachronism of Boer rule. From his public utterances, it was evident that Lloyd George had read neither *Das Kapital* nor the *Fabian Tracts*, and Bernard Shaw contemptuously dismissed his social legislation as "the blundering efforts of this ignoramus to regurgitate what he had swallowed of Socialism." At first, the Webbs were similarly skeptical: the Liberal reforms, they thought, would palliate rather than destroy existing social evils and would prolong the life of the Poor Law instead of sweeping it away. The more they watched his struggle against vested interests, however, the more sympathetic they became.

"He is a clever fellow," wrote Mrs. Webb in 1908, "but has less intellect than Winston, and not such an attractive personality —more of the preacher, less of the statesman." Within a year, however, the Webbs were announcing: "We admire Lloyd George and Winston Churchill and openly state that they are the best of the party." The battle for the Parliament Act they considered a "great triumph for Winston and Lloyd George who behaved with loyalty and discretion." Asquith, on the contrary, had in their judgment "shown himself careless, unintelligent and cowardly—without foresight or firmness." Mrs. Webb's conclusion was that the "two Radical leaders" were the men of the future. "The big thing that has happened in the last two years," she wrote in her diary toward the end of 1910, "is that Lloyd George and Winston Churchill have practically taken the *limelight*, not merely from their own colleagues, but from the Labour Party. They stand out as the most advanced politicians." The Duke of Beaufort growled that he would like to see Lloyd George and Churchill thrown among forty foxhounds.

In the years before 1914, Lloyd George had shown slight interest in European affairs. This was partly the result of a provincial education—he was sometimes found to be ignorant of the basic facts of geography—and partly the result of his total absorption in domestic politics. In 1911, however, he was largely responsible for getting his friend Churchill transferred from the Home Office to the Admiralty, a post in which the latter immediately made his mark. In that year also, in the belligerent Mansion House speech during the Moroccan crisis, the Chancellor made his initial pronouncement upon European affairs, admonishing Germany that, in the event of war, Britain would stand firmly by her ally France. Thus was revealed for the first time a new aspect of Lloyd George, which the war years would develop more fully. As yet, however, he displayed small knowledge of the situation, for on July 9, 1914, nearly two weeks after the murder of the Austrian Archduke at Serajevo, he told an audience of bankers in the Guildhall that in European politics "the sky has never been more perfectly blue."

When, in August 1914, war broke out over the German invasion of Belgium, no one knew whether Lloyd George would support the war or whether, like the aged Gladstonian Morley and the labor leader John Burns, he would resign from the Cabinet. As Jones records, even his closest friends were in doubt up to the very last moment. This was the first instance in which, to their surprise, Lloyd George's friends observed a certain indecisiveness, even a certain slipperiness, in his behavior. Before long, such vacillation would be recognized as one of his leading characteristics.

In England, as in all Europe, it was generally believed that the war would be over within a few months. Lord Kitchener, the new Secretary of War, was almost alone in warning the nation to prepare for an indefinitely protracted conflict: it was, unfortunately, almost the sole instance in which his judgment was correct. It took the bloody stalemate on the Western Front, and the tragic failure at the Dardanelles—for which Churchill was made the scapegoat—to shock the public out of its wishful thinking.

As if the King and the Prime Minister between them did not afford enough emotional security, Lord Kitchener was now established—and who more eligible than the soldier in uniform?—as the father figure of the nation in arms. Throughout the land, from thousands of posters, that formidable presence, with square jaw, level gaze, and accusing finger, intimidated able-bodied men into volunteering for service. If Kitchener was not a great man, said Elizabeth Bibesco, at least he was a great poster. By 1915 it was clear that the hero of Omdurman was not equal to the European war and that the Germans were a more dangerous enemy than the dervishes. The holocausts of Neuve Chapelle and Loos were caused by a fearful shortage of munitions, and especially of high-explosive shells, a shortage that the Secretary of War long refused to admit.

Kitchener's ineptitude was Lloyd George's opportunity. With the help of the Northcliffe press, the Chancellor had for months been urging an all-out effort to end the scandal of the munitions shortage. In May 1915, he himself became Minister of Munitions —a new office within the Cabinet which was created to increase war production. In this hazardous and unprecedented post, for which he relinquished the safety and the prestige of the Exchequer, Lloyd George proved a brilliant success, and from it he emerged as by far the strongest organizing genius in the government. Beginning, as he liked to recall, with two secretaries, two tables, and a chair, Lloyd George built up a Headquarters Staff "organized into departments—guns, explosives, shells, bombs, machine guns, rifles, factory building, labour—and a Records Office." Beneath these were established fifty local Boards of Management, which distributed orders to the engineering firms throughout the nation.

What Lloyd George accomplished was nothing less than the reorganization of "the engineering capacity of Britain for war production." In the words of Malcolm Thomson, his official biographer, "it was a gigantic task, the like of which had never before been attempted or even conceived." Not till 1940, under the direction of Winston Churchill, was this amazing feat duplicated. In order to staff the new ministry, Lloyd George had no hesitation in demanding from other departments their finest civil servants. He boasted of having commandeered some of the best brains in the country. Under him served such men as the future Lord Beveridge, the future Lord Layton, Sir Eric Geddes, Sir Hubert Llewellyn Smith, Seebohm Rowntree, Lord Moulton, and many other figures prominent in science or in industry. Unlike Neville Chamberlain at a later date, Lloyd George was so confident of his own abilities that he never feared to be outclassed by others. Hence he always made use of the best talents available. He was intolerant of, not reassured by, mediocrity.

His chief enemy was the War Office, which resisted all plans to expand war production, to multiply weapons, or invent new ones. Kitchener once declared that four machine guns to a battalion was the maximum needed on the Western Front—anything above four was "a luxury." By the end of the war each battalion averaged eighty. Lloyd George ordered guns and shells on a scale far exceeding the official estimates of the War Office, endorsed as they had been by Kitchener, but had to fight hard to gain Cabinet approval for them. In the course of these struggles with the War Office, in his initial year at the new ministry Lloyd George increased the output of shells by a thousand per cent and gained control over the invention and production of new weapons. The result was the first appearance, in 1916, of the tank. Churchill, while still at the Admiralty, had already ordered the first experiments with this new weapon: he and Lloyd George were, in fact, the two civilians responsible for thrusting it on a sluggish and incredulous War Office.

There was also the problem of labor, since the trade unions were suspicious of any relaxation of the privileges they had gained over the years. They were especially hesitant about admitting large numbers of women workers into the munitions industry, particularly since Lloyd George insisted on equal pay for piecework between the sexes. With the possible exception of Churchill, who at this period was in disgrace over the failure at the Dardanelles, no one but Lloyd George could have mobilized millions of workers so enthusiastically behind the war effort. His prewar championship of the working class now stood him in good stead. A. J. P. Taylor describes the abandonment of restrictive practices by the unions for the duration of the war as "the most significant event in the history of British Trade Unions" in modern times.

When, in June 1916, Kitchener was drowned off the Orkneys, Lloyd George at once succeeded him as Secretary of War. In place of the stubborn, inarticulate soldier, who once stiffly referred to his fellow ministers as "the twenty-three gentlemen in the Cabinet with whom I am barely acquainted," there now appeared the most voluble and dynamic personality in English public life.

From the War Office it could only be a matter of months before Lloyd George rose to the premiership. For Asquith, though an adroit parliamentarian and competent administrator, was totally lacking in the drive and initiative that Lloyd George possessed. "Wait and See" was a nickname the premier had not acquired without deserving it. He also lacked the personal magnetism and the oratorical power necessary to inspire a nation in time of war. Nor was he ever aware of the need to establish good relations with the press, whose influence was now thrown overwhelmingly against him. "For the first time," wrote Mrs. Webb in December 1916, "a Cabinet has been created not by a party political organization or by any combination of political organizations, nor by the will of the House of Commons, but by a powerful combination of newspaper proprietors. The House of Commons, in fact, almost disappears as the originator and controller of the Cabinet."

Always in later years Lloyd George protested that he had nothing to do with these attacks mounted by the press lords on his chief. Certain it is that he was fully aware of the power of the fourth estate and of the value of publicity: Northcliffe, Beaverbrook, and Lord Riddell were at this time among his closest friends. Lloyd George also maintained that he had never coveted the position of premier. "I never said 'Make me Prime Minister!'" he declared in 1922. "On the contrary, I begged Lord Balfour, Mr. Bonar Law, or anybody to take that position. I begged Mr. Asquith to remain, so long as the conditions were ensured in his Premiership that I thought were necessary to conduct the war efficiently." This last is perhaps a significant reservation. Nearly twenty years later, in his *War Memoirs*, he declared emphatically: "I neither sought nor desired the Premiership."

One might have thought—many did—that Lloyd George protested too much. Asquith described later how his colleague had once come to him with tears in his eyes and disavowed any knowledge of the press campaign against his leader. He "assured me," said the premier, "that sooner than take part in such disloyalty . . . he would prefer (i) to break stones (ii) to dig potatoes (iii) to be hung and quartered. And I am quite sure that he was sincere." But Asquith still did not believe him. At a later date, Keynes and others were to notice Lloyd George's power of convincing himself and others of the absolute truth of what he was saying, no matter how much it might contradict what he had just said previously. Asquith, at any rate, two days after his forced resignation, was convinced that it had been the result of "a well-organized, carefully engineered conspiracy." As the Clydeside rebel Willie Gallacher sardonically observed, the "knock-out blow" that Lloyd George so often boasted would win the war "missed the Kaiser, and hit old man Asquith instead, knocking him clean out."

There is no documentary evidence to show that Lloyd George

did in fact aspire to the premiership: this may, however, indicate merely the inadequacy of documents as a means of substantiating truth. For given all else that we know about Lloyd George—his ambition, his competitiveness, his egotism, his complete self-confidence—it is hardly credible that he did not wish to be Prime Minister in 1916, knowing himself to be certainly the fittest man for that office. It was thirty-six years since in his daydreams he had seen himself as William the Conqueror.

When Lloyd George became Prime Minister on December 6, 1916, nearly two more years of terrible conflict had yet to be endured. From the nerve center of the war, the premier now exhibited on a larger scale the same inspiring and energizing qualities that he had already shown at the Ministry of Munitions. Even the Tories, who in prewar days had loathed the little Welshman, were now loud in their praises of him as the one indispensable man, symbol of the nation's will to victory.

Bonar Law himself, the head of the Conservative party, said of the Prime Minister that "he thought of nothing, and aimed at nothing, and hoped for nothing, except the successful end of the war. That was his life, and he had no other life. In good report and evil, we saw what courage meant. It was not merely the courage of dogged determination, but was accompanied by a brilliant hopefulness which was an example and inspiration to everyone who worked with him." Lloyd George's old Ulster enemy Sir Edward Carson, who in 1912 would gladly have seen him hanged, now proclaimed that history would record that Lloyd George "did more than any other man to preserve the liberties of the world." The austere Lord Milner, during the Boer War his bitter foe, now extolled his "genius and absolutely amazing courage," and once, after dinner at the Ritz, asserted that the Prime Minister had been a greater war minister even than Chatham in the eighteenth century, and that victory had been due chiefly to his "incomparable drive." Nearly thirty years later, Lord Vansittart, who abominated the politics of Lloyd George, wrote that what he chiefly remembered and admired in him was his courage in adversity. The Orangeman Sir Henry Wilson, whose contempt for civilians exceeded—if it were possible —that of Kitchener, once admitted that Lloyd George alone could win the war. Colonel House, on first meeting the Prime Minister, wrote Woodrow Wilson that Lloyd George had "something dynamic within him which his colleagues have not and which is badly needed at this great hour." Another former political opponent, Lord Birkenhead, praised him later as "incomparably the greatest living English statesman," while according to a distinguished foreign observer, Field Marshal Smuts of South Africa, Lloyd George was "the biggest Englishman of them all" (a mistaken compliment to a son of Wales).

Much of Lloyd George's success was due to the power of words. The Frenchman Pierre Maillaud, who, like Smuts, had listened to Churchill in 1940, nevertheless called Lloyd George "the greatest British orator I have ever heard." General Seely testified that the premier was the only politician who could "electrify" that most disenchanted of audiences—the men in the trenches: all others bored them. One of his biographers has described the almost hypnotic power that Lloyd George could exert over his hearers. "Tense, straining forward, silent, hardly breathing—then suddenly, clapping, cheering, laughing almost hysterically, or near to tears again. As Lloyd George spoke, he waved his hand gently from side to side. The silver magic of his voice, and the throbbing current of his passion, gradually possessed the entire audience and they swayed as one man in rhythm with the compelling hand." An audience in wartime, of course, is easy enough to rouse; for as Lloyd George once told Albert, King of the Belgians: "Man is a creature of conflict, in whom it is always possible to develop warlike sentiments."

In his *Unfinished Autobiography*, the well-known Oxford historian H. A. L. Fisher has left us an intimate picture of the Prime Minister in time of war:

> His animated courage, and buoyancy of temper, his gift of witty speech and unconquerable sense of fun, his easy power of confident decision in the most perilous emergencies, injected a spirit of cheerfulness and courage into his colleagues which were of extraordinary value during those anxious years.

There was one quarter, however, where Lloyd George's eloquence made no appeal, and where his charm was wasted. Not even the Germans detested the Prime Minister as heartily as did the British Commander-in-Chief. For whereas Lloyd George, like Churchill, was an "Easterner" in strategy, Sir Douglas Haig, despite the fearful losses on the Somme and at Ypres, was a confirmed and impenitent "Westerner." He believed, in other words, that only on the Western Front would the ultimate decision be gained; he opposed all diversionary operations, especially in the Mediterranean, whether aimed at Austria-Hungary or at Turkey. Lloyd George, on the contrary, appalled by the four hundred thousand British casualties at the Somme in 1916, a disaster repeated in 1917 beneath the mournful ridge of Passchendaele, wished to assume the defensive in the West, and attempt to overthrow the Central Powers by an attack upon their vulnerable southeastern flank.

In disputes over strategy, Haig, who was accustomed to give orders to everyone around him, had to listen in silence while Lloyd George lectured him, and with a wave of his hand over the map airily disposed of difficult military problems. When driving in a car, with no refuge from the incessant flow of words, Sir Douglas found the premier especially "fatiguing." As he moaned in his diary, "he talks and argues so." Lloyd George's persecution of him was perhaps the greatest ordeal that Sir Douglas had to face on the Western Front. Like Kitchener, Haig was inarticulate. But his silence served him well, since had he sought to argue, he would have been no match for the premier's lightning rapidity of mind. The pose of silent, outraged dignity was one that suited Sir Douglas, a very handsome man, to perfection.

In his diary, however—though it was not to be published till after both of them were dead—Haig was always the hero of these encounters. "I gave L. G. a good talking to," he would boast, "and I felt I got the best of the arguments. He seemed quite 'rattled' on the subject of Italy." No witnesses exist to corroborate the Field Marshal's complacent account of these forensic victories, which appear, in fact, to have been as illusory as his successes in Flanders.

In 1916, during one of Lloyd George's visits to the Front, Haig summed him up as being "astute and cunning, with much energy and push, but I should think shifty and unreliable." Nine months later he endorsed this unflattering judgment. "He seems to me so flighty—makes plans and is always changing them and his mind. . . . I have no great opinion of L. G. either *as a man or a leader.*" "L. G. seems a 'cur,' " he wrote in 1918, "and when I am with him I cannot resist a feeling of distrust of him and his intentions." Not long before victory, he declared him "a thorough impostor."

Haig was above all suspicious, and not without reason, that behind his back Lloyd George was compromising him with the French. Thus Marshal Foch once told him how the British Prime Minister had actually solicited his criticisms of various British generals, though not of the Commander-in-Chief himself (from Sir Henry Wilson's diary, however, we learn that Lloyd George had in fact criticized Haig directly to Foch). "I would not have believed," wrote Haig indignantly, "that a British Minister could have been so ungentlemanly." When a French Cabinet minister was visiting the Front, the Commander-in-Chief did his best to keep Lloyd George out of the way. "It seems almost dangerous," he reasoned, "to allow L. G. to be out alone, as he is capable of promising the Frenchman anything."

When, in December 1918, Lloyd George wanted Haig to take part in a victory procession in London, the Field Marshal indignantly refused to cross over from France. "The real truth, which history will show," he wrote in his diary, "is that the British Army has won the war in France in spite of L. G., and I have no intention of taking part in any triumphal ride with Foch, or with any pack of foreigners, through the streets of London, mainly in order to add to L. G.'s importance and help him in his election campaign." He had already had enough of Lloyd George's "conceit and swagger," and also of his boastfulness.

Nor could Haig forgo the pleasure of alluding to a foible of the premier about which gossip was rife—his lack of physical courage. "The P.M. looked as if he had been thoroughly frightened," he gloated in April 1918, when Lloyd George visited him not far behind the lines, "and he still seemed in a funk." It was well known that the premier did not care to be in London during a Zeppelin raid. His friend Thomas Jones and his enemy Viscount Hardinge both considered him a physical coward. "His courage," commented Beaverbrook dryly, "was always more of the moral than the physical order." Similarly, during the Second World

War, his private secretary believed that one of the reasons why Lloyd George gave up attending Parliament, and retired from London to Wales, was to escape the danger of Nazi bombs.

The Prime Minister for his part never attempted to conceal his scorn for what he regarded as Haig's stupidity and callousness to loss of human life. Here was a general who, in an age of tank warfare, still put his trust in a cavalry breakthrough—as if, in any case, the almost impregnable fortifications in the West, with pillboxes, barbed-wire entanglements, and machine-gun nests, had not long ago proved that the *arme blanche* was as obsolete as the feudal cavalry at Agincourt. In conversation, and later in his *War Memoirs,* Lloyd George ridiculed Haig mercilessly—and with good warrant.

The question naturally arises, why did he never remove Haig from his command? Two factors may perhaps account for this: first, that Haig was strongly supported by the King and idolized by the British public, from whom a severe censorship had concealed the truth about the ghastly failures on the Somme and at Ypres; second, that Lloyd George's own position as head of the coalition, with his former chief leading an opposition that was both vigilant and resentful, was so precarious that to proceed against so popular a figure as Haig might have brought about his own downfall.

On Armistice Day 1918, Lloyd George stood at the highest point of his career (only twelve years before, he had been no more than a back-bencher in Parliament). The Prime Minister decided to capitalize at once upon victory, and thereby prolong his power. The "Victory election" of December 1918 was held so precipitately that, contrary to what was to happen in 1945, large numbers of soldiers overseas were never able to vote at all. It resulted, however, in the greatest personal triumph in the history of parliamentary elections in England: neither Gladstone nor Disraeli had ever commanded such a majority as Lloyd George now gained as head of the war coalition thus prolonged into the peace. The rival group of Asquithian Liberals was almost annihilated, their leader suffering the loss of his own seat. An acute observer, however, might have surmised difficulties in a coalition where the leader belonged to one party and the great bulk of the members to the other. For about three quarters of the coalition were Conservatives.

The election, which Keynes thought "an act of political immorality," was fought largely upon cheap popular slogans such as "Hang the Kaiser," "Make Germany pay," and "Make Britain a land fit for heroes to live in"—none of which promises was to prove capable of realization. "I feel physically sick," wrote Beatrice Webb while the campaign was still in progress, "when I read the frenzied appeals of the Coalition leaders—the Prime Minister, Winston Churchill and Geddes—to hang the Kaiser, ruin and humiliate the German people. . . . It may all be election talk, but it is mean and brutal talk degrading to the electorate. It is the Nemesis of having as Premier a man of low moral and intellectual values." Or, as Keynes put it satirically, "a vote for a Coalition candidate meant the crucifixion of Anti-Christ and the assumption by Germany of the British National Debt."

Even Churchill was to maintain that in this famous parliamentary contest "the blatancies of electioneering . . . robbed Britain in an appreciable degree of her dignity." He went on to relate how he himself, in his successful contest at Dundee, felt compelled, against his convictions, to exploit the popular fury against the Kaiser. Beatrice Webb later provided an amusing glimpse into Lloyd George's own reflections, a few months after his triumph, upon the way in which he had gained it. "The P.M. looked meditative as he lay back in his armchair smoking his big cigar: 'That stunt about indemnities from Germany that *they* started during the election—with an emphasis on *they*—he said slowly, as if thinking aloud, 'was a very foolish business.' This left us gasping, but being fellow guests we agreed cordially with him." Fifteen years later, meeting the Kaiser's grandson Prince Louis Ferdinand, Lloyd George told him that in 1918 he had neither expected nor desired the fall of the Hohenzollerns.

The "Victory election" not only returned Lloyd George to power, but filled the House of Commons with what a future Tory premier, Stanley Baldwin, called "a lot of hard-faced men who look as if they had done well out of the war." Sir Harold Nicolson, in a more indulgent vein, described them as "the most unintelligent body of public school boys which even the Mother of Parliaments has known." It was to make possible the triumph of such mediocrity that the graveless dead, whose names are inscribed in letters of gold upon the Menin Gate, had perished in the gas-poisoned salient of Ypres.

As for the Prime Minister himself, if during the slaughter of Passchendaele he never lost his buoyancy or his high spirits; and if, twenty years later, fighting the war over again with German generals, he enjoyed himself immensely recalling agonies which both to him and to Haig had never been more than statistics, or names on a map—if such lack of imagination seems shocking, one must also remember that had he felt more compassion, the Prime Minister could hardly have preserved the determination necessary to win the war. His extraordinary energy, conceded Lord Birkenhead, inevitably involved "some degree of natural insensibility."

The problem, at any rate, was now the winning of the peace, and to Paris Lloyd George proceeded, there to confer with the diplomats of Europe, dominated as they were by the French Premier, Georges Clemenceau, and also by Woodrow Wilson, President of the United States. As always, the problem of a durable peace was more complicated than any posed by war, no matter on how large a scale the latter might have been waged. No miracle of organization built up overnight could hope to resolve the innumerable conflicting interests that were now seething in Paris. For, notwithstanding the immense practical difficulties involved in the reconstruction of a battered continent, the real problems were not merely political or economic but, as in the world today, psychological, involving the control of human passion.

For the task that he faced so lightheartedly—the most searching test of his whole career—Lloyd George was singularly ill-equipped. Wholly insular in background, he had never had the least acquaintance, or desire for acquaintance, with foreigners. Like Woodrow Wilson, he never understood their minds, their aspirations, or their feuds. From their ardors and their hatreds he was equally exempt. Of European history and geography he knew very little. In the House of Commons, at a time when Poland and Czechoslovakia were fiercely disputing over the rich coal-bearing area of Teschen, he candidly admitted that he hadn't the slightest idea where such a place was. Of economics, a subject of utmost importance where reparations were in question, he was equally ignorant.

These limitations were not compensated for by his unfailing optimism and haphazard diplomacy, his impatience with detail, his preference for informal verbal agreements, and his reluctance to put anything in writing; still less by what Sir Harold Nicolson calls his "unequalled powers of improvisation." Referring to his talent for patching up hasty solutions to complicated problems, Thomas Jones, Assistant Secretary of the Cabinet, once said that Lloyd George had a mind like Clapham Junction. It "had few deep grooves, but was endlessly adjusting and accommodating." As a negotiator, the premier was the despair of trained diplomats, being as ignorant of their procedure as he was indifferent to it. He went to Paris, Keynes wrote scornfully, "to do a deal and bring home something which would pass muster in a week." His methods, reported Nicolson, who had frequent opportunity to watch him close at hand, were "personal, forensic, intuitive, imprecise, variable, conceited and far too private." He had, Sir Harold goes on to say, "an aversion to detail that was almost pathological." Lingering traces of his youthful resentment against aristocrats showed in his marked distaste for British diplomats and for the officials of the Foreign Office, whom he loved to circumvent and sometimes to humiliate. Where at the Ministry of Munitions he had once made use of the best brains available, now, in this new world of international diplomacy, he showed himself "temperamentally hostile to expert or even to educated opinion." In the phrase of A. J. P. Taylor, Lloyd George was "the great 'rogue' of English political life."

To balance these deficiencies, the British Prime Minister was, like Woodrow Wilson, free from the personal rancor and desire for revenge which animated most of the Allied delegates. Unlike France, Belgium, Italy, Serbia, or Poland, Britain herself had not been ravaged in the war. In addition to this, ever since his early days as a fervent Welsh nationalist, Lloyd George had always sympathized with the "underdog," in which category Germany now unmistakably found herself. Such sympathy, as the enraged Clemenceau was soon to discover, afforded a sentimental foundation for traditional balance-of-power politics, in which British would tend to favor the defeated enemy at the expense of France, her victorious ally.

At the peace conference in Paris, Lloyd George may also have counted upon personal gifts to enable him, as so often in the past, to establish an ascendancy over his colleagues. He was endowed with a magnetic personality and an abundance of charm. He also possessed considerable psychological flair, especially where the weaknesses and vanities of others were concerned. Witnesses as unlike one another as Winston Churchill and Beatrice Webb were agreed about the premier's engaging personal qualities. "One of the most admirable traits of Mr. Lloyd George's character," wrote Churchill in his *World Crisis*, "was his complete freedom at the height of his power from anything in the nature of pomposity or superior airs. He was always natural and simple. He was always exactly the same to those who knew him well; ready to argue any point, to listen to disagreeable facts even when controversially presented. One could say anything to him, on the terms that he could say anything back."

Meeting him just after the war, with the aura of victory fresh upon him, Mrs. Webb described how "we talked with the freedom and intimacy of old friends—it is impossible to do otherwise with Lloyd George. He is so easy in manner, so amusing, so direct and apparently spontaneous in his observations and retorts, and he enjoys like qualities in others." Such was the spell that he cast that he was able to make her forget, at least for the moment, the disgraceful election campaign he had conducted only two months earlier. Lloyd George and Churchill, she admitted, both possessed "the gift of accessibility and eagerness to know."

The impression of these two observers is confirmed by that of Alfred Duff Cooper. "There is something very remarkable about him," he noted after first meeting Lloyd George. "He creates the impression of a great man, and he does it without seeming theatrical and without seeming sincere." According to the historian Sir Bernard Pares, the premier was "absolute in his democracy. He talked to everyone as an equal. There was no question of authority." Such were the advantages of not having been educated at a Public School.

The question now, however, was whether men so temperamentally different from him and from each other as Clemenceau and Wilson, both of whom represented in addition such widely divergent national interests, would as readily succumb to his spell as had so many of the politicians with whom he had dealt at home—though even there he had been unable to influence military leaders like Haig and Robertson.

In *The Economic Consequences of the Peace*, a book which exerted so great an influence in 1919 throughout the English-speaking world, John Maynard Keynes represented President Wilson as the almost helpless victim of the British premier's superior subtlety and guile. "What chance could such a man have," he asked,

> against Mr. Lloyd George's unerring, almost medium-like, sensibility to everyone immediately around him? To see the British Prime Minister watching the company, with six or seven senses not available to ordinary man, judging character, motive, and subconscious impulse, perceiving what each was thinking and even what each was going to say next, and compounding with telepathic instinct the argument or appeal best suited to the vanity, weakness, or self-interest of his immediate auditor, was to realize that the poor President would be playing blind-man's-buff in that party.

Since both Wilson and Clemenceau remained unaffected by Lloyd George's powers of persuasion, Keynes's fears, at least in this respect, proved groundless. "The President, the Tiger and the Welsh witch," he observed, "were shut up in a room together for six months and the Treaty was what came out." Yet the treaty hardly reflects any special dominance by the British premier over his colleagues: Wilson got the League and Clemenceau got revenge, though not as much as he would have wished. If Lloyd George at Versailles, despite his hysterical election pledges, represented moderation, it can hardly be said that his viewpoint prevailed.

His subsequent animosity to Woodrow Wilson may reflect his chagrin over his failure to control the President. "There were lumps of pure unmixed clay," Lloyd George wrote maliciously in his memoirs, "here and there amidst the gold in every part of his character. . . . Spiritually he dwelt beyond the snow line, high above his fellows, in an atmosphere pure, glistening and bracing—but cold. Suddenly, he was precipitated into the swamps of petty personal or party malignity down below." The President, he thought, was in fact "the most extraordinary compound I have ever encountered of the noble visionary and the implacable, unscrupulous partisan." Clemenceau made the same point with Gallic concision. Wilson, he said, talked like Jesus Christ, but acted like Lloyd George. The latter he thought the most ignorant man he'd ever met.

The treaty accomplished, the Prime Minister no doubt expected to enjoy, after the long ordeal of war, a period of ease and prosperity. As the chief architect of victory, and the greatest war minister since Chatham, he was undoubtedly the most popular man in Britain. He was one of the chief arbiters of European peace, and the head of what appeared still to be the most powerful empire in history. "The British flag," his Foreign Secretary, Lord Curzon, proclaimed grandiloquently at this time, "has never flown over a more powerful or a more unified empire. . . . Never did our voice count for more in the councils of nations, or in determining the destinies of mankind."

Instead, however, of the tranquil enjoyment of power which he anticipated, the premier experienced a series of misfortunes— the economic depression of 1920, the outbreak of civil strife in Ireland, and the Greco-Turkish war. Their cumulative result was his ignominious overthrow after four years.

To the problem of permanent unemployment—in 1920 nearly two million men were out of work—Lloyd George had as yet devoted little serious thought. No one, of course, yet realized that this was a permanent, not simply a temporary situation. The premier's only contribution to relieving distress in the coal industry was to repudiate the recommendations of the commission headed by the eminent judge Sir John (later Lord) Sankey, which he himself had appointed. The report of the commission, among whose members were Sidney Webb and Professor Tawney, had included a suggestion for the nationalization of coal.

The result of Lloyd George's failure to address himself to the social and economic problems of postwar Britain had a decisive influence upon his future career. Before the war, especially in his fight against the Lords, he had been something of a hero to a large number of workingmen; and during the war, despite labor troubles on the Clyde and elsewhere, he had continued to dominate them by his eloquence and by the magnetism of his platform personality. It was not, therefore, inconceivable—and the thought may have crossed his mind—that when the war was over he might become the leader of the labor movement. Had he done so, very different would have been the course of British domestic politics in the twentieth century. Such a possibility however, was ruled out by his treatment of labor after the war. Mrs. Webb has described him at an industrial conference in 1919:

> He was looking more than ever the actor-conjurer—only instead of the malicious sly look he had when I watched him at the Bristol Trade Union Congress he had assumed the most beneficent air; he might have been the Heavenly Father of the World of Labour. With a combination of persiflage and emotional sympathy with the monotony and sordidness of wage-earning life, he ended in a somewhat forced peroration—a stale refrain of the song of victory.

The troubles in Ireland were none of his making, but the ever-increasing brutality by which Lloyd George sought to end them alienated most of his Liberal followers. In the end, few but die-hard Tories were prepared to countenance the policy of indiscriminate reprisals against the civilian population, the looting and burning of Irish towns and villages, and the infamous deeds of the Black and Tans. Condemned by Liberal and Labour parties, by an independent American commission of inquiry, and by an increasing body of public opinion at home, Lloyd George continued month after month to maintain blandly in the House that the "murder gang" in Ireland was about to be exterminated. He gave these assurances almost to the very day when, in July 1921, the leaders of that "gang" were invited as equals to sit down in No. 10 Downing Street and there negotiate peace.

It was embarrassing for the Prime Minister, who at Versailles had championed the right of self-determination for small peoples, to find himself in the position of using all the force at his command to deny that very right to the small people who were his nearest neighbors, and to whom he had always felt bound by sentimental ties. For Lloyd George was proud of being a Celt, and proud of the superior understanding of the Irish which he felt this gave him. The total failure of his policy in Ireland was, therefore, a personal humiliation and a blow to his vanity. When dealing with the French statesman Aristide Briand, he sometimes stressed the fact that between a Breton and a Welshman there would naturally be a special sympathy that should lead to understanding; and when, in 1921, the Irish delegates arrived in London, he greeted them as "fellow Celts," informing them confidentially that he "could never feel the same with these cold-blooded Saxons" as he did with the children of the twilight.

This myth of the Twilight, with its echoes of Cornwall and Brittany, of Matthew Arnold and Ernest Renan, captivated the imagination of Lloyd George, who appears to have taken it at least half seriously. It also provided a springboard for the wholly Teutonic fantasy of Keynes, who, in one of his most amusing passages, reduced the premier to a wraithlike baleful emanation from the world of Merlin appearing in the twentieth century. "How can I convey to the reader who does not know him," he asked,

> any just impression of this extraordinary figure of our time, this syren, this goat-footed bard, this half-human visitor to our age from the hag-ridden magic and enchanted woods of Celtic antiquity? One catches in his company that flavour of final purposelessness, inner irresponsibility, existence outside or away from our Saxon good and evil, mixed with cunning, remorselessness, love of power, that lend fascination, enthralment, and terror to the fair-seeming magicians of North European folklore.

Apart from leading the nation to victory in the European war, the signing of the Irish treaty in 1922 was probably the greatest act of statesmanship of Lloyd George's career—and certainly it was no small triumph thus to have ended a tragedy that had lasted for more than seven centuries. Beatrice Webb was quick to praise the "amazing skill" with which the Prime Minister had handled the negotiations and reconciled conflicting interests. "Few enlightened persons," she wrote, "believe that any other man could have got this peace by understanding; no other leader could have whipped the Tories to heel and compelled them to recognize the inevitability of Irish independence. Moreover, the peace put us right with the world." The effect, however, of the Irish treaty upon Lloyd George's personal fortunes was disastrous. For the Tories who composed the bulk of the coalition never forgave what they regarded as an unnecessary "surrender to murder," as well as a betrayal of the Protestant minority in the south of Ireland. They waited only for revenge.

As for the Near East, nothing could have been more rash or ill-advised than the Prime Minister's lighthearted encouragement of the Greek attack upon Turkey in 1921. Early memories of the aged Gladstone's passionate denunciation of the Armenian massacres in 1895 were awakened by the still more terrible atrocities perpetrated by the Turks against the Armenians during the First World War. Lloyd George's phil-Hellenism and Zionism both sprang from a common root—detestation of the Turk and the wish to dismember his empire. Lord d'Abernon saw in Lloyd George's support of the Greeks yet another instance of his "invariable devotion to what he conceived to be the oppressed." It was one thing, however, to give Smyrna to the Greeks, another for them to keep it; and when the Turkish armies, under the inspiring leadership of Mustafa Kemal, drove the Greek armies headlong out of Anatolia, Britain's aid was perforce confined to words. Public opinion at home would not have tolerated participation in a fresh war—against an enemy, moreover, who was being actively encouraged by Britain's ally, France. The terrible slaughter of the Greek population of Smyrna in 1922 and the almost total destruction of the city were the final fruits of Lloyd George's irresponsible Near Eastern policy. None of his biographers suggests that he felt any compunction, let alone guilt, for his role in the disaster that finally engulfed more than a million people.

In October 1922, at the famous Carlton Club meeting, Lloyd George's government was overthrown by a sudden revolt of the coalition Conservatives led by Stanley Baldwin. Among the reasons for this unexpected repudiation of the Prime Minister, recent events in Ireland and Turkey undoubtedly played a large part. But the premier's conduct of affairs at home, the way in which he ran the Cabinet and treated his colleagues, had also given rise to much dissatisfaction and had disgruntled many of his followers.

Lloyd George's behavior between 1918 and 1922 affords a striking illustration of Lord Acton's maxim about the way in which power corrupts. For in the fullness of power, the Prime Minister began to reveal signs of incredible folly and arrogance. The follies of his public career were compounded by the blazing indiscretions of his private life, over which the press, with extraordinary self-restraint, threw a veil of discreet silence. In the Cabinet he showed himself a complete autocrat, often interfering with the way in which his ministers managed their own departments. A rebel from childhood, Lloyd George had no sense of teamwork, and for the Public School tradition, which bred this collective discipline, he had nothing but contempt. He was wanting in loyalty to his colleagues, and in his dealings with them was both capricious and irresponsible. According as the situation might require, he would go over their heads to establish direct relations with foreign powers, with the press, or with their own subordinates. Thus Beaverbrook recalls how the premier often gave instructions to undersecretaries without having previously consulted the appropriate ministers. In the judgment of Professor Feiling, Lloyd George, by the way in which he aggrandized his own position at the expense of others, made the position of premier almost a presidential one. "He has demanded the price," wrote Edwin Montagu who served under him as Secretary of State for India, "which it is in the power of every genius to demand—and that price has been the total, complete, absolute disappearance of the doctrine of Cabinet responsibility ever since he formed his Government." Even the official biography by Malcolm Thomson deplores these dictatorial tendencies, which war no doubt had strengthened, and which now, in time of peace, ran riot. Where once he had conciliated opposition, says Thomson, Lloyd George now took pleasure in "bludgeoning" it.

He was much less willing than formerly to listen to independent advice, and surrounded himself with men who could be relied on to tell him what he wanted to hear. "Mr. Lloyd George," wrote Sir Frederick Pollock to Justice Holmes, "is wholly lacking in judgment, is very ill-informed, and has an inveterate habit of taking advice anywhere except in the right quarters." "Sycophants," exclaimed Sir Robert Vansittart, "were round him like bluebottles." After 1918, wrote A. J. P. Taylor over forty years later, "Lloyd George had no colleagues, only subordinates."

His faithful secretary, Frances Stevenson, whom he finally

married, admits that he had no qualms about hurting the feelings of others, and acknowledges that he was too self-centered to realize that there was scarcely a single man in his Cabinet whom he had not, at one time or another, insulted. Lord Milner at the War Office in 1918 was one of the first to resent being reprimanded in front of others. He had, in consequence, threatened to resign. "To submit to that sort of public rebuke without a protest," he told his chief, "or to expose myself to a chance of its repetition, is, I feel, not consistent with self-respect." While never forgetting what he called Lloyd George's "absolutely amazing courage," Milner found "his methods dubious and his manners often intolerable." In his autobiography, *The Mist Procession*, Vansittart recalls how once, when he himself produced "ethnic figures" to dissuade Lloyd George from encouraging the Greeks in Asia Minor, the premier "threw them back at me over the conference table. I told Curzon that I would walk out, if again insulted before foreigners."

At the Foreign Office, Lord Curzon, slow-moving, monumental, and given to pompous platitudes, never failed to draw upon himself the inexhaustible malice and mischief of his impatient, nimble-witted chief.

The Marquess complained to his friend Sir Austen Chamberlain that "the Prime Minister had more than once treated him with scant courtesy—almost with contumely—in the presence of his colleagues and attached little weight to his opinion on matters directly within the sphere of his departmental responsibility. . . . Surely no previous Prime Minister," he complained, "had ever addressed one of his Secretaries of State in such a way." Sir Austen himself told Bonar Law that he had "been shocked by the P.M.'s attacks on Curzon, thinly disguised sometimes as criticisms not of himself but of his department." The oddest part of it all, thought Chamberlain, was that although more than once Lloyd George had spoken to Curzon "in a tone and manner that are almost insulting," he didn't seem in the least anxious to get rid of him. But can there be a bullfight without the bull? And what else could be expected, Lord Curzon may have reflected, from a man who sometimes after lunch went to bed with his trousers on—a piece of "bad form" which the Foreign Secretary could not but deplore.

A detached observer like Sir Harold Nicolson, watching the

skillful placing of the banderillas in the massive aristocratic hide, was convinced that Lloyd George was deliberately avenging on the person of a lord the humiliations suffered in his youth at Llanystumdwy. The Prime Minister was, in fact, quite well aware —at least in this instance—of what he was doing, but excused himself to his secretary by maintaining that Curzon was the only man he ever bullied. With an air of injured innocence, he protested how he wouldn't dream of treating Bonar Law, Balfour, or Smuts in such a fashion.

The victims of Lloyd George's rudeness were usually "elder statesmen," a status that Churchill had not yet achieved. But Beaverbrook, for one, remembers how Churchill was sometimes bullied with the rest. Thus, in 1921, when the latter was Secretary for the Colonies, the premier accused him simultaneously of waste in Iraq, of "fatuous" policies at home, and of ungenerously blaming his own colleagues for the unemployment situation. Strangely enough, in the face of these reproofs, Churchill showed an unwonted meekness, and gave back the soft answer that averted wrath. Few colleagues, wrote Lloyd George's official biographer, "did not at some time or other come under the lash of a hasty anger that passed away as quickly as it rose." Unfortunately those who suffer injuries have longer memories than those who inflict them.

The Foreign Office and the diplomatic service, those last strongholds of aristocratic power, were the special targets of the premier's freebooting forays. Even at Versailles, he sometimes failed to consult his Foreign Secretary, at that time Lord Balfour, about important matters. Sir George Buchanan, when ambassador to Rome, complained to Count Sforza about the "intolerable life which Lloyd George led English ambassadors." What Nicolson calls his "opaque and volatile methods" filled professional diplomats with consternation. Instead of using the regular channels of diplomatic intercourse, the Prime Minister preferred to consult directly with whom he would, and where and when he would. According to Lord Vansittart, he discredited professional diplomacy, partly by the publicity which made privacy impossible, partly by his excessive fondness for round-table conferences at the highest level, and partly by his appointment to the highest posts of wealthy amateurs such as Lord Crewe and Lord Hardinge (both ambassadors to Paris), thereby hindering the preferment of career diplomats and injuring the morale of the foreign service.

Lloyd George's competitive instincts were well developed. "There can be no friendship," he once said, "between the top five men in a Cabinet." It was not for nothing that he was known as "the little Welsh bruiser." Thomas Jones, having served both masters, contrasted the bullying ways of his fellow Welshman with the "quiet decency" with which Baldwin made "mutinous colleagues" feel ashamed of themselves. In private, Lloyd George would refer to rivals like Baldwin or MacDonald in terms of utter contempt: "They are such worms, such insects." Neville Chamberlain was "a pinhead." Edwin Montagu was "a swine and a sneak." Lloyd George's manners could be execrable, wrote Vansittart, nor did he care to whom he gave offense. During the general strike of 1926, the same author reports Lloyd George as boasting of his tit for tat with "little Baldwin": "Baldwin knifed me, and I'll knife him." In Thomas Jones's diplomatic understatement: "None would claim that Lloyd George strove hard to raise the level of political ethics."

Baldwin's considered opinion of Lloyd George was that he was "neither simple, nor English, nor a gentleman." He let it be known that he would never sit in a Cabinet of which Lloyd George was a member. Neville Chamberlain, who had also been humiliated by the premier, made and kept a similar resolution with regard to "that little beast." But the favorite Conservative nickname for the premier was "the goat," a term of derision apparently coined by Frederick S. Oliver, which might refer either to his nimbleness in politics or to his well-known habits of promiscuity.

Even before Lloyd George had been corrupted by the plenitude of power, Lord Robert Cecil, a disinterested witness, wrote that he "profoundly distrusted" his fitness for the highest office. From his own knowledge Lord Robert affirmed that he "has tired out the patience of every man who has worked with him." Lord Balfour, who was reported to observe the ways of "the Little Man" as a scientist might examine an insect under the microscope, once commented: "Principles mean nothing to him—never have. His mind doesn't work that way." And Lionel Curtis, writing after Lloyd George's death, commented that he was "as great as a man can be without principle."

Such strictures upon the premier were by no means confined to the Conservatives. No one could have despised him more than the deposed leader "Squiff." The Asquithian Liberals whom Lloyd George had demolished in the "Victory election" naturally held him responsible for the fate of their once powerful party. In 1922 his portrait, along with that of Churchill, was taken down from the walls of the National Liberal Club and installed in the basement. The Liberal journalist J. A. Spender took special pleasure in denouncing "that scoundrel George," and expatiated endlessly upon the premier's ignorance of history, geography, and economics. So, too, Sir Ernest Woodward, the Oxford historian, depreciates Lloyd George's "sly malignant oratory," and blames him for the demoralization of the Liberal party.

Perhaps the most revealing and amusing account of Lloyd George's comportment at the height of his power is that given by Beatrice Webb. Meeting the premier at dinner at Lord Haldane's in March 1918, she observed him, as she observed everyone else, coolly and dispassionately, without illusions and without ill-will, but with a lively curiosity and an analytic mind. "Prime Ministers," she reflected that night,

usually excite, in all but the most sophisticated minds, a measure of awe and instinctive deference. No such feeling is possible with Lloyd George. The low standard of intellect and conduct of the little Welsh conjurer is so obvious and withal he is so pleasant and lively that official deference and personal respect fade into an atmosphere of agreeable low company—but low company of a most stimulating kind—intimate camaraderie with a fellow adventurer....

He is a blatant intriguer—and every word he says is of the nature of an offer "to do a deal." He neither likes nor dislikes you; you are a mere instrument, one among many—sometimes of value, sometimes not worth picking up. He bears no malice for past opposition; he has no gratitude for past services. He is no doubt genuinely patriotic and public-spirited, but all his ways are crooked and he is obsessed by the craving for power. His one serviceable gift is executive energy—he sees that things are done and not merely talked about. Unfortunately, he does not care whether or not they are thought about. He is the best of boon companions: witty, sympathetic, capable of superficial argument and quick retort, and brilliant in his observations on men and things.

The idealism of the young radical who once had had the courage to oppose the Boer War had given way to the opportunism and unscrupulousness of the practiced politician. "Somewhere in him," wrote the Christian pacifist George Lansbury, "there used to be the makings of a fine public servant, but like so many others he fell among thieves." Little by little Lloyd George's reputation for dishonesty and double-dealing, for chicanery and slipperiness, became something of a legend. His friend Lord Birkenhead, who admired him as being "incomparably the most profound and subtle political strategist in the country"—the only two things that Birkenhead could not forgive were failure and idealism—wrote that the Prime Minister was "like a Greek wrestler whose subtle body has been anointed with oil. He is not very easy to grip."

The fame of his political dexterity spread far beyond the British Isles. In his book *The Arab Awakening*, George Antonius tells how the old, blind king of the Hejaz, driven from Mecca by Ibn Saud in 1926, held Lloyd George responsible for his misfortunes, and told his son: "The English are an honourable kind, in word and in deed, in fortune and in adversity. I say honourable: Only his Excellency Luweed Jurj is something of an acrobat and a fox. I say a fox, saving your presence. God have mercy on the soul of his Excellency, Kitchener."

In his novel *Lord Raingo*, Arnold Bennett depicted Lloyd George as having "no scruples, no sense of justice, or of decency, no loyalties," and as always covertly observing the effect he was having upon others. He had "darting yellowish eyes," and when he smiled, he showed his "cruel teeth." Laurence Housman caricatured him with equal savagery as Mr. Trimblerigg, who "lied often and lied well," and whose creed was: "The Kingdom of Heaven is taken by tricks." An ex-preacher, Mr. Trimblerigg was "a curious combination of the tipster, the thimblerigger and the prophet." Those who knew him best were astonished by "the passionate sincerity with which he was always able to deceive himself."

Should it be counted a virtue, or mere brazenness, that Lloyd George was known to be amused by the questionable repute he had acquired? The difference between himself and Bonar Law, he once told Baldwin, was that the latter minded being called a liar, whereas he himself did not. He is also said to have relished the tribute of the anonymous satirist who once compared him to that scriptural prince of liars, Ananias:

Lloyd George, no doubt, when his life pegs out,
Will ride in a fiery chariot,
And sit in state, on a red-hot plate,
Twixt the devil and Judas Iscariot.
Ananias that day to Satan will say:
"My claim to precedence now fails:
Please move me up higher, away from the fire,
And make way for that liar from Wales."

In the chorus of criticism and abuse, one scarcely finds a single favorable witness. Except for Churchill and Birkenhead, two buccaneers with whom he was united in cynical comradeship, he had few friends in political life. Only among his own people was his popularity undimmed. Even so, when, in 1929, Aneurin Bevan arrived in Parliament from Wales, the new political genius showed scant respect for his famous fellow countryman. One member, listening to a passionate attack made by Bevan upon "the Father of the House," observed that Lloyd George was being "confronted with the ghost of his own angry youth." There was "nothing generous about Aneurin Bevan," the ex-premier curtly told Thomas Jones, his former secretary and later crony of his old age.

Another charge made against Lloyd George in his years of postwar power was that, for the sake of personal advantage, he debased the peerage more thoroughly than any other premier in modern English history. Betwen 1918 and 1922, he granted twenty-six peerages, one hundred and thirty baronetcies and four hundred and eighty-one knighthoods. Of such titles, since Lloyd George had always cultivated the fourth estate, a notable proportion went to the press: no less than five peerages, five baronetcies, and thirty-seven knighthoods. (Four press lords had been members of his wartime government—Northcliffe, Beaverbrook, Rothermere, and Rhondda.) When criticized for this abuse of honors—and even the official biography admits that he was guilty of "unseemly practices" in this regard—Lloyd George justified himself by referring facetiously to the precedent set over a century ago by William Pitt—of whom Lord Rosebery remarked that his baronets had been legion and his knights as the sands of the sea.

The iconoclast of 1911 must have derived considerable satisfaction from the knowledge that he was now the master of the

Lords, and that he could, whenever he chose, debase the currency in peers. According to Lord Vansittart, he actually created ninety-one peers during his six years in office. Not for over a century had the fountain of honors gushed so vigorously. The flow was highly profitable to the guardian of the well. It would no doubt be crude to intimate that titles were bought and sold as in the good old days of the eighteenth century: they were bestowed in return for services rendered, and the services often took the form of large donations to the party funds. Lord Vansittart, in his autobiography, recalls how touts like "nasty Maundy Gregory" were sometimes employed to drum up trade among prospective aspirants for honors, and that a regular tariff was established, with knighthoods costing up to £12,000 apiece, and baronetcies up to £40,000. Lloyd George was the first Prime Minister since Walpole in the eighteenth century to have left office a much richer man than when he entered it.

With the money thus acquired, there was built up a huge party fund, which was held absolutely and solely at the disposal of Lloyd George. Not till 1927 did he give any accounting of it, and according to Thomas Jones, the most trustworthy of his biographers, many of the papers essential to an understanding of what happened were "efficiently destroyed." That large sums were involved is evident from the fact that Lloyd George was able to purchase the *Daily Chronicle*, a paper he later sold for £2,000,000. He spent £160,000 on the 1923 election, and £300,000 in 1927. The bulk of the fund, however, was dissipated in the election of 1929, when the ex-premier made his last serious bid for power. It was, as Frank Owen says, "the greatest election effort of his life." He flooded the country with posters depicting himself as a knight in shining armor, slaying the dragon of unemployment—but all to no avail, for of the five hundred and twelve Liberal candidates who stood for Parliament, only fifty-eight were elected, while many forfeited their deposits.

As may be imagined, the Asquithian Liberals were furious with what they regarded as the misappropriation of Liberal party funds for Lloyd George's personal use. It was distasteful to come cap in hand before their old enemy seeking a handout at every general election. In the opinion of Thomas Jones, Liberalism might even have survived "had Lloyd George parted with his treasure."

For all his admiration of the wartime premier, Professor Jones reluctantly concluded that "he would have done better for Liberalism and for himself without his Fund."

The total eclipse of Lloyd George after 1922 is a remarkable phenomenon. On his leaving office, George V had written: "I am sorry he is going, but some day he will be P.M. again." With this forecast the great majority of the nation, his own political enemies, and not least, Lloyd George himself would no doubt have agreed. The Prime Minister, however, had alienated too many interests, bullied too many people, and wounded too many feelings ever again to command a following. For the desirability of excluding Lloyd George from office was one point upon which all parties—Conservative, Labour, Liberal—and all leaders—Baldwin, MacDonald, Asquith—were in agreement. The result was that, even in 1931, during the crisis of the depression, when the emergency national government was being formed, few considered inviting the most eminent living statesman—for that title not even his enemies could deny—to sustain it with his prestige or his ability. Over the B.B.C., Lloyd George declaimed bitterly that the election of 1931 was a "partisan intrigue under the guise of a popular appeal." By that time, however, no one cared much about what he thought on any subject.

That Lloyd George's career was virtually over was naturally slow to be realized. To many in England in the nineteen-twenties, he still seemed, fresh from his wartime triumph, the greatest figure in national life. In 1923 the Webbs would even have preferred him as premier to Baldwin, and with all his faults, they had considered him a better leader than Ramsay MacDonald. Three years later, during the general strike, they supported the middle course he then followed, since Lloyd George blamed equally the ineptitude of Baldwin's leadership and the irresponsible folly of unionists like A. J. Cook. For those who, like the Webbs, saw Britain being pulled apart by two extremes—the attraction from Communist Russia on the one hand, and that from Fascist Italy on the other—it sometimes seemed as if the wartime premier might yet have a significant role to play. "Out of this turmoil," wrote Beatrice Webb in 1926, "might emerge Lloyd George as arbiter; or Winston as Mussolini. It is clear that in their own imagination each of these two active politicians sees himself as the *Man of Destiny!* Of the two I back the Welsh wizard—a stronger and better fighter. But I think the British," she added, "will prefer cricket to melodrama."

When the depression came, it was unfortunate that through his own fault Lloyd George had been completely discredited, since he was one of the few men with vision enough to realize that the situation demanded bolder and more imaginative measures than either MacDonald or Baldwin—two former enemies now united—were willing to take. The challenge of the depression, in fact, aroused in Lloyd George something of the old spirit he had put into the winning of the war. His economic ideas appear to have been shaped in part by the theories of Keynes, in part by the practice of Franklin D. Roosevelt. Lloyd George now envisaged what he termed a "British New Deal," and called for a national development board to take stock of Britain's industrial and agricultural needs so as to mobilize the nation's resources. He proposed to nationalize the Bank of England, and urged the adoption of a great program of public works—including the development of Britain's hydroelectric potential and the modernizing of her archaic road system. These proposals, praised by Churchill as being "at once virile and sober," and deserving of "the closest attention," were ignored by almost everyone else. Only in the labor movement might Lloyd George have won popular support for such radical suggestions, but, unhappily for himself, he had irretrievably antagonized labor by what Beatrice Webb calls his "bitter and insulting" attacks on the Labour party in 1929, and by the "undignified and futile rage" he showed in public as a result of the Labour victory in the general election of that year.

The result was that in the nineteen-thirties, having no other outlet for his energies, Lloyd George devoted himself to the agreeable task of justifying to posterity both his wartime leadership and the part that he had played in making the peace. Between 1933 and 1937, six large volumes of his *War Memoirs* appeared, followed in 1938 by two more massive tomes, entitled *The Truth about the Peace Treaties*. In order to refresh his memories of the First World War, the ex-premier, in high good spirits, toured the battlefields of France and Flanders. The book itself was written mainly at Churt, his country home in Surrey, but partly in the winter sun of Marrakesh. Sir Maurice Hankey, who had been secretary to the war Cabinet, and Captain Liddell Hart, the military expert, helped him with advice in their respective fields. Trained clerks from the Cabinet indexed his papers for him.

Lloyd George derived much pleasure from fighting the old battles once again, and from once more deriding the generals—though some of them, like his old adversary Haig, were no longer alive. Chiefly because of their unconcealed vanity and egotism, his memoirs make a disagreeable impression. Lloyd George was more concerned to exonerate himself of charges brought against him by various critics than to convey to the reader any sense of the mingled grandeur and horror of the tragedy in which he had taken a leading part. As a writer, moreover, he lacked the gifts with which Churchill made so stirring an epic out of his recollections of the same tragedy. For Lloyd George lacked in point Churchill's sense of proportion and design, his strong dramatic feeling, and his power of infusing his immense vitality into every subject upon which he touched. The rseult is that his *War Memoirs* are frequently lifeless, circumlocutory, and overloaded with detail. In similar fashion, most of his speeches have lost their power with the passing years. Today, in Vansittart's vivid phrase, they "stand like superannuated spells."

"All he can do," wrote Keynes scornfully, "is to work over his hoards of paper, snipping out anything capable of being made to do duty in an unrelieved tirade of self-justification." Political enemies were quick to see that the ex-premier had not added to his reputation, and at the University of Toronto in 1939, Baldwin referred to him ironically as one of those "statesmen who have never made a mistake." Though it came with ill-grace from one who had supported Chamberlain at Munich and after, there was truth in the gibe. Even such admirers as Thomas Jones were distressed by the rhetorical insincerity of many passages of the book and by what Jones called its "cheap sneers, petty vindictiveness and deliberate suppression." In truth, the author was not equal to his subject, and the greatness of the theme was lost in the smallness of the man.

When the project of writing his memoirs had originally suggested itself to him, Lloyd George negotiated to sell the press rights for £90,000, but so great was the public outcry against what then seemed like a selfish exploitation of tragedy that he declared the money would be devoted to war charities. After this the project languished for some years, and, according to Beaverbrook, when the *War Memoirs* finally appeared, though they brought their author something like £60,000, not a penny of it went to charity.

Before his final retirement Lloyd George made one last extraordinary appearance on the international scene: his visit to Hitler at Berchtesgaden in 1936. Doubtless he knew already that *Mein Kampf* had praised his oratory and power over the masses. "The speeches of this Englishman [!]" wrote Hitler, "were the most wonderful achievements . . . they gave proof of the most astonishing knowledge of the soul of the greatest layers of the people." And when he arrived at Berchtesgaden, Hitler sprang forward to greet him with outstretched hand, welcoming him effusively as "the actual victor of the World War."

Although Lloyd George was now seventy-three, his surrender to the Führer's influence was probably due to vanity rather than to senility. The old man was captivated by Hitler, by "his gestures, his eyes, his voice, his talk." He called him "a great and wonderful leader . . . the Saviour of Germany." When Hitler gave him his photograph, he asked if he might put it on his desk along with those of Foch, Clemenceau, and Woodrow Wilson. The tea party ended with an invitation to the Führer to visit England in person.

On returning home, Lloyd George wrote an article in Beaverbrook's *Daily Express*, a leading organ of appeasement, in which he declared that the Germans had no desire to attack any other country. Hitler had fought personally in the World War, and knew what war meant. "The Germans," he asserted, "have definitely made up their minds never to quarrel with us again." It was not Hitler's fault, he believed, that no "friendly arrangement" between Britain and Germany had as yet been reached. With Dachau only a few miles away and the Night of the Long Knives only two years ago, one wonders how any sane man could so completely have deceived himself. Concentration camps and blood purges, to be sure, are not pleasant topics for the tea table; but *Mein Kampf*, which Lloyd George ought at least to have known about, was an explicit statement of the ruthlessness with which Hitler intended to pursue his aim of territorial aggrandizement in Europe, with world dominion as his ultimate goal.

There were in England at this time not a few who regarded Hitler with as much enthusiasm as did Lloyd George—Arnold Toynbee, for example, was another devout, deluded pilgrim to the shrine of Berchtesgaden, and Neville Chamberlain was soon to fly there hopefully. If at first you don't succeed, said wags in London, fly, fly again. The war over, Lloyd George's official biographer saw fit to remind the public that originally Hitler's work was "in many ways inspiring, constructive and beneficient," and Thomas Jones continued to believe that at their meeting it was the ex-premier who dominated Hitler, not vice versa. "Lloyd George easily dominates any company," Jones wrote in 1936 to his friend Abraham Flexner, who just then was sending him from Princeton appalling firsthand accounts of cruelties practiced against Jews and others in Germany. In *The Gathering Storm*, Churchill commented on the gullibility of his former leader. "No one was more completely deluded," he wrote, "than Mr. Lloyd George, whose rapturous accounts of his conversations make odd reading today."

Lloyd George's behavior at this time is contradictory and baffling. While flirting with Hitler, he condemned Mussolini as "temperamentally an aggressor," and was willing to go to war over Abyssinia. He was furious with the Hoare-Laval Pact, and favored blocking the Suez Canal against Italian troops. In what Churchill later called "one of the greatest Parliamentary performances of all time," he condemned as a "cowardly surrender" the government's relinquishment of sanctions against Italy in 1936. The pleasure of publicly belaboring Baldwin was no doubt as great as that of attacking Mussolini—a fact that may have accounted for Lloyd George's unusual warmth on this occasion. Then, in 1936, when General Franco rose in arms against the legitimate government of Spain, the old Welsh Baptist radical revolted at the notion of a clerical Fascist dictatorship and urged Britain and France to aid the Spanish Republic and stop the farce of nonintervention. He also confessed himself puzzled to see his new friend Hitler unaccountably dropping bombs on undefended Spanish towns like Guernica.

After the Munich Pact in 1938, despite the fact that Chamberlain, having capitulated to Hitler's demands, had done just what Lloyd George had recommended, the latter turned upon the Prime Minister with a vehemence that matched Churchill's. "China, Abyssinia, Spain, Czechoslovakia!" he declaimed (in private, he termed Beneš "a little French jackal"). "We have descended during these years a ladder of dishonour, rung by rung. Are we going, can we go, any lower?" Especially, he condemned the exclusion of Russia from the Munich Conference. The harassed Chamberlain replied by reminding his critic that even in totalitarian countries statesmen did not "foul their own nests" in public.

One cannot help wondering whether Lloyd George at this time realized, or was capable of realizing, his own motives. Was not Neville Chamberlain, perhaps, more offensive to him than Adolf Hitler? For no sooner did the Prime Minister, after the German invasion of Poland, belatedly proclaim his intention to fight to the end than Lloyd George urged him to invite Hitler to state his peace terms, and not to reject any offer that the Führer might make! In the early months of 1940, his secretary remembers his personal attacks upon Chamberlain as being "vitriolic." "Hypocrisy," "mendacity," and "cowardice" were some of the accusations that Lloyd George leveled at the Prime Minister. The ex-premier's last important intervention in debate was on the dramatic occasion in the Commons, on May 8, 1940, which resulted in Chamberlain's resignation. The Prime Minister had spoken of the need for sacrifice. "I say solemnly," said Lloyd George with kindling fervor, "that the Prime Minister should give an example of sacrifice, because there is nothing which can contribute more to victory than that he should sacrifice the seals of office."

With Chamberlain out of office, and Churchill in full control, Lloyd George's interest in the war waned perceptibly. He complained to the new Prime Minister that though he had "in public thrice offered to help the Government in any capacity, however humble," he had been thrice ignored; nor was he mollified when Churchill offered him a post in the war Cabinet—subject to Chamberlain's approval! There was talk of sending him, though he was now nearly eighty, as ambassador to Washington—but President Roosevelt indicated that someone else would be more acceptable.

From this point onward, the ex-premier degenerated more and more into a surly and cantankerous critic of the government. "I am not going in with this gang," he declared in 1941. "There will be a change. The country does not realize the peril it is in." He did "not believe in the way or in the persons with which the War Cabinet is constituted. It is totally different," he complained peevishly, "to the War Cabinet set up in the last war." Visiting him in November 1942, Smuts found him "frustrated, knowing that he was the biggest man about the place and unused." Lloyd George now condemned the policy of unconditional surrender which he himself had supported in 1918, and criticized Churchill's secret sessions of Parliament as "a pernicious sham." He blamed the Allies for not doing more to help Russia in the West and noted almost regretfully how small were the losses of the Eighth Army in Africa compared to those at Passchendaele. The inference seemed to be that this was hardly worth calling a war. On one occasion Churchill, stung by his former chief's captious criticisms, lost patience and made a sharp allusion to Pétain. The shaft went home, and Lloyd George retired ignominiously to Llanystumdwy.

As the tide turned at Alamein and Stalingrad, and victory came within sight, the old man lost all interest in the mighty struggle then unfolding. He refused to concern himself with the thrilling events culminating in the invasion of Normandy, and fell back instead upon Dickens and other favorites of his childhood.

He had long ago abandoned all interest in religion. No memories of the ardent evangelism of his youth stirred in him now. His mind, as Thomas Jones observed, was in fact "neither speculative nor devout." The old man was content to sit for hours at the window gazing out vacantly at the mountains of Snowdonia, or across the bay at Harlech, as the buzz bombs and rockets fell upon London. He had never had any interest in art or in music (apart from hymn-singing), so that such things could not solace him now. More and more his mind reverted to the experiences of childhood.

Whatever his thoughts, Lloyd George can hardly have realized the significance of that childhood or of the way in which it had shaped his future life. For such knowledge we are indebted to two biographies, which appeared not long after his death, written by men who knew him well and who had worked with him for years—Malcolm Thomson and A. J. Sylvester. Mr. Thomson's life was written at the request of Lloyd George's widow, the Countess Lloyd George, and was based upon the official papers she possessed. These two writers, both of them warm admirers of Lloyd George, are in substantial agreement about the main features of his character. They disclose new aspects of his private life and thus enable us to glimpse something of the psychological basis on which the public personality rested.

Never having known his father, the child had been brought up by his mother, his grandmother, and his uncle Richard Lloyd, the village shoemaker of Llanystumdwy. At the time of his father's death there were two children—himself and a slightly older sister; soon a younger, posthumous brother was born. All through childhood, the precocious boy appears to have been petted and spoiled by his adoring maternal relatives. The result, as his widow later pointed out, was that from his earliest days he took for granted that someone else would always look after him. Waited on hand and foot, he was free to indulge his studies and his daydreams. The practical details of life were beneath him, and to the end of his days he was incapable of doing the simplest things for himself. His hands were almost useless: he could scarcely dress himself or button up his clothes; he fumbled with doorknobs and could not open windows. He could never find documents, even when they had passed directly through his hands, which gave him the additional pleasure of scolding his secretaries for having mislaid them.

Later, when he was installed as Prime Minister at Downing Street, the faithful Sarah Jones came from Wales to look after his children and to manage his household, which she soon came to dominate. When others were apprehensive before the great man, anxious to indulge his every whim, Sarah Jones, who washed and mended his clothes, would scold him like the naughty boy she knew he was. "Great God, must you always act like a spoiled child?" Or perhaps, her patience exhausted, she would break out suddenly: "Great God, there you go again. It's ashamed of you I am." In public life also, Lloyd George needed someone to look after him, nor was he always fortunate enough to have C. P. Scott at hand to stitch and mend his speeches. Mr. Sylvester has preserved an amusing impression of the genial editor of the *Manchester Guardian* going over something Lloyd George had written. Correcting it, deleting carefully, and stroking his white beard, Scott could be heard chuckling to himself from time to time: "Naughty, naughty."

The early impatience with detail and incapacity in the practical affairs of daily life was reflected throughout Lloyd George's public career. His genius lay in moving others by his eloquence to matters of great pith and enterprise—hence his successes at the Ministry of Munitions and in the premiership: he failed whenever, as at Versailles, the situation required not so much inspired vision or grandiose schemes (to be executed by others), as patient, persistent, daily attention to a mass of detail—political, economic, social, cultural, geographic. As Sir Harold Nicolson noticed, his "aversion to detail was almost pathological."

The spoiled child is usually vain and egotistical, inconsiderate of others, and incapable of admitting himself in the wrong. Lloyd George's public life was one long illustration of these weaknesses. As Mr. Sylvester says, though he always preached democracy, "no greater autocrat ever lived." Autocrats, however, have few friends—and Lloyd George, as his widow testifies, had hardly any. There was, she says, a certain secretiveness about him which forbade any real intimacy. Most of those who knew him would have agreed with the remark of Frederick S. Oliver: "He does not understand what friendship means." Of all his acquaintances in his public life, Churchill was the only one who was ever close enough to call him "David."

Whenever crossed or thwarted, Lloyd George was liable to fall into a towering rage: the scene at Paris when he lost his temper with Poincaré, banging his fist on the table and accusing the French premier of "insulting the whole British race"—such a scene may have been rehearsed many times, long years before, in the cobbler's cottage at Llanystumdwy. When his secretary, Frances Stevenson, once reproached him "after a savage hurt which he had inflicted," he simply answered: "I wound where I know I can hurt most." Indifferent to the feelings of others, he would conceal his plans from his assistants, and then rebuke them for not having anticipated his wishes. He refused to read letters, even about important matters, and then blamed his secretaries for not having informed him about their contents. He liked to place people in embarrassing situations, and when they attempted to explain he would get up and walk away. He would cause consternation at No. 10 by not mentioning, till a few moments before he was due to arrive, that a very important visitor was expected for lunch. Had he confined his bullying ways to his inferiors, only a few feelings might have been injured, and all would have been well; but when he humiliated his own Cabinet members and treated Lord Curzon like an office boy, he made it certain that, once fallen from power, he would never again be called to office.

Another trait of Lloyd George was extreme vanity. He was sufficiently confident of his own intuitive ability to believe that he had only to glance at a person's face in order to judge his character. If he made a speech, he was hurt not to receive congratulations from those who might have heard it. Especially where his personal appearance was concerned, his self-love was evident. He was particularly proud of his small hands and feet, and of his carefully groomed, abundant silky hair. One of Mr. Sylvester's duties was to be in attendance when the barber came, so as to insure that not too much was taken off. When, during the war, the Prime Minister developed a new *persona*, he cultivated an appearance to match it. All England soon became familiar with the tossing snow-white mane that fell about his shoulders as he spoke. The Tyrolean cloak and the beribboned pince-nez were admirably contrived stage effects.

Perhaps the most amusing illustration of Lloyd George's vanity was his belief in phrenology. When he was a child, someone had examined his cranium and declared it to be the head of a future Prime Minister. Thereafter, phrenology was the standard by which Lloyd George privately measured the capacity of others. "Simon and Neville," he would observe meaningly, "have big bumps of conceit." No wonder Chamberlain had made a fool of himself at Munich. "Look at his head!" Lloyd George would exclaim. "The worst thing Neville Chamberlain ever did was to meet Hitler and let Hitler see him." Bonar Law, it appears, was the only person exempt from such phrenological scrutiny.

That Lloyd George's personality was to a large degree infantile may actually have been one of the sources of his strength
as a war leader. The crisis of the war enabled him to identify his
own infantile ego with the national interest, so that the satisfaction of his private urge to power seemed no more than a patriotic
duty, and was accepted as such by the nation. Since in time of
war to kill becomes a virtue, and even civilized societies undergo
a reversion toward infantilism, there is, in this perfect coincidence
of public and private ends, a certain ironic appropriateness.

The war once won, the two ends diverged; and the premier
was now abused for continuing to be what in fact he had always
been. This infantile type of personality is not seldom the foundation of the kind of greatness typified by what Ludendorff called
Lloyd George—"a man of iron." It is true, of course, that other
gifts—intuitive understanding of the needs and weaknesses of
others, a certain degree of intelligence (not necessarily high),
and perhaps, above all, a capacity for oratory—are essential before
the infantile potential can be raised to political greatness. Yet a
little man in a rage (or a big one for that matter) is still no more
than an infant that has grown large without ceasing to be infantile. Adolf Hitler provides a sinister illustration of this not uncommon phenomenon.

In the New Year's honors list of 1945, his previous consent
having been obtained, an earldom was conferred upon Lloyd
George. Those who idolized him in Wales had hoped that, like
Gladstone, he would die a commoner. His acceptance of a peerage disillusioned some of his admirers. He chose the title Earl
Lloyd-George of Dwyfor, but he lived neither to take his seat
in the Lords nor yet to see the end of the war. He died of cancer
on March 26 of that year, and at his own request was buried,
not in Westminster Abbey, but in his native village—today a
place of pilgrimage for Welshmen from all over the principality.
He was, said Winston Churchill, the greatest Welshman since
Henry VII.

After Lloyd George's death, of his two children who had entered politics, one, Lady Megan, joined the Labour party, while
the other, Major Gwilym Lloyd George, became Home Secretary in a Conservative government. Thus was symbolized in

Lloyd George's own family the disruption of the Liberal party, which he himself had done so much to promote. His own seat at Carnarvon, which he had held for fifty-five years, was immediately captured by the Tories.

VIII

Sir Winston Churchill

(1874-1965)

AT THE TIME of his death, a few weeks after his ninetieth birthday, adored by his fellow countrymen and admired by the world, Sir Winston Churchill was not just a man, but also a revered institution. "He was the greatest man of his time," wrote Lord Vansittart in his autobiography, "probably of all time," and when Field Marshal Montgomery called Sir Winston the greatest Englishman in history, he spoke for the entire nation.

Churchill's genius is universally recognized, his place in history secure: time itself has silenced his detractors, once so numerous and vocal. During the larger part of his long parliamentary career, he was more often attacked by his own party as being twice a renegade than by the Labour party, which was the object of his own implacable lifelong hostility. Now all that is forgotten, for human beings when at last they bow before greatness cannot bear to find in it the least flaw or imperfection. Idolatry takes the place of respect founded on rational judgment, and sentimentality envelops the object of worship, blurring its outlines and obscuring its true nature. To sentimentalists extreme old age is specially hallowed and hence exempt from critical scrutiny. The maxim *De mortuis nil nisi bonum* is invoked. Like so many distinguished figures of English history whom he himself praised, Sir Winston in fact became a myth; nor did he have to wait for death to bring this about—it happened during his own lifetime. He did "bestride the narrow world like a Colossus."

History, however, is not respectful of myth, and by surrounding eminence with awe we do not render it the homage it deserves. True greatness—that of Abraham Lincoln, for example—

is not diminished by a recognition of faults perhaps inseparable from its composition. Sir Winston Churchill's faults loom as massive as his virtues, and it would be a poor compliment to him to pretend that they did not exist. Perhaps the most discerning tribute one can pay him is to admit that only some extraordinary, perhaps unique quality of personal greatness could have endeared to his fellow countrymen a character in many ways so forbidding—insensitive, egotistical, arrogant, aggressive—and a mind in many respects so limited and so often lacking in sympathy with the problems, aspirations, and sufferings of all who found themselves outside the particular class in which he himself happened to be born. To have transcended such limitations, to have put democracy so notably in his debt, and to have become for millions the most cherished symbol of their lives—this suggests something of the unusual depth and many-sided nature of the personality that concludes this series of studies.

Of the public figures in English history whose lives have already been discussed, probably the one who most resembled Winston Churchill was David Lloyd George. The fact alone that both, like Chatham before them, were great war ministers, links their names inseparably. Beyond that, they shared many qualities in common: unquenchable vitality, restless energy, personal magnetism, and an inspiring power of oratory. They were alike also in their defects: opportunism, total lack of consideration for others, and a degree of egotism that can only be termed infantile. Lloyd George, however, whom Lord Haldane once called "an illiterate with an unbalanced mind," lacked both the versatility and the intellectual power of Churchill. Where Sir Winston found relaxation in Macaulay or Gibbon, Lloyd George in his prime amused himself with cheap detective fiction. The latter, cast in an inferior mold, lacked also the personal courage of his younger colleague and successor.

Since Gladstone detested both imperialism and war, and since he not only became, but remained, a Liberal in politics, it may seem strange to compare him with Churchill. Yet in certain personal attributes the great Victorian is closer to Sir Winston than any figure in modern English politics, not excluding Lloyd George. He alone displayed a similar combination of intellectual power with emotional depth. He alone dominated his generation, as Churchill did his, by sheer moral force—for whatever the other gifts of the Welsh wizard, this is a quality no one would attribute to him. Though wearing an altered aspect and harnessed to different political ends, pugnacity and aggressiveness were features as prominent in Gladstone as in Churchill. As a boy of nine the latter once heard Gladstone speak on Irish Home Rule. All his life he recalled the "great white eagle, fierce and splendid." The G.O.M. was then eighty-four and, in the vigor of his ninth decade, surpassed even Sir Winston at a similar age. Nor must it be forgotten that Gladstone lacked the supreme instrument for the magnification of personality which was at Churchill's disposal: in the days of Midlothian there was no B.B.C.

Since at the time of Disraeli's death Churchill was but six years old, he could preserve no personal memory of him. He was brought up, however, to revere him as the founder of the modern Conservative party and as the creator of British imperialism. Nevertheless, despite certain traits they shared in common—opportunism (Churchill also tended to regard domestic politics as "play and gambling"), a considerable literary gift, and the invaluable asset of a sense of humor—one is struck more by the differences than by the similarities between the two great Conservative leaders of modern England. In his cleverness and ability to manipulate people, Disraeli suggests not so much Churchill as Lloyd George. Above all, he was lacking in that moral fervor and emotional power which both Gladstone and Churchill possessed.

The man of action seldom troubles himself about the origin and purpose of life, the meaning of the universe or what place in it may be assigned to man. As Churchill, with equal candor and cynicism, tells us in his autobiography: "I adopted quite early in life a system of believing whatever I wanted to believe." That so crude a process of rationalization, however convenient, could not serve truth, was a matter of perfect indifference. To him as to the young Disraeli, the world was and always remained—his oyster. Churchill's lighthearted pragmatism settled philosophic problems that have vexed man ever since he learned to think—the question, for example, of free will versus determinism. Such difficulties the impatient subaltern in India solved by declaring them nonexistent: free will and determinism were one and the same thing. The solution thus happily achieved sustained Churchill throughout life. The warlike approach to philosophy— the cutting of metaphysical knots by the sword of the will— distinguishes men like Churchill from genuine thinkers like Bentham or Mill almost as much as if they inhabited different planets.

The gulf between Churchill and social philosophers such as Jeremy Bentham, or social scientists like the Webbs, is equally wide. For they hopefully regarded man as primarily a rational creature, and thought habitually in terms of mankind, not just in terms of any particular group or nation. The touchstone of "the greatest happiness" was to be applied to the whole human race, not merely to a favored portion of it. Ironically enough, the future of the nation which in 1940 Churchill helped to save was to be molded after the war chiefly by ideas such as those of the Fabians, ideas that all his life Churchill held in abhorrence and which he never ceased to combat. In a sense, therefore, it may be said that final victory lay with the Webbs and their friends.

It is no accident that in Churchill's most popular historical work philosophers and social thinkers are almost entirely excluded from consideration. In the fourth volume of his *History of the English-Speaking Peoples*, where Churchill devotes half a page to Wellington's duel with Winchelsea and four pages to Queen Caroline's trial in 1820 (still without comprehending its significance), he allots a single line to Bentham, and never even mentions figures as significant as Newman and Mill, Malthus and Owen, Darwin and Huxley. In his mind, such men had no real existence.

A similar bias is reflected in his preference for General Robert E. Lee over Abraham Lincoln. Despite the conventional tribute he pays to the Emancipator, it is evident that the imagination that kindled to the battles of the Civil War remained unmoved by Lincoln's profound humanity and by his tragic greatness; and though Churchill quotes at length from Daniel Webster, he makes no allusion to the Gettysburg Address or to the Second Inaugural address.

The Churchill whom the world justly delights to honor, and whom, as long as civilization lasts, men will not readily forget,

is the Churchill of 1940. That year will forever remain inseparable from his image. That was his year of glory, to which
the whole of his previous life served but as a prelude. Of that
May night in 1940 when at the age of sixty-five he became
Prime Minister, thus achieving the ambition of a lifetime, he
writes: "As I went to bed at about 3 a.m., I was conscious of a
profound sense of relief. At last I had the authority to give instructions over the whole scene. I felt as if I were walking with
Destiny, and as if my whole past life had been but a preparation
for this hour and for this trial."

In 1940 he provided the inspiration that produced out of almost
irretrievable disaster the will to victory. That hour of unparalleled
danger was the superb climax of his existence. From a whole
nation, nerved to unequaled effort by the eloquence of the beloved leader, came a well-nigh miraculous response. In a single
week—the week of Dunkirk—the weariness and fecklessness of
twenty squalid years were sloughed away. In a crisis where to
a rational observer no hope existed, a nation facing imminent
destruction was renewed in hope. Two thousand years of history
had brought the people of Britain to this confrontation, to this
hour of testing, in which all they had ever achieved—freedom,
law, decency itself—hung suspended in the balance: and not for
Britain alone, but for the world. In the scales of this tremendous
challenge Churchill was weighed and not found wanting. He
not merely attained victory; he also did what no other living
Englishman could have done: for by commemorating it in deeply
felt and deeply moving words, he handed down its memory to
future ages. As Clement Attlee observed in his graceful tribute
on Churchill's eightieth birthday, the old warrior was in this
like Julius Caesar: he had not only conquered, but had written
his own version of his triumph. No passage in the *Gallic Wars*
could surpass the splendor of the rhetoric with which Churchill
clothed the heroic episode of Dunkirk—the hope of ultimate victory snatched from almost overwhelming disaster:

There was a white glow, overpowering, sublime, which ran through
our island from end to end. . . . In the midst of our defeat glory
came to the island people, united and unconquerable; and the tale
of the Dunkirk beaches will shine in whatever records are preserved
of our affairs. . . . We shall not flag or fail. . . . We shall go on

to the end, we shall fight with growing confidence and growing strength in the air, we shall defend our island, whatever the cost may be, we shall fight on the beaches, we shall fight on the landing-grounds, we shall fight in the fields and in the streets, we shall fight in the hills; we shall never surrender, and even if, which I do not for a moment believe, this island or a large part of it were subjugated and starving, then our Empire beyond the seas, armed and guarded by the British Fleet, would carry on the struggle, until, in God's good time, the New World, with all its power and might, steps forth to the rescue and the liberation of the Old.

In 1940 Churchill not only saved Britain but became also the supreme symbol of hope to the unhappy peoples of Europe who had fallen under Hitler's domination. Frenchmen, Poles, Norwegians, Dutch, Danes, Greeks, and Yugoslavs saw in him their sole chance of freedom, however remote the hour of that freedom might be. Listening in some clandestine corner to the B.B.C., hundreds of thousands, perhaps millions, throughout Europe risked danger of death. This they did nightly, to be heartened in their resistance by hearing that dogged angry defiance of the monstrous tyranny that held them in its grip. Innumerable hearers thus sustained their courage and prolonged their hope; and for years after, many could never hear without a constriction in the throat that rasping inimitable voice with its still not quite conquered lisp, that occasional stutter, and that staccato delivery whose phrases were chopped up regardless of sense or punctuation, the better to hurl them against the enemy.

It was to those dark days that Pierre Mendès-France, Prime Minister of France, referred in 1954 when he spoke of "the immense debt of gratitude" that the French people owed to Churchill for having helped to release them from slavery. "Few statesmen," he wrote, "have inspired so much admiration and respect among so many peoples as the one who today crosses the threshold of his ninth decade in a life crowded with risks, honours, battles and triumphs." The wartime premier Paul Reynaud had already termed him "the most popular of all living men in France"; while in liberated Belgium, Paul Spaak, the Foreign Minister, extolled him as having "marked his country and the world with his personality. He is a poet of action. In war he saved the free world. In peace he has always been, in success as in defeat, the perfect example of the man who deserves to live in the world which he saved."

Above all, however, in the concentration camps of Nazi Germany—in Dachau and Belsen and Buchenwald—among the doomed and tormented, who had once been simple human beings, Churchill was the name whose syllables they dwelt on with gratitude and hope, the name they clung to in the midst of despair. For them it was like a glimmer of light showing faintly at the distant end of a tunnel, reminding those who were trapped that the normal world still existed.

In his *Story of a Secret State*, the valiant Polish fighter Jan Karski tells how, far away in Eastern Europe, as he lay in the hospital, crippled after a savage beating by the Nazis, the tidings of the fall of France filled him with despair. Soon came the further news that England and her indomitable premier had not surrendered—and in the hospital bed in Slovakia, in the broken body of a tortured man, the name of Churchill renewed the will to fight and the determination never to yield.

From his Norwegian prison camp, Odd Nansen—the son of the great explorer who had been one of Hitler's youthful heroes —testified how Churchill was the mainstay of the prisoners' morale. Nansen himself has told how merely by repeating those "immortal words—blood, sweat and tears," he gained the strength to continue; while in dark moments, as after the fall of Singapore or Tobruk, Churchill was so candid in defeat, that all prisoners knew that there was one man whom they could trust.

And in 1944, from her fugitive lair in the heart of Amsterdam, where, in the city of Rembrandt and Spinoza, human beings were marked for extermination and hunted down like animals, a young Jewish girl named Anne Frank listened eagerly for the voice of her "beloved Winston Churchill" coming over the airwaves across the North Sea with its message of hope. Yet not even Churchill could avert the evil fate whereby that sensitive and intelligent being, for whom the beauty of life was just beginning to unfold, was shipped by cattle truck to Belsen, there to be gassed to death.

No people at war's end had more reason to be grateful to Churchill, none had more reason to cherish his name, than the people of Israel. Hence, when at last their ordeal was over, the Israeli Foreign Minister, Moshe Sharett, paid tribute to the man whom, more than any other, the Jewish people considered as their savior. "Israel," he told Churchill, "unites with Britain and the nations of the world in paying homage to your matchless record and statesmanship. In one of the bleakest crises in the history of civilization, it was given to you by supreme feat of personal determination and inspired national leadership, to save the cause of freedom, to give sublime expression to the faith and fervor of man in his resistance to tyranny, and to lead your own brave people from defeat to victory. Your staunch advocacy of the Zionist cause," Mr. Sharett concluded, "has earned you the gratitude of the Jewish people."

When, on Sir Winston's eightieth birthday, both Houses of Parliament assembled in the ancient palace of Westminster to salute him, in the words of *The Times*, as "the greatest man of his time and to admit him . . . as a Freeman of British History," Churchill himself observed that there had "never been anything like it in English History." Neither the elder nor the younger Pitt, neither Marlborough nor Wellington, not Disraeli or Gladstone, or Lloyd George had ever been similarly honored.

In returning thanks, Sir Winston, in one of his last great speeches, referred again to 1940, that year of incandescence when his own mind and heart had fused so perfectly with the mind and heart of the nation he led. "I have never accepted," he declared, "what many people have kindly said, namely, that I inspired the nation. Their will was resolute and remorseless, and as it proved, unconquerable. . . . It fell to me to express it, and if I found the right words, you must remember that I have always earned my living by my pen and my tongue. It was the nation and the race dwelling all round the globe that had the lion's heart. I had the luck to be called upon to give"—and here his voice rose menacingly as he glanced above his spectacles—"the roar."

It is time to look back over what Sir Winston called his "variegated career." But how to disentangle reality from myth, or do justice to the elements of a personality at once so simple and so complex, and formed moreover on what seems a scale that is larger than human life? The least one can attempt is to trace the stages of his strange development, and mark the growth —or rather the lack of growth—of his ideas. For just as in early photographs one sees, above the white collar of the Harrow schoolboy, the same resolute, determined look in the widely spaced eyes, the same pugnacious expression of the mouth with which half a century later the world would be familiar, similarly in the realm of ideas, whatever the boy learned the man never forgot. "I have held certain beliefs for sixty years," he once told Mrs. Roosevelt truculently during the Spanish Civil War, "and I'm not going to change now." The question of the correctness or incorrectness of such beliefs did not arise. It was sufficient that he had always held them.

One of the most striking features of Churchill's personality is the immense emotional power that he could generate at will. This ability to concentrate all of his resources at any given moment, excluding everything else, was one of the chief sources of his strength. One may imagine with what zest in childhood he seized each new idea that presented itself, and made it his own. Ideas were not so much to be assimilated as taken by storm. Even in his hobbies, his language was Nelsonian. At seventy-six he described how in middle age he had first started to paint: "I seized the largest brush and fell upon my victim with berserk fury. I have never," he added, "felt any awe of a canvas since." "Painting a picture," he wrote, "is like fighting a battle. . . . Audacity is the only ticket."

Terms like "race" and "blood" were among the earliest tro-phies he acquired from his reading, and just because their use was unscientific was no reason why he should give them up. To the lessons of anthropology, unknown in his youth, Sir Win-ston was deaf. He took an impish delight in brandishing before the world such terms as "the British race and nation," and in attributing to genetic inheritance the moral and cultural traits of a people. In writing about the battle of Hastings, for example, he gratefully remembered how some Bretons fought with the Conqueror, thus linking England with "some of the best stocks from Roman Britain." His own military genius—an attribute that to his generals was of dubious value—he ascribed to his direct descent from the great Duke of Marlborough. As with a naughty boy, the knowledge that such terms were forbidden lent an added flavor to their use. Not even the proof supplied by the Nazis of the evil latent in the misuse of words like "race" served as a corrective: in 1956, still unrepentant, he told the Primrose League that the blood strain of Israel was bound to prevail over that of the Arabs.

As with anthropology, so with psychology. In learning to

paint, Churchill tells how he was always attracted by the brightest colors; and in reading, the unsubtle motivation of characters in Macaulay or Sir Walter Scott, their sharp dramatic contrasts unrelieved by shading, satisfied equally his youthful imagination and his adult sense of reality. The revolution wrought by Freud in psychology, and by Lytton Strachey in biography, left him unmoved. Churchill, moreover, never loved books for their own sake, but valued them for the spoils they might yield. They were "hammered on the anvils of his mind, and afterwards ranged in an armoury of bright weapons ready to hand." His object in reading was not so much to understand life as to dominate it.

As Smuts once remarked, Churchill mentally inhabited the eighteenth century—not the world of the Enlightenment, however, but of that corrupt aristocracy which Burke had defended so passionately. Sir Winston thus carried with him into the twentieth century a host of ideas which, like his clothes, were long out of date. The London *Times* recorded how in Westminster Hall, on that memorable eightieth birthday, he sat arrayed in "a morning coat of outmoded square cut, with the usual gold chain looped across his waistcoat, and wearing one of those spotted bow ties that always look so much alike that one suspects he ordered a gross of them many years ago." One is tempted sometimes to suppose that his ideas may also have been acquired by the gross from the stock of late Victorian England. His imperialism, his jingoism, his contempt for "native" peoples and their aspirations, his distrust of democracy, and his resistance to the political equality of women, all derive their origin perhaps from those twin male nurseries, Harrow and Sandhurst, in which he had been reared. So strong are habits formed in childhood that not until 1940 could Churchill break himself of the practice of alluding to the French as "frogs." As for the Irish, he never did quite succeed in ridding himself of grotesque notions implanted in him at the tender age of three by his nanny.

By far the strongest influence in Churchill's early life, as he himself made clear in his autobiography, was that of his father. A ruthless guerrilla fighter in the parliamentary wars, Lord Randolph had astonished his contemporaries by becoming Chancellor of the Exchequer in 1886. Carried away perhaps by *hubris*, he had overplayed his hand and pushed his luck too far. A resignation that was probably never seriously intended was suddenly accepted, and at the early age of thirty-seven, Lord Randolph found himself rejected by the party whose leader he had aspired to be. He failed to retrieve his position in the House and became increasingly bitter and morose, absenting himself from England and his family for long periods of travel abroad. He died in 1895 at forty-six. Winston was then in his twenty-first year.

An intense attachment to Lord Randolph's memory, an ardent desire to vindicate his name, and a stubborn resolve to succeed where his father had failed: this triple motive sustained much of Churchill's public life. He *looked* like his father—bulldog crossed with cherub, pugnacity tempered by naughtiness—he dressed like his father, and he spoke like his father. Gibbon was an equal inspiration to both. Sir Winston deliberately modeled his early career upon that of his father, and for the greater part of his life was judged and condemned by his contemporaries in precisely the same way that his father had been judged and condemned by *his*—brilliant, erratic, unstable, endowed perhaps with a touch of genius, but too clever by half, too intolerant of others, and doomed after spectacular early success to final failure.

Seldom has history seen a more perfect example of the Oedipus complex triumphantly resolved, of a son taking over so completely his father's whole personality—his ideas, his ambitions, his resentments, his shortcomings. For Sir Winston, the way to self-fulfillment lay through initial submission—the deliberate subduing of his own proud, headstrong nature before the dominant personality of Lord Randolph. This self-willed subjection on the part of one so independent is all the more remarkable since Churchill had never really known his father, had never enjoyed a moment's intimacy with him, had been, in fact, rejected by him. The boy's subjection to his father, however, was compensated for by a rebelliousness that raged all the more strongly against all other symbols of authority.

For the father—egotistical, self-absorbed, unapproachable, brooding in his later years under the bitter stigma of failure—had no time to waste upon the son who, he was convinced, was a ne'er-do-well. Lord Randolph failed to detect the least hint of promise in his elder son; after all, Winston had been near the bottom of his class at Harrow and had gotten into Sandhurst only after three attempts. If ever the boy exerted himself to please his father, he had been snubbed instantly for his pains.

In the world of Winston's childhood, his mother's presence had been equally remote. In his autobiography, he recalled how she had glittered in the distance like the evening star—like those glittering diamonds that, to the fascinated gaze of a little boy, she wore in her dark hair as the crown of a mysterious, unapproachable beauty. Deprived of normal parental care and devotion, of mother's love and father's guidance, Winston's emergent personality was nonetheless founded securely as upon a rock— the rock being Mrs. Everest, his nurse, who supplied for him in infancy and early childhood the place of both his parents.

In the short, stout figure of this formidable woman, a generation of Victorian nurses found their apotheosis and justification. England and the world owe much to Mrs. Everest, who provided for her young charge the indispensable element of unquestioning love wherein he was enabled to grow secure and to develop freely, without fear of ridicule or blame. It was an early mark of Winston's greatness that even as a boy he realized the debt he owed to Mrs. Everest. When, careless of what his schoolfellows might think—most of them would probably have died of shame sooner than admit they had ever had a nurse—Winston brought Mrs. Everest to Harrow and walked with her through its precincts, he was giving signal proof of that same independence, that same willingness to stand alone, that was to serve England in such good stead in 1940. The Churchills had no hereditary connection with Kent, but Kent was Mrs. Everest's favorite county. In Kent, therefore, the mature Churchill resolved to fix his home, so that the names Chartwell and Churchill were to become synonymous in the minds of Englishmen.

Yet, if Mrs. Everest provided the foundation, Lord Randolph remained the lodestar of Churchill's ambition, and after Lord Randolph's death, it was his image that dominated the ambitions of his son. "A man's relation to his father or his nurse," writes the eminent historian Sir Lewis Namier, "may determine the pattern of his later political conduct or of his mental faculties and may even create the appearance of cold, clearsighted objectivity."

It is perhaps not too fanciful to regard Winston's later parliamentary triumphs as so many trophies raised to vindicate his father's memory and to propitiate his shade. In one sense, life for Sir Winston, apart from its own intrinsic excitement, was a continuous self-justification before an austere remembered presence whose approval now could no longer be given or withheld.

From earliest childhood, Winston had been a rebel against all external authority, and such he remained through life. Refractory to authority, he broke all rules. At Harrow he was regarded as utterly incorrigible. Not for nothing does a boy have that particular look in his eye: a look that bodes no good to anyone who thwarts him. Nor did the adult Churchill ever feel it necessary to conceal from mediocrity the contempt he felt for it. He never bothered to learn the elementary lesson suggested by Voltaire: that it is not sufficient to have genius—one must also persuade others to forgive one for having it. In course of time, however, Churchill, like Disraeli, overcame massive prejudices, and like that statesman, forced his enemies to accept him at his own evaluation. He was "a rebel against routines and conformities," wrote *The Times*, a paper that had once been one of his severest critics, "a character' outstanding in a race [!] that has for many centuries prided itself on producing characters, full of whims and foibles, impulsive and wayward, sometimes apparently rash and irresponsible, intractable always in word and deed." Sir Winston's victory, like that of Disraeli, was complete.

In his autobiography, Churchill has described how the collection of fifteen hundred toy soldiers which he possessed as a child determined his subsequent choice of a military career. When asked at Harrow what profession he intended to follow, the young Winston promptly replied: "The Army, of course, so long as there's any fighting to be had. When that's over I shall have a shot at politics." He correctly predicted his future. At twenty-two, he was already a subaltern in India, playing polo in Mysore and taking part in punitive expeditions upon the North-West frontier.

It was in India that he first evinced signs of unusual character and intelligence. Regarded as a dunce at Harrow, where he had remained in the lowest form three times as long as anyone else, he now developed a passion for history. In the cantonment at Bangalore, while his brother officers devoted themselves to polo or pig-sticking by day, to cards or flirtation by night, the young Churchill read avidly in Gibbon and Macaulay, thereby acquiring a command of rhetoric, a fund of knowledge, and a vigor of style that were to stand him in good stead throughout life. He likewise read Plato's *Republic* and the *Politics* of Aristotle, as well as Schopenhauer, Darwin, Lecky, and Winwood Reade's *Martyrdom of Man*—a book that made a powerful if transient impression upon him. At this time also, he wrote an autobiographical novel, *Savrola*, whose hero was a thinly disguised portrait of himself, and whose martial deeds were his own daydreams. The books just mentioned were all in the library of Savrola; and like his creator, Savrola was an agnostic and positivist: an odd circumstance for an officer in the Fourth Hussars. But Churchill's youthful agnosticism gradually succumbed to what proved to be his real religion—the tribal cult of nationality.

More than thirty years later, Churchill lightheartedly recalled his first experience of war on the North-West frontier: the systematic destruction of the miserable mud hovels of "savages," fighting fiercely in defense of "their own kitchens and parlours." The tribesmen watched sullenly from the hills as their wells were stopped up, their crops burned, and the great shade trees cut down. "At the end of a fortnight," Churchill concluded mischievously, "the valley was a desert—and honour was satisfied." Such was imperialism in the good old days, set down with equal candor and callousness by one of its leading exponents. Sometimes, complained the young soldier-journalist, "just when we were looking forward to having a splendid fight," a war would be prevented by some busybody of a politician. Although a lot of people were killed, some widows pensioned, and the "badly wounded hopped around for the rest of their lives," still it was all rather exciting, and "very jolly."

Hearing that Kitchener was about to conquer the Sudan, Churchill used all his mother's influence—she left, he tells us, no stone unturned, no cutlet uncooked—to get posted from India to Egypt. He was present in 1898 at the decisive battle of Omdurman, where Gordon was avenged and the Mahdi's head defiled. Churchill himself charged on an Arab pony with the Twenty-First Lancers, and shot down half a dozen dervishes—

"ugly, sinister brutes," who had presumed to defend their desert wastes.

"Talk of fun. Where will you beat this?" he exulted, re-living the "excitement and thoughtless gaiety" of the Omdurman campaign. Twenty years later, he recalled how modern weapons had prevailed over the spears and black bodies of the Fuzzy-Wuzzies. "It was the last link in the long chain of those spectacular conflicts whose vivid and majestic splendour has done so much to invest war with glamour. . . . This kind of war was full of fascinating thrills. It was not like the Great War. Nobody expected to be killed." It was, in fact, the world of Rudyard Kipling and of Colonel Blimp.

Within a week of Omdurman, Churchill was home, enjoying the reputation gained by his brilliant journalism. Finding a subaltern's pay inadequate, he decided to give up the army as a career—a decision that was perhaps partly due to the resentment aroused at headquarters by his blunt criticisms of military leadership. When, in 1899, the Boer War broke out, the ultra-Tory *Morning Post* appointed him, at the unprecedented salary of £250 a month, its correspondent in South Africa. His capture by the Boers and his subsequent escape, thrillingly narrated, made Churchill at the age of twenty-six "the most discussed and admired figure in the British Empire." Smuts, his future war-time comrade, remembered him in captivity as "a scrubby, squat figure of a man . . . furious, venomous, just like a spider." He undertook a series of lecture tours through England, Canada, and the United States which proved to be highly successful. In New York, his chairman was Mark Twain, who argued gently with him about imperialism, Churchill defending the thesis "My country right or wrong." He was already making £20,000 a year—far more than most generals.

In her diary for July 1903, Beatrice Webb gives us an acute analysis of Churchill's character at this period. He was then twenty-eight, and the qualities so shrewdly observed were to characterize his personality for the next fifty years.

Went into dinner with Winston Churchill. First impression: restless—almost intolerably so, without capacity for sustained and unexciting labour—egotistical, bumptious, shallow-minded, and reactionary, but with certain personal magnetism, great pluck and some originality—not of intellect but of character. More of the American speculator than the English aristocrat. Talked exclusively about himself and his electioneering plans—wanted me to tell him of someone who would get up statistics for him. "I never do any brain-work that anyone else can do for me"—an axiom which shows organizing but not thinking capacity. . . . But I daresay he has a better side—which the ordinary cheap cynicism of his position and career covers up to a casual dinner acquaintance. Bound to be unpopular—too unpleasant a flavour with his restless, self-regarding personality, and lack of moral or intellectual refinement. . . . His bugbears are Labour . . . and expenditure on elementary education or on the social services. Defines higher education as the opportunity for the "brainy man" to come to the top. No notion of scientific research, philosophy, literature or art: still less of religion. But his pluck, courage, resourcefulness and great tradition may carry him far unless he knocks himself to pieces like his father.

In the "khaki election" of 1900, the cotton spinners of Oldham in Lancashire elected the *enfant terrible* to the House of Commons as a Conservative. Herbert Asquith, future Liberal premier, described contemporary Oldham as being "one of the most dismal places in the country, peopled by wan-faced, tired artisans who have never known life in its real sense and will never know it till their dying day." No doubt the artisans of Oldham felt honored that the grandson of a duke should condescend to represent them, and bring, at least during election time, some color into the drabness of their lives. In his maiden speech, the new member praised his late captors, the Boers, and pleaded for a magnanimous peace, such as was actually made at Vereeniging in 1902.

After three and a half years as a Conservative, on May 31, 1904, Churchill astonished friends and foes alike by deserting his party and going over to the Liberals. Just before crossing the floor of the House, he criticized his own leader, Arthur Balfour, so vehemently that one evening the Tories ostentatiously walked out on him while he was speaking. In unmeasured terms he censured the premier's "gross, unpardonable and flagrant ignorance," and condemned what he called his "slipshod, slapdash, haphazard methods of business." An ex-officer, he criticized the army estimates and attacked "the military hydrophobia with which we are afflicted." The feelings of the generals may be imagined when he announced that "the honour and security of the British Empire do not depend, and never can depend, upon the British Army." No wonder Conservatives felt the keenest indignation toward this "renegade," this "traitor to his class." Even twenty years later, when he rejoined them, many had not forgiven his defection, and few were inclined to welcome the cheerful prodigal, whose confident bearing seemed to indicate that in returning, he was conferring a favor upon them.

Churchill's motives in leaving his party, and cutting himself off from his own class, may well have been self-interested. For in 1904 it was evident that a decade of Tory rule was nearly over: Balfour's leadership was weak, and Joseph Chamberlain's campaign for tariff reform had split the party. Churchill correctly anticipated the victory of the Liberals in 1906 and joined them at a moment when they were to hold office for sixteen years. When he finally left them, in 1924, the Liberal party was clearly doomed, and he rejoined the Conservatives when they in turn were to enjoy power for nearly twenty years. If Churchill was only part of that time in office, the fault was his, since his domineering attitude toward India was too blatant even for most Tories to accept. Certain it is that each of his changes in party affiliation occurred at just the right moment for his own parliamentary fortunes—a fact that did not pass unobserved.

Even before he left them to join the Liberals in 1904, the Conservatives had never trusted Churchill. Earl Winterton, on his retirement in 1951, the "Father of the House," recalled that most Tories always entertained toward Churchill feelings of "suspicion and distrust." They explained his leaving the party on grounds of personal discontent. He was piqued, they said, because Balfour had not offered him high office. Behind his back, his colleagues used to jeer at him as the "Blenheim Rat." When he spoke in the House they ridiculed his lisp, and showed by hissing their own mastery of the letter "s" that baffled the victim they were tormenting.

In her entertaining autobiography *The Glitter and the Gold*, Consuelo Vanderbilt Balsan, the American-born Duchess of Marlborough, described the anxiety of the Tories to see her produce offspring, in order to keep that insufferable young redheaded nuisance out of the dukedom. On one occasion, the formidable

Dowager Duchess fixed her cold gray eyes upon the young American girl and took her aback by inquiring if she were already "in the family way." It would be "intolerable," said the old lady, "to have that little upstart Winston become Duke."

Fifty years later, it is difficult to realize the hostility that Churchill at this time inspired among his former friends and associates. Lord Haldane's sister overheard a famous Conservative hostess, after hearing Churchill speak in Parliament, cry out to a friend: "Wretch, I'd like to kill him." Lord Alfred Douglas' resentment of him verged upon insanity (Lord Alfred later got six months in jail for libeling Churchill). As early as Omdurman, Sir John Maxwell (later the executioner of the Irish rebels in 1916) wrote to a friend: "Winston Churchill is a   . I will leave you to fill in the blank, but use brown paint." The indecent play often made with Churchill's initials may be imagined. This almost hysterical anger on the part of the Conservatives was perhaps aggravated by a not unjustified suspicion that in his heart of hearts the renegade had never left them. As early as 1912, Wilfrid Scawen Blunt predicted that one day Churchill would return to the Tory fold.

To some degree, Churchill could hardly escape his fate, which had been that of Canning and Disraeli before him—brilliance engulfed by mediocrity. But Churchill himself, by his arrogance and conceit, by his rudeness and truculence, added needlessly to the enemies he could not help but make. "Tactfulness," wrote that Olympian peer Lord Rosebery, "has not been considered the strongest element in his Corinthian composition." Like his friend Sir John Fisher, Churchill positively delighted in the number of his foes. The problem that every Prime Minister had to face, said Lloyd George later, was whether Winston would be a greater nuisance outside, or inside, the Cabinet.

People were offended by Churchill's colossal egotism and by his insulting indifference to the opinions of others. With him monologue took the place of conversation. The fact that his monologues were so witty, and his witticisms so devastating, only added to the wrath of his enemies. The malicious said that while Winston was speaking, one could always see his next speech in process of gestation. Confident of his own genius, and unable to deny himself the pleasure of deflating pomposity,

Churchill certainly never went out of his way to conciliate opposition.

In politics as in war, the best method of defense is attack. So, far from showing compunction for his defection from the Tories, the youthful renegade made a special point of deriding them and attacking the House of Lords. "The Conservative Party," he declared at Nottingham in 1908, "is not a party but a conspiracy." Its leaders were "unscrupulous and reckless adventurers." Its politics, he said, were like those of the Republican party in the United States—"rigid, materialist and secular." In language reminiscent of Disraeli in his Young England period, he maintained that while there were rich men in the Liberal party and poor men who voted Conservative, yet "in the main the lines of difference between the two parties are social and economic . . . lines of cleavage between the rich and the poor." "Whenever private privilege comes into collision with the public interest," he stated in 1908, "the public interest must have the right of way."

The House of Lords he ridiculed as "a Punch and Judy show." Vying in derision with his colleague Lloyd George, he denounced the "vulgar joyless luxury" of the peers, "a minute minority of titled persons, who represent nobody, who are answerable to nobody, and who only scurry up to London to vote in their own party interests, in their class interests and in their own interests." Reviewing the nineteenth century, and tracing the successive struggles over Catholic and Jewish emancipation, the reform bills, and the ballot, he defied the Conservatives "to produce a single instance of a settled controversy in which the House of Lords was right." The veto over legislation wielded by the peers he called "the evil, ugly and sinister weapon . . . which they have used so ill so long." Such language gave much offense to the King and later caused the French historian Elie Halévy to bracket Churchill with Lloyd George as the "two great demagogues" of the time.

The best known, perhaps, of all Churchill's attacks upon his old party was delivered in 1908 in Manchester, the citadel of free trade, against Chamberlain and his protectionist policy. "We know perfectly well what to expect," he told his cheering audience, should the Tories return to power.

A party of great vested interests, banded together in a formidable confederation; corruption at home, aggression to cover it up abroad; the trickery of tariff juggles; the tyranny of a well-fed party machine; sentiment by the bucketful; patriotism and imperialism by the imperial pint; an open hand at the public exchequer, an open door at the public house; dear food for the million, cheap labour for the millionaire. That is the policy of Birmingham, and we are going to erect against that policy of Birmingham the policy of Manchester.

In 1945, incidentally, the Communist party used this passage in its election campaign. It is likewise amusing to note how, in the last volume of his *History of the English-Speaking Peoples*, which appeared in 1958, Churchill so lightly glossed over the very thing that he had earlier condemned so severely—the role of the Lords in obstructing change throughout the nineteenth century.

The discomfiture of the Tories was increased by the fact that among his new colleagues Churchill was an outstanding success. In the six years between 1908 and 1914—first at the Board of Trade, then at the Home Office, and finally at the Admiralty—he established himself as one of the strongest men in the Cabinet. Excepting only the Exchequer, held by Lloyd George, whatever post Churchill held became at once the best publicized and the most controversial in the government. The alliance between the "barefoot boy from Wales," as Birkenhead ironically called Lloyd George, and the grandson of the Duke of Marlborough was the effective driving force within the Liberal Cabinet; and the Welshman, eleven years older than Churchill, was the one person in politics whom, because of his energy, audacity, and eloquence, the younger man unfeignedly admired and whose disciple he was willing to acknowledge himself.

In his years at the Board of Trade (1908–10), Churchill took advantage of Herbert Gladstone's supineness at the Home Office to pass the Trade Boards Act, setting up a minimum wage in "sweated industries," and of John Burns's indolence at the Local Government Board to establish, as a measure against unemployment, the first labor exchanges in Britain. Working men, he declared, should have time to read and think, and "cultivate their gardens." Had not the Marxian H. M. Hyndman once observed that reading *Candide* was bad for socialism?

As Home Secretary (1910–11), Churchill took a special interest in prison reform—partly, it is said, as a result of his three weeks in a Boer prison in Pretoria. One of his first acts was to invite the aristocratic rebel Wilfrid Scawen Blunt, who had once been jailed for anti-imperialist activities, to send him a memorandum on prison conditions. He warmly sympathized with John Galsworthy's denunciation of solitary confinement. He soon became known as one of the most active of Home Secretaries in visiting prisons and correcting abuses. More than twenty years later, in his book of prison reminiscences called *Walls Have Mouths*, W. F. Macartney recorded how many "old timers" in prison thought of Churchill as the only Home Secretary who had ever taken an interest in their welfare and treated them as human beings.

While still at the Home Office, Churchill in 1911 became a national figure by superintending in person an assault launched in the East End of London by the police upon some Russian Anarchists, whose leader was a sinister figure called Peter the Painter. The Prime Minister himself expressed astonishment that the Home Secretary, attired in frock coat and silk hat, should have exposed himself to fire and supervised an operation best left to the constables of the metropolitan police force. There never had been the least doubt about Churchill's personal courage, but now his appetite for melodrama made him once more a public hero.

It was at the Admiralty, however, from 1911 to 1915, that Churchill found maximum scope for his ruthless energy, infectious enthusiasm, and powers of organization. Abandoning his earlier critical attitude toward naval expenditure, he now made it his business to strengthen and modernize the Royal Navy and to continue the reforms that his volcanic friend Sir John Fisher had begun. As First Lord of the Admiralty, Churchill also paid close attention to the comfort and morale of the ordinary seaman. The outbreak of war with Germany in 1914 triumphantly vindicated his policies, and found the Navy in the highest state of efficiency and readiness for action that it had ever reached in time of peace.

Two months after World War I began, there occurred a curious episode in Churchill's career—one that might well have ended his public service. By late September 1914, from the cautious naval strategy followed by the Germans it was evident that the naval battle between the two strongest fleets in the world, which Churchill so greatly desired, was not likely to take place. (Nearly two years were to elapse before the battle of Jutland.) The result, as unexpected as it was undesired, was that just when the fate of Europe was being decided on the battlefield, Churchill was condemned to remain in Whitehall, a passive spectator of events.

The German investment of the port of Antwerp gave him the opportunity for military distinction which he craved. Just as three years earlier he had taken charge at Sidney Street, so now he proceeded to the Scheldt with the Royal Naval Division, consisting of about eight thousand men, transformed already into heroes in Churchill's ebullient imagination. To the Prime Minister, Asquith, however, it seemed that the majority of the Naval Division were "a callow crowd of the most raw recruits, most of whom had never fired off a rifle while none of them had ever handled an entrenching tool." The First Lord, wrote his friend Sir Ian Hamilton, later commander at the Dardanelles, "handles them as though he were Napoleon and they were the Old Guard. He flings them right into the enemy's open jaws." Churchill wired from Antwerp, offering to resign his post at the Admiralty and take command in the field. The ex-lieutenant of Hussars, observed the premier ironically, would "have been in command of two distinguished Major Generals, not to mention Brigadiers, Colonels, etc." Needless to say, the irrepressible Winston desired substantial reinforcements. "His mouth," wrote Asquith, "waters at the thought of Kitchener's armies. Are these glittering commands to be entrusted to dug-out trash, bred on the obsolete tactics of twenty-five years ago, mediocrities who have led a sheltered life, mouldering in military routine?"

Had Churchill remained in Antwerp, he would have run a fair chance of being interned in Holland for the duration of the war, a fate suffered by a considerable portion of his force during its precipitate retreat. The Prime Minister reported, after seeing him on his return:

For about an hour he poured forth a ceaseless invective and appeal and I much regretted that there was no shorthand writer within hearing as some of his unpremeditated phrases were quite priceless. He was, however, three parts serious and declared that a political career was nothing to him in comparison with military glory.

Soon after the fiasco at Antwerp, a still more glittering prize transfixed Churchill's sanguine imagination: the Dardanelles. With one successful stroke, as it appeared to him, Turkey might be knocked out of the war, Germany assaulted on her ill-protected southeastern flank, and a sea route opened to Russia by which the munitions of the Western powers could equip the almost unlimited manpower of their ally in the East. Had that happened, Churchill later maintained, the Russian Revolution might well have been averted, and the course of history changed.

The Dardanelles campaign, the chief amphibious operation of the war, was in fact a costly failure. More than forty thousand British, Australian, and New Zealand troops lie buried on the thorny sun-baked hillsides of Gallipoli. Forty per cent of the half-million Allied troops who landed were destined to be casualties. Yet though the campaign was mismanaged and starved of troops by Kitchener, with proper handling it might well have been a brilliant success. Admiral Sir Roger Keyes, the most dashing of British naval officers in the First World War, praised the audacity of the conception and declared that properly executed, it would have shortened the war by two years. Forty years later, Clement Attlee, then leader of the Labour Opposition, magnanimously called the assault upon the Dardanelles "the only imaginative idea of the war."

Robert Rhodes James, in his recent survey of the campaign, finds Churchill at fault for the precipitate haste with which he launched Britain into an ill-prepared campaign, riding roughshod over the opposition of naval and military professionals. The official Australian history also held Churchill's ignorance of military matters to be partly responsible for the failure. His old friend Admiral Fisher had always doubted the feasibility of the project, and angrily resigned as First Sea Lord while the campaign was still in progress. It is impossible to settle controversies about what might have been, and Stalin in 1942 at the Moscow Conference was to jeer at Churchill for the failure at Gallipoli. In any case, public opinion at home demanded a scapegoat, and Churchill was sacrificed. He had been nine years in office.

For the next two years he was out of power, and during part of that time saw service as a battalion commander on the Western Front. In 1917, however, Lloyd George, having succeeded Asquith as premier, determined to bring back into the government his old friend and ally. As soon as Churchill's name was mentioned, Bonar Law, the leader of the Conservatives in the coalition, declared that, if he had to choose between Churchill in or out, he "would rather have him against us every time." Conceding that Churchill possessed energy and drive, he considered his mind to be "entirely unbalanced." Lord Curzon likewise believed that, while Churchill would be "a potential danger in opposition," he would be "an active danger in our midst." Domesticated fowl are fearful of the hawk. Leading Conservatives like Lord Milner, Austen Chamberlain, and Lord Robert Cecil were all opposed to Churchill's rejoining the government. The party chairman, Sir George Younger, declared him to be directly "responsible for two of the greatest disasters of the war"—Antwerp and the Dardanelles—a judgment in which Field Marshal Sir Henry Wilson concurred. Lord Derby reported that army leaders were unanimous against Churchill; and because of the navy's failure at the Dardanelles, many admirals also condemned him. Admiral Sir Charles Beresford declared that he had "gambled with the lives of men in the most reckless way," and that he ought never to hold office again. The *Morning Post*, which had once sent Churchill to cover the Boer War, now derided him as "a floating kidney in the body politic." Was it really the failures at Antwerp and Gallipoli that rankled with the Tories, or the memory of the humbling of the Lords in 1911? "Never before in history," wrote Beaverbrook, "had the selection of a Minister of the Crown given rise to such vehement opposition."

"I knew something of the feeling against him amongst his old Conservative friends," wrote Lloyd George in his *War Memoirs*, "but the insensate fury they displayed . . . surpassed all my apprehensions, and for some days it swelled to the dimensions of a grave ministerial crisis which threatened the life of the Government." It is a tribute to Lloyd George's political courage and to his high estimate of Churchill's abilities that he was willing to jeopardize his own career for the sake of strengthening the ministry. Field Marshal Smuts, with his detached judgment and unique influence, supported the premier, and Churchill duly became Minister of Munitions, a post originally created for Lloyd George himself. "It is interesting," reflected the Prime Minister in retrospect, "to observe . . . the distrust and trepidation with which mediocrity views genius at close quarters. Unfortunately genius always provides its critics with material for censure—it always has and always will. Churchill is certainly no exception to this rule."

The new minister was an unqualified success—with all but his colleagues. From the moment of Churchill's appointment the latter began to fear for their own jobs. Within a month, for example, Sir Eric Geddes at the Admiralty was seeking Bonar Law's help in defending that institution against depredations from the Minister of Munitions.

Among Churchill's most important war services was his early sponsorship, against the opposition of military men, of the tank, and against the wishes of the Admiralty, of the convoy system at sea. One reason for Churchill's unpopularity was certainly the fertility and originality of his imagination, which put his colleagues to shame, while his aggressiveness threatened their posts.

Transferred to the War Office in 1919, he was immediately responsible for quelling a series of dangerous postwar mutinies which threatened to break out among the troops. Unfair and inadequate plans having been made for the mobilization of several million men, Churchill promptly improvised new and superior ones. He alone, declared the Commander-in-Chief, had saved a situation in which four million troops were on the verge of chaos.

In the last year of Lloyd George's coalition, Churchill, as Secretary for Air and the Colonies (1921–22), championed the independence of the Royal Air Force against the demands of the army and the navy. Even at the Admiralty before the war, he had been one of the earliest to grasp the significance of the new air arm and was largely responsible for the initial mounting of machine guns in planes and for the launching of the first aerial torpedoes. "Even more than in the fleet," wrote Sir Ian Hamilton at Gallipoli, "I find in the Air Force the profound conviction that, if they could only get into direct touch with Winston Churchill, all would be well. Their faith in the First Lord is, in every sense, touching." As early as 1913, Churchill himself had taken flying lessons, but had had several narrow escapes in taking off and landing. After an accident at Croydon in 1919, in which his companion broke both legs and he himself was badly bruised, he was persuaded to give up flying altogether.

A few years later, as Colonial Secretary, he flew out to Cairo to deal with the grave problems arising from newly won Arab independence. The result of his visit was the establishment of the Emirs Feisal and Abdullah as rulers of Iraq and Transjordan respectively, and the achievement of a solution of Arab grievances which Colonel T. E. Lawrence, gravely concerned for British honor in the Middle East, felt fulfilled the promises which had been made to King Hussein.

It was likewise as a member of Lloyd George's Cabinet that Churchill took part in the Irish peace negotiations in 1921. Erskine Childers, that enigmatic and ill-fated figure of the Irish War, soon to be executed by the Free State, has described the atmosphere of loaded menace brought to the conference by Churchill and Birkenhead. With scowl and jowl and menacing cigars, Lord Pakenham confirmed, they seemed the incarnation of all that was most oppressive in the spirit of imperialism. It was, as Churchill later admitted, with the gravest misgivings that he brought himself to sign the "treaty" of 1922—"the most hazardous enterprise on which a great empire in the plenitude of its power ever embarked." He nevertheless supported Lloyd George in pushing the measure through the Commons.

Denied all part in peacemaking at Versailles, Churchill fretted impatiently for some new field in which to distinguish himself. In 1919 he conceived what was for twenty years to be the dominant motive of his political life—a hatred of Communist Russia.

In 1919, Lloyd George told Bonar Law that Churchill seemed to have "Bolshevism on the brain." In applying the lessons of the past, it is curious how little Churchill was sometimes able to profit by his intense devotion to history. "His ducal blood," wrote Lloyd George satirically, "revolted against the wholesale elimination of Grand Dukes in Russia." Churchill seems to have taken the Russian Revolution almost as a personal affront. His position in the twentieth century was, in fact, precisely that of Burke in the eighteenth, and as the latter in a fury of unreason had denounced the French Revolution, so now Churchill stormed against its modern counterpart in Russia. He failed to realize that much of the misery of the Russian people was due to the corruption and tyranny of the tsarist regime, to its ineptitude in war, and to the chaos that inevitably followed its collapse. "Of the political and social philosophy of the Russian Revolution," as Emrys Hughes observes, "he had not the slightest understanding." Churchill's interest in history was always personal and romantic rather than philosophic or analytical. To economics and the history of ideas he was equally indifferent.

If the Webbs were blind to one aspect of Russian society, Churchill was blind to the other. His vision distorted by hatred, it was impossible for him, with all his experience of men and affairs, to realize that Soviet Russia was not wholly evil and destructive or that with infinite travail it was bringing a new civilization to the birth.

The result of his failure to learn the lesson of the French Revolution was that Churchill as War Secretary in 1919 repeated the mistakes of the allies in 1792. He was, wrote the Prime Minister, "the most formidable and irresponsible protagonist of an anti-Bolshevik war." Regardless of the fate of Charles XII and Napoleon, nothing would have pleased him more than to lead an invasion of Anglo-French armies into Russia. According to Lloyd George, when, in 1919, General Denikin made his closest approach to Moscow, Churchill was talking about entering the Russian capital in person, mounted on a white charger, at the head of the victorious White forces.

Fortunately, Lloyd George was resolved "not to commit the country to what would be purely a mad enterprise, out of hatred of Bolshevik principles." A war against Russia, he foresaw, would be "the direct road to bankruptcy and Bolshevism in these islands; . . . it would do more to incense organized labour than anything I can think of; and what is worse, it would throw into the arms of the extremists a very large number of thinking people who now abhor their methods." Hence he begged Churchill "to throw off this obsession which, if you will forgive me for saying so, is upsetting your balance." On account of the war-weary temper of the British and French peoples, such a project was, in any case, impossible. (A small French force in Odessa actually mutinied in 1919.) The most that Churchill could do was to give military aid to adventurers like Kolchak, Denikin, and Yudenich, prolonging the civil war by nearly two years and greatly intensifying the terror inside Russia.

In his *Memoirs of a British Agent*, Bruce Lockhart, who as an observer for the British government was in Russia at the time, affirms that Churchill's injudicious intervention in Russia led only to disaster. "For the intensification of that bloody struggle," he writes, "allied intervention with the false hopes it raised was largely responsible." A government white paper estimated the cost of Churchill's lighthearted support for aggression at £100,000,000—a cost that the Secretary of War himself did not find excessive, since the munitions sent "were only an unmarketable surplus of the Great War. Had they been kept in our hands till they mouldered they would only have involved additional charges for storage, care and maintenance." Killing communists was one way of preventing war matériel from going to waste.

Unable to sway the premier to his way of thinking, Churchill compensated for his frustration by the violence of his invective. In almost hysterical language he raged against what he called "the foul baboonery of Bolshevism." When Lloyd George once shook hands with Krassin, the Russian Ambassador, Churchill inquired sarcastically what it had felt like to touch the hairy hand of a baboon. Descending into personal abuse of the Russian leaders, he declared that "even the slaughter of millions . . . will not attract future generations to their uncouth lineaments and outlandish names." Trotsky had "the ferocity of Jack the Ripper, the toughness of Titus Oates." In the Russian Revolution he saw Sidney Street spread over a continent. Ignorant of the elementary fact that Anarchists were bitterly opposed to communism, it struck him that Peter the Painter "was one of those wild beasts who in later years were to devour and ravage the Russian state and people." Though Peter had perished in London in 1911, Churchill now was willing to believe that he was still alive. He described him as "one of the Bolshevik liberators and saviours of Russia. . . . But of this," Sir Winston added hastily, "rumour is alone the foundation." Where communism was concerned even Churchill's sense of humor deserted him.

"Of all tyrannies in history," he fulminated, "the Bolshevist tyranny is the worst, the most destructive, the most degrading." Ten years later, in his book *The Aftermath*, with apocalyptic fervor he identified the Revolution with "the 'nameless beast' so long foretold in Russian legend." No one was more adept at making the flesh of his readers creep. "Russia, self-outcast," he ruminated in 1929, "sharpens her bayonets in her Arctic night, and mechanically proclaims through self-starved lips her philosophy of hatred and death." A decade later, he still envisaged the Russian people as "congealed into the long night of another glacial period."

Not many years after this rodomontade, Churchill was to hail Stalin as his personal friend and Russia as the savior of democracy; and to proclaim at Yalta in 1945, after a banquet at the Yussupov Palace:

> It is no exaggeration or compliment of a florid kind when I say that we regard Marshal Stalin's life as most precious to the hopes and hearts of all of us. There have been many conquerors in history, but few of them have been statesmen, and most of them threw away the fruits of victory in the troubles which followed the wars. . . . I walk through this world with greater courage and hope when I find myself in a relation of friendship and intimacy with this great man, whose fame has gone out not only over all Russia, but the world.

In this effusive praise of the dictator, as in his previous diatribes against him, one sees striking confirmation of Churchill's early remark that he had adopted a system of believing whatever he wanted to believe. This belief in what psychologists call the "omnipotence of words"—the delusion that by words alone we can master the objective world and bend it to our will—was also, however, the source of much of Churchill's actual power over others.

If Churchill's off-stage thunder had small effect upon the Kremlin, it served another purpose by embarrassing the Labour party at home. Between the wars, Sir Winston's chief platform stock in trade was the dubious theme that socialism and communism were indistinguishable, and that the British Labour party was the agent and dupe of Moscow. "A vote for the Socialists," he announced in his 1924 address to the "educated constituents" of Westminster, "is a vote for the Communists. . . . They pretend to be separated, but at every crisis we find them together. The same sinister power directs them both, and they both march to the pipers of Moscow under the shadow of the Red Flag." One of his election leaflets warned that, should Labour win, "the monarchy will be ended and a Bolshevik Republic set up. Religion will be stamped out. The Home will be destroyed. . . . Children will be taken from their mothers and made the property of the State." Such bloodcurdling threats recall the good old days when mothers frightened naughty children with the name of "Boney," the Corsican ogre. They also anticipate the demagoguery of Senator McCarthy in the United States.

In Mrs. Webb's diary we have already seen how mild and ineffectual a socialist was Ramsay MacDonald, but to Churchill's fevered vision he was the counterpart of Kerensky, "pretending that he meant to do the best he could for his country, and all the time apologizing behind the scenes for the wild, dark, deadly forces which had him in their grip." Whether Churchill really believed such nonsense it is hard to say, but with his capacity for systematic self-deception, it is likely that he did. The fact that, by 1925, the Labour party had expelled Communists from its ranks counted for nothing with him. He had forgotten his prewar definition of a Liberal as "a man who should keep a sour look for scaremongers of every kind and of every size, however distinguished, however ridiculous."

The attempt to discredit Labour by identifying it with communism was a grave disservice to the cause of parliamentary democracy in England, for had it succeeded, it would have meant the end of the party system. The Liberals having ceased to be an effective force in politics, nothing would have been left to fill the vacuum created by the disappearance of the Labour Opposition except a genuinely revolutionary party on the left. Had there actually been any truth in the conservative slogan of the nineteen-twenties, that labor was unfit to govern, a believer in democracy should have hoped for its education, not for its destruction.

Churchill had his personal reasons for resenting labor. Its growth throughout Britain had weakened liberalism everywhere and had deprived him of his own seat in the Commons. In December 1923 he had failed at West Leicester as a Liberal; a month later he announced himself once more a full-blown Tory. His pretext for leaving the Liberal party after nearly twenty years was that it had helped to put Ramsay MacDonald in power as head of a minority government, and that Labour, as he wrote in a letter to the press, was "innately pledged to the fundamental subversion of the existing social and economic civilization, and organized for that purpose and that purpose alone."

The difficulty was how to persuade the Tories to accept him once more. "If I am able to cooperate cordially with the Conservative Party," he wrote in 1924, "it is not because I have changed my position. It is because they have very wisely and rightly returned or are in the process of returning to a broad and progressive platform."

Churchill, in fact, had performed an almost unprecedented feat. Once, during a quarrel in 1910, Lloyd George had warned him angrily that he could never leave the Liberal party: "No man can rat twice." Yet this was precisely what he had now done. Not only that, but the returning prodigal had been rewarded with the fattest calf at Baldwin's disposal—the Exchequer. The reason for this surprising preferment was perhaps the Tories' urgent need of Churchill's parliamentary gifts in the struggle against Labour; to which may be added the powerful influence of the ex-Lord Chancellor Birkenhead, whose special brand of cynical materialism was much relished by Churchill.

At the Exchequer (1924–29), an office for which, like his father before him, he was temperamentally unsuited, Churchill was an acknowledged failure. It was the first post in which he had failed to make good—but statistics are less amenable to emotional appeal than are human beings. In 1925, following the advice of the experts at the Bank of England, he prematurely returned England to the gold standard, from which she had departed during the war. In a second witty book, *The Economic Consequences of Mr. Churchill*, John Maynard Keynes accurately forecast the result of such a policy: a loss of export markets, lower wages, and increased unemployment at home. "At this very hour," declared Lloyd George in 1925, "coalowners and miners have been driven to the brink of a yawning chasm of strife, largely through this deed of egregious recklessness by the Chancellor of the Exchequer."

Churchill's deflationary policies, however unfortunate for the nation, and especially for the mining industry, provided him with the greatest opportunity of his career up to this point, for they led directly to the coal strike and hence to the general strike of 1926. For nine days, together with his friend Birkenhead, he wielded in effect the chief power in the government (since Baldwin, as G. M. Young remarks, was at this time no more than "a passenger in his own Cabinet"). For the upper and middle classes, Churchill now emerged as the savior of Britain against revolution—a revolution that existed solely in their overheated imagination. The press being paralyzed by the general strike, he brilliantly edited a government paper called the *British Gazette*, which in a single week achieved a circulation of two million two hundred thousand—except for the B.B.C., it had a monopoly of news, all other papers having been put out of action by the strike. Churchill also tried to commandeer the B.B.C., but failed to overcome the resistance of its director, Sir John Reith—a fact that may have been not without significance for the career of the latter when, during the Second World War, he found himself without public employment. No one opposed Churchill with impunity.

The *British Gazette*, "this ephemeral and unpleasant journal," as Sir Osbert Sitwell calls it in his autobiography, naturally wielded immense influence over public opinion during the nine days of the strike—nine days that failed to shake the world. In its rhetorical columns, Churchill referred to the strikers as "the enemy," and though they remained peaceful, denounced them as violent revolutionaries. The Archbishop of Canterbury's appeal for conciliation he suppressed outright. "Jimmy" Thomas, that mildest of mild trade unionists, later asserted that Churchill had confided to him personally that "a little bloodshed would do no harm." If this be true—and to anyone familiar with Churchill's impulsive temperament, there is nothing improbable in the remark—he must have been disappointed, since no bloodshed occurred. A section of the Cabinet, headed by Churchill and Birkenhead, was "spoiling for a fight," believing that this was as good a time as any to break the power of the trade unions. Even the usually equable Baldwin was so alarmed as to declare that England was closer to civil war than she had been for centuries.

In the late nineteen-twenties Churchill, as the mythical hero who had crushed the general strike and saved the country from revolution, seemed destined to succeed Baldwin as Prime Minister, a position which those who had known him in his youth had confidently predicted he would attain before he was fifty. In 1931, however, as an impenitent imperialist, he quarreled with the premier over the promise of dominion status for India. Even though the promise was hedged with numerous reservations and predicated for a distant future, the very idea of such "absurd and dangerous pretensions" on the part of the Indian people alarmed Churchill and the die-hard Tories immeasureably. An aged colonel, reports G. M. Young, was going about denouncing Baldwin and Lord Irwin, the Viceroy, as "negrophiles."

In language redolent of the mood of Victoria's Diamond Jubilee, Churchill condemned "the casting away of that most truly bright and precious jewel in the Crown . . . which more than all our other Dominions and Dependencies constitutes the glory and strength of the British Empire. . . . The loss of India," he warned, "would mark and consummate the downfall of the British Empire. That great organism would pass at a stroke out of life into history. From such a catastrophe there could be no recovery."

It was not solely of Britain, however, that he professed to be thinking. If India should gain dominion status, the fabric of civilization built up during two centuries of British rule would at once collapse. India would "fall back quite rapidly through the centuries into the barbarism and privations of the Middle Ages." "To abandon India to the rule of the Brahmins would be an act of cruel and wicked negligence. It would shame for ever those who bore its guilt."

At one moment he maintained a point of view common among British officers in India—that the Hindus, not being "a fighting race," would inevitably be overwhelmed by the Moslems and the martial peoples of the north; at another, he asked rhetorically, who but the British could protect from Hindu domination the eighty million Moslems, the sixty million untouchables, and the five hundred and sixty Indian princes? As the Calcutta *Statesman* commented on this sudden concern for the untouchables, "Does anyone believe that they cost Mr. Churchill a night's sleep, or doubt that they are nearer to Lord Irwin's heart than to his?"

"Mr. Churchill has sincerity," wrote Robert Byron scornfully in his *Essay on India* in 1931. "But it is only the transitional sincerity of a monkey at a nut, and is based neither on moral principle, nor on intellectual conviction—virtues which Providence and disputatious temperament have denied him. . . . Yet how many times has not the phoenix risen purged from the ashes to hatch another clutch of misfortunes on the English nest?"

Gandhi, of course, was the special object of Churchill's contempt. "It is alarming and also nauseating," he wrote,

> to see Mr. Gandhi, a seditious Middle Temple lawyer, now posing as a fakir of a type well-known in the East, striding half-naked up the steps of the Viceregal palace, while he is still organizing and conducting a defiant campaign of civil disobedience, to parley on equal terms with the representatives of the King-Emperor.

Albert Einstein, however, on the occasion of Gandhi's seventieth birthday, praised him as "a man who had confronted the brutality of Europe with the dignity of the simple human being, and thus at all times risen superior to it; . . . generations to come, it may be, will scarce believe that such a man as this ever in flesh and blood walked upon this earth."

According to Field Marshal Smuts, during the Second World War Churchill held Gandhi personally responsible for the troubles in India and believed that there would never be a settlement so long as he remained alive. He even regretted that he had not done away with the Indian leader when he had been in prison. "Winston," Smuts told Sir John Kennedy at this time, "is his own malign influence. . . . In great things he is very great, in small things not great."

Of the various dire prophecies made by Churchill concerning the consequences of dominion status for India, none has been fulfilled. His intransigence, however, had serious results for his own political future, since it led to the irreparable breach with Baldwin and hence to his own exclusion from the national government in the nineteen-thirties. If Churchill lacked authority to urge the necessity for rearmament against Hitler, it was partly because he had ruined his position within his own party. Once again, unable to disguise his impatience with mediocrity, he incurred the hostility of his colleagues, and became the chief object of Conservative distrust.

When, during the abdication crisis of 1936, he again defied
Baldwin's leadership and supported Edward VIII, it seemed
certain that his political career was finished. Never in his life,
he admitted, had he experienced greater personal hostility—not
so much from Labour as from his fellow Conservatives—than at
this time. When he rose in the Commons to plead the King's
cause, they refused to let him be heard. Momentarily stunned
by the torrent of catcalls, shouts, and jeers which poured upon
him from all sides, he sat down in despair. Stanley Baldwin could
now afford to treat him as an object of pity. "I have a dismal
prospect before me," complained the premier ironically as he
contemplated his own retirement. "Look at the flotsam and jet-
sam of political life thrown up on the beach: Lloyd George,
Winston, Horne, Gilmour."

The last word, however, as usual was with Churchill. History
would deal severely with Baldwin, he prophesied. "I know, because I shall write it." Always behind the menace lurked the
impish grin. Baldwin's last years, in fact, were to be darkened
by the flood of angry and abusive letters which poured in upon
him from all parts of the country—once the outbreak of war had
exposed the folly of appeasement.

Churchill's ideas upon the subject of democracy, exposed
as it now was to attack from extreme right and left, were succinctly stated in his Romanes Lecture at Oxford in 1930. He was
then fifty-five years of age.

Democracy, he told his audience, "seems to lose much of its
authority when based on universal suffrage"; adding, with reference to the depression, in words that sound strange on the lips
of the great parliamentary leader of the war years soon to come:
"The House of Commons, to which the anxious nation looks
to provide a solution, is unsuited both by its character and the
conditions which govern its life to fulfill such a task. Nevertheless, the task has to be done. Britain is unconquerable, and will
not fail to find a way through her difficulties." But if the British
way did not lie through the House of Commons, in what direction did it lie? In that of Fascism?

Two years later, in his book *Amid These Storms*, Churchill declared his position still more unequivocally. "Democracy as a
guide or motive to progress has long been known to be in-

competent." No wonder Mrs. Webb had thought it possible that he might some day play the role of a "British Mussolini." Actually, as early as 1927, Churchill had paid a visit to the Duce in Rome, and had been warmly greeted and lavishly entertained. Before leaving Italy, he told a press conference that Mussolini "thought of nothing but the lasting good, as he understood it, of the Italian people." Had he himself been an Italian, he declared, he would certainly have been a Fascist, but in Britain fortunately there were other ways of "grappling with Communism and choking the life out of it." "I could not help being charmed," he admitted, "as so many other people have been, by Signor Mussolini's gentle and simple bearing and by his calm, detached poise in spite of so many burdens and dangers." Only three years before, the man of "gentle and simple bearing" had ordered the murder of the courageous leader of the opposition, Giacomo Matteotti, and in a few more years would connive at the assassination of King Alexander of Yugoslavia. The Roman press, for its part, united in complimenting Signor Churchill on "having understood the real spirit of *fascismo*."

A week before the outbreak of the Abyssinian war, Churchill was still praising Mussolini as "so great a man and so wise a ruler." Since this tribute, however, was as ineffectual in checking Fascist aggression as Canute's command to halt the rising tide, Churchill took a second look at Mussolini, and did not like what he saw. Even at the risk of war, in 1936 he urged sanctions against Italy, and expressed his conviction that the British fleet in the Mediterranean would be more than a match for any Fascist attack.

By 1940 Mussolini had revealed his true nature so completely that no one could now mistake it. Churchill, accordingly, now referred over the B.B.C. to his former friend as "this whipped jackal Mussolini" and as Hitler's "little Italian accomplice, trotting along hopefully and hungrily but rather wearily and very timidly at his side." After the Duce's overthrow in 1943, the Prime Minister denounced him as "one of the principal criminals of this devastating war." No reader of the first volume of Churchill's war memoirs, *The Gathering Storm*, would suspect that the writer had ever had any sympathy either for fascism or for its creator.

In 1936, when General Franco rose in arms to overthrow the elected government of the Spanish people, Churchill showed a similar myopia. So blinded was he by royalist prejudice that from its inception he had condemned the Spanish Republic. When, in the bloodless revolution of 1931, the monarchy had been peacefully abolished, Churchill, unlike such Spanish liberals as Unamuno and Ortega y Gasset, failed to realize that Spain was seeking desperately to emerge from the eighteenth century into the twentieth. He saw only that, as in Russia in 1917, monarchy had been abolished. To realize how useless and insignificant, as well as how offensive, was such a figure as Alfonso XIII, that roué, gambler, and race-track enthusiast who was the last Bourbon to style himself "Most Catholic King," it is sufficient to read *In Place of Splendour,* the poignant autobiography of Constancia de la Mora, a leading Spanish aristocrat. Churchill, however, as a personal friend of Alfonso XIII, saw in that fatuous simulacrum of a king only "a modern, democratic man of the world . . . a practical, genial man of the world, with a noble air but without a scrap of conceit or humbug." He even praised that quality in him which was most conspicuous by its absence—"his vigilant care for the interest of his country." It is rather like hearing Burke descant on the domestic virtues of Louis XVI. Before the Spanish Civil War, however—after three years of anguish and at least a million dead—had fully run its course, Churchill had begun to have second thoughts about a situation that so evidently had played into the hands of Hitler and Mussolini.

Even where the former was concerned, Churchill, despite his reading of *Mein Kampf,* was still hopeful—still willing, as late as 1937, when he published a sketch of the Führer in *Great Contemporaries,* to give him the benefit of the doubt. Though he took note, as Lloyd George had not done, of the abolition of freedom in Germany, of the destruction of the law courts and the trade unions, of the persecution of the Jews and the concentration camps, of the "stern, grim and even frightful methods" by which Hitler achieved power, Churchill in 1937 still thought it possible that the Führer might someday be accounted one of the "great figures whose lives have enriched the story of mankind," that he might yet save "the great Germanic nation"—"the most industrious, tractable, fierce and martial race in the world"—and restore it "serene, helpful and strong, to the forefront of the European family circle." Of Hitler's rise to power, punctuated as it was by violence and murder, Churchill then wrote: "The story of that struggle cannot be read without admiration for the courage, the perseverance, and the vital force which enabled him to challenge, defy, conciliate, or overcome, all the authorities or resistances which barred his path." "We may yet live," he concluded, "to see Hitler a gentler figure in a happier age."

After the war, at least, Sir Winston realized the significance of the night of the thirtieth of June 1934 when Hitler had Ernst Roehm and other leaders of the S.A. simultaneously liquidated. "This massacre," he wrote in *The Gathering Storm*, "however explicable by the hideous forces at work, showed that the new Master of Germany would stop at nothing, and that conditions in Germany bore no resemblance to those of a civilized state. A dictatorship based upon terror and reeking with blood had confronted the world. . . . I was deeply affected by the episode." Some years later, in his *Triumph and Tragedy*, he added a warning: "Those who are only wise after the event should hold their peace."

Since Sir Winston is universally esteemed for his political insight, one wonders why he was so slow to recognize the evil nature of this "bloodthirsty guttersnipe," as he was to call Hitler during the war. No doubt, at first, his own wishful thinking led him to accept at face value Hitler's assurance that he would be the savior of Europe against Bolshevism, but equally it is clear that Churchill's own faith in democracy was by no means as staunch as his belief in imperialism. When Hitler eliminated the labor movement in Germany, Churchill may well have reflected that he was only doing a more thorough job than he himself and Lord Birkenhead had been able to do in 1926. In no case could he have felt the deep personal hostility to Hitler which animated a trade union leader like Ernest Bevin. Only when Germany's rearmament began to pose an unmistakable threat to the British Empire did Churchill finally cast aside illusion and begin to speculate upon the possibility of Russia as an ally.

One turns with relief from the years of the locust, those twenty years when, in Auden's phrase,

> Upon each English conscience lie
> Two decades of hypocrisy,

to the years of Sir Winston's splendor. When at length he realized Hitler's true intentions, he devoted all his energies to the task of awakening Britain and Europe to a sense of the peril that confronted them. One sympathizes profoundly with that anguish, as of a Titan in chains, through the years when Churchill fumed and fretted over the prospect of a disaster looming more threateningly with every passing month. The answer alike to angry charges and to anguished pleadings was the fatuous self-complacency of the Baldwin and Chamberlain governments. When someone asked him in 1938 if there were not some extenuating factors in Chamberlain's deal with Hitler at Munich, Churchill replied irritably: "No, in the depths of that dusty soul there is nothing but surrender." To a friend he confided: "The Government had to choose between war and shame. They chose shame, and they will get war too!"

In his memoirs, however, Churchill showed himself singularly magnanimous to the memory of Chamberlain, but Baldwin—"that astute and relentless politician," as he called him, "the greatest party manager the Conservatives ever had"—he never forgave for his deliberate deception, in the vital matter of rearmament, of the electorate in 1935. For after the Conservatives had won the election in that year, Baldwin, with what he himself termed "appalling candor," had confessed in the Commons that had he admitted the truth about Britain's unpreparedness, nothing "would have made the loss of the election, from my point of view, more certain."

For Churchill, however, perhaps the greatest disappointment of these years was the selection of an arch-mediocrity, Sir Thomas Inskip, later Lord Caldecote, as Defense Minister in 1936. Churchill had all along taken the lead in urging as an absolute necessity the coordination of the three armed services under a common director. He had made this point of view so thoroughly his own that almost everyone, both Conservative and Labour, both among politicians and the press, believed Churchill to be the one man for the post—the one person with the requisite energy, enthusiasm, and genius for organization. When the platitudinous Sir Thomas was announced as Britain's retort to Hitler's Rhineland invasion, which had occurred the previous week, incredulity was general. "There has been no similar appointment," said a wag, "since the Roman Emperor Caligula made his horse a consul." In the Upper House, Lord Salisbury admitted: "My confidence is shaken a little bit. I must confess I am surprised at the appointment." Even that irreproachable Tory Sir Austen Chamberlain could not help observing: "Mr. Churchill has great courage, infinite energy, and great and wide experience in the matter of defence. Many in the House of Commons regret that Mr. Baldwin has not thought fit to call him to the office to which he has greater qualifications than any living politician."

When, in 1937, on his seventieth birthday Baldwin retired from the premiership, taking with him what *The Times* appreciatively termed "the fragrance of the fields, the flavour of apple and hazelnut" (not very potent specifics against the poison now emanating from Germany), the great steel owner turned gentleman farmer was replaced by the Birmingham industrialist. At a huge rally in the Albert Hall, Baldwin announced that he was handing on the torch to youth. The particular youth whom he had in mind was Neville Chamberlain, then aged sixty-eight. The new Prime Minister was hard-working where his predecessor had been indolent, and determined where his predecessor had been slack. Unfortunately, he also had infinite self-conceit and small knowledge of European politics. What so critical an hour needed was not the prim morality and the limited outlook of the successful businessman but the ferocious energy, bulldog tenacity, and scowling defiance of Winston Churchill. Chamberlain, too, was suspicious of talent, and filled his Cabinet with nonentities. In May 1938—with Churchill in full view—he could look around him and lament: "I do not see anyone to hand over to without undermining confidence." His very last act in office was to be an ineffectual effort to keep Churchill out of the premiership.

Meanwhile, the annexation of Austria and the surrender at Munich had occurred; and as reward for his foresight and independence Churchill was stigmatized by his own party as a wanton warmonger. "Mr. Churchill has spoken about Ethelred the Unready," said Sir Thomas Inskip. "There is nothing unready about our Air Force; . . . our citizens do not want to be hoodwinked. . . . I believe that we have at last got on the road to friendly relations with Germany." Almost on the eve of the conflict, the Defense Minister was still dispensing soporifics to the nation. "War today," he proclaimed on August 3, 1939, "is not only not inevitable but is unlikely. The Government have good reason for saying that." At this very moment, Hitler was completing his final plans for the destruction of Poland.

On September 3, 1939, Britain declared war upon Germany, and at such a moment even Chamberlain felt impelled to summon Churchill back to the Admirality. It was ten years since he had last occupied a post in the Cabinet. Now he found himself in the same seat at the same desk in the same office as that which, on the outbreak of the First World War, he had occupied twenty years earlier. Two words flashed from Whitehall to electrify the Royal Navy: "Winnie's back." Churchill's own thoughts were somber, and he felt "oddly oppressed" as he recalled how many of his old naval comrades—Fisher, Jellicoe, Beatty—were dead. "No one," he mused, "had ever been over the same terrible course twice with no interval between." The omen-freighted situation brought back old memories of *Richard II:*

> For God's sake, let us sit upon the ground
> And tell sad stories of the death of kings.

As in 1914, once again the early months of the war were discouraging to so fiery a spirit. There was the relative inactivity of the so-called phony war; the ignominious loss, in the supposedly safe anchorage of Scapa Flow, of the battleship *Royal Oak*; and the disastrous failure, in April 1940, of the attempt to save Norway from the Nazis. "Considering the prominent part I played in these events," wrote Churchill later, "and the impossibility of explaining the difficulties by which we had been overcome, or the defects of . . . our methods of conducting war, it was a marvel that I survived and maintained my position in public esteem and parliamentary confidence. This was due to the fact that for six or seven years I had predicted with truth the course of events, and had given ceaseless warnings, then unheeded but now remembered."

Then, on May 10, 1940, came the German invasion of the Low Countries, and Churchill found himself at last Prime Minister. Although Chamberlain, even in this crisis, still had a majority in the Commons, he knew that Labour would never accept his leadership in a national government, and hence was reluctantly forced to resign. For notwithstanding the long and bitter antagonism between Churchill and Labour, and despite the memory of the unscrupulous manner in which, as it seemed to them, he had suppressed the general strike, Churchill was the one man in the Conservative party in whom Labour could have confidence as a war leader and under whom Labour would serve in a war Cabinet.

Within three weeks of his taking office, there occurred the disaster of Dunkirk. In a heroic and unprecedented naval operation, the bulk of the British army was ferried in safety across the narrow seas, but with the loss of its arms and equipment. Huge stores of supplies fell into the hands of the enemy. At that moment, as Churchill later revealed, there were in the island sufficient weapons to equip only two divisions. Had the Straits of Dover—that tank-trap twenty miles wide—not existed, Britain would have ceased to count as a community of free men.

Now all the resources of Churchill's ebullient spirit were called simultaneously into play. The man and the moment matched one another to perfection. The unparalleled danger of 1940 was to discover in the Prime Minister qualities of heart and mind and speech such as he himself could hardly have realized that he possessed. As the world well knows, Churchill now rose to heights of courage and resolution, of eloquence and inspiration, which no past occasion in his life had ever been able to call forth. Years before, he had characterized the Russian exile Boris Savinkov as having "the wisdom of a statesman, the qualities of a commander, the courage of a hero and the endurance of a martyr." Here, as so often, the portrait of the sitter was that of the painter himself. The Grand Anachronism of modern English history suddenly found himself recognized by all as the most compelling force in contemporary politics. From being a lone survivor from the past, Churchill suddenly became the chief hope of the future.

The first achievement of the Prime Minister—of which no other man was capable—was to hearten the nation in the hour of disaster, and transform the fact of failure into a pledge of victory. The regeneration of public spirit which followed the evacuation from Dunkirk was a miracle of morale. On June 18, 1940, in the first of many memorable speeches, Churchill told the House of Commons:

> What General Weygand called the Battle of France is over. I expect that the Battle of Britain is about to begin. Upon the battle depends the survival of Christian civilization. Upon it depends our own British life, and the long continuity of our institutions and our Empire. The whole fury and might of the enemy must very soon be turned on us. Hitler knows that he will have to break us in this island or lose the war. If we can stand up to him, all Europe may be free and the life of the world may move forward into broad, sunlit uplands. But if we fail, then the whole world, including the United States, including all that we have known and cared for, will sink into the abyss of a new Dark Age, made more sinister, and perhaps more protracted, by the lights of perverted science. Let us therefore brace ourselves to our duties, and so bear ourselves that, if the British Empire and its Commonwealth last for a thousand years, men will say, "This was their finest hour."

Churchill's versatility had always been astonishing. He had compressed into the space of a single life eight or nine separate careers, each lived at the highest intensity, and all with conspicuous success. He had been successively, and sometimes simultaneously, soldier, journalist, politician, lecturer, military and naval expert, historian, painter, and builder. Now every resource at his command was compressed into a single moral quality—the will to victory. The plenitude of power, which for the first time in his life he now wielded, gave him the opportunity to reveal on a grand scale his extraordinary powers of organization, as well as the capacity to coordinate large masses of detail. His vitality was never more intense, his resilience never more pronounced.

As for personal courage, should the Germans ever land in England, everyone knew that they would never take Churchill alive. Should misfortune come, he urged his fellow countrymen to sell their lives as dearly as might be. Should German parachutists land, he grimly reminded the public, "You can always take one with you." As with Lloyd George in the First World

War, his chief virtue was his unshakable confidence in victory. The terrible difference, however, between then and now was that, with Germans holding the coast of Western Europe from the North Cape of Norway to the Pyrenees, the situation was immeasurably more grave than it had ever been in the earlier conflict.

Churchill's native truculence and pugnacity now at last found occasion worthy of their employment. On the eve of war in 1914, when the Cabinet had been almost overpowered by the tragic solemnity of the occasion, and the Prime Minister and his wife were both in tears, Margot Asquith recalls seeing "Winston Churchill with a happy face," exulting in the declaration of hostilities." Fifty years later, Lady Bonham Carter remembered how Churchill once admitted at this time: "I think a curse should rest on me because I am so happy. I know this war is smashing and shattering the lives of thousands every moment—and yet—I cannot help it—I enjoy every second I live." In the trenches in 1915, Churchill's regimental adjutant recalled how he had positively "revelled in war"; while Siegfried Sassoon remembered how on one occasion Churchill, with a big cigar in his mouth, glorified war as being the finest thing on earth.

In 1940, therefore, with the supreme direction of affairs at last in his own hands, Churchill was in his element. "Alas, I must write it," he confessed in his war memoirs. The conditions of conflict were "like one ruffian bashing the other on the snout with a club, a hammer, or something better." In this primordial situation of mankind, one suspects that—adapting the phrase of La Rochefoucauld—there was something not altogether unpleasing to Winston Churchill. He delighted in coining revengeful phrases, such as the oft-repeated adjurations to make the enemy "burn and bleed," to "strike him in his soft under-belly," or "thrust in a dagger under the Adriatic armpit." His natural sadism bubbled without restraint. Lord Alanbrooke remembered a personal bayonet demonstration in the ancestral hall at Chequers, given by the premier even though he was then ill with bronchitis. On another occasion Sir Winston, finding himself amid the ruins of the ancient amphitheater of Carthage, sustained the morale of the Eighth Army by reminding it with gusto how once "the cries of Christian virgins rent the air while lions devoured them."

In spite of the imminence of danger—perhaps because of it—Churchill no doubt enjoyed himself more during the Second World War than at any other period of his life. "Considering the burden of responsibility which he was bearing," wrote Lord Alanbrooke, "his lightheartedness was unbelievable." At odd moments, Churchill would suddenly break into snatches of music-hall melodies. "We're here because we're here," he would hum energetically at Stranraer, as if to account thereby for his unlikely presence in that remote little Scottish port. Alanbrooke could not help contrasting such gaiety and exuberance with his own "heavy sense of responsibility and frequent need for prayer." Like a naughty boy, Churchill particularly enjoyed defeating the security precautions devised on his behalf. He flew persistently in weather that the Royal Air Force deemed impossible for flying, and in 1944 left home and family on Christmas Eve in order to fly to Athens, then torn by civil war and impending revolution, there to settle by his presence such irritating disturbances.

All who worked with Churchill in these years have testified to his incredible exuberance, energy, and vigor. He literally wore out some of those who were serving under him: Sir John Dill, Chief of the Imperial General Staff in 1940, is an unhappy example. The nation responded to such leadership. Many a bombed and blasted town saw the Prime Minister striding through the ruins, dispensing the V-sign as a benediction, heartening those who had suffered, and radiating his own great strength and courage. The nation admired him for refusing to move the seat of the government from London, and for his determination to share the fiery ordeal of the capital; and when he wept to see the ruins of the Commons—that chamber in which he had spent more than forty years of public life—he and his people were united in a bond of perfect sympathy.

Not even in those dreadful days did Churchill's sense of humor desert him. At the age of sixty-six, his buoyancy of temper and volatility of spirit were such that in a single speech he could pass in a minute from grimness to gaiety, and from menace to merriment. At one moment his hearers were uplifted by passionate emotion; at the next they were chuckling over some malicious thrust at the enemy. No matter how grave the occasion, no one could tell when the tension would not suddenly be dissolved in laughter. He once threatened General de Gaulle, whose obstinacy and patriotism he so much admired: "Si vous m'obstinerez, je vous liquiderai." And his saying soon became proverbial, that of all the crosses he had had to bear, the Cross of Lorraine was the heaviest. A general who had divulged information was forcefully reminded that the enemy was eager for every scrap of cheese it could get, "and you go and give them a whole ruddy Stilton." Once after a discussion of the always difficult question of supply, Churchill convulsed his hearers by summing up the problem in a pithy phrase: "Too many little pigs and not enough teats on the old sow." A favorite expression, picked up during a visit to America, was "a gone coon," and, like Gladstone in this respect, once he had made a saying his own, he never let it go. If Japan should ever enter the war, Hong Kong, he used to say with a mournful air, was "a gone coon"; and during Hitler's advance into Russia, he was heard to lament that Moscow, likewise, was "a gone coon." Sometimes his humor was grim. When his formal declaration of war upon Japan after Pearl Harbor was criticized as being too ceremonious, he disarmed his critics by expostulating: "After all when you have to kill a man it costs nothing to be polite."

Yet despite his exhilarating leadership and the revival of morale which he inspired, Churchill's first two years in office saw an unbroken series of reverses—Greece, Crete, North Africa, Malaya, Singapore, Burma. Perhaps the most humiliating to British self-esteem was the escape of the *Scharnhorst* and the *Gneisenau* in February 1942 from Brest, through the English Channel and the Straits of Dover, back to their own home ports. No one but Churchill could have retained, through such a series of misfortunes, the confidence of the nation; and throughout this perilous period there was no curtailment of Parliament's right to criticize the government.

Nor could anything, throughout these dark and hazardous months, be more admirable than the fortitude and courage of the Prime Minister. He never failed or faltered, or showed sign of discouragement or doubt. Even when, as in the dreadful winter of 1940–41, Britain was at her weakest, Churchill was constantly devising new offensive plans. The fact that the requisite resources were lacking made no difference; for no one knew better the moral importance of thinking always in terms of attack, and not waiting passively, as in the days of Chamberlain, upon the initiative of the enemy.

The personal relations that Churchill established with President Roosevelt and Marshal Stalin, dramatized as they usually were by his unfailing flair for the great occasion—whether at Moscow or at Casablanca, at Teheran or at Cairo—were helpful in coordinating the activities of all partners in the Grand Alliance. In that combination the British Prime Minister was the linchpin, and it is doubtful whether any other leader could so well have harmonized the various conflicting aims and personalities.

There was another aspect of the Prime Minister which, however, at that time was naturally concealed from the public. Among the first to reveal it was one of Churchill's oldest and closest friends. During the early part of the war, Lord Brabazon of Tara was Minister of Aircraft Production. In his autobiography, *The Brabazon Story*, published in 1956, he described how the premier behaved to his colleagues and subordinates. "The way that Churchill treated everyone was almost unbearable. . . . He usually appeared after his early afternoon sleep in the vilest of tempers . . . he behaved as if he were a bullying schoolmaster. Everyone, in his opinion, was a half-wit: and if anyone said anything he was jumped on and snubbed." The premier's favorite target was Sir Archibald Sinclair, later Lord Thurso, then Secretary for Air. "The abuse and insults which Winston heaped upon him were almost unbelievable." Even allowing, wrote Brabazon, for the almost intolerable strain under which Churchill was laboring, his "general cursing of everyone was not the best way to inspire incentive and imagination."

These accounts of the premier's domineering ways, which so far exceeded those of Lloyd George, are fully corroborated by such witnesses as Lord Alanbrooke, wartime Chief of the Imperial General Staff, and Sir John Kennedy, Director of Military Operations. On accepting his appointment as C.I.G.S. in November 1941, the former wrote in his diary: "I hope I may be able to stand the storms of abuse which I may well have to bear frequently." Once, during the campaign in France in 1940, the Prime Minister, at a time when the situation was extremely fluid, tried to bully Alanbrooke by issuing tactical instructions over the telephone from London! The latter admitted that he was "infuriated" by the premier's insinuation that he had "cold feet." If practical objections were raised to any plan that he himself had suggested, Churchill immediately became angry and accused his generals of cowardice. The C.I.G.S. once got "a very unpleasant gruelling . . . in a full room." It was laden with sarcasms and lasted two full hours. "I sometimes think," said Sir Winston tauntingly, "that some of my generals don't want to fight the Germans." "He shoved his chin out," Alanbrooke recalled, "in his most aggressive way." The premier was fond of lecturing generals for "thinking only about themselves and their reputations and never attacking till matters were a certainty." This sounds rather like a dig at Montgomery, and in fact at one point during the struggle at Alamein, when for three days no great change had taken place, Churchill was much annoyed with "Monty" for thus "allowing the battle to peter out."

He was fond of referring to the fate of Admiral Byng in 1757, and of intimating that if he could have his way, some of his own generals would likewise be shot. On one occasion, in April 1941, at dinner at Chequers, the Prime Minister became enraged with his Director of Military Operations. With flushed face and flashing eyes, he declared that if Egypt were lost, "blood will flow. I will have firing parties to shoot the generals." Such threats, according to Sir John Kennedy, became routine, and the generals soon learned to discount them; but Sir John recalls his own "blazing anger" at being called a "defeatist," and his difficulty in repressing his anger. Lloyd George at his worst had never dared treat Haig or Robertson in such a fashion. After these displays, Churchill would sometimes lecture his generals on the folly of losing one's temper.

Three days before Pearl Harbor there was a terrible scene at a midnight meeting of the Chiefs of Staff. Attlee and Eden tried in vain to calm the premier down, but he stalked out of the room without even saying good night. "It was pathetic and entirely unnecessary," wrote Alanbrooke. "God knows where we should be without him, but God knows where we shall go with him." The C.I.G.S. could not help ruefully contrasting his own situation with that of his American counterpart: whereas General Marshall saw Roosevelt only once a month, or even once in six weeks,

Alanbrooke thought himself lucky if he escaped Churchill for as much as six hours. The latter once interrupted one of Alanbrooke's extremely rare holidays to harangue him over the telephone about some unimportant matter, and scold him for having lost touch with things. Churchill himself, of course, unless convalescing from illness, never took a holiday, and never felt the need for one. Why should he, when he had never enjoyed himself so much?

It was Sir John Dill, however, Alanbrooke's predecessor as C.I.G.S., who suffered most from the Prime Minister's aggressiveness. He told the Director of Military Operations how Churchill had once got in a "fury" with him, declaring that some firing squads ought to get busy among the British forces in the Middle East. "I could see the blood coming up his great neck," said Dill, "and his eyes began to flash." But what the C.I.G.S. never could forgive was the humiliation of being told by the premier how much he wished he had the Greek General Papagos to run his army for him. "I cannot tell you how angry the P.M. had made me," Dill confessed to Kennedy. And once, as the Chiefs of Staff filed out from a meeting, Churchill, in a heavy stage aside, whispered to a bystander: "I have to wage war with such ancient weapons." Nor did the premier confine his bullying to his own commanders. On one occasion he summoned the Canadian General McNaughton to Chequers. Alanbrooke found the latter "looking limp" after "a ghastly weekend. He had been kept up till all hours in the morning till he did not know which way he was facing." "The effort left for the war after dealing with him," wrote Sir John Kennedy in 1944 after a meeting with Churchill, "is really negligible." When Field Marshal Wavell, unable to sleep all night after a severe dressing-down by the premier, wrote out a letter of resignation, Alanbrooke persuaded him to withdraw it, saying that if he himself were to take offense every time Churchill abused him, he would "have to resign at least once every day."

To professional military men, it was the premier's interference with strategical problems that caused most alarm. Ignoring his Chiefs of Staff, he would issue directives that, at least in the judgment of the Director of Military Operations, were "not only unsound but extremely dangerous." "His strategical imagination," wrote Sir John Kennedy, "was inexhaustible; very many of his ideas seemed to us wild and impracticable." Against the advice of his professional chiefs, he would set his heart on projects that were "wild, or unprofitable, or even impossible." As early as December 1939 he had a crackbrained scheme for taking the heavily fortified island of Pantelleria, then held by the Italians, "and a vast amount of time and energy were wasted on it." "I do wish Winston would give up strategy as his special fun," sighed Sir John.

In 1941, when Britain was woefully short of shipping, the Prime Minister was contemplating assaults upon Norway, Sicily, Italy, and French North Africa. To his sanguine imagination all these projects seemed equally feasible: the difficulty was to choose among such an embarrassment of (hypothetical) riches. According to Kennedy, in October 1941 Churchill regarded Sicily as "virtually taken already." A little while later, he was thinking of attacking Cherbourg or Madagascar. In May 1942, writes Alanbrooke, he wanted to land a brigade of guards at Alderney in the Channel Islands, and "establish lodgments all round the coast from Calais to Bordeaux with little regard to strength and landing facilities." The following month, he once kept up the weary C.I.G.S. from 10:30 P.M. to 1:00 A.M. discussing the capture of places as widely separated as northern Norway, Petsamo in Finland, Spitzbergen, and Rangoon. In 1943, an "obsession" with a landing in Sumatra developed. Such projects Sir Winston whimsically described as "eating the porcupine quill by quill."

Alanbrooke was appalled to find British strategy conceived thus on a "day to day . . . hand to mouth existence." The Prime Minister, he realized, arrived at the solution of any problem by sudden intuition, "without any kind of logical examination." The Chiefs of Staff, said Kennedy, all thought Churchill a gambler, acting on "impulse and intuition," not by reason. "The mistake you people make," one of the premier's secretaries told Sir John, "is that you think what the P.M. wants is a logical reasoned argument. There is nothing he dislikes more." Another close associate of Churchill reported to Kennedy in 1942 that "Winston was all over the place. He is difficult enough when things are going badly, more difficult when nothing is happening, and quite unmanageable when things are going well."

Once in a while, however, Churchill got his way—as in the case of the disastrous raid of August 19, 1942, on Dieppe, which both Alanbrooke and Montgomery opposed. The R.A.F. threw in fifty-six squadrons, a greater number than had been involved in the Battle of Britain, and suffered twice the losses of the Germans. The Canadian ground troops lost 75 per cent of their effectives.

In similar fashion, the Prime Minister was responsible in the spring of 1941 for the heavy British losses in Greece. The Greek government had asked only for naval and air assistance, and the Chiefs of Staff had been dubious about sending any military help. Admiral Cunningham, the British naval commander in the Mediterranean, declared that Churchill had done much harm by his "ungracious and hasty" interference in that theater. Rear Admiral Sir Henry Harwood (of *Graf Spee* fame), when he learned that the premier had urged another convoy to be sent directly to Egypt, "swore heartily" for five blistering minutes at Sir Winston. In 1941 the Prime Minister, having overruled Admiral Pound and the Admiralty, was responsible for the loss of the great battleships the *Prince of Wales* and the *Repulse* by sending them into the South China Sea without air protection against Japanese bombers. Field Marshal Smuts had also urged strongly against this suicidal course of action.

Another source of irritation was that the Prime Minister compelled others to adjust their hours of work to his own eccentric schedule. Having slept before dinner, he was full of vitality in the hours after midnight, at a time when everyone else, weary from a long day's work, was badly in need of sleep. "It is the night work after dinner till 1 a.m. with him that kills me," complained the C.I.G.S. Often at a moment's notice, just when he felt "a desperate longing for bed," Alanbrooke would be summoned to a nocturnal meeting. Sometimes he would be fetched out when already undressed and just about to step into his bath. He suspected that Churchill deliberately counted on the fact that people's powers of resistance were lowest in the early morning hours. During the First World War, Admiral Sir Reginald Hall had noticed how Churchill followed the same procedure, so that "tired Admiralty officials were hypnotized into accepting opinions which differed vastly from those they really held."

So serious was this matter of the premier imposing his eccentric routine upon others that Lord Hankey and Lord Chatfield made formal protests in the Upper House. The former declared that such hours of work were "perfectly intolerable. . . . Nobody is at his best in the Middle Watch. . . . I believe," he added, "it is the height of inefficiency and bad administration to work such hours, which really cannot be necessary." He went on to imply that in this regard the premier should make some sacrifice of his own personal convenience.

Lord Hankey, who as Sir Maurice Hankey had been secretary of the war Cabinet in the First World War, also complained of Churchill's meddling with professional military matters. "It had been the same in some ways with Lloyd George—but Lloyd George, though a rogue elephant, had had two steady old elephants to push him in the right direction, in the shape of Smuts and Milner." There were numerous resemblances between the behavior of the two wartime premiers. Churchill was as inconsiderate of his associates as Lloyd George had been. He too delighted in embarrassing them by last-minute decisions and last-minute changes of plan. Even Sarah Jones had a counterpart in the valet Sawyer, who would lecture Sir Winston upon the right way to wear a Panama hat.

The Cabinet suffered similarly from the autocratic habits of its chief. One minister commented that whereas Lloyd George had made his colleagues feel big, Churchill made them feel small. As soon as the latter came into the room, wrote Sir John Kennedy, everyone watched anxiously to see what humor he was in—whether he was smiling or scowling. If he made little jokes, everyone laughed—"rather like schoolboys with their headmaster." Alanbrooke stresses that if one had a favor to ask of Churchill, it was essential to wait before approaching him till he was in the right mood.

Yet when due allowance has been made for Churchill's egotism, truculence, irascibility, and ill-humor, he still remained, in the opinion of all who knew him, the indispensable man. Much as the generals might complain of the premier's conduct, they never considered the possibility of anyone else replacing him. Never, during their severest strictures upon him, did they lose sight of his transcendent virtues as a war leader. "He is quite the most wonderful man I have ever met," wrote Alanbrooke. "Occasionally such human beings make their appearance on this earth." And at the Quebec Conference in August 1943, when "Winston made matters almost impossible" by interfering constantly in matters of strategy, the exasperated C.I.G.S. was still calm enough to observe: "He is quite the most difficult man to work with that I have ever struck, but I would not have missed the chance of working with him for anything on earth." And no doubt many who had smarted under the premier would still have agreed with Admiral Sir Dudley Pound: "You cannot help loving that man."

Sir John Kennedy likewise rose above the frequent vexations that he had suffered. Churchill, he wrote, "towers above all others in vigour, drive and in his grasp of the situation." As with Lloyd George in the earlier conflict, "there is one thing," said Sir John, "that Winston's enemies and critics must admit—he has only one interest in life at the moment, and that is to win the war. Every waking moment is devoted to that. He lives his peculiar life, indoors, and rarely going out. Yet this seems to suit him well, and he shows little sign of wear and tear." "No soldier," he concluded in a final tribute, "ever had more generous and forbearing masters than I. The massive figure of the great Prime Minister towers above them all. Neither his stature nor his place in our annals can be diminished by glimpses of his petulance, or revelations of how difficult it was to chase all the butterflies conjured up and released by his limitless fancy. His glory remains."

The truth is that with Churchill, as with Lloyd George, his faults were inseparable from his greatness. His faults and virtues were so interwoven that one could not eliminate either without risk of losing both.

It is worth observing, finally, that although Churchill's postwar critics were widely condemned in the press for having dared to criticize the wartime leader, Sir Winston himself never deigned to acknowledge or reply to any of them. Yet surely it was better that criticism be heard while Churchill was still alive and able, if he chose, to reply, than that it be postponed till after his death, in which case his critics would certainly be charged with cowardice in waiting till the great man could no longer defend himself.

It has frequently been said, and not without truth, that in waging war Churchill was not concerned merely with military prob-

lems, but with political ones as well. Equally with the winning of
the war, his object was the winning of the peace. To a greater
degree, perhaps, than his friends Franklin Roosevelt or General
George C. Marshall, he thought realistically about the future and
the problems of postwar Europe. Here he brought to bear something that Lloyd George had never possessed—an intimate knowledge of European history, geography, and politics. Had he had
his way—and Churchill was still the confirmed "Easterner" with
unforgettable memories of the bloodbaths of the First World War
—the Western Allies might well have been the first to occupy
Vienna, Budapest and even Berlin, with incalculable consequences
for the future. Churchill was similarly perceptive in seeing how
weak was the Nationalist regime of China under Chiang Kai-shek,
and how mistaken was American policy in regarding that government as a world power—even as one of the Big Five.

The soundness of Churchill's judgment, however, was offset by
frequent lapses. Thus at Casablanca in 1943 he endorsed the dubious policy of unconditional surrender, and later consented to the
Morgenthau Plan for the dismemberment of Germany. By the
"terror bombings" that destroyed open German cities such as
Dresden, he not only miscalculated the effect upon German civilian morale, but put Britain in the same moral category with the
destroyers of Warsaw, Rotterdam, and Coventry. Although in
the context of the time perhaps no other course was possible, one
might also question, on grounds of pure expedience, the advisability of the trial and execution of the Nazi war criminals: for
whatever their guilt, which was as undeniable as it was monstrous,
there could be no doubt that future generations, above all in
Germany, would regard such trials rather as acts of revenge than
as occasions of justice. Nor was unprejudiced opinion reassured
by the fact that Russia, responsible among other atrocities for
the ghastly Katyn massacre, was one of the powers sitting in
judgment.

As for the controversial Yalta Conference of February 1945,
what may be criticized is not the acceptance by the Western
Allies of the Lublin government of Poland or Russia's dominance
over the satellite states of Eastern Europe—these were already
established facts, which it would have taken a third World War
to reverse—but the mood of self-deluding optimism which saw in

such dominance the hope of a just and lasting peace. In dealing with Stalin during the Second World War, Churchill was as much deluded by his oversanguine hopes as he had formerly been victimized by his own hysterical obsession with Bolshevism. In both instances, and in conformity with his whole life's pattern, the Prime Minister believed too easily what he wanted to believe. "I know of no Government," he told the House of Commons on his return from Yalta, "which stands to its obligations, even in its own despite, more solidly than the Russian Soviet Government. I decline absolutely to embark here on a discussion about Russian good faith." This expression of misplaced confidence preceded only by twelve months the famous speech at Fulton, Missouri, in 1946, in which Churchill warned the West to beware of its wartime ally. "How the Great Democracies triumphed, and so were able to resume the Follies which had so nearly cost them their life." Such is the epigraph prefixed to the sixth and final volume of Churchill's *History of the Second World War*. But can it be denied that he himself shared some responsibility for the raising of the false hopes on which such follies were founded?

The cruelest sacrifice to political realism was that of the Free Government of Poland, which during the war had made its headquarters in London. At Yalta, the Western Allies had not only recognized the Communist government of Poland, but had agreed to allow Russia to keep the eastern half of that country which she had occupied, in concert with the Germans, in 1939. After the war Churchill was furious with Mikolajczyk for not accepting this arrangement, and for standing in the way, as Churchill conceived it, of Anglo-Russian understanding.

In his autobiography, the leader of the Polish Peasant party described the brutal treatment he had received from the British Prime Minister:

> "You are no government," Churchill said. "You are callous people who want to wreck Europe. I shall leave you to your own troubles. You have no sense of responsibility. . . . You have only your miserable, petty, selfish interests in mind. . . . You ought to be in a lunatic asylum. . . . You hate the Russians. I know you hate them."

In Sir Winston's *Triumph and Tragedy*, there is no reference to such an interview; but the keen annoyance that Churchill felt with the government of Free Poland is evident in his references to it. At Yalta, he admitted to Stalin that its action "had been foolish at every stage." Toward Russia, on the other hand, his mood was euphoric: his hatred of Bolshevism had entirely evaporated. "My heart went out to mighty Russia, bleeding from her wounds," he told Stalin, "but beating down the tyrants in her path." The full irony of the situation is realized only when we remember that in 1939 it was the Free Government of Poland that Britain was pledged to defend, and that twenty years earlier Churchill, as Secretary for War, had encouraged the Poles in a resistance to Russia which he now stigmatized as criminal. It may be foolish to expect consistency in politics, but Churchill, with his capacity for surrendering himself wholly to each new situation, exhibited an extreme instability.

Shortly after Germany had been defeated, and before the war with Japan had reached its climax, Churchill decided to hold an election—the first in Britain in ten years. No doubt influenced by Lloyd George's spectacular success in the "Victory election" of 1918, he hoped to receive a similar mandate to continue as head of a coalition government.

In order to be present on polling day, July 26, 1945, Churchill flew home from the Potsdam Conference. Supremely confident of victory, he told his friends: "I feel it in my bones." So certain was he that, whereas Labour had issued a manifesto setting forth in detail its proposals for the future of Britain, Churchill had campaigned upon his name alone. Clearly he felt that the prestige of his wartime leadership enabled him to dispense with the tedious details of electioneering. As an additional insurance against defeat, he attempted to cast Harold Laski, one of the chief theoreticians of the Labour party, in the sinister role of leader of a postwar British "Gestapo"—a term that Churchill actually used in this connection. This ill-conceived propaganda recoiled on his own head.

Amid universal astonishment, Clement Attlee—"the sheep in sheep's clothing," as Churchill called him—gained an overwhelming victory at the polls, and the premier, after five years of unparalleled power, was abruptly dismissed from office. When his wife, attempting to console him, suggested that his defeat might well have been a blessing in disguise, he replied that at the moment the blessing appeared to be "quite effectively disguised." Privately he complained that the nation had given him "the order of the boot," but publicly he issued a dignified message to the people he had served so well:

> It only remains for me to express to the British people, for whom I have acted in these perilous years, my profound gratitude for the unflinching, unswerving support which they have given me during my task, and for the many expressions of kindness which they have shown towards their servant.

Future historians may well consider that, second only to the opportunity which Hitler gave him in 1940, Churchill's defeat in 1945 was the most fortunate thing that ever happened to him. For had he remained in office, he would certainly have refused to India, Pakistan, Ceylon, and Burma the independence that the Labour party was to grant in 1947. It was not his intention, he had stated emphatically, to preside over the liquidation of the British Empire. A Conservative government would have meant further imprisonment for Gandhi and Nehru, and the proscription of the Congress party. The freedom proclaimed in the Atlantic Charter would have been denied to the Indian people, and four hundred million human beings left seething with discontent. Whether Gandhi in such a crisis could still have held the Indian masses to nonviolence is problematical. Equally doubtful would have been the reaction of the British electorate to the forcible suppression of Indian freedom, and of the British taxpayer to the financial burden he would have been called upon to bear. The prospect of a subcontinent held down by the artillery, tanks, and airplanes of a country which had just vindicated its own freedom is not pleasant to contemplate. Communism would have been the probable beneficiary of a policy of repression, and it is likely that a catastrophe similar to that was soon to befall the French in Indochina would have taken place in India.

No wonder Stalin, foreseeing such probable results from Churchill's continuance in office, expressed his desire for a Conservative victory in 1945—but then the Russian leader, realizing that throughout Western Europe democratic socialism was the chief bulwark against communism, had always hoped for the defeat of Labour. And how far, one wonders, would American public opinion—at a time when the United States, through its overwhelming financial resources, controlled the fate of Britain and Western Europe—have tolerated a ruthless policy of repression in India, for which in the end, as in Indochina, it would probably have been called upon to bear the cost?

Only when we recall how in 1947 Britain and India parted with feelings of mutual friendship and respect, and how thereafter India, Pakistan, and Ceylon chose freely to remain members of the Commonwealth—a partnership that survived even the Suez invasion of 1956—can we gauge the full extent of the almost criminal folly to which Churchill, had he been victorious in 1945, would have committed Britain in India. The glory of 1940 would have been obscured by disaster; Churchill would have figured in history as a tyrant rather than a hero; and enemies of Britain throughout the world would have rejoiced. Such a calamity was averted in India by the statesmanlike policy of the Labour party— the party that for more than twenty years Churchill and the Tories had stigmatized as "unfit to govern."

For the next six years, while Labour established the welfare state, Churchill found himself condemned to the role of an impotent but angry spectator. Even his admirers admit that as leader of the Opposition from 1945 to 1951 he was a failure. For the sake of guerrilla warfare in the House—a warfare as futile as it was embittered—he eschewed constructive criticism of the government. To be sure it was galling to see Aneurin Bevan, "that squalid nuisance," as Sir Winston called him, dominating the treasury bench with the hosts of Labour massed behind him and enacting into law free medical care for rich and poor alike— indeed, for the entire nation.

So durable, however, was Labour's achievement that when Churchill, in the election of 1951, was once more returned to power, it was in effect—with the notable exceptions of the denationalization of road transport and steel—to conserve the moderate measure of socialism which the Labour government had introduced. Churchill's second and final ministry (1951-55) was memorable for the coronation of Queen Elizabeth II on June 2, 1953, an event signalized by the bestowal upon him of the Order of the Garter. Since Clement Attlee, despite his able leadership, was incapable of sounding such depths of national feeling as Sir Winston, it was a happy chance that the latter, at this supreme moment of symbolism and pageantry, should occupy once more the highest position in the state. It would have been churlish to have grudged the old warrior, with his deep and abiding interest in the long drama of English history, his happiness on this occasion as the tears glistened in his eyes.

Churchill's public life had begun with a queen upon the throne, and now after the vicissitudes of fifty years, it was ending in the same manner. To the young woman of twenty-six who was now his royal mistress, Sir Winston at seventy-eight brought the same chivalrous devotion that as a subaltern he had felt for Queen Victoria. He had witnessed the passage of five reigns, and had seen Britain emerge victorious from the two greatest wars in human history. He told the young Queen how vividly he recalled her great-great-grandmother, and, as Lord Melbourne had been Victoria's first tutor, so would he now be hers "in the anxious and darkling age through which we are passing."

The chief event of Churchill's final term of office was his announcement on March 1, 1955, that Britain was developing her own hydrogen bomb. In a last ringing speech to the House of Commons, Sir Winston at the age of eighty proved that he had not lost his mastery of the spoken word. "It may well be," he suggested, "that we shall by a process of sublime irony have reached a stage in the story where safety will be the sturdy child of terror and survival the twin brother of annihilation." Britain, he said, had decided to produce the hydrogen bomb in order to decrease her dependence on the United States and to recover, in the realm of global politics, her power to act independently. At the same time, he warned Russia that "continents are as vulnerable as islands." "The Hydrogen bomb," he concluded, "has made an astounding incursion into the structure of our lives and thoughts. Its impact is prodigious and profound."

The sole survivor, after Stalin's death in 1953, of the Big Three who dominated the Second World War, Churchill had as his last ambition the desire to meet the new leaders of the Kremlin in a "Summit Conference"—an expression that, like the terms "Iron Curtain" and "Cold War," he now added to the English language. "In spite of all the uncertainties and all the confusion in which world affairs are plunged," he wrote two months after Stalin's death,

> I believe that a conference on the highest level should take place between the leading powers without long delay. . . . I do not see why anyone should be frightened of having a try. . . . If there is not at the summit of the nations the will to win the greatest prize and the greatest honour offered to mankind, doom-laden responsibility will fall upon those who now possess the power to decide.

Despite his sanguine hopes, Churchill was unable at the Bermuda Conference of 1953 to overcome the reluctance of President Eisenhower to meet in person with the Soviet leaders. This was the last disappointment in Sir Winston's public life, for the most successful war minister in English history had set his heart upon going down to posterity as a man of peace. "Peace," he declared with fervor in 1955, "is the last prize I seek to win." It has even been suggested that when, in 1953, chosen above Hemingway and other writers for the Nobel literature prize, he could scarcely conceal his chagrin that he had not been given instead the Nobel prize for peace. Had the latter actually been granted to the warrior who in youth had charged at Omdurman and all through life had glorified war, the award would not have been lacking in piquancy.

When at last, in July 1955, the hysteria of McCarthyism having subsided, President Eisenhower went to the Summit Conference in Geneva, Sir Winston was no longer in office. Like Gladstone at a similar age, he was half deaf, and his health was giving way. He now revealed that two years previously he had been incapacitated by a paralytic stroke; physicians noted that he owed his recovery to his remaining physical vitality and his superb will to live. On April 6, 1955, after rumors of discontent within the Tory party, he had reluctantly submitted his resignation to the Queen. Ten years earlier, like Lloyd George, he had been offered an earldom, which he had declined. He was now offered a still higher rank—that of his great ancestor, the Duke of Marlborough; but the old House of Commons man, unlike his opponent Clement Attlee, steadfastly refused to go to "the other place," and rejected the proffered dukedom, even though it was more than eighty years since such an honor had been bestowed upon a commoner.

Even from his retirement, on one final occasion Sir Winston's words reverberated through the chancelleries of Europe and over the airwaves of the world. On May 10, 1956—the anniversary of Hitler's attack on the Low Countries—in receiving the Charlemagne Prize in Aachen, Sir Winston made the last great speech of his public life. It was to be expected that, as a good European, he would invoke the spirit of Charlemagne as a symbol of the unity of Europe, but to the astonishment of his hearers in the bombed-out German city, he went on to declare that "in a true unity of Europe Russia must have her part." Once again, the old horror of Bolshevism forgotten, he sought to bridge by words the gulf dividing East from West. "We must realize," he reminded an audience which included Chancellor Adenauer, "how deep and sincere are Russia's anxieties about the safety of her homeland from foreign invasion." If the Kremlin proved sincere in its repudiation of Stalinism, Russia and her East European satellites should be invited to join the North Atlantic Treaty Organization.

Whatever one may think of this proposal today, in 1956 its audacity took people's breath away, and in the American press it met with a bad reception. Some there were, however, who maintained that Sir Winston, with his lifelong flair for bold, imaginative solutions, was hinting at a peril now obscurely taking shape on Russia's Siberian flank—the danger from an awakening China with its land-hungry millions, which might one day drive Russia in self-defense to value her unity with Europe rather than her divergence from it.

Within a few months of Churchill's speech at Aachen, this possibility of an extraordinary reorientation among the great powers was made explicit by statesmen as distinguished as de Gaulle in France, Adenauer in Germany, and Adlai Stevenson in the United States. Curiously enough, the victory of Chinese communism never drew from Sir Winston any of the diatribes that, thirty years earlier, he had lavished upon Soviet Russia. He now accepted calmly and without hysterics the prodigious regeneration of China which the Webbs had long ago foreseen. In this regard, therefore, he showed himself more realistic at eighty than he had been in his prime.

In taking leave of Sir Winston's public life, one should stress how much he always owed to the unfailing sympathy and devotion of his wife. One suspects that she must have been endowed with patience in unlimited abundance. Probably no one is better able than she to confirm the truth of Dryden's aphorism—that men are but children of a larger growth. Whatever the difficulties or disappointments of his public life, Sir Winston could always count on perfect understanding and support at home: that was one empire, at least, over which his rule was never challenged. As he wrote gaily in his autobiography, in September 1908 "I married and lived happily ever afterwards."

More and more in his later years, Churchill came to see in the substantial unity of the English-speaking peoples the future hope of mankind. "Its maintenance, its stimulation and its fortifying," he declared in one of his last speeches as Prime Minister, "is one of the first duties of every person who wants to see peace in the world and wishes to see the survival of this country." To this object, therefore, he devoted the energies of his last years. Between 1956 and 1958 appeared the four volumes of his *History of the English-Speaking Peoples*. This was the fulfillment on a grand scale of a project that he had cherished for more than a quarter of a century. It was also his final contribution to a theme that had been dear to him through life, and of which, with his mingled ancestry, he was the chief living symbol—the theme of Anglo-American unity. These four volumes—even allowing for the research scholars whom he employed and for the fact that much of it appears to have been written during his enforced absence from front-bench politics during the nineteen-thirties—were an astonishing achievement for a man in his eighties. In point of total historical output—aside from any question of value—Churchill is said to have written more than Gibbon and Macaulay together.

Through skillful publicity in America, advance sales before publication reached the figure of fifty thousand, and Sir Winston's publishers were thought to be aiming at a sale of a million copies. Such a sale would mean that the work would reach more people in America than all previous histories of England combined. A leading novelist, John P. Marquand, affirmed that Churchill was equal to Gibbon "in depth, scope and wisdom," while surpassing him as being "more eloquent and convincing." Professional historians, both in England and in America, evaluated the work more cautiously.

The truth is that, as a serious work, the *History of the English-Speaking Peoples* is of relatively slight importance. One reads it not as a contribution to existing knowledge but as a further piece of self-revelation on the part of an extraordinary personality. Since Sir Winston goes out of his way to mock at scholars and scholarships, it is not surprising that his old-fashioned pages contain nothing new. There is an amusing irony in the fact that this prince of Tories should produce a belated example of the Whig version of history that was current in his youth. He shows almost no acquaintance with modern scholarship and is as indifferent to the work of Sir John Neale in the sixteenth century as to that of Sir Lewis Namier in the eighteenth. Edmund Burke is still a hero—"perhaps the greatest man that Ireland has produced"; and he is indignant with contemporary iconoclasm. Reluctantly he admits that in some details the version of his childhood may have to be modified—"if caution must be the hall mark of history," he sniffs disdainfully, "it is not much of a conclusion to come to about a great age of Parliamentary debate."

He himself is not unduly hampered by the tyranny of fact, and whenever it suits his purpose—as with the legends of King Arthur or Fair Rosamond—he impishly discards fact for fiction. Half in jest and half in earnest, he reproaches those "tedious investigators," the professional scholars, not only for being dull but for allowing themselves to be bound by a pedantic adherence to truth. "It is all true," Sir Winston remarks gaily about one of his own flights of fancy, "or it ought to be, and more and better besides." It seems almost churlish not to surrender oneself wholly to the charm of an entertainer so accomplished and so lighthearted.

Nothing will ever persuade him, since that was what he learned in childhood, that Richard III may possibly not have murdered the little princes in the Tower. By nature a partisan, no historian had less of the judicial temper. He cannot resist taking sides on every issue. In his condemnation of the Peasants' Revolt of 1381, one hears again the voice of the *British Gazette* denouncing the general strike of 1926. Popular movements never won Sir Winston's sympathy. To suspend judgment, to admit that one may never know the truth—this is intolerable to so ardent a man of action. He would rather defend the wrong convictions than not have any at all. Well knowing that anthropologists and other tiresome persons had cast doubt upon the validity of old-fashioned concepts such as "blood" and "race," Churchill takes mischievous pleasure in stressing them throughout his writings.

He delights in hyperbole and lavishly scatters superlatives. The highest estimate—of the length, for example, of prehistoric periods, or of casualties in battle—is the one that pleases him most. He moralizes about the death of sovereigns and the vanity of human hopes. Yet where fundamental issues are concerned, as in the Hundred Years' War, he sometimes shows himself completely amoral. He recognizes that England was the aggressor, but treats the long-drawn-out tragedy as rather a good joke. He idealizes the Black Prince and Henry V, while admitting "the wasteful and useless campaigns which followed their victories." He is proud of "those rugged, lusty, violent Islanders," and like General de Gaulle, will forgive anything for the sake of "glory."

His concept of human nature is marked by an extreme simplicity. For him, as for Sir Walter Scott, human beings are heroes or villains, saints or sinners. For him, even more than for Trevelyan, Freud might never have written. As a result, Churchill's characterizations of rulers like Canute, Richard the Lion Heart, Edward I, and Henry V are shallow, sentimental, and at times incredible. Thus Edward I, who was responsible for the cruel expulsion of the Jews, the terrible sack of Berwick, and the savage execution and dismemberment of Wallace is praised for his "magnanimity." Sir Winston's concept of what constitutes national character is equally arbitrary and superficial.

Two of the most serious limitations of his history are the narrow compass of its subject matter and the lack of proportion in the selection of events. For Churchill, as for E. A. Freeman, history is mainly politics and war. Constitutional history is slighted and economic history ignored. Nor is Sir Winston concerned with ideas. He lacks interest in cultural and intellectual history and discusses religion not for its own sake, but only in relation to politics. He fails even to mention great religious monuments such as Stonehenge or the Gothic cathedrals. He ignores alike the founding of the universities and the coming of the friars. He is interested neither in the ferment of new ideas called the Renaissance nor in the religious and moral ardors of Puritanism: hence he fails to appreciate the significance of either. The scientific revolution in the seventeenth century, on which the world of modern technology depends, is disregarded—Sir Isaac Newton along with Sir Christopher Wren; while the Enlightenment of the eighteenth century, which was the intellectual background of Jefferson, Franklin, Paine, and other leaders of the American Revolution, requires just half the space allotted to the insignificant battle of Steinkirk in Belgium in 1692.

What Sir Winston really loves are battles, and he describes them in masterly fashion. They absorb him so completely that he devotes as much space to the campaign of Crécy in 1346 as to the whole development of common law, and as many pages to the Wars of the Roses as to the first seven centuries of English history. He allots ten pages to Waterloo and eight to Trafalgar, but only half a page to the Industrial and Agrarian revolutions combined. Such disproportion is grotesque, if for no other reason than that Britain could not have defeated Napoleon without the Industrial Revolution. In the nineteenth century, nearly twice as much space is devoted to the four years of the American Civil War as to the previous half-century of American history with all its political, social, and industrial developments.

The basic philosophy of history implicit in Churchill's work is confused and contradictory. At first sight, Sir Winston's leading historical concept would appear to be derived from Carlyle—the idea that history is the biography of great men. We encounter a series of heroes—Alfred the Great, Canute, Richard the Lion Heart, Edward I, the Black Prince, Henry V, Queen Elizabeth, Marlborough ("Churchill, on whom the light of history now begins to fall"), Chatham, Burke—most of whom are projections of the author's own personality.

Even heroes, however, are subject to external necessity, known to some as providence, to others as fate. "The means by which Providence raises nations to greatness are the virtues infused into great men." This supramundane power acts sometimes to thwart human designs, as when Charles I intended to relieve La Rochelle "but Fate moved differently." At one moment, everything appears controlled by "chance"; at another, by some ineluctable purpose, or by "destiny"—a word of which Churchill is fond.

Sir Harold Nicolson has commented on Sir Winston's "deep compassion" in this book. More apparent is the latter's harshness toward failure in men or nations and his admiration of success, no matter by what ruthlessness it may have been achieved. There is little tenderness for the universal human plight or concern for human suffering. The sense of the mingled poetry and pathos of history which suffuses Trevelyan's writing is absent from this emphatic narrative proceeding briskly to the sound of drum and trumpet.

The strong aggressive component in Sir Winston's nature, which in 1940 was put to such good use in the service of Britain and of civilization, is much in evidence. At times his sadism seems gleeful, mischievous, and adolescent, like that of Evelyn Waugh; but often it is accompanied by a grim, sardonic humor.

Churchill's view of mankind alternates between sentimental hopefulness and despair. His accurate statement that paleolithic man was "capable of all the crimes, follies and infirmities definitely associated with mankind" echoes the famous dictum of Gibbon which Churchill, fifty years before, had quoted in *Savrola*. Neolithic man, he observes, learned to polish flint for killing: "This betokened a great advance, but others were in prospect." Thus, the Bronze Age achieved "another great improvement in human methods of destruction." With the Iron Age modern man unmistakably emerged.

> At this point we can plainly recognize across the vanished millenniums a fellow being. A biped capable of slaying another with iron is evidently to modern eyes a man and a brother. It cannot be doubted that for smashing skulls, whether long-headed or round-headed, iron is best.

One can almost hear Sir Winston chuckle as he reminds us of such comfortable truths.

Repeatedly he emphasizes the salutary lesson that throughout history man's nature has not changed essentially. A Romanized Briton reading modern history would find "worse tales than those of Tacitus or Dio." William the Conqueror was "a prime exponent of the doctrine so well-known in this civilized age as 'frightfulness.'" When Becket's brains are spilled in the transept of Canterbury, Churchill reminds us that in the twentieth century archbishops are sent to concentration camps. "What claim," he asks defiantly, "have we to vaunt a superior civilization?" In praising Simon de Montfort for not "purging" his enemies in 1265, "in the brutal manner of modern times"—did not Sir

Winston approve of the Nuremberg trials?—he makes the dubious generalization that in the Middle Ages, "for all their cruelty in individual cases, nothing was pushed to the last extreme": he has just described how the Inquisition annihilated the brilliant civilization of the Albigensians.

The insistence upon man's ever-present savagery, justified as it is by man's behavior in the twentieth centry, does not lead Churchill to give up his Victorian faith in progress. Thus, despite the cruelties of the Middle Ages, he feels that during those centuries "the forces of progress moved doggedly forward." Even Cromwell, "the harsh, terrific, lightning-charged being" who "grasped a heavy, sharp and reeking sword"—even Cromwell "cannot be wholly barred from his place in the forward march of liberal ideas." (Ideas, in Sir Winston's active mind, are martial: they assume the offensive and march like soldiers.) Like Trevelyan, Churchill is by nature so sanguine that he cannot help believing that in the end everything turns out for the best; and at one point refers to "the astounding, illogical knack for success that is part of the British heritage."

Sir Winston fails to discuss seriously how far civilization, despite man's inherent atavism, may really be said to have progressed. His own uncertainty of moral standards, his lack of an adequate knowledge of psychology and his impatience with any speculation that does not readily yield positive answers—such factors all preclude any fruitful approach to problems of fundamental importance.

Churchill's attitude to religion reveals an odd persistence of the positivism of his youth. In his last history, as in his early novel *Savrola*, one finds a strong undercurrent of the rationalist ideas that, as a subaltern in India, he acquired from Gibbon, Darwin, and Winwood Reade. Sir Winston is usually playful at the expense of the Almighty. Following the convention of the Enlightenment, deity is urbanely taken for granted and is introduced at intervals, usually with diverting effect, into the narrative. In this ironic laughter, in this mockery at the expense of the gods, Churchill comes closest, perhaps, to the practice of his admired Gibbon.

The comet of 1066 (later named after the astronomer Halley) was interpreted by Saxon and Norman alike according to their respective hopes. "At this very moment," observes Sir Winston impishly, "the Almighty, reaching down from His heavenly sphere, made an ambiguous gesture." In speaking of the Middle Ages, he notes urbanely how the elements "in those days were believed to be personally directed by the Almighty," and gravely cites a battle of Henry II, in which "the sleet, especially directed by Almighty God, beat upon the faces of his foes." His irony in speaking of Pelagius is worthy of Gibbon himself. This early British heretic, says Churchill, "cast a slur" upon the doctrine of original sin, and thereby "threatened to deprive mankind, from its very birth, of an essential part of our inheritance."

"If a God of Mercy rules the world," he asks in discussing the Black Death, "what sort of rule was this?" Like Pilate, however, he stays not for an answer. His most serious flight into eschatology occurs in a passage where he pictures Arthur, Roland, and Coeur de Lion seated "at some Eternal Round Table, which we trust the Creator of the Universe in His comprehension will not have forgotten to provide." There, too, no doubt, if anywhere, Sir Winston is now seated, discoursing on strategy among his peers.

The vitality of the narrative is most evident in the opening volume. Except where campaigns and battles are described, the later books tend to be tame and spiritless. The Reformation fails to move one for whom religion is so largely a bore. Cromwell, with his "smoky soul," momentarily rouses Sir Winston to fierce invective; but with the eighteenth century he sinks back into a tired narrative where, beneath the false glitter of a contrived rhetoric, there is little life. Churchill sees history as pageant and as drama: he observes it in its flow rather than in its depth. He is often entertaining: one might say, perhaps, that he has written a child's history for children of all ages.

A considerable portion of the work appears to have been written, at least in rough draft, during Churchill's enforced absence from office in the nineteen-thirties; and the remainder while Labour was in power during the late forties. In the Preface, dated from his country house, Chartwell, at Westerham in January 1956, Sir Winston expressed the hope that his history might play "some small part in uniting the whole world." His stated object was not to "favour national ambition at the expense of world peace," or "to stir a new spirit of mastery." To condone the aggressions of the Black Prince or Henry V, and to glorify the brutalities of the Crusaders against the "infidel," seems a curious way to fulfill these laudable aims; nor can Moslems be gratified to see "Arab infidels" equated with "Nordic pirates," or to read of Saladin's "warlike hordes." Over a century ago, Sir Walter Scott in *The Talisman* did more justice to the world of Islam. Sir Winston's attitude is closer to Belloc's frenzied zeal than to Sir Walter's magnanimity. Nor will Churchill's concluding assumption that Anglo-American cooperation is the climax of world history commend itself to more than a fraction of the world's population.

The nature of Churchill's long interest in history is perhaps best illustrated by a highly revealing comment in *Their Finest Hour* upon what he conceived to be its function. "History with its flickering lamp," he writes, "stumbles along the trail of the past, trying to reconstruct its scenes, to revive its echoes, and to kindle with pale gleams the passion of former days." In this romantic conception of the historian's task, the emphasis is clearly placed not upon intelligence or understanding, but upon imagery, feeling, and above all, upon passion. And when later, in *The Grand Alliance*, Churchill observes that upon all the events that he has been discussing, history will one day "pronounce its cool, detached and shadowy verdict," the final adjective suggests perhaps his skepticism about the unreality of historical judgments.

Fundamentally, no doubt, Churchill represented elemental force, vitality incarnate. Instead of reproaching him with what he was not, nor could ever be, perhaps it is more fitting to admire those extraordinary gifts with which nature so richly and uniquely endowed the great Romantic of our age.

On January 24, 1965, Sir Winston Churchill died at the age of ninety. It was the exact day of his father's death seventy years before. Is it too fanciful, remembering his deep lifelong fixation on his father's memory, to suppose that, even while dying, in the inmost recesses of his being he determined to die on that particular day and on no other? that some deep unconscious awareness sustained him through long days of semicoma until the appointed day arrived and at length he was ready to go. All his life he had believed in observing ceremonial occasions with due respect, and this was for him the most important of all.

Most Englishmen took it for granted that Sir Winston Churchill would some day be buried in one or other of the two great burial places of the nation—either in Westminster Abbey, where lie so many sovereigns and statesmen, or in St. Paul's Cathedral, where lie so many of Britain's foremost sailors and soldiers, among others Nelson and Wellington. All along, the great man himself had made quite other plans: in one last splendid gesture of self-assertion and defiance, Sir Winston had determined to break with tradition in the matter of a final resting place, and to lie forever in a little country churchyard close to his father and mother at the village of Bladon in Oxfordshire. In making this decision, Churchill must have realized that his roving, adventurous life, so tumultuous and wide-ranging, would thereby describe a perfect circle; for in returning to Bladon, he was returning to the place of his origin—the village lying just outside the walls of Blenheim Palace where he was born.

So it was that, after London had paid its final unforgettable tribute along the crowded thoroughfares from Westminster to St. Paul's and over the gray waterway of Thames, which had witnessed so many stirring scenes in England's history, the body of Winston Churchill was borne through the wintry countryside to lie at last beside his father. England must now come to Bladon —and during the following year more than a million Englishmen were to do so.

The death of Churchill symbolized the end of an epoch. He was the last survivor of the Victorian age, the last voice of the old imperialism, the last leader in two world wars, the last link with a heroic past. For the youth of England—for all who at the time of his death were under thirty years of age, and who therefore could not remember the Battle of Britain—Sir Winston was more symbol than reality. For older people, however, he was the past incarnate: during his funeral it must have seemed to them almost as if history itself had come momentarily to a close. A profound grief pervaded the nation, and millions felt themselves bereaved. The supreme father figure that had sheltered all their lives was gone; and even though Sir Winston had so long been failing in health that, in effect, he had several years ago withdrawn from public life, yet in this moment the nation faced a future without him with feelings of sorrow and foreboding. The gloom of the January day that enshrouded his funeral procession was emblematic of the desolation of a fatherless people between whom and the harsh reality of the modern world no august, protective presence could any longer interpose.

The sense of loss felt throughout Britain over the passing of Winston Churchill was as poignant and as universal as that felt in America after the murder of John Fitzgerald Kennedy. But where the mourning for Kennedy centered inevitably upon the tragedy of youth cut down untimely, of brilliant promise unfulfilled, the mourning for Churchill was more like grief for the human condition itself: it was the expression of an immemorial sadness over the fact that even the most intense vitality must some day wane and flicker and die. Churchill's passing was but the latest affirmation of the power of ancient death: of that force upon which Stoic emperors like Marcus Aurelius and Christian philosophers such as Pascal had brooded so obsessively—death mighty and inexorable. Some comprehension of this must surely have entered the consciousness of Englishmen that winter day.

Bibliography

JEREMY BENTHAM

ATKINSON, CHARLES M., *Jeremy Bentham, His Life and Work* (1905).

BAUMGARDT, DAVID, *Bentham and the Ethics of Today* (1952).

BENTHAM, JEREMY, *Works*, ed. Sir John Bowring, 11 vols. (1843–59).

———— *Fragment on Government* (*1776*), ed. F. C. Montague (1891).

———— *Handbook of Political Fallacies*, ed. Harold A. Larrabee (1952).

———— *Introduction to the Principles of Morals and Legislation* (1789).

DAVIDSON, WILLIAM L., *Political Thought in England: The Utilitarians from Bentham to J. S. Mill* (1935).

EVERETT, CHARLES WARREN, *The Education of Jeremy Bentham* (1931).

HALÉVY, ELIE, *The Growth of Philosophic Radicalism* (1928).

HAMBURGER, JOSEPH, *Intellectuals in Politics* (1966).

KAYSER, ELMER L., *The Grand Social Enterprise: A Study of Jeremy Bentham in Relation to Liberal Nationalism* (1932).

KEETON, GEORGE W., *Jeremy Bentham and the Law, A Symposium* (1948).

LETWIN, SHIRLEY, The Pursuit of Certainty (1965).

LUNDIN, HILDA G., *The Influence of Bentham on English Democratic Development* (1920).

MACK, MARY P., *Jeremy Bentham: An Odyssey of Ideas, 1748–92* (1962).

PLAMENATZ, JOHN, *The English Utilitarians* (1958).

STEPHEN, SIR LESLIE, *The English Utilitarians*, 3 vols. (Vol. I, *Jeremy Bentham*) (1900).

JOHN STUART MILL

BAIN, ALEXANDER, *John Stuart Mill* (1882).

BORCHARD, RUTH, *John Stuart Mill, the Man* (1957).

COURTNEY, W. L., *Life of John Stuart Mill* (1889).

COWLING, MAURICE, *Mill and Liberalism* (1963).

CRANSTON, MAURICE, *John Stuart Mill* (1958).

HAYEK, F. A., *John Stuart Mill and Harriet Taylor* (1951).

MILL, JOHN STUART, *Autobiography* (1873), ed. John Jacob Coss (1924).

———— *James and John Stuart Mill on Education*, ed. F. A. Cavenagh (1931).

———— *Letters*, ed. Hugh Elliot, 2 vols. (1910).

—— *Mill on Bentham and Coleridge,* ed. F. R. Leavis (1950).
—— *On Liberty* (1859).
—— *The Subjection of Women* (1869).
—— *Utilitarianism* (1863), ed. John P. Palmenatz (1949).
MORLAN, GEORGE K., *America's Heritage from John Stuart Mill* (1936).
MUELLER, IRIS W., *John Stuart Mill and French Thought* (1956).
NEFF, EMERY, *Carlyle and Mill* (1924).
PACKE, MICHAEL ST. JOHN, *Life of John Stuart Mill* (1954).
REES, JOHN C., *John Stuart Mill and His Early Critics* (1956).
STEPHEN, SIR LESLIE, *The English Utilitarians,* 3 vols. (Vol. III, *John Stuart Mill)* (1900).
WHITTAKER, THOMAS, *Comte and Mill* (1908).

JOHN HENRY NEWMAN

CAMERON, JAMES MONROE, *John Henry Newman* (1956).
CULLEN, ARTHUR D., *The Imperial Intellect: A Study of Newman's Educational Ideal* (1955).
FABER, GEOFFREY, *Oxford Apostles* (1936).
FROUDE, JAMES ANTHONY, *Short Studies on Great Subjects,* 4th series, *The Oxford Counter-Reformation* (1883).
HARROLD, CHARLES F., *John Henry Newman* (1946).
HOLLOWAY, JOHN, *The Victorian Sage* (1953).
KENNY, TERENCE, *The Political Thought of John Henry Newman* (1957).
McGRATH, FERGAL, *Newman's University: Idea and Reality* (1951).
MOZLEY, JAMES B., *Letters* (1885).
MOZLEY, THOMAS, *Reminiscences of the Oxford Movement,* 2 vols. (1882).
NEWMAN, JOHN HENRY, *Apologia pro Vita Sua* (1864).
—— *Autobiographical Writings* (1874), ed. Henry Tristram (1957).
—— *The Idea of a University* (1852).
—— *Loss and Gain* (1850).
—— *Parochial and Plain Sermons,* 8 vols. (1900–1901).
—— *The Second Spring* (1911).
—— *Tracts for the Times,* 6 vols. (1840–42).
O'FAOLÁIN, SEAN, *Newman's Way* (1952).
TREVOR, MERRIEL, *Newman: The Pillar of the Cloud and Light in Winter* (1962).
WARD, WILFRID, *Life of John Henry, Cardinal Newman,* 2 vols. (1912).
WILLIAMS, ISAAC, *Autobiography* (1892).

BENJAMIN DISRAELI

BLAKE, ROBERT, *Disraeli* (1966).
DISRAELI, BENJAMIN, *Works,* 20 vols. (1904).
—— *Letters to His Sister, 1832–52* (1904).
—— *Wit and Wisdom of Benjamin Disraeli* (1881).

FROUDE, JAMES ANTHONY, *The Earl of Beaconsfield* (1890).
GRAUBARD, STEPHEN, *Burke, Disraeli and Churchill* (1961).
GREVILLE, CHARLES C. F., *The Greville Memoirs, 1814–60*, ed. Lytton Strachey and Roger Fulford, 6 vols. (1938).
HARDIE, FRANK, *The Political Influence of Queen Victoria, 1861–1900* (1938).
JERMAN, B. R., *The Young Disraeli* (1960).
KEBBEL, THOMAS E., *Lord Beaconsfield and Other Tory Memories* (1907).
MASEFIELD, MURIEL A., *Peacocks and Primroses: A Survey of Disraeli's Novels* (1953).
MAUROIS, ANDRÉ, *Benjamin Disraeli* (1928).
MONYPENNY, W. F., AND BUCKLE, G. E., *Life of Benjamin Disraeli, Earl of Beaconsfield*, 6 vols. (1910–20).
O'CONNOR, T. P., *Lord Beaconsfield: A Biography* (1879).
ROTH, CECIL, *Benjamin Disraeli, Earl of Beaconsfield* (1952).
SICHEL, WALTER, *Disraeli* (1904).
SOMERVELL, DAVID C., *Disraeli and Gladstone* (1926).
SYKES, JAMES, *Mary Anne Disraeli* (1928).

WILLIAM EWART GLADSTONE

BASSETT, A. TILNEY, *The Gladstone Papers* (1930).
——— *Gladstone to His Wife* (1936).
BIRRELL, FRANCIS, *Gladstone* (1933).
EYCK, ERICH, *Gladstone*, tr. Bernard Miall (1938).
FLETCHER, C. R. L., *Mr. Gladstone at Oxford* (1890).
GARRATT, GEOFFREY T., *The Two Mr. Gladstones* (1936).
GLADSTONE, HERBERT (VISCOUNT), *After Thirty Years* (1929).
GLADSTONE, W. E., *Gleanings of Past Years, 1848–73*, 7 vols. (1886).
GREVILLE, CHARLES C. F., *The Greville Memoirs, 1814–60*, ed. Lytton Strachey and Roger Fulford (1938).
GUEDALLA, PHILIP, *The Queen and Mr. Gladstone*, 2 vols. (1933).
HAMMOND, JOHN L., *Gladstone and the Irish Nation* (1938).
HAMMOND, JOHN L., AND FOOT, MICHAEL R. D., *Gladstone and Liberalism* (1952).
KILBRACKEN, ARTHUR GODLEY, *Reminiscences* (1931).
KNAPLUND, PAUL, *Gladstone and Britain's Imperial Policy* (1927).
——— *Gladstone's Foreign Policy* (1935).
MAGNUS, SIR PHILIP, *Gladstone* (1954).
MORLEY, JOHN, *Life of William Ewart Gladstone*, 3 vols. (1903).
PAUL, HERBERT, *Life of Gladstone* (1901).
RENDEL, STUART, *Personal Papers of Lord Rendel* (1931).
SCHLUTER, AUGUSTE, *A Lady's Maid in Downing Street* (1922).
SMITH, GOLDWIN, *My Memory of Gladstone* (1904).
——— *Reminiscences* (1910).
WEST, SIR ALGERNON, *Private Diaries* (1922).
WILLIAMS, WILLIAM E., *The Rise of Gladstone to the Leadership of the Liberal Party, 1859–68* (1934).
YOUNG, G. M., *Mr. Gladstone* (1944).

BEATRICE AND SIDNEY WEBB

COLE, MARGARET, *Beatrice Webb* (1946).
—— *The Webbs and Their Work* (1949).
HAMILTON, MARY AGNES, *Sidney and Beatrice Webb* (1933).
LETWIN, SHIRLEY, *The Pursuit of Certainty* (1965).
WEBB, BEATRICE, *Diaries, 1912–24*, ed. Margaret Cole (1952).
—— *Diaries, 1924–32*, ed. Margaret Cole (1956).
—— *My Apprenticeship* (1926).
—— *Our Partnership*, ed. Barbara Drake and Margaret Cole (1948).
WEBB, BEATRICE AND SIDNEY, *The Co-operative Movement in Great Britain* (1899).
—— *The Decay of Capitalist Civilization* (1923).
—— *English Local Government: Poor Law History*, 2 vols. (1927–29).
—— *History of Trade Unionism*, revised ed. (1920).
—— *Methods of Social Study* (1932).
—— *Soviet Communism: A New Civilization?* 2 vols. (1935).
—— *The Truth about Soviet Russia* (1942).

DAVID LLOYD GEORGE

BEAVERBROOK, LORD, *The Decline and Fall of Lloyd George* (1963).
—— *Men and Power* (1956).
CLARKE, TOM, *My Lloyd George Diary* (1939).
JONES, THOMAS, *Lloyd George* (1951).
KEYNES, JOHN M., *The Economic Consequences of the Peace* (1919).
LLOYD GEORGE, DAVID, *The Truth about the Peace Treaties*, 2 vols. (1938).
—— *War Memoirs*, 6 vols. (1933–37).
LLOYD GEORGE, RICHARD (EARL), *Lloyd George* (1960).
McCORMICK, DONALD, *The Mask of Merlin* (1963).
OWEN, FRANK, *Tempestuous Journey* (1954).
RIDDELL, GEORGE, *Lord Riddell's War Diary 1914–18* (1933).
SYLVESTER, ALBERT J., *The Real Lloyd George* (1947).
TAYLOR, A. J. P., *Lloyd George: Rise and Fall* (1961).
THOMPSON, EDWARD RAYMOND, *Mr. Lloyd George* (1922).
THOMSON, MALCOLM, *David Lloyd George* (1948).
WEBB, BEATRICE, *Diaries, 1912–24*, ed. Margaret Cole (1952).
—— *Diaries, 1924–32*, ed. Margaret Cole (1956).
—— *My Apprenticeship* (1926).
—— *Our Partnership*, ed. Barbara Drake and Margaret Cole (1948).

SIR WINSTON CHURCHILL

BIBESCO, PRINCESS MARTHE, *Sir Winston Churchill, Master of Courage* (1959).
BONHAM-CARTER, LADY VIOLET, *Winston Churchill as I Knew Him* (1965).

BRABAZON, LORD, *The Brabazon Story* (1956).

BROMAGE, MARY C., *Churchill and Ireland* (1964).

BRYANT, SIR ARTHUR, *The Turn of the Tide* (1956).

CHURCHILL, RANDOLPH, AND GERNSHEIM, HELMUT, *Churchill: His Life in Photographs* (1955).

CHURCHILL, SIR WINSTON, *Blood, Sweat and Tears* (1941).

—— *Great Contemporaries* (1937).

—— *History of the English-Speaking Peoples*, 4 vols. (1956–58).

—— *Marlborough: His Life and Times*, 6 vols. (1933–38).

—— *Maxims and Reflections*, ed. Colin Coote (1949).

—— *Painting as a Pastime* (1950).

—— *A Roving Commission: My Early Life* (1930).

—— *Savrola* (1956).

—— *The Second World War*, 6 vols. (1948–53).

—— *Secret Session Speeches*, ed. Charles Eade (1946).

—— *Step by Step, 1936–39* (1939).

—— *While England Slept: A Survey of World Affairs, 1937–38* (1938).

—— *The World Crisis*, 4 vols. (1923–29).

COWLES, VIRGINIA, *Winston Churchill* (1953).

EADE, CHARLES, *Churchill, by His Contemporaries* (1953).

GRAUBARD, STEPHEN, *Burke, Disraeli and Churchill: The Politics of Perseverance* (1961).

GUEDALLA, PHILIP, *Mr. Churchill* (1942).

HIGGINS, TRUMBULL, *Winston Churchill and the Dardanelles* (1963).

HUGHES, EMRYS, *Winston Churchill: British Bulldog* (1955).

KENNEDY, SIR JOHN, *The Business of War* (1957).

THE LONDON *Times*, *The Churchill Years* (1965).

MARSH, SIR EDWARD, *A Number of People* (1939).

MORAN, LORD, *Churchill: The Struggle for Survival, 1940–65* (1966).

PAWLE, GERALD, *The War and Colonel Warden* (1963).

RABINOWICZ, OSCAR, *Winston Churchill on Jewish Problems* (1956).

ROBERTSON, JOHN HENRY, *Winston Churchill* (1956).

ROWSE, A. L., *The Churchills: From the Death of Marlborough to the Present* (1958).

THOMPSON, REGINALD W., *The Yankee Marlborough* (1963).

WINGFIELD-STRATFORD, ESMÉ, *The Making of a Hero* (1942).

Index